DATE DUE

The Dark Side
of
Interpersonal Communication

LEA's COMMUNICATION SERIES
Jennings Bryant/Dolf Zillmann, General Editors

For a complete list of other titles in LEA's Communication Series, please contact Lawrence Erlbaum Associates, Publishers.

The Dark Side
of
Interpersonal Communication

Edited by

William R. Cupach
Illinois State University

and

Brian H. Spitzberg
San Diego State University

LEA LAWRENCE ERLBAUM ASSOCIATES, PUBLISHERS
1994 HILLSDALE, NEW JERSEY   HOVE, UK

Lawrence Erlbaum Associates, Inc., Publishers
365 Broadway
Hillsdale, New Jersey 07642

Cover design by Cheryl Minden

Library of Congress Cataloging-in-Publication Data

The dark side of interpersonal communication / edited by William R.
Cupach and Brian H. Spitzberg.
    p.   cm.
Includes bibliographical references and index.
ISBN 0-8058-1167-2
1. Interpersonal communication. 2. Interpersonal conflict.
I. Cupach, William R. II. Spitzberg, Brian H.
BF637.C45D335 1994
302 – dc20   93-26764
                                    CIP

Books published by Lawrence Erlbaum Associates are printed on acid-free
paper, and their bindings are chosen for strength and durability.

Printed in the United States of America
10 9 8 7 6 5 4

CONTENTS

PREFACE

The dark side of human interaction has always intrigued us. Indeed, we suspect that most people are naturally curious about it. The dark side always makes for an engaging story; it implies mystery, intrigue, and dramatic irony. Its very elusive and enigmatic nature compels us to explore it, though perhaps with some trepidations.

We are struck by the fact that competent interpersonal communication is not merely a matter of good persons speaking well. Rather, social actors are faced routinely with the symbolic reality that humans are "rotten with perfection," as Kenneth Burke (1966) would say. To fully understand how people effectively function requires us to consider how individuals cope with social interaction that is difficult, problematic, challenging, distressing, and disruptive.

We realize that the dark side is not a new angle on human behavior. Nevertheless, it remains elusive, enigmatic, and inscrutable. So we set out to revisit this territory, inviting some of the sharpest social scientists in their respective fields to share their unique insights regarding the dark side of interpersonal interactions. The goal was not to map the entire territory of darkness in human relations. Rather, we attempted to illuminate a representative sample of phenomena lurking in the dark side. We considered numerous potential topics and somewhat arbitrarily settled on the chapters contained in this book. The authors of these chapters provide a state-of-the-art picture of their respective corners of academic interest.

The chapters contained in this book are divided into four, somewhat overlapping, divisions. Part I provides an overview of the myriad issues entangled in the dark side. In the opening chapter, Duck substantiates the importance of scrutinizing the dark side of interpersonal relationships. He illustrates that the dark side has been understudied, and he identifies numerous intriguing avenues that are ripe for exploration. Along the way, Duck makes some important arguments about how the dark side is situated integrally in the broader context of relationships. Spitzberg, in chapter 2, considers the notion of competence in social interaction. His analysis reveals that what we tend to view as competent communication often is not so competent, and what we view as incompetent can actually be quite competent.

Part II contains three chapters that explore the "maze of messages" commonly associated with the dark side. Vangelisti reviews a series of empirical studies designed to reveal the nature and complexities of hurtful messages. Drawing on an attributional framework, she presents evidence distinguishing socially elicited feelings of hurt from other emotions, such as anger and guilt. In addition to delineating the content of hurtful messages, Vangelisti identifies factors that influence the consequences of hurtful messages for interpersonal relationships. Wilder and Collins survey the landscape of interactional paradoxes. They argue that paradoxical communication is most appropriately viewed as normative rather than deviant. Drawing from such diverse fields as philosophy, psychotherapy, and rhetoric, the authors employ the notion of paradox to illustrate a variety of common social interaction patterns. Chovil focuses on a specific type of paradoxical communication in the form of equivocal messages. Equivocal messages are distinguished from related phenomena such as double binds, disconfirmation, and deceptive messages. In analyzing different communication situations that elicit equivocation, Chovil suggests that equivocal messages are often communicatively competent.

Chapters in Part III investigate the "face beneath the masks" in communication episodes considered to be problematic. Daly, Diesel, and Weber present original data on the nature of conversational dilemmas. Their research reveals the types of dilemmas that social interactants commonly face, and explores the role of communication competence in coping with them. This is followed by a chapter on social predicaments, where Cupach outlines the communicative manifestations and remedial processes associated with episodes in which persons are caught behaving ineptly, inappropriately, or foolishly. O'Hair and Cody discuss various types, functions, and consequences of deception in everyday interpersonal interaction. In addition to offering taxonomies of deceptive acts and motives for deception, the authors consider the ethical and pragmatic ramifications of deceptive behavior.

Part IV, "relational webs," scrutinizes some of the darker intricacies attendant on managing various types of interpersonal relationships. Metts offers a conceptualization of relational transgressions in personal relationships.

She considers how transgressions are semantically constructed as well as behaviorally negotiated by relational partners. The next two chapters in this section focus on aspects of communication within families. Petronio presents an original program of research grounded in the theory of communication boundary management. Specifically, she applies the theory to the context of parents invading the privacy of their college-aged children. Her work illuminates how parents and children manage privacy invasion as well as the consequences for parent–child relationships. In contrast, the chapter by Stafford and Dainton investigates presumably "normal" family interaction in broader strokes. The authors debunk myths regarding the institution of family in America, and illustrate the darker side of certain aspects of routine, day-to-day interaction among members of "ordinary" families. The authors also briefly review social–political and feminist critiques of the family. The final chapter in section four by Marshall thoroughly overviews the concept of abuse in relationships. Following an explication of key findings regarding physical abuse and violence, she offers a fresh perspective on the elusive phenomenon of psychological abuse. Marshall suggests that some of the deleterious effects previously associated with physical violence may actually stem from the more subtle forms of psychological abuse.

In the closing chapter, we offer a brief epilogue to the numerous provocative issues raised in this volume. We consider what the darkness metaphor implies for the study of human interaction. We also forecast some themes that could be profitably elaborated in supplementary volumes on the dark side.

We sincerely thank our friends and colleagues who supported us in our endeavor to illuminate the dark side. We are especially grateful to the talented authors whose provocative contributions comprise this book. We also acknowledge the contribution of Michael Hecht, who facilitated critical discussion about the dark side during a program at the Western States Communication Association in Albuquerque. Thanks are also due to Mary Doud and Emily Reece who carefully and patiently assisted us with manuscript minutiae.

—*William R. Cupach*
—*Brian H. Spitzberg*

REFERENCE

Burke, K. (1966). *Language as symbolic action*. Berkeley: University of California Press.

SHADES OF DARKNESS
IN INTERPERSONAL RELATIONS

1

STRATAGEMS, SPOILS, AND A SERPENT'S TOOTH: ON THE DELIGHTS AND DILEMMAS OF PERSONAL RELATIONSHIPS

Steve Duck
University of Iowa

In contrast to the clinical research that warms considerably to emotions such as anxiety, anger, depression, hostility, and aggression, researchers in personal relationships have proved remarkably nice and optimistic. For instance, of the 58 articles published in the *Journal of Social and Personal Relationships* for 1991–1992, 34 deal with support, intimacy, love, romance, coping, maintenance of relationships, facilitation of relationships, and competence (one title even contains the words "optimism about love"). Of the remainder, 12 deal with the positive role of relationships as a moderator of various stresses, and only 7 look at rejection, dissolution of relationships, loneliness, and other negative aspects of relating (the remaining papers deal with scale development, etc.).

The impression that personal relationships researchers are somewhat over-balanced in focusing on the positive is reinforced by the fact that only certain sorts of unpleasantness in relationships are studied much (especially loneliness, conflict, and insecure attachment). The full range of difficulties—from the commonly experienced turmoils of everyday life to outright betrayal considered in this chapter—has been given almost no theoretical attention either as a part of relating as a whole or even in their own right as fun things to study, at least when they happen to someone else. While pop psychologists are churning out books on people who love too much or who never grow up in relationships, academic relationship writers are writing about *Close Relationships* (Kelley et al., 1983), *Intimate Relationships* (Brehm, 1992), or *Meaningful Relationships* (Duck, in press). Those who study close relationships develop not scales of alienation as ancient sociologists would have urged but scales of closeness (Berscheid, Snyder, & Omoto, 1989). Those who explore love write more about passion and companionship than about the human desolation of lovelessness or unrequited love (Berscheid & Walster, 1974). Those who study marital interaction or attachment or intimacy usually presume that closeness and so on are the natural state of things, but also that the obverse of these phenomena is to be construed in terms of the positive and in the hopes of helping to prevent social problems such as divorce. In particular, work on "problems" in marriage has focused on conflict, miscommunication, abuse, and divorce (Gottman, 1979), but always with the implication that these are *mistakes* in relationships rather than a fundamental part of them. Indeed, some argue that relationships have been treated as normal and healthy only to the extent that negativity is absent from them (Prager, personal communication, Aug. 10, 1992).

By contrast this chapter argues that the relational significance of the unpleasant in the real lives of everyday mortals has been seriously underrepresented in theory and research that has taken too euphoric and decontextualized a view of the ways in which relational life can be nasty, brutish, and short, certainly insofar as it is *practiced*. Instead, the "negative" and the "positive" sides of relationship need to be incorporated together theoretically into one set of principles that can deal with both.

It should be clear that I am calling for the redress of balance, not for a change of focus to relationship difficulties rather than on the enjoyable. I argue for a rethinking of the role of those behaviors and experiences that these subjects probably get in real life but never show up in the lab, where other questions are asked. My claim is that a simple dichotomy into "positive" and "negative" is ultimately misleading and that both elements, however labeled, are conjoint parts of relationships.

... OF NICE AND THEN WHAT?

I suppose we should be flattered or encouraged by the fact that so much research in the relatively new and flourishing field of personal relationships is so nice. Researchers have built up a heroic list of theories and research studies on such nice relational topics as love (including selfless love), adult romantic attachment (dressed in white), deep and significant relationship quality, the development of ideal courtships, open and healthy disclosure, the valued provisions of relationships, the growth of deep personal intimacy, fairness and reciprocity in relationships, closeness, dating success, long-term friendship, and the resolution of different sorts of relational dissatisfaction. Matched with these are some research studies attempting to do the good work of discovering how to deal with issues that are typically depicted as "occasional problems" in these relationships, such as those that may be due to human error or faulty functioning or simple misunderstanding, or to curable loneliness, understandable jealousy, minor family distress, or other difficulties experienced by very nice people in relationships that are also essentially pleasant, rewarding, and to-be-sought-for.

In the bulk of personal relationships research, the underlying assumption is not only that relationships should be nice but also that people are nice: They set out constructively to develop relationships, help others in need, provide support to their friends, do nice things to maintain their relationships, occasionally use cute and funny little strategies to test out commitment, follow rules of relating, or act in playful and amusing manners that sustain and develop the human community of which relationships play so important (and so nice) a part. Occasionally, of course, one has naturally to admit that these well-meaning people experience unfortunately negative emotions in the course of their relationships, but these are typically explained as due to some faulty functioning or to a momentary and thoroughly understandable circumstance that provokes the negative emotion in essentially tolerable ways. Hence, the negative side of relating is depicted as a deviation from the positive rather than as a phenomenon that also composes the totality of relational experience.

The picture is an alluring one, being permeated with the fading light of a successful day, the plaintive call of geese in homeward flight, and the all-pervading scent of honeysuckle. However, it omits much that is the basis of human experience and simultaneously indicates an interesting trend in the development of the social sciences. As discussed in this chapter, social scientists tend to take a positive and excited view of new topics as soon as their star rises, only gradually becoming dissatisfied with its rosiness. Then they edge into a more complex eventual picture that takes account of the difficulties of sustaining the "positive" side of things in real life, as well as an awareness and acknowledgment of the continual existence of a countervailing side.

This is all to the good and something that this chapter proposes. As well as being an ever-present thread in the rich tapestry of our lives, the "dark side" is not always dark in its effects. Some of the best resolutions of relationship issues come out of conflicts, as Cicero (46 B.C.) and Braiker and Kelley (1979) have both taught. In learning to cope with relationship disasters, people sometimes grow stronger, more resilient, and better able to deal with others—indeed this argument has been put forward as the basis for some relationship accounts (Harvey, Weber, & Orbuch, 1990). Equally, and as a balance, remember that not all rosy aspects of relationships are experienced as positive: For some people, intimacy and closeness are terrifying (cf. Prager, in press); for others, love is maniacally disruptive and jealousy provoking (Hendrick & Hendrick, 1986); for yet others, the thought of acceptance is deeply revolting (as in Groucho Marx's aphorism that he would never join a club that would have him as a member). Of course, for others, close relationships are just not the most preferred priority in the rhythm of life—as compared to, say, a career or desires for personal control or solitude.

It is important to bear this in mind not only because it is true, but also to avoid the naiveties of the use of a dichotomous black–white way of thinking about the "positive" and "negative" of relationships. This latter would unconsciously shape the thinking of reader, writer, and researcher into a formulation of the issues that contrasts with the "right" way to act, rather than allowing researchers to welcome the "negative" as "equal sheep" into the field, even if they are black. One central point in this chapter is that the "dark side" is integral to the experience of relationships, not separate from it. It is part of living life, not something that knocks down theories, merely something that cries out to be included in them to make them better and stronger, just as the resolution of difficulty in relationships themselves can increase their strength. When it is recognized that real lives are richly entwined with begrudging, vengeful, hostile, conflictive tensions and struggles, it will perhaps begin to be realized that one must also start to look at the ways in which people cope with them in life and then to theorize about them. After all, many of the things that might immediately be thought of as being "dark" are for the most part common and usual, rather than bad, awkward, or to be spoken of in suppressed whispers. A part of building and sustaining relationships is the acceptance, perhaps with some grace, of one's partner's ongoing or persistent faults, in hopes of reciprocal graciousness in respect of one's own. Such a forbearance is a part of being in relationships, not something occasional, temporary, or unusual. Indeed, any recognition that relationships have cultural, social context and are not the splendid dyadic islands of much lab research requires that it must be acknowledged that tensions and conflicts are intrusive elements of relating. As partners attempt to please not only themselves but also others in the networks or kin group, so the tensions of relationship management will become at least as important as the intensity of their own closeness or emotion toward one another, as these are used to be experienced in splendid isolation. With the in-laws comes reality.

In a number of senses the personal relationships field has hitherto tended to neglect such social contexts and also relationships that are difficult for the participants or for researchers, not just those that represent the negative side of human relationships. Recently this has changed. For instance, researchers into social support have recently begun to comment on its negative, demanding, and wearing side (La Gaipa, 1990; Rook, 1984). Commentators on friendship have noted that it contains binds as well as bonds (Wiseman, 1986), that dating or courtship is sometimes tainted by violence (Deal & Wampler, 1986; Lloyd & Cate, 1985; Sugarman & Hotaling, 1989), that relationships occasionally end in punishing and disturbing ways (Duck, 1982; Orbuch, 1992), and that even personal rejection occurs now and again, though usually only in the playground, one will be glad to hear—at least that is the only place where researchers have studied it extensively (Asher & Coie, 1990). More than this, a recent volume (Wood & Duck, in preparation) has been devoted to those relationships that are "off the beaten track" and have been largely disregarded by research, such as gay and lesbian relationships, long-term marriages, and the relationships between members of minority populations, which have featured hardly at all in previous attempts to provide general theoretical accounts of commitment, relationships, and social exchange (Kelley et al., 1983). Another whole book looks at issues in relationships that seem to have been felt by researchers to be too unpleasant or too awkward to be featured at all in general theories or models of relationship processes as a whole, namely, those relationships that present special challenges to the individuals in them, such as the relationships of the handicapped, reconfigured families, or noncustodial parents (Duck & Wood, in preparation).

Despite these hopeful trends toward pessimism, the field still theoretically neglects relationships that are unusual or problematic, whether because they are problematic in themselves or merely problematic for existing methods and social exchange models. It also hardly ever devotes equivalent amounts of research effort to those that are actually quite common in human experience but are tinged with hatred (Shoenewolf, 1991), hostility, or enmity (Wiseman, 1989). It is not a new observation that this needs to be done. Harré (1977, pp. 345–347) gave a detailed argument for the study of "Feindschaft" rituals, humiliation, needlings, and the study of enemyship over 15 years ago, but no empiricists took much notice: Such relationships and relationship events are quite hard to initiate or imitate in the lab, and an ethnographic method was not terribly fashionable in 1977. Interestingly, Harré even pointed out that the distinction between negative and positive relationships is not that clear nor well drawn, with many apparently vicious things being said by friends to one another in play or when teasing. He discussed the uses of the "Cut" (the stylized refusal to acknowledge or greet someone—a version of the "silent treatment"—see Adams, 1977; Bruhn & Murray, 1985), as well as feuds, and less ritualized "needlings" of others out of resignation, irritation, or the desire to annoy the partner (Semin & Rubini, 1990).

Despite the cogency and astuteness of Harré's observations and the cleverness of his analysis of some of the elements of such negative twists to relationships, the work has not been taken up thoroughly nor assiduously by research. He did not go on, as others have done (Delia, 1980), to point to the simplemindedness of the view that assumes that relationships have an implicit and ubiquitous cycle from nonintimacy to intimacy (or from attraction to beginning to continuation, etc.). Nor did Harré castigate the notion that all courtship ever does is move ponderously and satisfactorily toward eventual commitment, nor the idea that friendships only develop rapturously toward new depths of intimate nirvana, nor the view that everyday life is replete with instances of friends arguing but getting over it. No one until Billig (1987) focused on the fact that life is variable unfinished business, leading others, such as Shotter (1992) and Duck (1990) to claim that relationships are also unfinished business in which friends can be irritating or might change their minds or can be indecisive or have debates or dialogues and discussions with one another, or act in variable and inconsistent manners with one another over time. These observations have had to wait for a later generation of observers who call for a more fully differentiated view of the true nature of daily experience of relationships in a world without sophomores (Allan, 1989; Duck, 1991).

There are many possible explanations of the fact that researchers have been less willing to look at the negative side of relationships or are late in treating relationships as more complex, interactive, socially performed phenomena than scores on a scale of closeness. For one thing, research has to begin somewhere (Berscheid, 1986). For another, there were not many who researched relationships in the old days—and finding and collecting researchers doing close analysis of, say, relationship development was quite a feat (Mark Cook and Glenn Wilson, two British psychologists having been the first—in 1977—to arrange, in Swansea, Wales, an international conference on relationships or "attraction love" as they called it in the language of the time—see Cook & Wilson, 1979). Thus the pioneers addressed only the issues that they could handle, because there was too much labor and not enough laborers. Thirdly, the reaction against lab studies of attraction (or lab studies of any kind) had not really taken much of a grip on relationship researchers, some of whom had never even met a postmodernist. Fourthly, researchers, like other human beings (although one tends to resist the label), have human tendencies that encompass poor processing of information, difficulty in doing hard, complex thinking, and a tendency to oversimplify incoming information (cf. Kahneman & Tversky, 1973).

An Observation on the Development of Fields of Study

Another way of looking at the positivity bias is in terms of the sociology of knowledge and the ways in which research is undertaken. The study of both attribution and of social support, for example, tended to begin with the enthusiastic study of all that could be concluded from the basic notions that people attributed causes on the basis of quasi-scientific observation of the world (Jones et al., 1972) or that social support was good for one's health (Berkman & Syme, 1979; Caplan, 1974; Cobb, 1976) or helped people to avoid loneliness (Cutrona, 1982). Reinterpretations of old research problems were offered, indicating that this orientation had properties similar to the philosopher's stone sought by ancient alchemists as the miracle substance that could turn other metals into gold. The new approach could solve practical problems, make people deliriously happy, and get research grants. As the research developed, so it became embarrassingly clear that attribution was a process that was subject to systematic error (Ross, 1977) or had no relevance at all to a lot of social behavior (Langer, 1978), or that social support was not always a blessing (La Gaipa, 1990; Rook, 1984). Indeed, in some cases attribution leads people up such pathways of confusion that they are better off not doing it at all (Nisbett & Ross, 1980), and in other cases the obligations of social support are so overwhelming that they destroy not only relationships but people (Nadler & Fisher, 1986), or else the attempts are so crude and unhelpful that they make everyone feel worse (Lehman & Hemphill, 1990).

The maniacal cheeriness and sense of relief that usually greet the discovery of a newly fashionable research area seem to be followed some 10–15 years later with a gently revised negative picture. One first begins to see papers claiming that the fashionable topic, while, of course, still inherently worthy and likely to solve the problem of global warming and world hunger, is possibly flawed. Thus one finds critics asking why, after 15 years of research in the topic of social support, researchers know so little about the central variable of study (Hobfoll, 1990). Similar sorts of claims have been made also in respect to openness and disclosure (Parks, 1982), attraction (Bochner, 1991), and competence (Spitzberg, 1993). One also begins to become uncomfortably aware that the topic leaders are edging conveniently nearer to the lifeboats by publishing reviews of the topic that are much less enthusiastic about it than some of their earlier work. They now suggest caution, counsel others of the difficulties and Gordian complexities in the area, and generally detach themselves discreetly, like realtors carefully standing in front of a damp patch newly discovered in the basement.

In an earlier analysis of the ways in which this happens in disciplines as a whole (Duck, 1980), I had the fancy that it bore a relationship to the life cycle of graduate students. Because researchers typically train their students to do what they do but also to be critical scholars, it follows that if researchers are dealing in fashionable topics and also being successful advisors, then their students will leave the programs 5 years later as scholars knowing what their teachers do but being somewhat critical of it. *Their* students will be trained by them and will leave their programs being even more critical of the original works. Thus, when these students begin to publish their work 10–12 years after the cycle started, it will tend to be highly critical of the work that their scholarly grandparents taught their advisors. Of course, I have never gathered either empirical or archival data to test this whimsy, but I still kinda like it. [The editors assure me that Martindale (1990) offered the more respectable argument that what is not new ceases to be arousing for

scientists (and artists) and the pressure for novelty itself leads to the slough-
ing off of previously favorite research skins.]

Given that such trends are determinable in research reports, it is important that future work on the field of relationships takes vigorous early steps
to counteract it as best it can by making early moves to incorporate the negative and the complex into theory. In this way researchers can forestall the
shifty abandonment of a field that seems to follow such disillusionment and
instead offer it as an exciting challenge even more inviting than the original
one of exploring all the sickly sweet aspects of relationships. In this case the
discovery and exploration of a neglected aspect of relating does not so much
negate or nullify the original area as some disillusionment seems to do, rather
it shows that, like the moon, it is not a flat disc as our (research) ancestors
used to think, but rather a lifesome three-dimensional orb. A first step, but
only a first step, is to identify rapidly those topics that make up the experience
of real human relationships but do not yet get sufficiently accounted in
research. Others have called for descriptive work, indeed that call was one
of Hinde's (1979) early and distinctive contributions to the field. However,
a descriptive approach to topics that researchers had previously studied by
other means, while a distinct addition to the scientific enterprise, is not the
same as systematically describing the phenomena that one wishes to understand *first*, and *then* doing so without preconceptions created by adherence
to particular research paradigms.

A useful but less adequate way to approach this possibility is the careful
observation of relationships in life or reflection on one's own experiences.
Going beyond this, Bochner (1990) caused many a raised eyebrow and incre-
ment in blood pressure by actually suggesting that researchers could even
gain insights from novels, films, plays, diaries, and other artistic human
products that had not been preconceived by an experimenter and scored on
a 7-point scale. Even these results of human cognition could be seen as a
form of report on the human experience, argued Bochner, that are popular
or widely accepted precisely for the very reason that they give remarkable
insight into the collective experience of the human readership. For instance,
Hinde (personal communication, Aug. 14, 1992) indicated that Black (1975)
did a relevant systematic survey of a number of works of art, ranging from
the Greek dramatists to *Lady Chatterley's Lover*, and explored the ways in
which the social mores of the time conflicted with the issue of marital or sexual fidelity depicted in the art. Davis (1983) also used both literary and relational research sources to explore the construction of sexuality and sexual
standards in society and so created a stunningly evocative and insightful analysis of the ways in which society regulates and interprets sexuality.

Had researchers been prepared to warrant such experiences and literary
sources, it is almost inconceivable that it could have taken 13 years from
Hinde's (1979) call for descriptive work to the first careful analysis of the role

of play in relationships (Baxter, 1992), or 10 years before anyone wrote about enemies (Wiseman, 1989), or more than a decade before a book appeared on hatred (Shoenewolf, 1991), or one-tenth of a century before someone proposed that researchers explore everyday relational talk as a factor in relationships (Duck & Pond, 1989), or that any of this could happen 10 years after some had already begun to congratulate themselves on the arrival of a thoroughgoing science of relationships.

Yet even now it has been pointed out that there are no papers on the role of disappointment in relationships, or of regret, or remorse, or many other emotional events that relate experience at one time point to experience at another or the views of one perceiver of a relationship to those of another (Duck, 1991). Equally few studies note that decisions to do something in life (especially things in relationships) or to pursue one course of action are implicit or explicit rejections of other lines of action that may come back to visit one's moments of reflective solitude once in a while (Billig, 1987). Thus, the unfinished business of relating likely involves mixtures and decoctions of regrets, joys, pleasures, remorses, forgivings, and mistakes. Nevertheless, most research misses this transactive point by focusing on only one of the partner's beliefs about encapsulated interactions separated from other emotional or social or cultural contexts, whether positive or negative, and without any reference to the symbols that the people traffic when they have interactions. It is as if it has been decided that all there is to know about handshaking can be found in an analysis of the structure of the back of one of the hands and the neural activity that goes into extending it.

It is important for a *real* science of relationships that studies attempting to create theoretical advances in the understanding of relationships in human beings do not simply focus on convenient populations or rather unrepresentatively happy relationships that are made the basis of lightsome claims to scientific generality and truth. It is not sufficient merely to nod in the direction of negative experiences without actually trying to include them in the general theory of relating. Simply to regard them as merely no more than the negative side of an otherwise positive and interpretable life is to denigrate something that may play a much stronger role in the human processes of relating that can widen the vision of the fuller enterprise. For example, to acknowledge that real people really do have to deal not only with liking and loving but also with hate and dislike is to ask very serious questions about the social management and psychological consequences of the range of relational experiences, rather than simply to note that a negative side exists and then move on like a research butterfly to a new and richer topical flower.

If the positive and negative sides of relationships are managed in the same ways, then the theories do not need modification, although it would be a good idea to demonstrate that similarity before assuming it. If they are managed in different ways, then some sort of theoretical explanation is needed for the differences; one is needed that can still tie into the general human enterprise in a theoretically meaningful way. More than that, researchers need to modify and broaden theories that are all too rapidly turning into blissful dispositional accounts of merely close relationships and not even looking at the episodic variability that occurs within them nor at all the other sorts of personal and social relationships that normal people deal with rather often (see Duck, in press, for an extended critique and discussion of this point).

Organizing Overlooked Topics for Further Research

The editors of this volume took a big step in correctly identifying the dark side of relationships as one that has hitherto received very little attention. The field had been going for several years before the first book of collected papers devoted solely to the dissolution of personal relationships as a whole (as distinct from divorce alone) was published in 1982, for example. But break-down of relationships is not the only difficult facet of relationships, and many unpleasant aspects have still not received any attention at all, many of which are reported in the chapters that follow. This volume correctly includes some discussion of indirectness, incompetence, deception, hurtful messages, paradoxes, predicaments, dilemmas, privacy binds, negative family relations, transgressions, and abuse.

The list of topics that researchers have failed to account or study is monumentally impressive in a tragic sense, for all the time while it has become increasingly common for writers to congratulate themselves for their theoretical advances in the field, these topics have lain neglected as silent accusers and pointers to the very limits of those theories. Some of the topics are studied a little, but most are not, or are studied only in some contexts and not others. For instance, there are studies of bullies at school (Olweus, 1989; Smith, Bowers, Binney, & Cowie, 1993), but not at work or in adulthood (and I have found no work on hectoring or overbearing adults, although I have met some). There are studies of date rape and violence in courtship, some of which even consider the role of verbal violence (Deal & Wampler, 1986; see also Vangelisti, this volume), but there are few thoroughgoing studies of intentional verbal humiliation or sharp tongues out of the dating context (Adams, 1977). Although James (1890) first noted the cruelty of the situation when a person is ignored by everyone, only a handful of attempts have followed up on the significance of being ignored or despised (e.g., Geller, Goodstein, Silver, & Sternberg, 1974). Some studies explored the consequences of rejection or neglect at school (Asher & Coie, 1990), but there seems to be none on such neglect in adulthood—notwithstanding the U.S. Constitution's (Article iii, Section 3) acknowledgment of its effects on enemies and its claim that good citizens should be able to do it. There are studies of betrayal

(Hansson, Jones, & Fletcher, 1990; Jones, 1988), but not of the vendettas that filmmakers used to like to portray in such films as *Cool Hand Luke*.

In part this may be because most of this work looks only at voluntary interdependence rather than at collegial or work relationships, which most spend the majority of their days dealing with when they are not just researching other people's happy and ideal relationships (cf. Hepburn & Crepin's, 1984, studies of relationships between prisoners and guards). The "needlings" which Harré (1977) noted as a regular and frequent feature of relationships that are enmeshed have not become the topic of investigators' studies of real life, much less of laboratory life. When teasing is studied (Pawluk, 1989; Shapiro, Baumeister, & Kessler, 1991), its negative and hurtful side is not given exceptional prominence. There has been a discussion on "bullshit" (Frankfurt, 1986), and there has been work on the derogation of sexual rivals (Buss & Dedden, 1990), although there has not been a study on male or female "bitchiness" or petty mean-spiritedness. How is this well-known and well-recognized behavior different from the "hurtful messages" that are given a chapter here (cf. Garfinkel, 1956)? Does it not evidence a deeper and dispositional strategic tendency that implicates an enduring intent or style that needs clarification (Semin & Rubini, 1990)? Nor are there many studies exploring the ways in which people undermine others, whether as rivals or as equals (but see Campbell & Tesser, 1985). There is a lack of study of the relational "stratagems and spoils" that Shakespeare identified for empirical scrutiny in 1598, yet at least people in the business world (and in-flight magazines about the business world) have an image of it as a world in which this must be expected to happen almost daily and which needs careful attention (and so money must be paid to entrepreneurs who can help one to prevent or avoid it and also to "Get One Up on Your Rivals Before They Do It to You").

It was 1986 before Miller, Mongeau, and Sleight (1986) published "Fudging with Friends and Lying to Lovers," the first discussion of the effects of deception in personal relationships (but see Shippee, 1977, on social relationships). This is despite the existence of large amounts of work on deception in other impersonal relationships (usually dealing with mock customs officers or simulated police officers). Those who study conflict still devote more time to looking at how to resolve it, rather than at how it is triggered or escalated in conversations.

Boring communicators are met much more frequently in life than in the research literature (Leary, Rogers, Canfield, & Coe, 1986; Leatham & Duck, 1992), in which researchers instead devote whole journals to competent and interesting communication, in defiance of their own experience of faculty meetings. The *Journal of Communication* devoted an issue in 1977 to gossip, but since then there has been almost not a peep out of any researchers on the effects of gossip on network functioning or on the personal relationships that are studied (but for one peep see Eder & Enke, 1991), even though researchers have recognized the effects of reputation in the network and network discussion on the formation and break up of relationships (La Gaipa, 1982; Parks & Barnes, 1988) and even of the importance of the daily gossipy chats that friends have with one another (Emler & Fisher, 1981).

In addition to these common experiences that in real life color one's willingness to approach, like, or get involved with someone else, there is a host of difficulties that two friends or lovers can experience in relationships, or which make the conduct of relationships strenuous. I am thinking here of some of the things that are well studied, such as conflict, or alternative relationship possibilities or time management problems in relationships (Clarke, Allen, & Salinas, 1985), as well as the disappointments, slights, and quarrels that occur from time to time. But where are the studies of *under*development of relationships, the ones that got away? Or of suspicion, that fertile ground for jealousy and dissatisfaction? There are studies of trust, but only very recently any on distrust (e.g., Eloy, Guerrero, Andersen, & Spitzberg, 1992; Levine & McCornack, 1991). Is distrust merely the opposite of trust, or is it a fundamentally different relational experience with behavioral consequences that affect people profoundly? What about the strongly motivating effects of the "dish best served cold," namely revenge? Emmons (1992, p. 3) pointed out that "the only prior [to 1992] attempts to measure revenge have been broadly based measures of fantasy in which revenge fantasies are a minor component . . . [and only a] small number of experimental social psychological studies have included revenge conditions."

This list of topics is astonishing in itself but by no means exhaustive. A moment's reflection on personal experience, or a day spent reading a novel instead of the *Journal of Personality and Social Psychology* or *Human Communication Research,* will lead almost any reader to some critical parts of relational life that have received so little attention that it is scientifically embarrassing and contrasts badly with the mountains of effort put into the other overstudied molehills of life.

Shaping Up the "Dark Side"

An understanding of the full range of relationship processes can only be increased if one extends our timely detailed lists of overlooked behaviors that doom, disturb, or challenge relationships; or of the distressing side effects of relationships themselves; or of the incompetent performance of the behaviors that normally promote relationships. The list of topics that require further study in this field is virtually endless, but the important point is that the focus on the favorable, positive, close, and nice side of relating misses entirely the point that, at the very least, such behavior and the processes of cognition that go with it are always implicitly contrasted with something else in human life. Part of the delights of intimacy comes from knowledge of the horrors of rejection; a certain measure of the satisfaction from being in good relationships comes from reflection on the opposite situation (as has been detected in studies of loneliness and ratings of the importance of relationships, though few go on to note that the importance given to relationships has to be seen in this context). The key point is that the process of balancing things out is itself a positive thing, rather than the positive end of the contrast being the thing itself alone.

The issues can be separated into: (a) those that affect the occurrence of relationships in the first place (thus obnoxious behavior presumably is negative enough to cancel the chance for a relationship to start, but what if it happens in a relationship that has already started?) , (b) those that affect the chances of continuance of a relationship, and (c) those that affect the enjoyment of relationships that are already well established and essentially not likely to be dismantled wholesale as the result of minor currents and eddies. Rodin (1982), in a wrongly neglected piece of insightful work that predates Rosenbaum's (1986) work on repulsion, discussed the negative behaviors and inferences that lead to a "failure to engage," and she wisely differentiated between "non-engagement," "failure to engage," and "disengagement" based on the idea that "liking and disliking are not complementary, as is usually supposed, but are completely distinct from one another" (p. 31). (The essay is well worth reading, and I refer the interested scholar to that intriguing chapter, while I focus on the negative behaviors that deal with the continuance of relationships or enjoyment of them.)

Basically the topics can be organized conceptually into four categories: (a) those that constitute different (negative) sorts of relationships from the positive ones usually studied (e.g., Enemies, Bullies); (b) those that represent attempts to sabotage relationships, prevent them from developing, cause them to deteriorate, or gain revenge for the breakdown of a previously positive relationship (e.g., Revenge, Undermining, Needling); (c) those that constitute a spoiling of positive relationships (e.g., Betrayal, Disappointment); and (d) those that illustrate the inherent downside—the daily hassles and difficulties— of being in positive relationships (e.g., Occasional Tensions, Conflict, Binds and Obligations of Relating). These four categories seem to come down to two distinctions, one on a positive/negative intent dimension, and the other on an inherent versus emergent dimension (as in Fig. 1.1).

This categorization of relational behavior points to the significance of partners' intent and the structural/management issues inherent in conducting *any* relationship. Thus, it is essentially a proposal with social consequences, insofar as Fig. 1.1 places the importance of negative behavior and structures at the interactive social management and communicative levels, not at the insulated, private, individual psychological level. Whereas negativity presumably has its source in individuals, it is manifested in dyads or in relational

	INHERENT	EMERGENT
BAD INTENTIONS TOWARD THE OTHER PERSON	NEGATIVE RELATIONS (Bullies; Enemies)	SABOTAGE (Needling; Revenge; Silent treatment)
GOOD INTENTIONS TOWARD THE OTHER PERSON	DIFFICULTY (Conflict; Binds)	SPOILING (Betrayal; Regret)

FIG. 1.1. A taxonomy of "dark" relational forms.

effects. Thus, insofar as the categorization has any heuristic potential, this comes from a metatheoretical overview and concerns the ways in which negativity affects the conduct of relationships rather than the individual's beliefs about conduct.

Yet what is really needed is a deeper analysis of the theoretical importance of such behaviors which presently take too little—if any—space in most books on relationships (see Duck, in press). The dark side of relationships needs a lot of the close theoretical attention that it presently does not get at all, not only to each topic in its own right, but also to its place in theories of relationships as a whole. For example, much of the dark side of relating is rather problematic, on the face of it, for exchange theories or theories of interdependence that act as if people stay together because things work out pretty positively for them most of the time. Yet there are plenty of examples of negative things happening in daily relationships fairly often. Is one supposed to ignore the negative side or to believe that, despite continual reports and experiences to the contrary, it happens only rarely or presents only cognitive and not behavioral dilemmas to people? Or should one be rethinking relational theories in a way that focuses them on the opposing forces that real live human beings buttering their daily bread outside the lab are forced to confront and resolve in the course of conducting their lives? Hatred and having enemies does not merely mean the absence of closeness or a lack of interdependence, but they are enmeshing relationships that challenge one's very notion of what a relationship is (Shotter, 1992). They place relational essence strongly in behavioral interaction, conversation, and the ways in which one person treats (not "thinks about" or "feels about" but "treats") another person. One has to face the possibility that existing theories of relationships appear to work well enough, merely because they are based on the sorts of research that choose to study the kinds of relationships in which they work well!

What is needed to incorporate the challenging side of relationships into the rest of what is known is an approach to the human enterprise that takes account of the different levels of experience that the human being encounters in social life and which incorporates an explanation of the negative (and why it is that it is experienced as negative) as well as an account of its significance in relational life for most people. Researchers should not merely package that life up into segments, some of which have one explanation and some another, but rather they should seek explanations that incorporate both. As theorists of relationships, one has the choice of explaining relational behavior (both positive and negative) as a compartmentalized human activity (though even so one needs to explain the role of the dark side in that) or as a further manifest expression of general human tendencies that can be seen in many different guises.

The important point is not to simply add to the list of topics in the field but to establish the significant theoretical observation that all sides of relating have to be included in any fully rounded comprehension of the nature of relating. Researchers can study closeness and develop as many scales of intimacy as they wish, but they shall not have fully comprehended the nature of relating until such attention is balanced by a theoretical appreciation of the significance of the tensions produced by management of the negative side of all this in human experience. I argue that these tensions are essentially a manifestation of other sorts of human behavior, showing the ways in which problematic events are conceptualized and given *meaning* by individuals.

It is also worth making a general point about the field that contributes to the state of affairs that this book decries. One of the astonishing gaps in the research on relationships is a reasonable descriptive base of the ways in which ordinary folks carry on their relating, whether positive or negative. Most research has been research-driven, that is, it takes questions that previous important researchers have addressed and then goes on to study them in refined and inventive ways. However, it is rare to find researchers studying first what real people think or do in their relationships before the methodological wagons begin to circle and set up camp for the night in a very small area of the larger prairie. This absence of a real comprehension of the activities of real people leads to such anomalies as the mountainous compilation of studies about self-disclosure and large theoretical treatises on its importance in developing relationships when those studies that have investigated it in real life (Dindia, Fitzpatrick, & Kenny, 1989; Duck, Rutt, Hurst, & Strejc, 1991) both find that it occurs only 2% of the time in a range of relationships from acquaintances, through friendship, to marital relations. It is a fair bet that such subtle misrepresentation of the geography of relationships is occurring all the time as teachers and their graduate students relentlessly pursue the clarification of established topics, without looking over their shoulders to see if real people are following them at all.

One way to do this would be to remind others of the contributions of those scholars who point out the dialectical and dialogical or dilemmatic nature of life. Positivity or negativity in relational behavior is not a state of a relationship, as is all too often and all too erroneously assumed (Duck & Sants, 1983). Rather, they both occur occasionally, one more than the other in most relationships, as part of the continuous and continually unfolding experience of relationships that constitutes the unfinished business of relating. People's daily experience of relationships is far more variable than the theories of closeness allow. For researchers as well as for most subjects, the daily experience of any given relationship taken over a week-long or month-long period is one with good and bad parts, intimate and distant days, positive and negative moments. Research that seeks to reduce the whole thing to a single and all-soaking statement that claims a state of closeness or positivity is making one big mistake, just as would be naive statisticians who suppose that the mean of a distribution tells all that one needs to know about it (Duck, 1990, 1991). Relationships are variable experiences, even though people may report them in single dispositional ways when asked to do so by experimenters or other researchers.

When this view is given its theoretical roots in the recent interest in dilemmas or in dialectics, then one begins to see the glimmerings of a way to conceptualize the negative and the positive sides of relationships. But one has to see them as more than a merely cognitive experience and as an issue for social management and social organization inaccessible to the scrutiny of mere social cognition theorists. For although the approach that I take is rooted in meaning, meaning is found in social action as well as in individuals' cognitive content (Burkitt, 1991). Billig (1987) and Shotter (1992) have argued that life is unfinished business which is devoted to the solving of dilemmas that are the basis of human thought. When this is applied to the area of relationships (Duck, 1990; Shotter, 1992) and also tied into the theoretical work on the use of language on social and personal relationships (Duck & Pond, 1989), then a model can be created for the negative and positive effects on relationships. This model is based on the idea that people talk to one another in daily discourse in a way that has both the purpose and the result of reifying their relationship and giving it meaning in their lives. The talk of everyday life, which has seemed so trivial that it was thought not to merit systematic study, is in fact a crucible for both the positive and negative sides of relationships.

First, one must recognize that relationships are conducted almost daily and that the experiences that are had there can be variable. Persons experience these daily fluctuations when friends are grouchy or lovers are inaccessible or undemonstrative, even though they remain friends and lovers. In such cases, the items from others' behavior which are likely to be interpreted and treated as significant are those that have personal meaning to the perceiver (Duck, 1991) or have meaning to the person within the relationship—which is one reason why one should not rush to characterize something as objectively "positive" or "negative" in relationships, nor even to characterize some types of relationships as close (I know a lesbian and a homosexual man who married in order to obtain a green card for him; they are friends but not close because they are married). Those behaviors that are the subject of talk are likely to be given such meaning, but other behaviors can also acquire it. Thus, some negative behaviors have the effect of denying the relationship (e.g., the silent treatment denies the responsibility of relationship partners to participate actively in the behaviors of relating), or else of denying the validity of the person in them (e.g., "defaces" the person or derogates him or her in some way, such as the behaviors of needling or bullying, both of which deny and reduce the person's rights in the encounter and diminish "face" recognition). In their own ways the behaviors that occur in a positive environment but have negative effects tend toward the same results: The binds of relationships tend to "deface" the person by countering his or her own needs for autonomy with pressures to put the relationship first. Betrayal also serves to diminish one of the persons by indicating that he or she was placed second to some other need or desire or preference of the partner, although regret seems to be a recognition that one has diminished oneself by performing an action that does not live up to one's expectations for oneself.

This interpretation puts the negative and positive behaviors in the same theoretical pile, in the sense that relational acts are positive when they impinge on the meanings that a person has for the relationship and the persons in a positive way, and negative when they affect those images negatively. The behaviors in themselves are not inherently positive or negative in this analysis, but become so only in the context of what they mean for the relating partners specifically. Thus, one is able to distinguish the "cruel remark" that is taken in a given relationship to be teasing, from the "cruel remark" that really is intended and perceived to be cruel by the interactants in the context of their knowledge of one another in the relationship. In the daily talk of relating which has been given so little attention partners construct, share, and interpret the meanings of one another as they conduct their perpetually unfinished relational business. (Even when relationships are over people can still think about them in ways that affect their moods and even their behavior.)

Talk thus serves to create and establish the meanings that exist for the partners in the relationship (Duck, in press) and against which standard the behaviors of the relationship are judged as positive or negative. It is in the personal meaning systems of the two relational partners that acts are given their negative or positive spin, whether at the early stages or the later stages of relationship formation and maintenance. Thus, by seeking to lift the curtain on the dark side of relationships we should look closely at the meaning systems of the persons in them, just as we should when the spotlight is put on the good stuff (Duck, 1991). Personal systems of meaning are the basis for all the relationship effects that researchers study, whether dark or light. All the same, I am not arguing that one should cast aside cheery research and now all do investigations of depressing negativity amidst an atmosphere of sackcloth and ashes. It would be a grievous intellectual error to regard the "dark side" as a separate aspect of relating (Altman, personal communication, Sept. 1, 1992). Instead, we need to theorize it as an integral part of the unified process of relating. Like the dark side of the moon, the dark side of relationships can be found to co-exist in the same entity as the light side. We need to explore and understand it not in itself but in its relation to everything else that has ever been learned about relationships. More important, we need to understand how normal people leading everyday lives resolve and manage the "dark side" of those working, throbbing relational lives.

ACKNOWLEDGMENTS

I gratefully acknowledge the insights, advice, and suggestions of Irwin Altman, Anita Barbee, Bill Cupach, Robert Hinde, Karen Prager, Catherine Radecki-Bush, Phil Shaver, Brian Spitzberg, and Julia T. Wood who read and commented on the first draft.

REFERENCES

Adams, R. M. (1977). *Bad Mouth: Fugitive papers on the darkside*. Berkeley: University of California Press.

Allan, G. (1989). *Friendship*. Hemel Hempstead, UK: Harvester Wheatsheaf.

Asher, S. R., & Coie, J. D. (1990). *Peer rejection in childhood*. Cambridge University Press.

Baxter, L. A. (1992). Forms and functions of intimate play in personal relationships. *Human Communication Research, 18*, 336–363.

Berkman, L. F., & Syme, S. L. (1979). Social networks, host resistance and mortality: A nine year follow-up of Alameda County residents. *American Journal of Epidemiology, 109*, 186–204.

Berscheid, E. (1986). Mea culpas and lamentations: Sir Francis, Sir Isaac and the "slow progress of soft psychology." In R. Gilmour & S. W. Duck (Eds.), *The emerging field of personal relationships* (pp. 267–286). Hillsdale, NJ: Lawrence Erlbaum Associates.

Berscheid, E., Snyder, M., & Omoto, A. (1989). Issues in studying close relationships: Conceptualizing and measuring closeness. In C. Hendrick (Ed.), *Close relationships* (pp. 63–91). Newbury Park, CA: Sage.

Berscheid, E., & Walster, E. H. (1974). 'A little bit about love.' In T. L. Huston (Ed.), *Foundations of interpersonal attraction* (pp. 355–381). New York: Academic Press.

Billig, M. (1987). *Arguing and thinking: A rhetorical approach to social psychology*. Cambridge: Cambridge University Press.

Black, M. (1975). *The literature of fidelity*. Cambridge: Cambridge University Press.

Bochner, A. P. (1990, July). Invited address. Paper to the Fifth International Conference on Personal Relationships, Oxford, UK.

Bochner, A. P. (1991). The paradigm that would not die. In J. Anderson (Ed.), *Communication yearbook 14* (pp. 484–491). Newbury Park, CA: Sage.

Braiker, H. B., & Kelley, H. H. (1979). Conflict in the development of close relationships. In R. L. Burgess & T. L. Huston (Eds.), *Social exchange in developing relationships* (pp. 135–168). New York: Academic Press.

Brehm, S. S. (1992). *Intimate relationships* (2nd ed.). New York: Random House.

Bruhn, J. G., & Murray, J. L. (1985). "Playing the dozens": Its history and psychological significance. *Psychological Reports, 56,* 483–494.

Burkitt, I. (1991). *Social selves: Theories of the social formation of personality.* London: Sage.

Buss, D., & Dedden, L. A. (1990). Derogation of competitors. *Journal of Social and Personal Relationships, 7,* 395–422.

Campbell, J., & Tesser, A. (1985). Self-evaluation maintenance processes in relationships. In S. W. Duck & D. Perlman (Eds.), *Understanding personal relationships* (pp. 107–135). London: Sage.

Caplan, G. (1974). *Support systems and community mental health: Lectures on concept development.* New York: Behavioral Publications.

Cicero, M. T. (46 B.C.). *De amicitia.* Horti Novabaculae, Rome: Libri Sapientis.

Clarke, D. D., Allen, C. M. B., & Salinas, M. (1985). Conjoint time budgeting: Investigating behavioral accommodation in marriage. *Journal of Social and Personal Relationships, 3,* 53–70.

Cobb, S. (1976). Social support as a moderator of life stress. *Psychosomatic Medicine, 3,* 300–314.

Cook, M., & Wilson, G. (1979). *Attraction and love.* Oxford: Pergamon Press.

Cutrona, C. E. (1982). Transition to college: Loneliness and the process of social adjustment. In L. A. Peplau & D. Perlman (Eds.), *Loneliness: A sourcebook of current theory, research and therapy* (pp. 291–309). New York: Wiley.

Davis, M. S. (1983). *SMUT: Erotic reality/obscene ideology.* Chicago: University of Chicago.

Deal, J., & Wampler, K. S. (1986). Dating violence: The primacy of previous experience. *Journal of Social and Personal Relationships, 3,* 457–471.

Delia, J. G. (1980). Some tentative thoughts concerning the study of interpersonal relationships and their development. *Western Journal of Speech Communication, 44,* 97–103.

Dindia, K., Fitzpatrick, M. A., & Kenny, D. A. (1989, May). *Self disclosure in spouse and stranger interaction: A social relations analysis.* Paper presented to the International Communication Association, New Orleans, LA.

Duck, S. W. (1980). Taking the past to heart: One of the futures of social psychology. In R. Gilmour & S. W. Duck (Eds.), *The development of social psychology* (pp. 211–238). London: Academic Press.

Duck, S. W. (Ed.). (1982). *Personal relationships 4: Dissolving personal relationships.* London: Academic Press.

Duck, S. W. (1990). Relationships as unfinished business: Out of the frying pan and into the 1990s. *Journal of Social and Personal Relationships, 7,* 5–28.

Duck, S. W. (1991, May). *New lamps for old: A new theory of relationships and a fresh look at some old research.* Paper presented to the Third Conference of the International Network on Personal Relationships, Normal/Blomington, IL.

Duck, S. W. (in press). *Meaningful relationships: Talking, sense, and relating.* Newbury Park, CA: Sage.

Duck, S. W., & Pond, K. (1989). Friends, Romans, countrymen, lend me your retrospections: Rhetoric and reality in personal relationships. In C. Hendrick (Ed.), *Close relationships* (pp. 17–38). Newbury Park, CA: Sage.

Duck, S. W., Rutt, D. J., Hurst, M., & Strejc, H. (1991). Some evident truths about communication in everyday relationships: All communication is not created equal. *Human Communication Research, 18,* 228–267.

Duck, S. W., & Sants, H. K. A. (1983). On the origin of the specious: Are personal relationships really interpersonal states? *Journal of Social and Clinical Psychology, 1,* 1–27.

Duck, S. W., & Wood, J. T. (in preparation). *Relationship challenges [Understanding Relationship Process 5]*. Newbury Park, CA: Sage.

Eder, D., & Enke, J. L. (1991). The structure of gossip: Opportunities and constraints on collective expression among adolescents. *American Sociological Review, 56,* 494–508.

Eloy, S. V., Guerrero, L. K., Andersen, P. A., & Spitzberg, B. H. (1992, May). *Coping with the green-eyed monster: Relational satisfaction and communicative reactions to jealousy.* Paper presented to International Communication Association Conference, Miami.

Emler, N., & Fisher, J. (1981, September). *Gossip among friends.* Paper presented to the annual convention of the Social Psychology Section of the British Psychological Society, Oxford.

Emmons, R. A. (1992, August). *Revenge: Individual differences and correlates.* Paper presented at 100th annual convention of the American Psychological Association, Washington, DC.

Frankfurt, H. (1986, Fall). On bullshit. *Raritan.* [Condensed and reprinted in *Harper's Magazine,* February 1987, pp. 14–17].

Garfinkel, H. (1956). Conditions of successful degradation ceremonies. *American Sociological Review, 61,* 420–424.

Geller, D. M., Goodstein, L., Silver, M., & Sternberg, W. C. (1974). On being ignored: The effects of violation of implicit rules of social interaction. *Sociometry, 37,* 541–556.

Gottman, J. M. (1979). *Marital interaction: Experimental investigations.* New York: Academic Press.

Hansson, R. O., Jones, W. H., & Fletcher, W. L. (1990). Troubled relationships in later life: Implications for support. *Journal of Social and Personal Relationships, 7,* 451–464.

Harré, R. (1977). Friendship as an accomplishment: An ethogenic approach to social relationships. In S. W. Duck (Ed.), *Theory and practice in interpersonal attraction.* London: Academic Press.

Harvey, J. H., Weber, A. L., & Orbuch, T. L. (1990). *Interpersonal accounts: A social psychological perspective.* Oxford: Basil Blackwell.

Hendrick, C., & Hendrick, S. S. (1986). A theory and a method of love. *Journal of Personality and Social Psychology, 50,* 392–402.

Hepburn, J. R., & Crepin, A. E. (1984). Relationship strategies in a coercive institution: A study of dependence among prison guards. *Journal of Social and Personal Relationships, 1,* 139–158.

Hinde, R. A. (1979). *Towards understanding relationships.* London: Academic Press.

Hobfoll, S. E. (1990). Introduction: The importance of predicting activating and facilitating social support. *Journal of Social and Personal Relationships, 7,* 435–436.

James, W. (1890). *Principles of psychology.* London: Macmillan.

Jones, E. E., Kanouse, D. E., Kelley, H. H., Nisbett, R. E., Valins, S., & Weiner, B. (Eds.). (1972). *Attribution: Perceiving the causes of behavior.* New York: General Learning.

Jones, W. H. (1988, July). *Betrayal.* Paper presented to the Fourth International Conference on Personal Relationships, Vancouver, British Columbia.

Kahneman, D., & Tversky, A. (1973). On the psychology of prediction. *Psychological Review, 80,* 237–251.

Kelley, H. H., Berscheid, E., Christensen, A., Harvey, J., Huston, T. L., Levinger, G., McClintock, D., Peplau, L. A., & Peterson, D. (1983). *Close relationships.* San Francisco: W. H. Freeman.

La Gaipa, J. J. (1982). Rules and rituals in disengaging from relationships. In S. W. Duck (Ed.), *Personal relationships 4: Dissolving personal relationships* (pp. 189–209). London: Academic Press.

La Gaipa, J. J. (1990). The negative effects of informal support systems. In S. W. Duck (Ed., with R. C. Silver), *Personal relationships and social support* (pp. 122–139). London: Sage.

Langer, E. J. (1978). Rethinking the role of thought in social interaction. In J. H. Harvey, W. Ickes, & R. F. Kidd (Eds.), *New directions in attribution research* (pp. 35–58). Hillsdale, NJ: Lawrence Erlbaum Associates.

Leary, M. R., Rogers, P. A., Canfield, R. W., & Coe, C. (1986). Boredom in interpersonal encounters: Antecedents and social implications. *Journal of Personality and Social Psychology, 51,* 958–975.

Leatham, G. B., & Duck, S. W. (1992, February). *Boring communication*. Paper presented to the annual convention of the Western States Communication Association, Boise, ID.

Lehman, D. R., & Hemphill, K. J. (1990). Recipients' perceptions of support attempts and attributions for support attempts that fail. *Journal of Social and Personal Relationships, 7,* 563–574.

Levine, T., & McCornack, S. (1991). The dark side of trust: Conceptualizing and measuring types of communicative suspicion. *Communication Quarterly, 39,* 325–340.

Lloyd, S. A., & Cate, R. M. (1985). The developmental course of conflict in dissolution of premarital relationships. *Journal of Social and Personal Relationships, 2,* 179–194.

Martindale, C. (1990). *The clockwork muse: The predictability of artistic change*. New York: Basic Books.

Miller, G. R., Mongeau, P., & Sleight, C. (1986). Fudging with friends and lying to lovers: Deceptive communication in personal relationships. *Journal of Social and Personal Relationships, 3,* 495–512.

Nadler, A., & Fisher, J. D. (1986). The role of threat to self-esteem and perceived control on recipient reactions to help: Theory development and empirical validation. In L. Berkowitz (Ed.), *Advances in experimental social psychology* (Vol. 19, pp. 81–122). Orlando, FL: Academic Press.

Nisbett, R., & Ross, L. (1980). *Human inference: Strategies and shortcomings of social judgement*. Englewood Cliffs, NJ: Prentice-Hall.

Olweus, D. (1989). Bully/victim problems among schoolchildren: Basic facts and effects of a school based intervention program. In K. Rubin & D. Pepler (Eds.), *The development and treatment of childhood aggression*. Hillsdale, NJ: Lawrence Erlbaum Associates.

Orbuch, T. L. (Ed.). (1992). *Close relationship loss: Theoretical approaches*. New York: Springer-Verlag.

Parks, M. R. (1982). Ideology in interpersonal communication: Off the couch and into the world. In M. Burgoon (Ed.), *Communication yearbook 5* (pp. 79–108). Beverly Hills, CA: Sage.

Parks, M. R., & Barnes, K. J. (1988, November). *With a little help from my friends: The role of third parties in the initiation of interpersonal relationships*. Paper to the annual convention of the Speech Communication Association, New Orleans, LA.

Pawluk, C. J. (1989). Social construction of teasing. *Journal for the Theory of Social Behavior, 19,* 145–167.

Prager, K. (in press). *The development of intimacy*. New York: Guilford.

Rodin, M. (1982). Non-engagement, failure to engage and disengagement. In S. W. Duck (Ed.), *Personal relationships 4: Dissolving personal relationships* (pp. 32–49). London: Academic Press.

Rook, K. S. (1984). The negative side of social interaction: Impact on psychological well-being. *Journal of Personality and Social Psychology, 45,* 37–54.

Rosenbaum, M. (1986). Interpersonal repulsion. *Journal of Personality and Social Psychology, 49,* 189–201.

Ross, L. (1977). The intuitive psychologist and his shortcomings: Distortions in the attribution process. In L. Berkowitz (Ed.), *Advances in experimental social psychology* (Vol. 10, pp. 173–220). New York: Academic Press.

Semin, G., & Rubini, M. (1990). Unfolding the concept of person by verbal abuse. *European Journal of Social Psychology, 20,* 463–474.

Shakespeare, W. (1598). *Serenade to music*. Quill-written manuscript, presented to the Annual Convention of Pendrivers and Inkslingers Association, University of Stratford-on-Avon, UK.

Shapiro, J. P., Baumeister, R. F., & Kessler, J. W. (1991). A three component model of children's teasing: Aggression, humor, and ambiguity. *Journal of Social and Clinical Psychology, 10,* 459–472.

Shippee, G. (1977). Preceived [sic] deception in everyday social relationships: A preliminary statement. *Psychology, 14,* 58–62.

Shoenewolf, G. (1991). *The art of hating*. New York: Random House.

Shotter, J. (1992). What is a "personal relationship"? A rhetorical-responsive account of "unfinished business." In J. H. Harvey, T. L. Orbuch, & A. L. Weber (Eds.), *Attributions, accounts and close relationships* (pp. 19–39). New York: Springer-Verlag.

Smith, P. K., Bowers, L., Binney, V., & Cowie, H. (1993). Relationships of children involved in bully/victim problems at school. In S. W. Duck (Ed.), *Understanding relationship processes 2: Learning about relationships* (pp. 184–212). London: Sage.

Spitzberg, B. H. (1993). The dialectics of (in)competence. *Journal of Social and Personal Relationships, 10*, 136–158.

Sugarman, D. B., & Hotaling, G. T. (1989). Dating violence: Prevalence, context and risk markers. In M. A. Pirog-Good & J. E. Stets (Eds.), *Violence in dating relationships* (pp. 3–32). New York: Praeger.

Wiseman, J. P. (1986). Friendship: Bonds and binds in a voluntary relationship. *Journal of Social and Personal Relationships, 3*, 191–211.

Wiseman, J. P. (1989, May). *Friends and enemies: Are they opposites?* Paper presented to the Iowa Conference on Personal Relationships, Iowa City, IA.

Wood, J. T., & Duck, S. W. (in preparation). Off the beaten track: Understudied relationships. *Understanding relationship processes 6*. Newbury Park, CA: Sage.

2

THE DARK SIDE
OF (IN)COMPETENCE

Brian H. Spitzberg
San Diego State University

In the ever-shifting eddies and currents, depths and shallows, tributaries and arroyos of relational waters, we discover the challenge of navigating to safe harbor and desired destinations. Relationships are often our greatest source of satisfaction, and just as often it seems, the source of our darkest tragedies, deepest regrets, and almost Sisyphean struggles. Given the potential importance of relationships to our well-being, we have long sought the best designs and the most accurate maps with which we might competently navigate the course of human relations. This chapter examines the history, importance, reigning ideologies, and paradoxical aspects of competence in human encounters and relationships. The objectives are to overview the centrality of competence in relationships and everyday communication, and to identify the extent to which that which we normatively take to be competent often is not, and vice versa.

HISTORY

Humans have probably been concerned with interpersonal competence ever since the evolution of self-reflective capacities and symbol systems complex enough to permit shades of subtlety (and therefore error) in meaning and interpretation. Nevertheless, scrutiny of the intellectual history of the concept reveals few clues of its more feral forms. Written histories say relatively little about interpersonal competence, or any of its cognate concepts, until relatively modern times. However, numerous small glimpses are available into the Western tradition of scholarly and social concern about social skills.

In ancient Greece and Rome, orality was highly valued, as it was commonly understood that public argument was a primary means to social influence and a better society. Little was written about interpersonal relations specifically until the Renaissance, at which time the courtly politics and ritualized customs of etiquette increasingly placed a premium on competent management of social encounters. Reductionist tendencies prevailed in scholarly conjecture through the faculty psychologies and elocutionist models of effective expression of the late 1800s. Contemporary models have evolved from a variety of models, including those that concentrate on individual traits enabling basic social functioning to more process-based models concerned with how complex interactional systems are created and recreated through communication (for review, see Spitzberg & Cupach, 1984, 1989). Competence as an intellectual concept is clearly subject to historical, cultural, and paradigmatic change over time (Benson, 1978; Dean & Youniss, 1991; Kasson, 1990; O'Neill, 1980; Wine, 1981) and continues to be a dominant theme of current relational ideologies (Dillon, 1986).

IMPORTANCE

The importance of competence can be considered in terms of two sequential questions. First, how incompetent are we? If incompetence is not a common occurrence, there is little cause for concern, theoretical or otherwise. Second, what are the consequences of our incompetence? If incompetence carries few costs to the individual or the society, then again there is little cause for concern.

The answer to the first question is exceedingly difficult to answer, given that any estimate of incompetence in society is entirely dependent on the meaning of the measure used to gauge incompetence and the audience making the judgment (Spitzberg, 1987, 1988; Spitzberg & Cupach, 1984, 1989). Rather than dissect the specifics of the various studies relevant to this question, a more impressionistic approach will suffice to suggest that communicative *in*competence is probably extensive.

Just as a general point of reference, estimates of competence in basic symbolic skills such as reading, writing, and arithmetic consistently indicate that approximately one-fifth to one-third of adult Americans are functionally illiterate (Adult Performance Level Research Project, 1977; Hunter & Harman, 1979; Kozol, 1985). Estimates regarding social and interpersonal illiteracy are not as standardized. However, there are several estimates relevant to the question.

Curran, Miller, Zwick, Monti, and Stout (1980) conservatively estimated that approximately 7.4% of the population is socially incompetent. Bryant, Trower, Yardley, Urbieta, and Letemendia (1976) found that 16.3% of their sample was consensually viewed by multiple raters as socially inadequate. These samples were of generally nonpathological psychiatric patients. In contrast, Hecht and Wittchen (1988) studied a nationally representative sample of German adults and estimated that approximately 10% fell below the level that was considered minimally functional. Closely related to social difficulty are social avoidance and anxiety. Estimates of serious or debilitating shyness and social anxiety in the general adult population vary from 20% (Richmond & McCroskey, 1985, p. 29) to 40% (Bryant & Trower, 1974, p. 15) to even higher (Zimbardo, 1977, p. 233). In light of such sources of information, Argyle (1980, p. 147) estimated that "at least 7 per cent of normal adults (more than this for young people), 25 per cent or more of neurotics, and most psychotics are seriously handicapped by lack of social skills."

Finally, two studies specifically provide evidence of communicative incompetence. Rubin's (1981) small-scale study of college students indicated that between 10% and 50% could not adequately perform each of several communication skills, such as asking a question and describing a point of view disagreeing with their own. Vangelisti and Daly (1989) studied a nationally representative sample of 208 adults (ages 21–25) who performed eight oral communication tasks (e.g., provide information about a fire in their home to an hypothetical fire department, describe a movie or TV show recently viewed, etc.). "Using liberal estimates of speaking skills the data suggest that approximately 15 to 20% of the population of 21–25 year olds cannot adequately communicate orally, at least on the sorts of tasks used in this assessment" (p. 132). It seems a small wonder, therefore, that a needs assessment of research in communication education identified communication competence as the highest priority facing the discipline (Rubin & Feezl, 1986).

Most of us can conjure manifold instances of incompetence in our everyday lives. It seems that our relationships with others are rife with informational error, both innocent and intentional. Research indicates that actors frequently experience uncertainty (Planalp & Honeycutt, 1985; Planalp, Rutherford, & Honeycutt, 1988; Turner, 1990) and second-guessing (Hewes, Graham, Doelger, & Pavitt, 1985), withholding of information (Berger & Kellerman, 1989), misinterpretations (Abbey, 1987), intentional miscommunications (Johnson, Palileo, & Gray, 1992; Muehlenhard, 1988), deception (Camden, Motley, & Wilson, 1984; Cochran & Mays, 1990; Rodriguez & Ryave, 1990), suspicion (Baxter & Wilmot, 1984; Bell & Buerkel-Rothfuss, 1990; Levine & McCornack, 1991), and things about which they cannot communicate (Roloff & Cloven, 1990; Rosenfeld, 1979). It is not surprising, therefore, that studies of interpersonal perception reveal that communicative inaccuracy is common, with dyads typically achieving no more than 25% to 50% accuracy in interpreting or representing each other's behavior (Christensen, Sullaway,

& King, 1983; Hawkins, Weisberg, & Ray, 1980; Kenny & Albright, 1987; Levinger & Breedlove, 1966; Margolin, Hattem, John, & Yost, 1985, May, 1991; Ozer & Buss, 1991; Robinson & Prince, 1980; Sillars, Pike, Jones, & Murphy, 1984).

Finally, relationships appear to be commonly inflicted with messages and situations that reflect or produce conflict (Straus & Sweet, 1992), violence (Marshall, this volume; Stets, 1992; Sugarman & Hotaling, 1989), sexual aggression (Koss, 1989), sexual harassment (McKinney & Maroules, 1991), communicative aggression (Felson, 1981; Fung, Kipnis, & Rosnow, 1987; Harris, Gergen, & Lannamann, 1986; Infante, Riddle, Horvath, & Tumlin, 1992), guilt (Miceli, 1992; Vangelisti, Daly, & Rudnick, 1991), defensiveness (Stamp, Vangelisti, & Daly, 1992), complaints (Alberts, 1989), degradation (Garfinkel, 1956), insults (Semin & Rubini, 1990), predicaments (Cupach & Metts, 1990; Harris, 1984), hassles (Perlman, 1990), betrayal (Hansson, Jones, & Fletcher, 1990), infidelity (Roscoe, Cavanaugh, & Kennedy, 1988), conversational abandonments (Kellerman, Reynolds, & Chen, 1991), narcissism (Vangelisti, Knapp, & Daly, 1990), and regrettable messages (Knapp, Stafford, & Daly, 1986). If we do not encounter these situations every day, their shadow seems to at least lurk around virtually every conversational corner.

The second question concerns the costs of this incompetence. House, Landis, and Umberson (1988) and Spitzberg and Cupach (1989) reviewed an extensive survey of research on this question and, despite several general methodological problems in the literature, found convincing evidence that social incompetence and isolation are very damaging, personally, relationally, and socially. Specifically, research indicated that interpersonally incompetent and relationally isolated persons are at higher risk of mental disorder, depression, shyness, loneliness, anxiety, stress, hypertension, academic failure, juvenile delinquency, drug abuse, sexual offense, morbidity, and mortality. The data reviewed by House et al. (1988) indicated that people who lack significant relationships are 1.5 to 2 times more susceptible to mortality than those who are more integrated into a network of meaningful social relationships. This also corresponds to the extensive evidence that married people are significantly benefitted in psychological and physical health relative to unmarried and divorced/widowed persons (Amato & Keith, 1991; Argyle, 1986; Kitson & Morgan, 1990; Stroebe & Stroebe, 1986). There is also evidence that regardless of the number of positive interactions one has, it is the negative or problematic interactions that seem to determine well-being (Rook, 1984). There is little question that the successful accomplishment and management of relationships is integral to one's well-being.

Despite the extensive evidence, there are discordant tones in the harmonious sound of these studies. For example, isolated studies can be found that either have failed to find expected relations to competence or have found unexpectedly small relationships. Segrin's (1992) meta-analysis estimated a correlation of only .26 between depression and observer ratings of social skills. Lepore, Evans, and Palsane (1991) found that the frequency of "social hassles" had relatively little independent influence on psychological well-being. Watkins and Eisler (1988) found that while Type A personality interactants displayed anger inappropriately, they were more socially skilled in other aspects of conversation, relative to Type Bs. Other studies have found no significant or substantial relationships between communicative competence or social skills and suicide risk (Ritter, 1990), juvenile delinquency (Renwick & Emler, 1991), mental disorders (Kelly, Farina, & Mosher, 1971; Numbers & Chapman, 1982), and sexual criminality (Stermac & Quinsey, 1986). Although these may just be methodological quirks, they may also reflect deeper problems in the ways in which competence is conceptualized. If competence is a far more complex phenomenon than either the conceptualizations or measures are reflecting, then research will continue to be inconsistent, and progress in understanding the full richness of relational processes will be slow indeed.

In order to disentangle some of the conceptual difficulties entailed in interpersonal competence, several paradigms of competence are reviewed next. This sets the stage for discussing several paradoxes of competence and incompetence. Specifically, it is argued that in several domains that which is normatively considered incompetent passes for competent, and that which normatively passes for competent is seen as incompetent. In order to establish this argument, however, it is important to make some distinctions that are central to understanding the concept of competence in interpersonal encounters and relationships.

REGNANT PARADIGMS

So amorphous is the available research and scholarly thought about competence, that to apply the term *paradigm* seems an exercise in optimism. Certainly several basic conceptual and methodological perspectives have been identified and contrasted (Rubin, 1990; Spitzberg, 1987; Spitzberg & Cupach, 1984, 1989; Wiemann & Bradac, 1985). Rather than analytically excavate these metatheoretical literatures, a more synthetic approach is provided. There are three basic core issues regarding how competence is viewed, about which the vast majority of conceptual and methodological treatments revolve: abstraction, location, and criteria.

Abstraction

Relational and interactional processes can be viewed from at least three levels of abstraction: macroscopic, mezzoscopic, and microscopic. These levels reflect the extent to which a unit of analysis is aggregated over time, space, and inference. Microscopic issues of competence typically refer to very discrete, relatively objective, and low-inference behaviors and skills such as eye contact, gestures, question asking, fluency, and specific manifestations of symmetry, compensation, and rhythmicity. Mezzoscopic levels are the more aggregated constructs such as speech acts, assertion routines, self-disclosure, jokes and story telling, and so on. Macroscopic levels of analysis are more aggregated still, tapping such constructs as empathy, cognitive complexity, adaptability, compatibility, and so on.

Although clearly not isomorphic, time is often closely aligned with abstraction judgments. For example, most microscopic inferences refer to a particular place and time (e.g., "O made frequent eye contact"), whereas most macroscopic inferences imply judgments that span place and time (e.g., "O is trustworthy"). In many instances, therefore, the abstraction continuum implies the time dimension of the state-trait continuum as well.

These levels have their parallels in most interpersonal research, in general, and topics in the "dark side," in particular. For example, topics such as courtship aggression, conflict, deception, family distortions, and so forth, can all be viewed at the level of specific discrete behaviors or as broad-based relational tendencies. Other topics (e.g., equivocation, hurtful messages, criticism, etc.) may be most fruitfully analyzed at more mezzo- and microscopic levels.

Location

Location concerns the place within which competence is presumed to reside. Historically, there have been three typical loci of competence: in abilities, in inferences, and in the social unit, which is a hybrid of abilities and inferences in a larger group (e.g., dyad, family, task group, etc.). Specifically, competence as ability has been the dominant paradigm and implies that an individual possesses the capacity for production and reproduction of goal-oriented behavioral routines (i.e., skills) related to the successful accomplishment of desirable interpersonal ends. The program of research in this paradigm attempts to identify the skills and abilities of actors that consistently produce preferred outcomes in interpersonal interaction. Typically, but not necessarily, the assumption is that these skills and abilities are cross-contextual and, therefore, dispositional.

The inference location identifies competence as an inherently subjective phenomenon and therefore properly located in the mind of the interpreter. The most obvious rationale for this perspective is that competence cannot inhere in the ability, or the manifest behavioral skill, because any given behavior can be competent in one context, yet incompetent in another. If the competence of a given behavior shifts from one relational, environmental, and functional context to another, then competence must reside in the social evaluations and attributions made about that behavior. The question in this tradition is no longer what skills are competent, but what skills and characteristics are perceived to be competent, and how these perceptions are derived. The program of research in this paradigm attempts to identify the systematic predictors of people's impressions of competence, whether these are skills or dispositions of the actor being judged, or inferential tendencies of the actor doing the judging.

The third location is the social unit, which involves more than one individual either producing a behavior or making a judgment or being judged. Current ideology insists that relationships are systemic, and that there must be dyad- or group-level wellsprings of competence that are unique and perhaps nonsummative. For example, criticisms, equivocation, deception, hurtful messages, and violence can be investigated at the actor or individual level, even if relational locations seem more informative. However, double binds, predicaments, conversational dilemmas, relational transgressions, and so on, tend to make sense only in the larger frame of patterned interaction in a particular relational context. This paradigm is much more recent and has been evolving as the methods of dyadic, group, and network analysis have been evolving. The program of research in this paradigm attempts to identify the mutual, *relational* sources of actor and coactor competence and the factors that influence these sources.

Criteria

The criteria of competence concern the standards by which something is considered competent. Criteria obviously differ from one research camp to another. For example, psychiatrists determining the capacity for a schizophrenic patient to function in society need different standards of judgment than a student deciding whether to consider a flirt's advances as a source of flattery or harassment. Yet, across such apparent gulfs as these, some consensus in principle does seem salvageable.

The vast majority of competence research and theory concerns some variant(s) of appropriateness and/or effectiveness. *Effectiveness* is defined as the accomplishment of relatively desirable or preferred outcomes. These outcomes do not necessarily have to be positive, as achieving the least punishing outcome may at times be the most competent alternative available. Further, effectiveness can subsume subordinate means such as understanding, clarity, efficiency, and so on. That is, to the extent that a given situation calls for efficiency in order to be effective, then the competent approach to this situation is to be efficient in achieving these outcomes.

Appropriateness is defined as enacting behavior in a manner that is fitting to the context, thereby avoiding the violation of valued rules, expectancies, or norms. Behavior does not have to conform or be polite to be appropriate, because there are novel situations in which there are no norms to conform to, and because one of the more competent maneuvers may be to renegotiate the existing norms or rules. Again, appropriateness may subsume subordinate means. For example, in any given situation, clarity (e.g., McCroskey, 1984), deception (Camden et al., 1984), or ambiguity (Eisenberg, 1984) may be the most appropriate tactic.

Appropriateness and effectiveness represent molar, fundamental criteria of competent action. Both the mental patient and the flirt need to negotiate the vicissitudes of daily life in a minimally appropriate and effective manner, and failure to do so represents incompetence to some degree or another in virtually all conceptions of adequacy and quality in interpersonal interaction. These standards may be viewed as mutually desirable criteria of competence, although in any given context, actor, coactor, or observer may be in the best position to judge the criteria. Consequently, the more that both criteria are achieved for all parties involved, the more presumptively competent is the performance.

The rationale for including both criteria is relatively straightforward. Specifically, when these dimensions are crossed to form a four-quadrant taxonomy, the desirability of mutual criteria becomes more obvious. An actor who is inappropriate and ineffective is manifesting a *minimizing* interactional mode that is incompetent a priori. An actor who is appropriate but ineffective is demonstrating a *sufficing* style that does nothing wrong, but also achieves no personal agendas in the process. The individual who is effective but inappropriate is engaging in a *maximizing* style with competitive (i.e., zero-sum) overtones, thereby permitting lying, cheating, deceiving, and coercion as legitimate forms of discourse. Certainly these acts, and this style, are defensible as potentially competent modes of interaction (see Parks, 1985). However, compared to the maximizing style of interaction, it seems self-evident that the *optimizing* style, which is both appropriate and effective, is a more defensible description of ideal communication (see Fiske, 1991, for a somewhat analogous taxonomy). The consideration of "ideal" forms naturally leads into considerations of ideology.

IDEOLOGY IN COMPETENCE

Developments in critical theory have increasingly made scholars aware of the often hidden ideological components of standard scientific endeavors (Martindale, 1979; Weber, 1991). The ideological underpinnings of interpersonal communication theory and research have also come under investigation (e.g. Bochner, 1982; Kursh, 1971; Lannamann, 1991; Lawrence, 1991; Parks, 1982). As Gergen (1973, p. 312) noted, "if we rely on the language of the culture for scientific communication, it is difficult to find terms regarding social interaction that are without prescriptive value." Competence scholarship is far from immune from such ideological presumptions (Parks, 1985). Aside from the instructional and therapeutic implications of competency research to the educational context, there are few personal and relational issues so ideologically contaminated as the definitional criteria used to anchor competence judgments and by which actions are guided.

There are at least two obvious ideological features that have gone relatively unnoticed in competence research. First, the criteria by which competence is judged are inevitably built on the hidden scaffolding of ideological architecture. For example, competence is sometimes equated with the accomplishment of clarity, accuracy, and understanding. Yet, ambiguity, deception, equivocation, and tentativeness are often highly competent communicative tactics. Cognitive or resource efficiency could be viewed as a primary criterion of competence, yet this smacks of corporate production mentality, cybernetic, and mechanico-physical laws of conservation. Such metaphors may be incompatible with more divergent, metaphorical, tangential, systemic, and creative realms of communicative accomplishment. Appropriateness and effectiveness contain their own ideological components, but when dialectically interconnected, they form a highly general and yet often enigmatic standard of competence. Their dialectical relations are the stuff of which this chapter is comprised.

The second ideological component lies in the selection of conceptual content. Many studies eschew theoretical grounding or explicit rationale for selection of criteria. Consequently, such research projects tend to produce a "list" of components of competence (Spitzberg, 1989). If components such as sensitivity, empathy, adaptability, politeness, confirmation, supportiveness, altercentrism, and self-disclosure are emphasized, a communal function is clearly being prioritized. This function tends to be more ideologically associated with some cultures (e.g., Asiatic) and co-cultures (e.g., females). In contrast, if components such as control, efficiency, interaction management, conflict management, assertiveness, planning, and strategic orientation are emphasized, then other cultures (e.g., Germanic) and co-cultures (e.g., males) are provided preferential status. Such metaphors may be so submerged in such lists, or so random in appearance, that their implications go largely unnoticed.

ON THE COMPETENCE OF THE INCOMPETENT, AND VICE VERSA

One acid test of ideology in a given area is the extent to which taken-for-granted presumptions begin to be overturned. In the area of interpersonal relationships, it seems that such coups are everywhere. What was once presumed to be competent in relationships is no longer representative of the fully functioning interactant. Conversely, what was once presumed to be *in*-competent is now often viewed as surprisingly competent. This section brief-ly examines a few of these toppled conceptual regimes. The survey is intended to be illustrative rather than comprehensive. Broader surveys are available in this text and elsewhere (e.g., Spitzberg, 1993).

The Bright Side

Competence is often virtually equated with adaptability or behavioral flexi-bility. The assumption is based on very straightforward reasoning. An actor is more likely to select the optimal lines of action in any given context to the extent she or he is possessed of a broad repertoire of tactics, good deci-sion making, and analytic abilities to interpret the situation and plan responses, and skilled capacity for production and implementation of these responses. Underlying this ability may be several more specific abilities that are com-monly presumed to facilitate adaptability, including empathy, role-taking, self-monitoring, and cognitive complexity.

Empathy is generally considered an affective mimicry, or modeling, of another's perceived affective state. This affect may be primarily physiologi-cal (e.g., arousal, facial expression reaction, etc.) or more a cognitive interpre-tation of another's affective state. Role-taking is generally considered a cognitive projection and imaginative construction of another person's views of a given situation or of the world in general. Thus, empathy is typically considered largely affective, whereas role-taking is considered a more cog-nitive phenomenon. Both constructs have been mired in an extended histo-ry of theoretical (Deutsch & Madle, 1975; Gladstein, 1984; Hickson, 1985; Schwalbe, 1988) and operational (Bryant, 1987; Chlopan, McCain, Carbonell, & Hagen, 1985) debate. Despite a lack of consensus regarding these forms of perspective taking, the general assumption has been that the more an ac-tor is able to take different perspectives, the more adept and adapted his or her actions will be for a given interactional audience. One presumed impli-cation of this adaptation is greater cross-situational and interpersonal altera-tion of actor behavior.

Self-monitoring is conceptualized as a tendency to be concerned about impressions of appropriateness within, and across, social encounters (Snyder, 1987). Self-monitors are expected to search for and accumulate social infor-mation so as to test social hypotheses (Dabbs, Evans, Hopper, & Purvis, 1980; Snyder & Cantor, 1980). Most theorists have predicted that higher self-monitors are likely to be better at adapting their responses to others and vary-ing their responses across audiences (Tunnell, 1980). However, like perspec-tive taking, self-monitoring has been the subject of extensive scholarly revision and rancor (Lennox, 1988; Lennox & Wolfe, 1984; Shuptrine, Bearden, & Teel, 1990; Snyder & Gangestad, 1986).

Cognitive complexity refers to the extent to which an actor has few, or many, dimensions along which the world is interpreted. Highly cognitively complex actors are able to construct many different interpretations of any given stimuli, and thereby are presumed to select the most adaptive response (Applegate & Leichty, 1984; Hale, 1980). However, there is again extensive disagreement over the meaning of complexity in terms of how it is measured (Beatty, 1987; Burleson, 1987; Burleson, Waltman, & Samter, 1987; Neimeyer, 1985) and how it relates theoretically to relevant constructs (Hall, Hecht, & Boster, 1985; Hecht, Boster, & Hall, 1987).

The constructs of perspective taking (i.e., empathy and role-taking), self-monitoring, and cognitive complexity are each considered an integral component underlying competent interaction. They are assumed to facilitate competent interaction, largely because they promote or enable adaptability of an actor's responses to the vicissitudes and demands of any given social encounter. Yet, these claims can be questioned on both conceptual and empirical grounds.

Conceptually, each of these constructs may be considered problematic in the realm of social interaction. Perspective taking may be detrimental if, in gaining an intimate knowledge of others' views, it (a) diminishes a person's objectivity by infusing too much of others' views into that of self's view, thereby making the competent accomplishment of tasks difficult (Steiner, 1955); (b) permits exploitation of self by unscrupulous or less empathic others (Tedeschi & Rosenfeld, 1980); or (c) provides so many interpretive perspectives that selecting the best becomes a debilitating or improbable task. Finally, being able to know what another feels or thinks is no guarantee that competent responses are forthcoming. This depends on the actor's motivation, knowledge, and skills. Knowing another person's perspective is not the same as knowing what to do about it and whether or not to do it. For example, knowing that a person is suffering and needs support or comfort does not imply that it is obvious what response best fulfills this person's needs.

High self-monitoring in an actor is at once both paradigmatic of a competent communicator, and at the same time, ambiguously close to implications of Machiavellianism, manipulativeness, ingenuousness, and even unpredictable flightiness of character. Furthermore, actors who constantly alter their performances to the audiences they encounter will eventually find themselves face to face with multiple audiences that have multiple and possibly mutually exclusive expectations for actor performance. Differing role expectations are often difficult to manage with consistency (Greenhaus & Beutell, 1985; Hoelter, 1985), yet inconsistency may create incompatible roles that intersect in curious ways, resulting in failed facework and audience distrust (Athay & Darley, 1981).

Cognitive complexity implies a linear relationship to communicative competence in response adaptation. Yet, at extremely high levels of complexity, an actor may be debilitated in fluency and tactic selection by the sheer overload of possible interpretations (Berger, Karol, & Jordan, 1989). Furthermore, as with perspective taking, being able to make multiple interpretations is no guarantee that a person is motivated to engage in more effortful cognitive processing, or that the effort of formulating more complex adaptive responses is considered worthwhile (Samter, 1991).

The empirical literature for all of these constructs, for the most part, has been supportive of their relationship to competent interaction. However, seldom mentioned by the proponents of these constructs are the studies that have not found support. Dillard and Hunter (1989) found the measures of empathy and self-monitoring so dimensionally messy, and the factor validity correlations so small across constructs, that at least the measures could not be recommended for further use. Eisenberg and Miller's meta-analysis (1987) found that empathy produced only a very small effect size in predicting prosocial behavior (a possible proxy for competence), despite the strong conceptual rationale for considering them closely associated. Brown (1989) found that people's views of what constitutes an empathic person do not correspond very closely with the characteristics of people they nominate as highly empathic. Jiujias and Horvath (1991) found that high self-monitors are evaluated somewhat negatively, presumably because they are unpredictable. Several studies have either failed to find a predicted relationship, or have only found small effects, between cognitive complexity and more adaptive responses (Bruch, Heisler, & Conroy, 1981; Campbell & Yarrow, 1961; Dowling & Bliss, 1984; Duran & Kelly, 1985; Henzl, Mabry, & Powell, 1983; Honess, 1976; Penley, Alexander, Jernigan, & Henwood, 1991; Rubin & Henzl, 1984; Samter & Burleson, 1990; Willihnganz, 1987).

Adaptability itself may not be unambiguously competent for several of the reasons identified earlier. Adaptable persons are more unpredictable and therefore somewhat threatening to coactors (Athay & Darley, 1981). Having a broad repertoire may make it more difficult to select the most competent actions from an array (Osborne & Gilbert, 1992). In contrast, competence may be more closely related to persistence, expertise at a narrow range of proven techniques, or the trustworthiness of a consistent image. The point is not that these studies are necessarily any more or less valid than those that support traditional predictions. The point is that there is both conceptual and empirical reason to suspect the connection between these constructs and communicative competence.

One of the reasons perspective taking is believed to facilitate competent interaction is that it promotes accuracy of understanding. The ideology of accuracy is everywhere in the competence domain. Coorientation, mutual understanding, perceptual accuracy, and clarity are all common metaphors of competence. Research consistently indicates that most of the time even well-established dyads share relatively little in the way of exact mutuality of meaning. Yet, there is also evidence that misunderstanding is often quite functional. Eisenberg (1984) points out many of the advantages of strategic ambiguity in maintaining cohesiveness among divergent audiences, avoiding premature closure, and managing intractable conflicts. Some data indicate that marital satisfaction among married couples is more dependent on perceived understanding than actual understanding (Burggraf & Pavitt, 1991; Sillars et al., 1984). It may be that highly accurate communication simply makes concrete all the manifold issues upon which couples may differ, thereby introducing numerous tenuous and loose threads into the fabric of the relationship. The sustenance of everyday relations may depend on, in larger part than one cares to envision, a large dose of ambiguity, vagueness, and opacity. Competence, therefore, may often be a function of the deft use of ambiguity in smoothing out the turbulence of the behavioral stream.

Assertiveness is the ability, or tendency, to voice and defend one's rights in interpersonal situations. It is typically viewed relative to a continuum from passive behavior (avoidance), to assertive behavior, to aggressive behavior (violating another's rights in the pursuit of self's rights). Because assertive behavior is seen as attempting to obtain self's valued objectives (i.e., effectiveness) while respecting the rights of others (i.e., appropriateness), it can be viewed as a virtual prototype of competence (Galassi, Galassi, & Vedder, 1981). For years, research in behavior therapy literatures continued to demonstrate that third parties consistently evaluated actor assertiveness as highly competent. Then researchers started assessing what the coactors thought of the actor's assertive actions. Such research has revealed that although uninvolved third parties consider assertive actions to be competent, the actual receivers tend to be put off by assertion and often view the assertive actor as incompetent, unattactive, or both (see Delamater & McNamara, 1986, 1991; Hull & Schroeder, 1979; Kern, Cavell, & Beck, 1985; Lowe & Storm, 1986). This effect is likely moderated by gender of actor (Gervasio & Crawford, 1989; Lowe & Storm, 1986). Thus, assertiveness is almost definitionally competent in principle, yet may be too blunt or too difficult to implement in a manner that is truly both appropriate and effective. This is also suggestive that perhaps all complex social behavior is potentially incompetent, and may reflect perceivers' balancing of competence criteria in their interpretive constructions of meaning.

Conflict is closely related to assertiveness, in the sense that a perceived interpersonal incompatibility exists, and interaction is employed to manage or resolve the incompatibility. Historically, "modern" societal and scholarly thinking on relational conflict began with the notion that conflict of virtually any sort was dysfunctional. The pendulum shifted, and conflict management and assertiveness were then prototypically presumed to be functional for relationships (Kidd, 1975). More recently, some form of synthesis appears to have evolved, in which strategic and situational conflict management is considered more appropriate (Hubbard, 1985; Megli & Morgan, 1991; Prusank, Duran, & DeLillo, 1991). Thus, resisting distributive actions and engaging in more constructive conflict behavior are found to be facilitative in relationships (Rusbult, Verette, Whitney, Slovik, & Lipkus, 1991). Yet, such findings may be an illusion. Roloff and Cloven (1990) found that both the number of expressed and unexpressed conflicts were negatively related to relational satisfaction. Even more telling is the research by Gottman and Krokoff (1989, p. 49), which found that when examined longitudinally rather than cross-sectionally, "positive verbal behavior and compliance expressed by wives may be functional in the short run but problematic in the long run. The opposite was true for both partners' conflict engagement, which predicted concurrent dissatisfaction with the marriage but improvement over time." Initial compliance may smooth over structural conflicts of interest that created delayed and displaced problems for the relationship later, but conflict permitted some degree of resolution despite its initial unpleasantness. Thus, much of the cross-sectional research on conflict may vastly oversimplify the systemic and chronological influence of behavior, thereby misrepresenting which behavior is competent, and which is not.

Shadows on the Bright Side

Virtually any behavior, when used in the extreme, is likely to be incompetent. This incompetence can derive from at least two sources. First, any behavior that is used too consistently or frequently is progressively likely to lose reinforcement value as its novelty and salience diminish and the recipients accommodate to the behavior. For example, compliments may be generally viewed as competent, but if employed continuously, they are likely to lose much of their role as reinforcers, and perhaps even be seen as evidence of ingratiation or manipulative intent. Second, social systems tend to develop rules for appropriate display, and many of these rules govern the extent of behavior considered appropriate. For example, evaluation is curvilinear to talk time, speech rate (Hayes & Meltzer, 1972; Street & Brady, 1982; Wheeless, Frymier, & Thompson, 1992), interpersonal distance (Patterson & Sechrest, 1970), conversational activity (Hayes & Sievers, 1972), self-disclosure (Derlega, Harris, & Chaikin, 1973), intimacy (Harper & Elliott, 1988), and impression management tactics (Baron, 1986). Most normatively positive forms of interaction can become pathological if taken to extremes (Wynne, 1988). On the other end of the continuum, minimal use of behavior also clearly has its role in competent interaction (Bennett & Jarvis, 1991). Thus, intimacy, if taken to extremes of expression or lack of expression, can range from denial of privacy, autonomy, and self-identity to alienation and loneliness.

The importance of this curvilinearity is difficult to overemphasize. The lay and scholarly literatures are littered with recommendations of a variety of skills in the satisfying management of interpersonal relations. However, rarely are the implications of curvilinearity, saturation, and interaction effects (Hayes & Sievers, 1972) among the dimensions of interpersonal activity considered.

Seeing the Light of the Dark Side

Just as most behaviors commonly presumed to be competent are often incompetent, there are many presumptively incompetent actions that can become functionally competent. Even that which is considered obnoxious can be seen as relatively acceptable (Tyler & Sears, 1977). Unfortunately, there is not an extensive literature exploring such domains, partly because such findings would be politically and ideologically unpalatable, and partly because such results often are not interpreted in light of a competence framework. A few brief examples are examined here to make the point.

Courtship violence is a prototype of a behavior that society at large considers incompetent. Yet, an extensive review of studies found that

> On average, the relationship has worsened because of the violence in about 40 percent of the cases, but in roughly six of every ten relationships that did not terminate, the violence is reported to have had no effect on, or to have actually improved the relationship. (Sugarman & Hotaling, 1989, p. 14)

Across three studies, a third of relationships are reported to have improved or become more deeply involved after the occurrence of violence (Cate, Henton, Koval, Christopher, & Lloyd, 1982; Henton, Cate, Koval, Lloyd, & Christopher, 1983; Makepeace, 1981). This is in part compatible with the finding that a third of episodes of courtship violence are interpreted as indications of "love" (Cate et al., 1982; Henton et al., 1983; Roscoe & Kelsey, 1986). It may be that violence represents a shock to the relational system that forces partners to confront deeper problems that previously were permitted to be avoided. Although there should always be means that are more competent than violence as relational "therapy," it would be empirically irresponsible to deny the possibility that violence, on occasion, plays a functionally adaptive role in relationships.

The intentional derogation of others is typically viewed as hurtful, both by society (Adams, 1977) and interactants (Vangelisti et al., 1991). However, all societies apparently engage in rituals of degradation (Garfinkel, 1956) and find a frequent need for insults (Adams, 1977; Semin & Rubini, 1990). Careful study of such rituals and normative practices have found that they are often quite functional. Insult and teasing rituals not only assist in facilitating intragroup identification and cohesion, but they also contribute to the development of communicative competence and identity formation (Bruhn & Murray, 1985; Pawluk, 1989). Similarly, research on intentional embarrassment has found that such actions fulfill a variety of interpersonal and systemic objectives that are generally seen by the actors as functional (Petronio & Snider, 1990; Sharkey & Waldron, 1990). When the long-term interests or interests of the larger social system are considered, interpersonal shame, degradation, derogation, and embarrassment often serve highly competent ends that may or may not be perceived by the targets at the time.

Another exemplar of socially disapproved behavior is deception. Both men and women claim that lies, guile, cheating, and cunningness are unpleasant forms of courtship activity (Laner, 1989a, 1989b). Yet, some research on the reported use of lies and deception concludes that most lies can be interpreted in terms of altercentric motivations and are relatively normative practices in relationships (Camden et al., 1984; Hample, 1980; Metts, 1989; Shippee, 1977). As Camden et al. (1984, p. 319) speculate,

> the lie exchange . . . could represent a nearly optimal communicative competency. The amount of conscious effort (costs) required to encode the white lie is minimal. Moreover, the positive benefits are more certain to both the liar and the victim when the lie is told. From a cost-effectiveness perspective, white lies may be viewed as a most appropriate strategem for the tact dilemma.

In a finding similar to the violence literature, the occurrence and unveiling of one form of deception—relational infidelity—has been found to produce relational discussion (27%) and work to improve the relationship (15%) much of the time (Roscoe et al., 1988). Deception often serves ends in relationships that are not entirely recognized by the participants at the time, but can be viewed as adaptive in retrospect or in the big picture of the relationship (Kursh, 1971).

CONCLUSION

In 1962, a chiropractor was charged with the murder of a young female patient. The chiropractor had advised the family that he could cure the girl of cancer, and that traditional health care could not, despite the consensual opinion of practitioners that at the time the cancer was highly operable. The key question of the trial was this:

> Can words alone be the instrument of a criminal killing. Putting it another way, can words alone be so employed as to make their author a murderer. . . . During the seven centuries that have passed from the time of Edward to the present, apparently, no case of murder by words has reached the courts in any of the English speaking countries of the world. (Miner, 1963, p. 6)

The decision of the jury hearing *People versus Phillips* was that the chiropractor was guilty of murder. It seems that sticks and stones may break your bones, and words can kill you. The competence with which we communicate and interact with one another potentially carries such dark consequences.

Yet, competence is an elusive phenomenon. Everyday behavior often makes it seem ephemeral, and its mercurial character has frustrated most scholarly investigation. The centrality of competence to relationship development has not been commonly recognized. Communicative competence is integral to relational functioning, in at least three fundamental ways (Spitzberg, 1993). First, competent communication facilitates the satisfactory development and management of relationships. Second, competence impressions moderate the influence of behavior in relationships. For example, research has shown that the role that conflict behavior plays in relational outcomes depends on how it influences the coactor's view of the actor's competence (Canary & Cupach, 1988; Canary & Spitzberg, 1987, 1989, 1990). Third, the self-inference of competence has significant impacts on confidence, motivation, efficacy, and the behavioral course of relational interaction (Bandura, 1990; Kolligian, 1990). Given the importance of competence to the functioning of relationships, it is essential that inquiry comes to grips with its nature. Traditionally, scholarship has oversimplified the construct of competence and fallen prey to ideologies that have steered theory away from potentially fertile fields of investigation. This book is an attempt to redress these deficits by focusing on the many ways in which the dark side is both normative and often quite competent.

REFERENCES

Abbey, A. (1987). Misperceptions of friendly behavior as sexual interest: A survey of naturally occurring incidents. *Psychology of Women Quarterly, 11,* 173–194.

Adams, R. M. (1977). *Bad mouth: Fugitive papers on the dark side.* Berkeley: University of California Press.

Adult Performance Level Research Project. (1977). *Final report: The adult performance level study.* Washington, DC: U.S. Office of Education, Department of Health, Education and Welfare.

Alberts, J. K. (1989). Perceived effectiveness of couples' conversational complaints. *Communication Studies, 40,* 280–291.

Amato, P. R., & Keith, B. (1991). Parental divorce and adult well-being: A meta analysis. *Journal of Marriage and the Family, 53,* 43–58.

Applegate, J. L., & Leichty, G. B. (1984). Managing interpersonal relationships: Social cognitive and strategic determinants of competence. In R. N. Bostrom (Ed.), *Competence in communication: A multidisciplinary approach* (pp. 33–56). Beverly Hills, CA: Sage.

Argyle, M. (1980). Interaction skills and social competence. In P. Feldman & J. Orford (Eds.), *Psychological problems: The social context* (pp. 123–150). New York: Wiley.

Argyle, M. (1986). The skills, rules, and goals of relationships. In R. Gilmour & S. Duck (Eds.), *The emerging field of personal relationships* (pp. 23–39). Hillsdale, NJ: Lawrence Erlbaum Associates.

Athay, M., & Darley, J. M. (1981). Toward an interaction-centered theory of personality. In N. Cantor & J. F. Kihlstrom (Eds.), *Personality, cognition, and social interaction* (pp. 281–308). Hillsdale, NJ: Lawrence Erlbaum Associates.

Bandura, A. (1990). Conclusion: Reflections on nonability determinants of competence. In R. J. Sternberg & J. Kolligian, Jr. (Eds.), *Competence considered* (pp. 315–362). New Haven, CT: Yale University Press.

Baron, R. A. (1986). Self-presentation in job interviews: When there can be "too much of a good thing." *Journal of Applied Social Psychology, 16*, 16–28.

Baxter, L. A., & Wilmot, W. W. (1984). "Secret tests": Social strategies for acquiring information about the state of the relationship. *Human Communication Research, 11*, 171–201.

Beatty, M. J. (1987). Erroneous assumptions underlying Burleson's critique. *Communication Quarterly, 35*, 329–333.

Bell, R. A., & Buerkel-Rothfuss, N. L. (1990). S(he) loves me, s(he) loves me not: Predictors of relational information-seeking in courtship and beyond. *Communication Quarterly, 38*, 64–82.

Bennett, M., & Jarvis, J. (1991). The communicative function of minimal responses in everyday conversation. *Journal of Social Psychology, 131*, 519–523.

Benson, P. G. (1978). Measuring cross-cultural adjustment: The problem of criteria. *International Journal of Intercultural Relations, 2*, 21–37.

Berger, C. R., Karol, S. H., & Jordan, J. M. (1989). When a lot of knowledge is a dangerous thing: The debilitating effects of plan complexity on verbal fluency. *Human Communication Research, 16*, 91–119.

Berger, C. R., & Kellerman, K. (1989). Personal opacity and social information gathering: Explorations in strategic communication. *Communication Research, 16*, 314–351.

Bochner, A. P. (1982). On the efficacy of openness in close relationships. In M. Burgoon (Ed.), *Communication yearbook 5* (Vol. 5, pp. 109–124). New Brunswick, NJ: Transaction.

Brown, N. W. (1989). Comparison of described empathic and nominated empathic individuals. *Psychological Reports, 64*, 27–32.

Bruch, M. A., Heisler, B. D., & Conroy, C. G. (1981). Effects of conceptual complexity on assertive behavior. *Journal of Counseling Psychology, 28*, 377–385.

Bruhn, J. G., & Murray, J. L. (1985). "Playing the dozens": Its history and psychological significance. *Psychological Reports, 56*, 483–494.

Bryant, B. K. (1987). Critique of comparable questionnaire methods in use to assess empathy in children and adults. In N. Eisenberg & J. Strayer (Eds.), *Empathy and its development* (pp. 361–373). Cambridge: Cambridge University.

Bryant, B., & Trower, P. E. (1974). Social difficulty in a student sample. *British Journal of Educational Psychology, 44*, 13–21.

Bryant, B., Trower, P., Yardley, K., Urbieta, H., & Letemendia, F. J. (1976). A survey of social inadequacy among psychiatric outpatients. *Psychological Medicine, 6*, 101–112.

Burggraf, C. S., & Pavitt, C. (1991, November). *Understanding on varying levels of abstraction and its association with marital satisfaction.* Paper presented at the Speech Communication Association Conference, Atlanta, GA.

Burleson, B. R. (1987). Cognitive complexity. In J. C. McCroskey & J. A. Daly (Eds.), *Personality and interpersonal communication* (pp. 305–350). Newbury Park, CA: Sage.

Burleson, B. R., Waltman, M. S., & Samter, W. (1987). More evidence that cognitive complexity is *not* loquacity: A reply to Beatty and Payne. *Communication Quarterly, 35*, 317–328.

Camden, C., Motley, M. T., & Wilson, A. (1984). White lies in interpersonal communication: A taxonomy and preliminary investigation of social motivations. *Western Journal of Speech Communication, 48*, 309–325.

Campbell, J. D., & Yarrow, M. R. (1961). Perceptual and behavioral correlates of social effectiveness. *Sociometry, 24*, 1–20.

Canary, D. J., & Cupach, W. R. (1988). Relational and episodic characteristics associated with conflict tactics. *Journal of Social and Personal Relationships, 5*, 305–325.

Canary, D. J., & Spitzberg, B. H. (1987). Appropriateness and effectiveness in the perception of conflict strategies. *Human Communication Research, 13*, 93–118.

Canary, D. J., & Spitzberg, B. H. (1989). A model of competence perceptions of conflict strategies. *Human Communication Research, 13,* 630–649.

Canary, D. J., & Spitzberg, B. H. (1990). Attribution biases and associations between conflict strategies and competence outcomes. *Communication Monographs, 57,* 139–151.

Cate, R. M., Henton, J. M., Koval, J., Christopher, F. S., & Lloyd, S. (1982). Premarital abuse: A social psychological perspective. *Journal of Family Issues, 3,* 79–90.

Chlopan, B. E., McCain, M. L., Carbonell, J. L., & Hagen, R. L. (1985). Empathy: Review of available measures. *Journal of Personality and Social Psychology, 48,* 635–653.

Christensen, A., Sullaway, M., & King, C. E. (1983). Systematic error in behavioral reports of dyadic interaction: Egocentric bias and content effects. *Behavioral Assessment, 5,* 129–140.

Cochran, S. D., & Mays, V. M. (1990). Sex, lies, and HIV. *New England Journal of Medicine, 322,* 774–775.

Cupach, W. R., & Metts, S. (1990). Remedial processes in embarrassing predicaments. In J. A. Anderson (Eds.), *Communication yearbook 13* (pp. 323–352). Newbury Park, CA: Sage.

Curran, J. P., Miller, I. W., III, Zwick, W. R., Monti, P. M., & Stout, R. L. (1980). The socially inadequate patient: Incidence rate, demographic and clinical features, and hospital and posthospital functioning. *Journal of Consulting and Clinical Psychology, 48,* 375–382.

Dabbs, J. M., Jr., Evans, M. S., Hopper, C. H., & Purvis, J. A. (1980). Self-monitors in conversations: What do they monitor? *Journal of Personality and Social Psychology, 39,* 278–284.

Dean, A. L., & Youniss, J. (1991). The transformation of Piagetian theory by American psychology: The early competence issue. In M. Chandler & M. Chapman (Eds.), *Criteria for competence: Controversies in the conceptualization and assessment of children's abilities* (pp. 93–109). Hillsdale, NJ: Lawrence Erlbaum Associates.

Delamater, R. J., & McNamara, J. R. (1986). The social impact of assertiveness: Research findings and clinical implications. *Behavior Modification, 10,* 139–158.

Delamater, R. J., & McNamara, J. R. (1991). Perceptions of assertiveness by women involved in a conflict situation. *Behavior Modification, 15,* 173–193.

Derlega, V. J., Harris, M. S., & Chaikin, A. L. (1973). Self-disclosure reciprocity, liking and the deviant. *Journal of Experimental Social Psychology, 9,* 277–284.

Deutsch, F., & Madle, R. A. (1975). Empathy: Historic and current conceptualizations, measurement, and a cognitive theoretical perspective. *Human Development, 18,* 267–287.

Dillard, J. P., & Hunter, J. E. (1989). On the use and interpretation of the emotional empathy scale, the self-consciousness scales, and the self-monitoring scale. *Communication Research, 16,* 104–129.

Dillon, G. L. (1986). *Rhetoric as social imagination: Explorations in the interpersonal function of language.* Bloomington: Indiana University Press.

Dowling, S., & Bliss, L. S. (1984). Cognitive complexity, rhetorical sensitivity: Contributing factors in clinical skill? *Journal of Communication Disorders, 17,* 9–17.

Duran, R. L., & Kelly, L. (1985). An investigation into the cognitive domain of communication competence. *Communication Research Reports, 2,* 112–119.

Eisenberg, E. M. (1984). Ambiguity as strategy in organizational communication. *Communication Monographs, 51,* 227–242.

Eisenberg, N., & Miller, P. A. (1987). The relation of empathy to prosocial and related behaviors. *Psychological Bulletin, 101,* 91–119.

Felson, R. B. (1981). An interactionist approach to aggression. In J. T. Tedeschi (Ed.), *Impression management theory and psychological research* (pp. 181–199). New York: Academic Press.

Fiske, A. P. (1991). *Structures of social life: The four elementary forms of human relations.* New York: Free Press.

Fung, S. S. K., Kipnis, D., & Rosnow, R. L. (1987). Synthetic benevolence and malevolence as strategies of relational compliance-gaining. *Journal of Social and Personal Relationships, 4,* 129–141.

Galassi, J. P., Galassi, M. D., & Vedder, M. J. (1981). Perspectives on assertion as a social skills model. In J. D. Wine & M. D. Smye (Eds.), *Social competence* (pp. 287–345). New York: Guilford.

Garfinkel, H. (1956). Conditions of successful degradation ceremonies. *American Journal of Sociology, 61,* 420–424.

Gergen, K. J. (1973). Social psychology as history. *Journal of Personality and Social Psychology, 26,* 309–320.

Gervasio, A. H., & Crawford, M. (1989). Social evaluations of assertiveness: A critique and speech act reformulation. *Psychology of Women Quarterly, 13,* 1–25.

Gladstein, G. A. (1984). The historical roots of contemporary empathy research. *Journal of History of the Behavioral Sciences, 20,* 38–59.

Gottman, J. M., & Krokoff, L. J. (1989). Marital interaction and satisfaction: A longitudinal view. *Journal of Consulting and Clinical Psychology, 57,* 47–52.

Greenhaus, J. H., & Beutell, N. J. (1985). Sources of conflict between work and family roles. *Academy of Management Review, 10,* 76–88.

Hale, C. L. (1980). Cognitive complexity-simplicity as a determinant of communication effectiveness. *Communication Monographs, 47,* 304–311.

Hall, S., Hecht, M., & Boster, F. (1985, November). *Artifacts in constructivist complexity research.* Paper presented at the Speech Communication Association Conference, Denver, CO.

Hample, D. (1980). Purposes and effects of lying. *Southern Speech Communication Journal, 46,* 33–47.

Hansson, R. O., Jones, W. H., & Fletcher, W. L. (1990). Troubled relationships in later life: Implications for support. *Journal of Social and Personal Relationships, 7,* 451–463.

Harper, J. M., & Elliott, M. L. (1988). Can there be too much of a good thing? The relationship between desired level of intimacy and marital adjustment. *American Journal of Family Therapy, 16,* 351–360.

Harris, L. M., Gergen, K. J., & Lannamann, J. W. (1986). Aggression rituals. *Communication Monographs, 53,* 252–265.

Harris, T. E. (1984). The "faux pas" in interpersonal communication. In S. Thomas (Ed.), *Studies in communication* (Vol. 2, pp. 53–61). Norwood, NJ: Ablex.

Hawkins, J. L., Weisberg, C., & Ray, D. W. (1980). Spouse differences in communication style: Preference, perception, behavior. *Journal of Marriage and the Family, 42,* 585–593.

Hayes, D. P., & Meltzer, L. (1972). Interpersonal judgments based on talkativeness: I Fact or artifact? *Sociometry, 35,* 538–561.

Hayes, D. P., & Sievers, S. (1972). A sociolinguistic investigation of the "dimensions" of interpersonal behavior. *Journal of Personality and Social Psychology, 24,* 254–261.

Hecht, H., & Wittchen, H. U. (1988). The frequency of social dysfunction in a general population sample and in patients with mental disorders. *Social Psychiatry and Psychiatric Epidemiology,* 17–29.

Hecht, M. L., Boster, F. J., & Hall, S. (1987, May). *Cognitive complexity, self-monitoring, and listener-adapted communication: A test of constructivist assumptions.* Paper presented at the International Communication Association Conference, Montreal, Canada.

Henton, J., Cate, R., Koval, J., Lloyd, S., & Christopher, S. (1983). Romance and violence in dating relationships. *Journal of Family Issues, 4,* 467–482.

Henzl, S., Mabry, E. A., & Powell, R. G. (1983, May). *The effects of cognitive complexity and gender on assessments of communication competence.* Paper presented at the International Communication Association Conference, Dallas, TX.

Hewes, D. E., Graham, M. L., Doelger, J., & Pavitt, C. (1985). "Second-guessing": Message interpretation in social networks. *Human Communication Research, 11,* 299–334.

Hickson, J. (1985). Psychological research on empathy: In search of an elusive phenomenon. *Psychological Reports, 57,* 91–94.

Hoelter, J. W. (1985). A structural theory of personal consistency. *Social Psychology Quarterly, 48,* 118–129.

Honess, T. (1976). Cognitive complexity and social prediction. *British Journal of Social and Clinical Psychology, 15,* 23–31.

House, J. S., Landis, K. R., & Umberson, D. (1988). Social relationships and health. *Science, 241,* 540–545.

Hubbard, R. C. (1985). Relationship styles in popular romance novels, 1950–1983. *Communication Quarterly, 33,* 113–125.

Hull, D. B., & Schroeder, H. E. (1979). Some interpersonal effects of assertion, nonassertion, and aggression. *Behavior Therapy, 10,* 20–28.

Hunter, C. St. J., & Harman, D. (1979). *Adult illiteracy in the United States: A report to the Ford Foundation.* New York: McGraw-Hill.

Infante, D. A., Riddle, B. L., Horvath, C. L., & Tumlin, S. A. (1992). Verbal aggressiveness: Messages and reasons. *Communication Quarterly, 40,* 116–126.

Jiujias, A., & Horvath, P. (1991). The evaluation of self-monitoring attributes. *Social Behavior and Personality, 19,* 205–215.

Johnson, G. D., Palileo, G. J., & Gray, N. B. (1992). "Date rape" on a Southern campus: Reports from 1991. *Sociology and Social Research, 76,* 37–43.

Kasson, J. F. (1990). *Rudeness and civility: Manners in nineteenth-century urban America.* New York: Hill and Wang.

Kellerman, K., Reynolds, R., & Chen, J. B-S. (1991). Strategies of conversational retreat: When parting is not sweet sorrow. *Communication Monographs, 58,* 362–383.

Kelly, F. S., Farina, A., & Mosher, D. L. (1971). Ability of schizophrenic women to create a favorable or unfavorable impression on an interviewer. *Journal of Consulting and Clinical Psychology, 36,* 404–409.

Kenny, D. A., & Albright, L. (1987). Accuracy in interpersonal perception: A social relations analysis. *Psychological Bulletin, 102,* 390–402.

Kern, J. M., Cavell, T. A., & Beck, B. (1985). Predicting differential reactions to males' versus females' assertions, empathic-assertions, and nonassertions. *Behavior Therapy, 16,* 63–75.

Kidd, V. (1975). Happily ever after and other relationship styles: Advice on interpersonal relations in popular magazines, 1951–1973. *Quarterly Journal of Speech, 61,* 31–39.

Kitson, G. C., & Morgan, G. C. (1990). The multiple consequences of divorce: A decade review. *Journal of Marriage and the Family, 52,* 913–924.

Knapp, M. L., Stafford, L., & Daly, J. A. (1986). Regrettable messages: Things people wish they hadn't said. *Journal of Communication, 36,* 40–58.

Kolligian, J., Jr. (1990). Perceived fraudulence as a dimension of perceived incompetence. In R. J. Sternberg & J. Kolligian (Eds.), *Competence considered* (pp. 261–285). New Haven, CT: Yale University Press.

Koss, M. P. (1989). Hidden rape: Sexual aggression and victimization in a national sample of students in higher education. In M. A. Pirog-Good & J. E. Stets (Eds.), *Violence in dating relationships: Emerging social issues* (pp. 145–168). New York: Praeger.

Kozol, J. (1985). *Illiterate America.* New York: NAL Penguin.

Kursh, C. O. (1971). The benefits of poor communication. *Psychoanalytic Review, 58,* 189–208.

Laner, M. R. (1989a). Competition and combativeness in courtship: Reports from men. *Journal of Family Violence, 4,* 47–61.

Laner, M. R. (1989b). Competition and combativeness in courtship: Reports from women. *Journal of Family Violence, 4,* 181–195.

Lannamann, J. W. (1991). Interpersonal communication research as ideological practice. *Communication Theory, 1,* 179–203.

Lawrence, S. G. (1991, November). *Is fidelity a goal of communicators?* Paper presented at the Speech Communication Association Conference, Atlanta, GA.

Lennox, R. D. (1988). The problem with self-monitoring: A two-sided scale and a one-sided theory. *Journal of Personal Assessment, 52,* 58–73.

Lennox, R. D., & Wolfe, R. N. (1984). Revision of the Self-Monitoring Scale. *Journal of Personality and Social Psychology, 46*, 1349–1364.

Lepore, S. J., Evans, G. W., & Palsane, M. N. (1991). Social hassles and psychological health in the context of chronic crowding. *Journal of Health and Social Behavior, 32*, 357–367.

Levine, T. R., & McCornack, S. A. (1991). The dark side of trust: Conceptualizing and measuring types of communicative suspicion. *Communication Quarterly, 39*, 325–340.

Levinger, G., & Breedlove, J. (1966). Interpersonal attraction and agreement: A study of marriage partners. *Journal of Personality and Social Psychology, 3*, 367–372.

Lowe, M. R., & Storm, M. A. (1986). Being assertive or being liked: A genuine dilemma? *Behavior Modification, 10*, 371–390.

Makepeace, J. M. (1981). Courtship violence among college students. *Family Relations, 30*, 97–102.

Margolin, G., Hattem, D., John, R. S., & Yost, K. (1985). Perceptual agreement between spouses and outside observers when coding themselves and a stranger dyad. *Behavioral Assessment, 7*, 235–247.

Martindale, D. (1979). Ideologies, paradigms, and theories. In W. E. Snizek, E. R. Fuhrman, & M. K. Miller (Eds.), *Contemporary issues in theory and research: A metasociological perspective* (pp. 7–24). Westport, CT: Greenwood Press.

May, B. A. (1991). The interaction between ratings of self, peers' perceptions, and reflexive self-ratings. *Journal of Social Psychology, 131*, 483–493.

McCroskey, J. C. (1984). Communication competence: The elusive construct. In R. N. Bostrom (Ed.), *Competence in communication: A multidisciplinary approach* (pp. 259–268). Beverly Hills, CA: Sage.

McKinney, K., & Maroules, N. (1991). Sexual harassment. In E. Grauerholz & M. A. Koralewski (Eds.), *Sexual coercion: A sourcebook on its nature, causes, and prevention* (pp. 45–58). Lexington, MA: Lexington Books.

Megli, J. M., & Morgan, L. G. (1991, May). *How to get a man and other advice: Articulation of the rhetorical visions present in popular women's magazines from 1974–1989*. Paper presented at the International Network on Personal Relationships Conference, Normal, IL.

Metts, S. (1989). An exploratory investigation of deception in close relationships. *Journal of Social and Personal Relationships, 6*, 159–179.

Miceli, M. (1992). How to make someone feel guilty: Strategies of guilt inducement and their goals. *Journal for the Theory of Social Behaviour, 22*, 81–104.

Miner, J. W. (1963). The Phillips case—A new dimension in murder. *Journal of Forensic Sciences, 9*, 1–10.

Muehlenhard, C. L. (1988). "Nice women" don't say yes and "real men" don't say no: How miscommunication and the double standard can cause sexual problems. *Women and Therapy, 7*, 95–108.

Neimeyer, R. A. (1985). *The development of personal construct psychology*. Lincoln: University of Nebraska.

Numbers, J. S., & Chapman, L. J. (1982). Social deficits in hypothetically psychosis-prone college women. *Journal of Abnormal Psychology, 91*, 255–260.

O'Neill, Y. V. (1980). *Speech and speech disorders in Western thought before 1600*. Westport, CT: Greenwood Press.

Osborne, R. E., & Gilbert, D. T. (1992). The preoccupational hazards of social life. *Journal of Personality and Social Psychology, 62*, 219–228.

Ozer, D. J., & Buss, D. M. (1991). Two views of behavior: Agreement and disagreement among marital partners. In A. J. Stewart, J. M. Healy, Jr., D. Ozer, & R. Hogan (Eds.), *Perspectives in personality: A research annual* (Approaches to understanding lives, Vol. 3B, pp. 91–106). London: Jessica Kingsley.

Parks, M. R. (1982). Ideology in interpersonal communication: Off the couch and into the world. In M. Burgoon (Ed.), *Communication yearbook 5* (pp. 79–108). New Brunswick, NJ: Transaction.

Parks, M. R. (1985). Interpersonal communication and the quest for personal competence. In M. L. Knapp & G. R. Miller (Eds.), *Handbook of interpersonal communication* (pp. 171–201). Beverly Hills, CA: Sage.

Patterson, M. L., & Sechrest, L. B. (1970). Interpersonal distance and impression formation. *Journal of Personality, 38,* 161–166.

Pawluk, C. J. (1989). Social construction of teasing. *Journal for the Theory of Social Behavior, 19,* 145–167.

Penley, L. E., Alexander, E. R., Jernigan, I. E., & Henwood, C. I. (1991). Communication abilities of managers: The relationship to performance. *Journal of Management, 17,* 57–76.

Perlman, D. (1990, July). *You bug me: A preliminary report on hassles in three types of relationships.* Paper presented at the International Society for the Study of Personal Relationships, Oxford.

Petronio, S., & Snider, E. (1990, November). *Planned strategic embarrassment.* Paper presented at the Speech Communication Association Conference, Chicago, IL.

Planalp, S., & Honeycutt, J. M. (1985). Events that increase uncertainty in personal relationships. *Human Communication Research, 11,* 593–604.

Planalp, S., Rutherford, D. K., & Honeycutt, J. M. (1988). Events that increase uncertainty in personal relationships II: Replication and extension. *Human Communication Research, 14,* 516–547.

Prusank, D. T., Duran, R. L., & DeLillo, D. A. (1991, May). *Interpersonal relationships in women's magazines: Dating and relating in the 1970's and 1980's.* Paper presented at the International Network on Personal Relationships Conference, Normal, IL.

Renwick, S., & Emler, N. (1991). The relationship between social skills deficits and juvenile delinquency. *British Journal of Clinical Psychology, 30,* 61–71.

Richmond, V. P., & McCroskey, J. C. (1985). *Communication: Apprehension, avoidance, and effectiveness.* Scottsdale, AZ: Gorsuch Scarisbrick.

Ritter, D. R. (1990). Adolescent suicide: Social competence and problem behavior of youth at high risk and low risk for suicide. *School Psychology Review, 19,* 83–95.

Robinson, E. A., & Price, M. G. (1980). Pleasurable behavior in marital interaction: An observational study. *Journal of Consulting and Clinical Psychology, 48,* 117–118.

Rodriguez, N., & Ryave, A. (1990). Telling lies in everyday life: Motivational and organizational consequences of sequential preferences. *Qualitative Sociology, 13,* 195–210.

Roloff, M. E., & Cloven, D. H. (1990). The chilling effect in interpersonal relationship: The reluctance to speak one's mind. In D. D. Cahn (Ed.), *Intimates in conflict: A communication perspective* (pp. 49–76). Hillsdale, NJ: Lawrence Erlbaum Associates.

Rook, K. S. (1984). The negative side of social interaction: Impact on psychological well-being. *Journal of Personality and Social Psychology, 46,* 1097–1108.

Roscoe, B., Cavanaugh, L. E., & Kennedy, D. R. (1988). Dating infidelity: Behaviors, reasons and consequences. *Adolescence, 23,* 35–43.

Roscoe, B., & Kelsey, T. (1986). Dating violence among high school students. *Psychology, 23,* 53–59.

Rosenfeld, L. B. (1979). Self-disclosure avoidance: Why I am afraid to tell you who I am. *Communication Monographs, 46,* 63–74.

Rubin, D. L. (1981). Using performance rating scales in large-scale assessments of oral communication proficiency. *Perspectives on the assessment of speaking and listening skills for the 1980's* (pp. 51–67). Proceedings of a symposium presented by Clearing House for Applied Performance Testing, Northwest Regional Educational Laboratory, Portland, OR.

Rubin, R. B. (1990). Communication competence. In G. M. Phillips & J. T. Wood (Eds.), *Speech communication: Essays to commemorate the 75th anniversary of the Speech Communication Association* (pp. 94–129). Carbondale: Southern Illinois University.

Rubin, R. B., & Feezel, J. D. (1986). Elements of teacher communication competence. *Communication Education, 35,* 254–268.

Rubin, R. B., & Henzl, S. A. (1984). Cognitive complexity, communication competence, and verbal ability. *Communication Quarterly, 32*, 263–270.

Rusbult, C. E., Verette, J., Whitney, G. A., Slovik, L. F., & Lipkus, I. (1991). Accommodation processes in close relationships: Theory and preliminary empirical evidence. *Journal of Personality and Social Psychology, 60*, 53–78.

Samter, W. (1991, November). *Competence, motivation, and interpersonal acceptance: What social knowledge and social anxiety will get you.* Paper presented at the Speech Communication Association Conference, Chicago, IL.

Samter, W., & Burleson, B. R. (1990). Evaluations of communication skills as predictors of peer acceptance in a group living situation. *Communication Studies, 41*, 311–325.

Schwalbe, M. L. (1988). Role-taking reconsidered: Linking competence and performance to social structure. *Journal for Theory of Social Behaviour, 18*, 411–436.

Segrin, C. (1992). Specifying the nature of social skill deficits associated with depression. *Human Communication Research, 19*, 89–123.

Semin, G. R., & Rubini, M. (1990). Unfolding the concept of person by verbal abuse. *European Journal of Social Psychology, 20*, 463–474.

Sharkey, W. F., & Waldron, V. R. (1990, November). *The intentional embarrassment of subordinates in the workplace.* Paper presented at the Speech Communication Association Conference, Chicago, IL.

Shippee, G. (1977). Preceived (sic) deception in everyday social relationships: A preliminary statement. *Psychology, 14*, 58–62.

Shuptrine, F. K., Bearden, W. O., & Teel, J. E. (1990). An analysis of the dimensionality and reliability of the Lennox and Wolfe Revised Self-Monitoring Scale. *Journal of Personality Assessment, 54*, 515–522.

Sillars, A. L., Pike, G. R., Jones, T. S., & Murphy, M. A. (1984). Communication and understanding in marriage. *Human Communication Research, 10*, 317–350.

Snyder, M. (1987). *Public appearances—Private realities: The psychology of self-monitoring.* New York: Freeman.

Snyder, M., & Cantor, N. (1980). Thinking about ourselves and others: Self-monitoring and social knowledge. *Journal of Personality and Social Psychology, 39*, 222–234.

Snyder, M., & Gangestad, S. (1986). On the nature of self-monitoring: Matters of assessment, matters of validity. *Journal of Personality and Social Psychology, 51*, 125–139.

Spitzberg. B. H. (1987). Issues in the study of communicative competence. In B. Dervin & M. J. Voight (Eds.), *Progress in communication sciences* (Vol. 8, pp. 1–46). Norwood, NJ: Ablex.

Spitzberg, B. H. (1988). Communication competence: Measures of perceived effectiveness. In C. H. Tardy (Ed.), *A handbook for the study of human communication: Methods and instruments for observing, measuring, and assessing communication processes* (pp. 67–106). Norwood, NJ: Ablex.

Spitzberg, B. H. (1989). Issues in the development of a theory of interpersonal competence in the intercultural context. *International Journal of Intercultural Relations, 13*, 241–268.

Spitzberg, B. H. (1993). The dialectics of (in)competence. *Journal of Social and Personal Relationships, 10*, 137–158.

Spitzberg, B. H., & Cupach, W. R. (1984). *Interpersonal communication competence.* Beverly Hills, CA: Sage.

Spitzberg, B. H., & Cupach, W. R. (1989). *Handbook of interpersonal competence research.* New York: Springer-Verlag.

Stamp, G. H., Vangelisti, A. L., & Daly, J. A. (1992). The creation of defensiveness in social interaction. *Communication Quarterly, 40*, 177–190.

Steiner, I. D. (1955). Interpersonal behavior as influenced by accuracy of social perception. *Psychological Review, 62*, 268–273.

Stermac, L. E., & Quinsey, V. L. (1986). Social competence among rapists. *Behavioral Assessment, 8*, 171–185.

Stets, J. E. (1992). Interactive processes in dating aggression: A national study. *Journal of Marriage and the Family, 54,* 165–177.

Straus, M. A., & Sweet, S. (1992). Verbal/symbolic aggression in couples: Incidence rates and relationships to personal characteristics. *Journal of Marriage and the Family, 54,* 346–357.

Street, R. L., Jr. & Brady, R. M. (1982). Speech rate acceptance ranges as a function of evaluative domain, listener speech rate, and communication context. *Communication Monographs, 49,* 290–308.

Stroebe, W., & Stroebe, M. S. (1986). Beyond marriage: The impact of partner loss on health. In R. Gilmour & S. Duck (Eds.), *The emerging field of personal relationships* (pp. 203–224). Hillsdale, NJ: Lawrence Erlbaum Associates.

Sugarman, D. B., & Hotaling, G. T. (1989). Dating violence: Prevalence, context, and risk markers. In M. A. Pirog-Good & J. E. Stets (Eds.), *Violence in dating relationships* (pp. 3–32). New York: Praeger.

Tedeschi, J. T., & Rosenfeld, P. (1980). Communication in bargaining and negotiation. In M. E. Roloff & G. R. Miller (Eds.), *Persuasion: New directions in theory and research* (pp. 225–248). Beverly Hills, Sage.

Tunnell, G. (1980). Intraindividual consistency in personality assessment: The effect of self-monitoring. *Journal of Personality, 48,* 220–232.

Turner, L. H. (1990). The relationship between communication and marital uncertainty: Is "her" marriage different from "his" marriage? *Women's Studies in Communication, 13,* 57–83.

Tyler, T. R., & Sears, D. O. (1977). Coming to like obnoxious people when we must live with them. *Journal of Personality and Social Psychology, 35,* 200–211.

Vangelisti, A. L., & Daly, J. A. (1989). Correlates of speaking skills in the United States: A national assessment. *Communication Education, 38,* 132–143.

Vangelisti, A. L., Daly, J. A., & Rudnick, J. R. (1991). Making people feel guilty in conversations: Techniques and correlates. *Human Communication Research, 18,* 3–39.

Vangelisti, A. L., Knapp, M. L., & Daly, J. A. (1990). Conversational narcissism. *Communication Monographs, 57,* 251–274.

Watkins, P. L., & Eisler, R. M. (1988). The type A behavior pattern, hostility, and interpersonal skill. *Behavior Modification, 12,* 315–334.

Weber, M. (1991). Value-judgments in social science. In R. Boyd, P. Gasper, & J. D. Trout (Eds.), *The philosophy of science* (pp. 719–732). Cambridge, MA: MIT Press.

Wheeless, L. R., Frymier, A. B., & Thompson, C. A. (1992). A comparison of verbal output and receptivity in relation to attraction and communication satisfaction in interpersonal relationships. *Communication Quarterly, 40,* 102–115.

Wiemann, J. M., & Bradac, J. J. (1985). The many guises of communicative competence. *Journal of Language and Social Psychology, 4,* 131–138.

Willihnganz, S. (1987, November). *Cognitive complexity, face support and social support.* Paper presented at the Speech Communication Association Conference, Boston, MA.

Wine, J. D. (1981). From defect to competence models. In J. D. Wine & M. D. Smye (Eds.), *Social competence* (pp. 3–35). New York: Guilford.

Wynne, L. C. (1988). An epigentic model of family processes. In C. J. Falicov (Ed.), *Family transitions: Continuity and change over the life cycle* (pp. 81–106). New York: Guilford.

Zimbardo, P. G. (1977). *Shyness.* New York: Jove/Harcourt Brace Jovanovich.

THE MAZE OF MESSAGES

3

MESSAGES THAT HURT

Anita L. Vangelisti
University of Texas

After my parents got divorced, my father sat down and had a long talk with me. He told me a lot of things that my mom did to hurt him and tried to explain his side of the story. I already knew most of what he said, but there was one thing that really surprised me. He said, "Your mother never really loved you as much as she did your brother or sister. . . . It was obvious from the start. You looked like me and she couldn't hide her feelings." He probably didn't mean this the way I took it, but it has bothered me ever since. I wish now he wouldn't have said it. I'm not sure why he did. I guess he was just expressing his anger.

Although most of us have used the old adage "sticks and stones may break my bones,"[1] few who study communication would argue that the impact of words on people and relationships is less than that of physical objects— whether those objects be sticks, stones, bats, or fists. Words not only "do" things when uttered (Austin, 1975), but they have the ability to hurt or harm in every bit as real a way as physical objects. A few ill-spoken words (e.g., "You're worthless," "You'll never amount to anything," "I don't love you anymore") can strongly affect individuals, interactions, and relationships.

Feeling hurt, by its nature, is a social phenomenon. Except in relatively

---

[1]Steve Duck has informed me of a German proverb that provides a more accurate representation of the association between words and feelings of hurt: "Böse Disteln stechen sehr, böse Zungen stechen mehr." A colleague from Germany, Jurgen Streeck, confirmed the translation: "Nasty thistles hurt/stick a great deal, but nasty words hurt/stick more."

rare circumstances, people feel hurt as a result of some interpersonal event—
something they perceive was said or done by another individual. The hurtful utterance may be spoken with the best of intentions or it may be overtly
aggressive. It may occur as a one-time event or it may be embedded in a
long history of verbal abuse. It may be spoken by a complete stranger or
by a life-long friend. Regardless of intentionality, context, or source, feelings
of hurt are evoked by and expressed through communication. Although theorists of emotion and of communication have acknowledged the potential
association between social interaction and the elicitation of emotions such
as hurt, theoretical work has only recently begun to explain the processes
that link communication and emotion (Averill, 1980; Bowers, Metts, & Duncanson, 1985; de Rivera & Grinkis, 1986; Shimanoff, 1985, 1987; Weiner, 1986).

Weiner (1986) suggested that emotions are determined, in part, by attributions. He and his colleagues have found, for example, that the attributions
people make about interpersonal events distinguish whether individuals feel
anger, guilt, or pity (Weiner, Graham, & Chandler, 1982). Given this, when
people feel hurt, their attributions concerning the messages that initially
evoked their feelings should distinguish those (hurt) feelings from other similarly "negative" emotions. Although researchers have begun to study the association between attribution and emotion, they have largely neglected the
relationship between communication and attribution. Because attributions
are based, in part, on individuals' observations of interpersonal events, the
messages that people believe evoked their feelings of hurt are central to understanding how hurt is elicited.

The purpose of this chapter is to begin to describe the social interactions
that people define as hurtful. First, evidence is presented that distinguishes
socially elicited feelings of hurt from other emotions on the basis of attributions. Second, messages that elicit hurt are described. Third, and finally, factors that influence the impact of hurtful messages on relationships are
examined.

DISTINGUISHING FEELINGS OF HURT

Eliciting Emotion

According to Mandler (1975) and other theorists (e.g., Berscheid, 1983), people are most likely to experience emotion when their usual patterns of behavior are interrupted. This interruption results in arousal (Burgoon &
Walther, 1990), which in turn produces a general positive or negative reaction. Weiner (1986) further specified that if the initial interruption or "outcome" is negative, unexpected, and/or important, individuals will assign a
causal attribution to the outcome. According to Weiner, the chosen attribu-

tion then produces a distinct set of emotions. For example, because individuals usually expect their conversational partners to be cooperative (Grice, 1975) and polite (Brown & Levinson, 1978), if a partner violates their expectations by being uncooperative or impolite, they will likely experience arousal. Because this violation is negative, the arousal will be labeled with a negatively valenced emotion—perhaps anger or hurt—depending on the attributions made about why the violation occurred.

Although theorists and researchers have pointed to the general processes underlying the social elicitation of emotions (Lazarus, Kanner, & Folman, 1980; Scherer, Wallbott, & Summerfield, 1986), empirical work testing these processes is sparse. The studies that have been conducted tend to fall either at one end or another of a "self" versus "other" oriented continuum. For example, works on anger (Buss, 1989) and love (Berscheid & Walster, 1974; Hendrick & Hendrick, 1986, 1988; Marston, Hecht, & Roberts, 1987) emphasize emotions that are directed toward others. These feelings, labeled "it" emotions by de Rivera (1977), are defined as social in part because they are oriented toward, and elicited by, other social interactants. In contrast, studies on emotions such as guilt (Vangelisti, Daly, & Rudnick, 1991; Wicker, Payne, & Morgan, 1983) and embarrassment (Metts & Cupach, 1989; Semin & Manstead, 1982; Sharkey & Stafford, 1990) emphasize feelings that are self-oriented (labeled "me" emotions by de Rivera). Although these "me" emotions are not directed toward other interactants, they are seen as social because they occur in social contexts and are often elicited through communication.

In contrast to emotions such as anger and guilt, feelings of hurt are more difficult to place on this self–other continuum. Hurt is neither directed toward others (as is anger) nor is it directed completely inward toward the self (as is guilt). Rather, feelings of hurt are located somewhere between the self–other endpoints. People feel hurt (self) because of something they perceive someone else (other) said or did.

Making Attributional Distinctions

The notion that hurt is neither wholly self- or other-oriented, however, does not clearly distinguish it from other emotions. Instead, Weiner (1986) suggested that the attributions associated with unexpected, negative, or salient social events distinguish one emotion (such as hurt) from another (such as anger or guilt). For example, Weiner et al. (1982) found that when causes were seen as controllable and internal, participants' feelings of anger exceeded their feelings of pity. In contrast, when causes were uncontrollable and internal, respondents tended to feel more pity than anger. Folkes (1982) further found that participants who were asked to imagine that they had turned down a request for a date anticipated different emotional responses based on the attributions they gave their imaginary partner for the rejection. Internal causes for rejection resulted in greater anticipations that the other's feelings would be hurt than did external causes for rejection. Weiner and Handel (1985) found similar results with a group of children who were asked to pretend that they rejected a peer's invitation to play.

Although these studies provide some hints as to the underlying attributions associated with socially elicited feelings of hurt, they do not provide a direct comparison between attributions associated with hurt and those associated with other similarly negative emotions. Because hurt is located somewhere between anger (an other-oriented, "it" emotion) and guilt (a self-oriented, "me" emotion) on the self–other continuum, it might be hypothesized that the causal attributions associated with hurt would also be located somewhere between those associated with anger and guilt. Given that anger is directed toward others, it is not surprising that people tend to attribute their feelings of anger to internal, stable qualities of other individuals (Weiner et al., 1982). In contrast, feelings of guilt are often associated with attributions of responsibility to the self (Wicker et al., 1983). If, however, guilt feelings are elicited through social interaction, many of these self-oriented attributions (e.g., "because I'm too impatient") may become interpersonal attributions ("because she was trying to make me realize how impatient I am") (see Newman, 1981). Indeed, Vangelisti et al. (1991) found that the most commonly cited reason for guilt-eliciting messages was to persuade (e.g., "because she wanted to convince me to do something")—an interpersonal attribution.

Because feelings of hurt are neither completely other-oriented nor self-oriented, attributions associated with hurtful messages should reflect others' internal, stable qualities less frequently than do attributions associated with messages that elicit feelings of anger (an other-oriented emotion), but more frequently than do attributions associated with guilt (a self-oriented emotion). In addition, attributions associated with hurtful messages should reflect interpersonal causes less often than do attributions associated with guilt-eliciting messages, but more often than do attributions associated with anger.[2]

Examining Attributional Distinctions

To examine the attributional differences between messages that elicit hurt, anger, and guilt, data were collected from a group of 183 undergraduate students enrolled in introductory communication courses. Respondents were

---

[2]Because little is known about the globality of attributions associated with guilt- or anger-eliciting messages, it is difficult to predict the relative globality of attributions associated with hurtful messages. Potential differences in globality between attributions associated with hurtful messages and those associated with messages that elicit anger and guilt, therefore, represent an interesting research question.

asked to complete a set of three, randomly ordered questionnaires. One of the questionnaires required them to recall a situation in which someone said something that hurt their feelings, another to focus on a situation in which someone made them feel angry, and another to remember a situation in which someone said something to make them feel guilty. In every case, participants were asked to describe briefly the situation and note what it was the other person said that made them feel hurt (angry or guilty). Two open-ended questions followed. Participants were asked to indicate whether or not they felt the other person intended to make them feel hurt (angry or guilty) and to explain why they felt the other person posited the statement or question that hurt their feelings (made them feel angry or guilty).

After the data were collected, the attributions provided by respondents were coded along three dimensions: source, stability, and globality. The *source* of each attribution was categorized as to whether it emphasized internal, external, interpersonal (Newman, 1981), or relational (Fincham, 1985) factors. The *stability* of each attribution was noted as either stable or unstable. Finally, *globality* was deemed as global or specific. Over 95% of the attributions were codable using these categories. (Interrater reliabilities for this and all subsequent coding can be obtained from the author.)

As expected, hurtful messages were found to be attributed to internal causes less often than were messages that elicited anger ($z = 3.38$) and more often than were guilt-eliciting messages ($z = -2.83$). Further, attributions for hurtful messages were seen as stable less frequently than were attributions associated with anger ($z = 1.70$) and more frequently than were those associated with guilt-eliciting messages ($z = -2.76$) (see Table 3.1).

TABLE 3.1
Frequencies of Attributions Made for Messages Eliciting Hurt,
Anger, and Guilt*

Attribution	Hurt	Anger	Guilt
Source			
Internal	103(.56)a	134(.73)b	76(.42)c
External	13(.07)	16(.09)	9(.05)
Interpersonal	57(.31)a	27(.15)b	87(.48)c
Relational	5(.03)	0(.00)	0(.00)
Stability			
Stable	30(.16)a	43(.24)b	13(.07)c
Unstable	148(.81)a	134(.73)b	159(.87)a
Globality			
Global	47(.26)a	46(.25)a	13(.07)b
Specific	131(.72)a	131(.72)a	159(.87)b

*Values labeled with different letters (a, b, or c) are significantly different ($p \leq .05$).
Note. Percentages may not sum to 100 because missing and uncodable data were not included in this chart.

Differences in the frequency of interpersonal attributions made for messages that elicited hurt, anger, and guilt were also expected. As hypothesized, hurtful messages were attributed to interpersonal causes more often than were messages that elicited anger ($z = -3.71$) and less often than were those associated with the elicitation of guilt ($z = 3.21$). The globality of attributions did not significantly differentiate hurtful messages from those that elicited anger. However, when compared to guilt-eliciting messages, hurtful messages were more often attributed to global ($z = -4.81$) causes and less often attributed to specific causes ($z = 3.61$) (see Table 3.1).

Discussing Attributions for Hurtful Messages

The findings of this investigation suggest that there are systematic distinctions between attributions associated with hurtful messages and those linked to messages that evoke anger and guilt. Hurtful messages were less frequently attributed to internal and stable causes than were messages that elicited anger and more frequently than were messages that evoked feelings of guilt. In addition, messages associated with hurt were seen more often as having an interpersonal source than those that elicited anger and less often than those that elicited guilt.

The interesting theoretical question that remains at this point is: Why? Why do attributions for hurtful messages differ from those associated with anger- and guilt-eliciting messages in these ways? On the one hand, it is possible that individuals possess a sort of cognitive "map" for emotions. A number of attributional dimensions may define this map—for example, positive versus negative, self-focused versus other-focused, active versus passive. Feelings of hurt, for instance, are negative, neither completely self- nor other-oriented, and are somewhat passive because they typically involve the individual being acted upon (hurt) by another. Given these qualities, hurt would likely be located on the map somewhere between anger and guilt. When people explain their feelings of hurt, therefore, the attributions that comprise these explanations should be similarly located "between" attributions typically made for anger and guilt.

On the other hand, it is also possible that people form their attributions for hurtful messages in a much more "ad hoc" (Garfinkel, 1967), much less rational fashion. For example, it may be more functional for individuals to attribute hurtful messages to interpersonal sources than it is to attribute them to internal sources. If people frequently attribute hurtful messages to the internal and stable qualities of their conversational partners, they are likely to find themselves with a partner they perceive is either unpleasant or insensitive to the feelings of others. Because people generally expect their conversational partners to be cooperative (Grice, 1975) and their relations with others to be positive (Taylor, 1989), these sorts of attributions may be relatively rare. Furthermore, many of the messages described by participants were uttered by friends (33%), family members (15%), and romantic partners (39%). It would probably be troublesome for people to make such attributions about the behavior of those they typically see as intimate relational partners (Knapp, Ellis, & Williams, 1980).

Although both of the explanations outlined here are possible, the data clearly do not provide evidence suggesting that one more accurately explains the attributional distinctions associated with hurtful messages than the other. Part of the answer to this "why" question involves the sequence in which emotions and attributions for emotion occur. Weiner (1986) suggested that people first feel a general positive or negative (primary) emotion, then they formulate an explanation for that feeling, and the explanation they choose, in part, determines their subsequent (secondary) emotion. If this is the case, as suggested by the work of Weiner and others (Graham, Doubleday, & Guarino, 1984; Weiner, Russell, & Lerman, 1978, 1979), the data that individuals look to in order to formulate their attributions become a vital link in the sequence. When people feel hurt, they have identified their feelings based in part on their observations of the messages that preceded those feelings.

Although the findings discussed in this section suggest that there are attributional distinctions between messages that elicit hurt and those that elicit anger and guilt, the results are limited in at least two ways. First, as analyzed, the data fail to provide a description of the messages that precede attributions associated with hurt. Second, the findings do not account for variations in degree or intensity of hurt experienced by respondents. The following section addresses these two issues.

DESCRIBING HURTFUL MESSAGES

Focusing on Messages

Weiner (1986) suggested that emotions are generated, in part, by particular patterns of attributions. He also notes, however, that the attributions associated with emotion do not emerge randomly. Instead, they are linked, in systematic ways, to antecedent variables. Previous experience, relational qualities, components of the situation, and behaviors that immediately precede the attribution all constrain people's attributional choices (e.g., Bryant & Veroff, 1982; Fincham, Bradbury, & Scott, 1990; Orvis, Kelley, & Butler, 1976; Sillars, 1980; Weiner et al., 1979).

Kelley (1983) noted that there are two sources of emotion. One is concrete and outcome-based (e.g., success or failure on an exam, pleasant or unpleasant behavior from a relational partner); the other is based on more global, interpersonal tendencies attributed to relational partners (e.g., love, kindness). Because hurt is an emotion that is elicited through social interaction, one source of hurt is the relatively concrete messages that participants perceive evoked their hurt feelings. The attributions associated with hurtful messages are not likely to occur at random. They are shaped, in part, by the messages that precede them—the acts of speech that people perceive hurt their feelings. An understanding of the social interactions people define as hurtful, therefore, includes a description of the form, content, and relative intensity of messages that hurt.

Examining Messages that Hurt

To begin to describe hurtful messages, data collected from two groups of undergraduate students were examined. The first set of data was collected from students (N = 179) enrolled in a large, introductory communication course. The second data set was collected approximately 1 year later and consisted of responses from individuals (N = 183) enrolled in one of several introductory communication courses.

Respondents were instructed to recall a situation in which someone said something to them that hurt their feelings. Then they were asked to write a "script" of the interaction as they remembered it. They were told to include what was said before the hurtful comment was made, what the comment was, and how they reacted to the comment.[3] After completing their script, participants were asked to look back on the conversation they described and to rate how hurtful it was (a high score indicated that it was "Extremely Hurtful" and a low score that it was "Not At All Hurtful").[4]

Inductive analysis (Bulmer, 1979) was used to develop a category scheme to describe the acts of speech that characterize hurtful messages.[5] With the exception of the data from five respondents (who could not recall any particularly hurtful messages), over 96% of the messages were codable into the

---

[3]Respondents participating in the second data collection session were also asked to indicate how long ago the hurtful message occurred.

[4]To reduce demand characteristics, participants were also informed that some people may not have experienced (or may not be able to remember) the type of conversations called for by the questionnaire and that part of the research project was to assess the percentage of people who could and could not do so. Subjects were further reminded that they would receive extra credit regardless of whether or not they completed the questionnaire (see Planalp & Honeycutt, 1985).

[5]Because the data were collected approximately 1 year apart, the analyses were conducted separately (also approximately 1 year apart). The initial category scheme, therefore, was primarily developed using the first data set. The second set of data was collected, in part, to demonstrate the applicability of the category scheme and to replicate the frequencies found using the first data set.

TABLE 3.2

Typology of Hurtful Message Speech Acts

Definition	Examples
Accusation: A charge of fault or offense.	"You are a liar." "You're such a hypocrite."
Evaluation: A description of value, worth, or quality.	"Well, if I met him and liked him, I would have remembered him." "Going out with you was the biggest mistake of my life."
Directive: An order, set of directions, or a command.	"Just get off my back." "Just leave me alone, why don't you!"
Advise: A suggestion for a course of action.	"Break up with her so you can have some fun." "I think we should see other people."
Express Desire: A statement of preference.	"I don't want him to be like you." "I don't ever want to have anything to do with you."
Inform: A disclosure of information.	"You aren't a priority in my life." "Well, I'm really attracted to Julie."
Question: An inquiry or interrogation.	"Why aren't you over this [a family death] yet?"
Threat: An expression of intention to inflict some sort of punishment under certain conditions.	"If I find out you are ever with that person, *never* come home again."
Joke: A witticism or prank.	"The statement was really an ethnic joke against my ethnicity."
Lie: An untrue, deceptive statement or question.	"The worst part was when he lied about something . . ."

typology. Definitions and examples of the categories are provided in Table 3.2. As can be seen in Table 3.3, the most commonly perceived hurtful messages across both data sets were accusations, evaluations, and informative messages, whereas the least common were lies and threats.

A brief perusal of these data suggested that the messages varied in terms of how hurtful they were to respondents. Interactions ranged from a former coach telling a respondent, "My, you seem to have put on a few pounds" to a physical education teacher exclaiming, "You are the worse [sic] player I've ever seen in my life!" In one case, a peer asked a respondent who was mourning her father's death, "When are you going to get over this?" In another, a respondents' stepmother told her, "You caused your grandmother's death. She died of a broken heart because you didn't show her how much you loved her." Although all of these examples were rated above the midpoint in terms of how hurtful they were to respondents, some were rated as more hurtful than others.

To determine whether any of the speech acts engendered extreme hurt more often than others, the messages coded into each category were divided

TABLE 3.3
Frequencies of Hurtful Message Speech Acts as a Function of
Overall Sample and High and Low Hurtfulness Ratings

	First Data Set			Second Data Set		
Message Type	Overall (N = 168)	High (N = 50)	Low (N = 75)	Overall (N = 183)	High (N = 73)	Low (N = 42)
Accusation	39(.23)	6(.12)	26(.33)*	39(.21)	14(.19)	15(.36)*
Evaluation	59(.35)	16(.32)	26(.33)	32(.17)	13(.18)	9(.21)
Directive	7(.04)	1(.02)	2(.03)	12(.07)	3(.04)	4(.10)
Advise	5(.03)	0(.00)	3(.04)	10(.06)	5(.07)	3(.07)
Express Desire	11(.07)	5(.10)	4(.05)	8(.04)	4(.05)	0(.00)
Inform	39(.23)	21(.42)	11(.14)*	63(.34)	29(.40)	8(.19)*
Threat	2(.01)	1(.02)	1(.01)	6(.03)	2(.03)	0(.00)
Joke	1(.01)	0(.00)	1(.01)	6(.03)	0(.00)	1(.02)
Lie	2(.01)	0(.00)	1(.01)	1(.01)	1(.01)	1(.02)

*A comparison between the proportion values obtained for high and low hurtful categories revealed a significant difference ($p \leq .05$).

Note. Percentages may not sum to 100 because missing and uncodable data were not included in this chart.

into two groups, using the median score on the item measuring message hurtfulness. Then, a series of t tests for proportions were conducted. As can be seen in Table 3.3, the analyses revealed that accusations were more often rated relatively low in hurtfulness ($z = 2.68$ for the first data set; $z = 2.02$ for the second data set), and informative statements were more frequently perceived as highly hurtful ($z = -3.57$ for the first data set, $z = -2.32$ for the second data set).[6]

The topics addressed by hurtful messages were coded using a procedure identical to the one outlined for the coding of message type. Initial categories were generated, the data were coded, the categories were refined, and the data were recoded. Table 3.4 provides a list of topic categories as well as examples of each topic. Over 93% of the messages reported were codable into the typology.

A frequency count of topics indicated that for both samples, the most commonly cited topics were romantic relationships and personality traits. The least common was ethnicity/religion. Table 3.5 contains the relevant information.

The topics of hurtful messages were similarly examined to determine if some topics were more likely than others to be seen as extremely hurtful. Topic categories were divided into two groups (one scoring above the median

[6]Given the number of tests conducted, these results should be interpreted with caution. However, because the differences were significant at well above the .05 level, the findings can be regarded with substantial confidence.

TABLE 3.4
Examples of Hurtful Message Topics

Topic	Example
Romantic Relations	"He never liked you anyway. He just used you to get back at me."
Nonromantic Relations	"You're trying too hard to be popular . . . you're ignoring your 'real' friends."
Sexual Behavior	"Why? Do you still want to sleep around?"
Physical Appearance	"God almighty you're fat!"
Abilities/Intelligence	"I guess it's hard for you teenage illiterates to write that stuff."
Personality Traits	"Well, I think you're selfish and spoiled!"
Self-Worth	"I don't need you anymore."
Time	"We don't do things together like we used to."
Ethnicity/Religion	"You're a stupid Jew!"

TABLE 3.5
Frequencies of Hurtful Message Topics as a Function of Overall Sample
and High and Low Hurtfulness Ratings

Message Topic	First Data Set			Second Data Set		
	Overall (N = 168)	High (N = 50)	Low (N = 71)	Overall (N = 183)	High (N = 73)	Low (N = 42)
Romantic Relations	45(.27)	19(.38)	17(.24)	51(.28)	25(.34)	7(.17)*
Nonromantic Relations	15(.09)	8(.16)	3(.04)*	26(.14)	12(.16)	5(.12)
Sexual Behavior	5(.03)	3(.06)	0(.00)	4(.02)	2(.03)	1(.02)
Physical Appearance	16(.10)	5(.10)	7(.10)	16(.09)	7(.10)	3(.07)
Abilities/ Intelligence	13(.08)	0(.00)	10(.14)*	16(.09)	4(.05)	4(.10)
Personality Traits	42(.25)	10(.20)	21(.30)	34(.19)	12(.16)	13(.31)*
Self-Worth	6(.04)	2(.04)	2(.03)	9(.05)	2(.03)	1(.02)
Time	15(.09)	3(.06)	10(.14)	7(.04)	1(.01)	5(.12)
Ethnicity/Religion	0(.00)	0(.00)	0(.00)	2(.01)	2(.03)	0(.00)

*A comparison between the proportion values obtained for high and low hurtful categories revealed a significant difference ($p \leq .05$).

Note. Percentages may not sum to 100 because missing and uncodable data were not included in this chart.

value on hurtfulness and the other scoring below the median value). Although the results of these analyses varied across the two data sets, the pattern of results were similar. For the first data set, hurtful messages focusing on non-romantic relationships were more often seen as extremely hurtful ($z = -2.28$), whereas messages addressing the respondents' abilities or intelligence were more frequently rated relatively low in hurtfulness ($z = 2.76$). In contrast, for the second data set, hurtful messages emphasizing romantic relationships were more often seen as highly hurtful ($z = -1.96$), and those involving time were more frequently rated as low in hurtfulness ($z = 2.60$) (see Table 3.5).

Why Some Messages Hurt More Than Others

Of the hurtful messages described, informative statements were the only speech acts that were rated extremely hurtful more often than they were rated low in hurtfulness. Informative statements, in short, were most typically seen as highly hurtful messages. Although potential explanations for this finding vary, the ability of recipients to "repair" or offer alternatives to the content of the message seems a particularly likely contributor. Whereas listeners are less likely than speakers to initiate repair (Schegloff, Jefferson, & Sacks, 1977), when accused or evaluated, recipients have the control to either overtly or covertly "defend" themselves against hurt. If the speaker does not initiate repair, the recipient may do so by offering alternatives to the accusation (e.g., accounts, excuses, justifications) and even verifying those alternatives with examples from his or her own experiences.[7] On the other hand, when informed of something, there are few such arguments available. The opportunities for recipients to repair any damage to their own face are severely limited. If, for example, a person is accused of being selfish and in-considerate, that person can point out instances in which that has not been the case. However, if the same person is informed by a lover that the lover is "seeing someone else," there is little the person can say to counter the statement.

Like informative statements, hurtful messages (in the second data set) centering on romantic relationships were, more often than not, perceived as extremely hurtful (although this difference was significant only for the second data set, messages in the first data set were similarly distributed). Given that over 54.5% of the informative messages concerned romantic relationships

---

[7]Work on accounts, blaming, excuses, and attributions (e.g., Cody & McLaughlin, 1988; Fincham, Beach, & Nelson, 1987; Fincham & Jaspers, 1980; Harvey, Weber, & Orbuch, 1990; Hilton, 1990; McLaughlin, Cody, & French, 1990; Weber & Vangelisti, 1991; Weiner, Amirkhan, Folkes, & Verette, 1987) certainly supports the notion that people generate such alternatives to explain unexpected social circumstances, potentially negative behavior, or broken social contracts.

(i.e., "I don't love you anymore," "I've been sleeping with someone else," "I decided we can only be friends"), this finding is not surprising. It is interesting, however, that participants tended to rate these relational hurts as more hurtful, whereas they tended to rate some personal or individual hurts (i.e., statements regarding self-worth) as less hurtful. One explanation for this contrast involves the potential recency of the messages concerning romantic relationships. Because the sample for this study was college students, events centering on romantic relationships may have been more recent and therefore more salient in the minds of respondents. However, this was not the case ($F(1,283) = 1.76$, ns). Furthermore, participants' ratings of hurtfulness were positively correlated with the amount of time that had passed since the hurtful event ($r(261) = .19$, $p \leq .001$).

A second explanation is that hurtful messages focusing on relational issues, like those comprised of informative statements, may be more difficult for recipients to repair than messages that emphasize nonrelational issues. This explanation is supported by the finding (in the first data set) that hurtful messages concerning nonromantic relationships were seen as extremely hurtful more often than not. (In the second data set this difference was not significant, but the data were distributed in a similar pattern.) Because relationships involve two people, they are at once controllable and uncontrollable. Each individual has the power to influence, but neither has complete reign. In contrast, many nonrelational issues such as time management are more controllable. Recipients may repair by excusing, justifying, or apologizing for their behavior or choices (McLaughlin, 1984). Further, because recipients have access to a great deal of information concerning their own behavior (e.g., the situational parameters they face), they may be able to rationalize their limitations by adjusting their own criteria for evaluating the behavior. Other nonrelational issues such as physical appearance and intelligence are relatively uncontrollable. Recipients therefore need not take responsibility for evaluative remarks or questions from others.

In comparison to nonrelational issues, relational issues present both recipients and speakers with a unique situation. Neither has complete control or responsibility for relational outcomes. As a result, when one partner evaluates ("You aren't going to make a very good husband") or makes an accusation ("You don't care about our friendship at all") concerning the relationship, the other is faced with a dilemma. He or she must seek a repair strategy that addresses the (relational) issue at hand without threatening the face of either partner. In many cases, these two goals are incompatible. The difficulties of dealing with such incompatible goals are reflected by the findings of a pilot study that suggest that recipients tend to react to extremely hurtful messages by withdrawing—either by crying or verbally acquiescing to their conversational partner (Vangelisti, 1989).

In addition to presenting participants with potentially difficult behavioral choices, extremely hurtful messages may also create some difficult cognitive tasks. When a loved one says something that hurts, participants may make one of at least two attributional choices. First, they may reason that the person did not intend to hurt their feelings. If this choice is made, the message may evoke feelings of hurt, but might not have a major effect on the relationship ("After all, she didn't *mean* to hurt my feelings"). Second, participants may believe that the message was intentionally hurtful. If so, they will likely have more difficulty discounting the impact of the message on the relationship ("How could anyone say something like that *on purpose?*"). In some cases, people may examine the available data to determine whether or not a message was intended to hurt. In others, the need or desire to maintain a close relationship may encourage participants to make attributions that minimize the intentionality they attach to hurtful messages.

The cognitive "effort" that individuals expend to make sense of hurtful messages should depend, in part, on the individuals' relationship with the person who uttered the message. For example, if a clerk in a department store hurts a person's feelings, that person is probably less likely to spend time contemplating the clerk's motives than if the same person was treated badly by a friend, parent, or spouse. Why? In part because people expect to be treated by intimate relational partners in relatively positive ways.

Obviously, there are exceptions to this rule. For instance, when explaining why his father said something hurtful to him, one respondent noted, "I don't understand why he always puts me down. I guess that's what fathers are supposed to do." Clearly this respondent did not expect positive feedback from his father. The rather bewildered account of his father's behavior suggests that the hurtful message described by the respondent may have been one of many—that it was contextualized in an ongoing stream of verbal abuse (Leffler, 1988; Vissing, Straus, Gelles, & Harrop, 1991; Yelsma, 1992) and/or intentional verbal aggression (Infante, Riddle, Horvath, & Tumlin, 1992; Martin & Horvath, 1992). Another example would be a physically abused wife who comes to expect negative behavior from her spouse. Even in such extreme cases, however, researchers have found that both the abused and the abuser use cognitive strategies to minimize the control and intentionality associated with abusive acts (Andrews, 1992; Herbert, Silver, & Ellard, 1991; Holtzworth-Munroe, 1992). In the context of close relationships, acts of violence are often interpreted as representing "love" rather than more obvious emotions such as anger or rage (Cate, Henton, Koval, Christopher, & Lloyd, 1982; Henton, Cate, Koval, Lloyd, & Christopher, 1983; Roscoe & Kelsey, 1986). In short, relational intimacy, the type of relationship people have with those who utter hurtful messages, and the intentionality attributed to the message should affect the impact of hurtful messages on relationships. The following section begins to address these issues.

STUDYING HURTFUL MESSAGES IN THE CONTEXT
OF RELATIONSHIPS

Theoretically, when people feel hurt, they have encountered an interpersonal event that is negative, unexpected, and/or particularly salient (Weiner, 1986). Because, as Taylor (1989) noted, individuals tend to expect a disproportionate amount of positivity in their associations with others, it is not surprising that their expectations are sometimes negatively violated. People are sometimes hurt by an unexpectedly negative message uttered by an acquaintance, friend, or family member.

Despite the feasibility of one person's utterance eliciting hurt in another, the perceived effect of hurtful messages on relational outcomes is less than straightforward. Bradac, Hopper, and Wiemann's (1989) claim that message effects both constrain and are constrained by contextual and relational factors adds a qualification to any predictions concerning the relational impact of hurtful messages. Initially, one would expect that extremely hurtful messages would negatively affect speaker–recipient relationships. Given that hurtful messages likely threaten the positive and/or negative face of the recipient (Brown & Levinson, 1978; Goffman, 1967), messages that are extremely hurtful should be associated with relational distancing (or decreased intimacy). If, for example, a father hurts a son by accusing him of lying and siding with his mother during family conflicts, one would expect the son to perceive less openness and intimacy between himself and his father. Similarly, if a spouse hurts his or her partner by threatening to leave the relationship, one would expect the relationship to become more distant than it was prior to the threat. Because, as Duck and Pond (1989) noted, communication "embodies" (p. 18) and shapes relationships, a message that hurts is likely to "hurt" the relationship between recipient and speaker. A review of related theoretical and empirical literature, however, reveals that at least three factors should affect the impact of hurtful messages on relational intimacy: (a) attributed intent, (b) relational intimacy (prior to the utterance), and (c) relational type (family versus nonfamily).

Attributed Intent

Attribution theorists have long contended that people's interpretations of the causes of social behavior affect social relationships (Heider, 1958; Kelley, 1973). Research on emotion often relies on a number of attributional dimensions (i.e., internal-external, stable-unstable, global-specific, controllable-uncontrollable) to distinguish one emotion from another. Although the literature on close relationships defines attributions along similar dimensions, one dimension that has emerged repeatedly in this literature is that of intentionality (Doherty, 1981; Orvis et al., 1976; Passer, Kelley, & Michela, 1978). In a synthesis of work on attributions in close relationships, Fincham (1985) noted that attributions of blame, intentionality, and motivation may be more important than other sorts of attributions in distinguishing relational outcome variables (i.e., distress) and in predicting the behavioral responses of relational partners. The comparative strength of attributions of intent to predict relational outcomes may lie in the fact that judgments of intentionality subsume many of the other dimensions traditionally used to define attributions. For instance, in order to judge the intentionality of a behavior, individuals might first note whether the behavior is internal, stable, specific, and controllable.

Empirical studies of married couples (Doherty, 1982; Fincham et al., 1987; Orvis et al., 1976) and roommates (Sillars, 1980) have demonstrated that attributions of blame and intentionality for negative interpersonal behaviors are associated with relational outcomes such as dissatisfaction, distress, conflict escalation, and negative criticism. Individuals who report that their relational partners intentionally engage in negative interpersonal behavior also tend to report negative relational outcomes. As Stamp and Knapp (1990) noted, the recipient's judgment of intent seems to "change the nature of the stimulus" for that person (p. 288). Given these findings, one would expect when hurtful messages are judged to be intentionally hurtful, they will have more of a distancing effect on the relationship. If recipients believe that a speaker uttered a hurtful message with the intention of hurting them, they will be more likely to report that their relationship with the speaker became more distant and less intimate as a result of the hurtful message.

Relational Intimacy

Research on romantic and marital relationships demonstrates that individuals' attitudes about their relationships are often associated with the way they interpret the interpersonal behavior of their partner (Noller & Fitzpatrick, 1990). For example, those who report having well-adjusted relationships tend to attribute their partner's negative behavior to unstable, specific causes, whereas individuals who are distressed tend to attribute the same negative behavior to stable, global causes (Fincham & O'Leary, 1983; Holtzworth-Munroe & Jacobson, 1985). Partners who are dissatisfied with their relationships also tend to be less accurate decoders of their significant other's nonverbal behavior (Noller, 1984).

Although it is important to acknowledge that the aforementioned findings are limited to romantic relationships, it is not unreasonable to suggest that they may have implications for other relationships as well. Individuals who report having very close or intimate relationships may interpret and/or cope with negative interpersonal events in different ways than people who have more distant, nonintimate relationships (Montgomery, 1988). Empirical studies of negatively perceived interpersonal behaviors (Knapp, Stafford, & Daly, 1986; Vangelisti et al., 1991) not only suggest that these behaviors are reported more frequently in the context of close or intimate relationships, but also that they seem to have little long-term effect on those relationships. In short, relational intimacy may serve to buffer the distancing effects of some negatively perceived interpersonal behaviors.

This is not to say that interpersonal behaviors such as hurtful messages will necessarily be perceived by intimates as any less negative or hurtful. Rather, the implication is that despite the hurtfulness of the message, the message will have less of a distancing effect on the relationship. Recipients who report having a close, intimate relationship with their conversational partners will report that the hurtful message had less of an impact on their relationship. People who have less intimate, distant relationships, on the other hand, lack the close relational history necessary to minimize the effect of the message's hurtfulness on their relationship (Knapp, 1984). In fact, individuals in the latter group may focus on their partner's negative interpersonal behaviors as a way of reinforcing their more distant relational state (Nisbett & Ross, 1980; Noller, 1984). Hurtful messages, therefore, should have more of a distancing effect on relationships that are initially distant or less intimate and less of an effect on relationships that are close or intimate.

Relationship Type

In his discussion of message variables, Bowers (1989) recommends that communication researchers continue to examine "established (and developing) social relationships and the ways in which they constrain and liberate messages" (p. 17). Although the study of close relationships has experienced incredible growth during the 1980s (Duck, 1990), communication researchers still know very little about the effects that different types of relationships have on the interpretation of communication messages.

Compared to friendships and romantic relationships, family relationships represent a unique context for interaction (Booth, 1991). There are at least two characteristics that set family relationships apart from other types of close, interpersonal relationships. First, as Galvin and Cooper (1990) noted, family relationships are involuntary. In contrast to friendships and romantic relationships, family members are not given the opportunity to choose their familial associations. If negative interpersonal behaviors are consistently performed by a family member, other members are not able to "terminate" their relationship with that individual in the same way as they might terminate a friendship, acquaintanceship, or romantic relationship. This sense of permanence may encourage them to take one another "for granted," thereby allowing for a variety of interpersonal behaviors that are hurtful, but do not change the nature of their relationships. As a result, family members may learn to deal with negatively perceived interpersonal behaviors, such as hurtful messages, in different ways than do nonfamily members. They may be less likely than nonfamily members to allow a single negative interpersonal behavior such as a hurtful message to affect their relationships with other members.

An extreme example of the involuntary nature of family associations can be seen in abusive parent–child relationships. Barring legal intervention, parents are able to bludgeon their children with psychologically damaging messages (e.g., "I wish you were never born," "If it weren't for you, your mother and I would still be married") (Vissing et al., 1991). Children are typically incapable—emotionally, intellectually, or physically—of stopping the abuse. Because family relationships are involuntary, many grown children not only endure the scars of past verbal abuse, but continue to endure the abuse into adulthood (Leffler, 1988). Such consistent negative interpersonal behavior may not create distance in their relationship with their parent, because it is the only pattern of parental behavior they have ever known.

A second characteristic of family relationships that distinguishes them from other relationships is the rich history that family members bring with them to every interaction. Kelley and his colleagues (1983) noted that two defining features of close relationships are: (a) the existence of interconnected activity over time, and (b) the experience of a diverse series of activities. Because family members are likely to have experienced a variety of interactions with one another over an extended period of time, they may place less weight on the impact of a single hurtful message. The message may, indeed, violate their expectations for how family members "should" interact (Galvin & Brommel, 1986), but the extended history they bring to each interaction may require an accumulation of hurtful messages (rather than a single message) to create relational distance.

Taken together, the involuntary nature of family relationships and the full histories that family members bring to any interaction may constrain the impact of hurtful messages on relational intimacy. If this is the case, hurtful messages that occur in the context of family relationships should have less of a distancing effect on those relationships than hurtful messages that occur in nonfamily relationships.

Examining the Impact of Hurtful Messages

To investigate the influence of attributed intent, relational intimacy, and relationship type (family versus nonfamily) on the impact of hurtful messages, data were collected from 290 undergraduate students enrolled in an introductory-level communication course. Prior to completing a 13-item questionnaire, respondents were asked to recall an instance in which someone said something to them that hurt their feelings. Then, for the first item, they were instructed to write a brief "script" of the interaction. As in the previous investigations, respondents were told to include what was said before the hurtful comment was made, what the comment was, and how they reacted to the comment.[8]

After describing the conversation, participants responded to several items. The first item required respondents to look back on the conversation they described and to rate how hurtful it was (a rating of 7 indicated that it was "Extremely Hurtful," and a rating of 1 indicated that it was "Not At All Hurtful"). Items 2 through 6 were designed to assess the impact of the hurtful message on relational intimacy. These items included statements such as "It made us more open," "It made us more intimate," and "It made us more distant." Item 7 asked that respondents note how close they were to the speaker at the time of the conversation (7 indicated "Extremely Close," 1 indicated "Not Close At All"). Finally, the last portion of the questionnaire required respondents to note whether or not the speaker intended to hurt them, to explain why they felt the hurtful message was uttered, and to describe the nature (e.g., friend, daughter, romantic partner) and length of their relationship with the speaker.

To test the hypothesized association between recipients' ratings of message hurtfulness and the perceived distancing effect of the message on the recipient–speaker relationship, the 5 items used to measure the perceived impact of the message on relational intimacy were summed (α = .90). As expected, message hurtfulness was positively associated with the perceived distancing effect that the message had on the relationship ($r(261)$ = .27, $p \leq$ .0005).

Although a positive association between message hurtfulness and the relational impact of hurtful messages was anticipated, relational impact was also expected to differ for messages that were seen as intentionally hurtful and for those that were seen as unintentional. When asked whether they felt the hurtful message they described was intentional, participants provided one of three responses: intentional, unintentional, or unknown. Of the 290 respondents who completed the questionnaire, 186 (64.1%) said that the hurtful message was unintentional, 87 (30.0%) reported that it was intentional, 14 (4.8%) said that they did not know, and 3 (1%) failed to respond. Messages attributed with intent (M = 28.61) had a significantly greater impact

---

[8]They were also told that they may not have experienced or may not be able to recall this type of conversation and were reassured that they would receive extra credit regardless of whether or not they completed the questionnaire (see Planalp & Honeycutt, 1985).

on the relationship than messages that were perceived to be unintentional (M = 24.44) (F(1,268) = 20.85, $p \leq$ .0001). There was no difference between intentional (M = 6.02) and unintentional (M = 5.77) messages with regard to ratings of message hurtfulness (F(1,245) = 2.73, ns).

Assuming that relational intimacy may mediate the negative impact of hurtful messages on recipient–speaker relationships, a negative association between relational intimacy and the perceived distancing effect that the message had on the relationship was anticipated. Results revealed a negative and significant correlation (r(283) = −.13, $p \leq$ .01) between intimacy and the composite measure of relational impact. There was no association between relational intimacy and message hurtfulness (r(260) = .04, ns).

The final hypothesis was based on the notion that family relationships provide a context for messages that is significantly different from the context provided by nonfamily relationships. Hurtful messages occurring in the context of family relationships were expected to have less of a distancing effect on the relationship than those occurring in nonfamily contexts. Participants' descriptions of their relationship with the person who uttered the hurtful message were divided into two categories: Relationships including son/daughter, sibling, mother/father, grandparent, and spouse were defined as family relationships;[9] friends, romantic partners, acquaintances, strangers, teachers, and bosses were defined as nonfamily relationships.

Hurtful messages uttered in the context of family relationships (M = 24.09) had less of an impact on the relationship than those uttered in nonfamily relationships (M = 26.32) (F(1,182) = 4.31, $p \leq$ .04). There was no difference between family (M = 5.80) and nonfamily (M = 5.90) relationships in terms of message hurtfulness (F(1,259) = .33, ns).

Given the nature of this sample (undergraduate students) and the fact that relational intimacy was negatively associated with the impact of hurtful messages on recipient–speaker relationships, it is possible that the differences found between family and nonfamily members were due, in part, to the higher level of intimacy in family relationships. College students may not have many nonfamily relationships that are as close or as intimate as their family relationships are. However, there was not a significant difference in intimacy between family (M = 5.19) and nonfamily (M = 5.09) relationships (F(1,283) = .18, ns). The finding that family members report that hurtful messages have less of a distancing effect than nonfamily members, therefore, is not due to a difference in intimacy between the two relationship types.

---

[9]For the purposes of this analysis, spousal relationships were defined as family relationships. Because there were only three spousal relationships in the current study, this distinction is not a problematic one, however, future studies should consider the potential issues involved in categorizing spousal relationships as "family" or "nonfamily."

Discussing the Impact of Hurtful Messages on Relationships

Although the vast majority (64.8%) of hurtful messages were perceived to be unintentional, those that were seen as intentional had a significantly greater distancing effect on the relationship. Recipients' remarks regarding intentionality reflected their willingness to make allowances for a variety of speaker difficulties. When asked whether the speaker intended to hurt them, recipients often made comments such as "she was mad at someone else," "he just doesn't know how to fight," "he has a personal problem with alcohol," or "he said it because he loves me." If speakers seemed to regret the hurtful message (Knapp et al., 1986), or if the message was offered for the good of the recipient (Weber & Vangelisti, 1991), the message did not have as strong an effect on the relationship. In contrast, when recipients perceived that the message was intentionally hurtful, their remarks frequently focused on stable personality traits of the speaker: "She's just that sort of person," "he is very cruel and unforgiving," "he doesn't care about anyone except himself."

Previous work (e.g., Holtzworth-Munroe & Jacobson, 1985) suggested that such global, stable attributions for negative behavior may be more closely linked to relational distancing than are specific, unstable attributions. To examine this issue, additional analyses were conducted. Participants' explanations were coded as to whether they were global or specific and whether they were stable or unstable. As expected, global ($M = 28.19$) attributions had more of a distancing effect on the relationship than did specific ($M = 25.53$) attributions ($F(1,268) = 5.97, p \leq .02$). Stable ($M = 28.21$) attributions were also perceived as creating more relational distance than unstable ($M = 25.09$) attributions ($F(1,269) = 11.65, p \leq .0005$). Because judgments of intent are partially based on recipients' knowledge of speakers' behavioral propensities across a variety of situations (Stamp & Knapp, 1990), these findings are consistent with the significant results found for attributions of intent.

The impact of hurtful messages on relational intimacy was also affected by ratings of relational closeness at the time the message was uttered. Ratings of relational closeness were negatively associated with the distancing effect of hurtful messages. Because there was not a similarly negative association between closeness and message hurtfulness, the apparent lack of distancing in more intimate relationships was not due to the fact that the messages hurt less. Instead, those who were involved in intimate relationships may be more willing to offer interpretations of the hurtful messages that are less harmful to the relationship. It is also possible that intimates have developed idiosyncratic patterns to deal with hurtful events (Montgomery, 1988), or that they have developed enough of a positive regard for one another that a single hurtful message does not affect relational intimacy (Knapp, 1984).

Similar explanations may be offered for the findings concerning family relationships. Although intimacy did not significantly differentiate between family and nonfamily relationships, results indicated that hurtful messages occurring in the context of the family had less of an effect on the relationship than did those occurring in nonfamily contexts. In contrast to intimate nonfamily relationships, family associations may encourage people to deal with hurtful messages by relying on the assumption that the relationships are involuntary and therefore virtually impossible to dissolve. One respondent noted in the margin of his questionnaire that "It seems if something happens with your family . . . [you are] a lot more apt to forgive them." Because family members are, for all practical purposes, irreplaceable, recipients of hurtful messages may feel more obligated to absorb the blow of a hurtful message without allowing it to impact the family relationship. In addition, the variety of circumstances family members have experienced together may create a sort of "immunity" to the impact of hurtful messages. Family members' experience with other negative interpersonal events may better prepare them for the feelings of hurt that can be elicited by other members.

CONCLUSIONS

Taken as a whole, the findings reported in this chapter begin to provide an interesting description of what hurtful messages look like and how they operate in interpersonal relationships. First, hurtful messages were distinguished from messages that elicited anger (an other-oriented emotion) and guilt (a self-oriented emotion) on the basis of the attributions people made for those messages. Hurtful messages were attributed to internal and stable causes less often than were messages that elicited anger and more often than were those that evoked feelings of guilt. Further, messages that hurt were attributed to interpersonal causes more frequently than were those that evoked anger and less frequently than those that created guilt. Obviously, these findings will be bolstered by future studies that present respondents with potentially hurtful messages and manipulate the attributions associated with those messages.

The second group of findings was based on the notion that people act as "naive psychologists" (Heider, 1958; Kelley, 1973; Ross, 1977) and that their attributions are constrained by their observations of available data. When people feel hurt, one source of data they may use to assess their emotion is the message they feel initially evoked the emotion. Hurtful messages most often described by respondents were accusations, evaluations, and informative messages. Informative messages were rated as extremely hurtful more often than not—perhaps due to the relative difficulty of repairing or offering an alternative to those messages. Further, if informative messages are viewed as relatively objective, they may be more difficult to rationalize away than more subjective messages. Participants also tended to rate messages focusing on relationships as extremely hurtful. When hurtful messages emphasized romantic relationships or nonromantic relationships, participants tended to report that they were extremely hurtful.

Finally, the third set of findings reported on factors that influence the impact of hurtful messages on relationships. Participants' ratings of message hurtfulness were positively associated with the perceived impact of the message on relational intimacy, such that highly hurtful messages tended to have more of an effect on perceived closeness. Messages that were seen as intentionally hurtful had a significantly greater impact on the relationship than messages that were perceived to be unintentional. In addition, relationships that were initially closer or more intimate were affected less by hurtful messages. Finally, hurtful messages spoken by family members had less of a distancing effect on the relationship than those that were spoken by nonfamily members.

Although the findings of these studies are obviously limited in the extent to which they tap actual interactions, the data are by no means superficial in nature. One participant discussed the break-up of a romantic relationship noting, "I felt anger. . . . I was helpless because she was supposed to be my wife in less than a year." Another discussed a situation in which her stepmother told her she was responsible for her grandmother's death. A third, after disclosing her fear that she was pregnant to her boyfriend, noted his response: "I don't have any money right now and I sure don't need the hassle of you being pregnant!" Yet a fourth wrote about a postdivorce discussion with his father, when his father told him, "I don't want anything to do with you anymore!" These are salient situations to recipients—regardless of their precise historical accuracy. In fact, one could argue that any inaccuracies reflected in participants' reports are vitally important to their present interpretations of the messages and their current interactions with the message senders (Cuber & Harroff, 1965; Harvey et al., 1990; Sillars & Scott, 1983). Whereas actual interactive data would, of course, enhance and extend the findings of these two studies, dismissing these self-reported accounts would leave a definite gap in the descriptions of messages that are perceived as hurtful.

In addition to providing a foundation for judgment studies and investigations focusing on actual interaction, the studies reported in this chapter have generated a number of questions for future research. For instance, the notion that hurtful messages may not have as much effect on intimate relationships as they do on less intimate relationships presents some interesting issues. What is it about the close relationships that may make them more able to absorb the blow of an extremely hurtful message? Is it relationship length, per se, or is it a perceived sense of "permanence" that lessens the impact of hurtful messages? Have the participants developed some type of coping strategy that helps them work through these situations? Although individuals who have been together for an extended period may have had more time to devise and practice the implementation of such strategies, it may also be that they have become "numb" to the effect of hurtful messages over time—they may have come to expect a given amount or particular types of hurtful messages and, as a result, may be less impacted by their occurrence.

Similar questions may be posited concerning hurtful messages that occur in the context of family relationships. In this chapter, the rich histories associated with family relationships were posited as a reason for the relatively low impact of hurtful messages on those relationships. Because family members typically observe one another in a variety of settings and across a number of circumstances, they are more likely to have seen one another behave in negative ways. Hurtful messages therefore may not be as much of a violation in family relationships as they are in other, less lengthy associations. In addition, the involuntary nature of family relationships may encourage people to use cognitive strategies that reduce the impact of the hurt on the relationship. Because it is difficult, if not impossible, for family members to dissolve their relationships with one another, the most functional way for them to deal with hurtful messages may either be to "forgive and forget" or to attribute the message to external, uncontrollable events. Obviously the length of family relationships and their involuntary nature are, in most cases, confounded. Examining family relationships that do not share a lengthy history of frequent interactions (i.e., mothers or fathers who do not live with their children, older sisters or brothers who moved away from home when their siblings were very young) may help to tease out some of these complex associations.

The relational effects of hurtful messages also might be examined in terms of a variety of situational variables. Some of these were hinted at in the data collected for the second study. For instance, in explaining what made the described message hurtful, one respondent noted that "It was my first time home after I'd enrolled in college and I had been missing my family very much." Another stated, "We had just had sex. I was not really getting anything from it especially." In these cases and others, contextual features such as timing and the intimacy of the setting seemed to have influenced respondents' perceptions of the message. In fact, it may be that in some instances, feelings of hurt are initially evoked by the content and structure of the situation. People may initially feel pain and frustration due to a poor performance, an unfulfilled expectation, or the dissolution of a relationship. The hurtful messages that occur in such contexts may represent the culmination of pain experienced over an extended period (e.g., when a distressed spouse "finally" asks for a divorce), or they may serve as markers that remind individuals of hurt that occurred on a one-time basis (e.g., when a coach or a teacher chastises a student for an unusually poor performance). In either case, hurtful messages likely play a pivotal role in the construction (and reconstruction) of people's emotions over time.

Whether researchers seek to further understand the contexts surrounding hurtful messages or the form and function of the messages themselves, it will be important to examine dyadic data in hurtful episodes. For example, the studies reported in this chapter suggest that recipients often feel hurtful messages are unintentional—that the speaker did not "mean" to hurt their feelings. Is this actually the case? Or do speakers often intend to hurt others? Infante and his colleagues (Infante et al., 1992; Martin & Horvath, 1992) have investigated some of the reasons individuals use intentionally aggressive speech. We do not know, however, why people utter hurtful messages when they do *not* intend to hurt recipients. Certainly, in some cases, the emotional consequences associated with a hurtful message are accidental and the speaker regrets what he or she said (Knapp et al., 1986). But, in other cases, it may be that speakers have a different goal in mind—one that overpowers their concern to avoid hurting their conversational partner. Speakers may even consciously decide that hurting another is "worth" achieving a particular goal. Some of the attributions respondents provided for hurtful messages in the present series of investigations hinted that this might be the case. For instance, one respondent noted that her best friend uttered a hurtful message in order to draw her attention to a problem in their relationship. She noted that this friend said what she did "so that I would realize our relationship was in trouble." Another respondent said that his coach "put down" his playing abilities in front of the other players to "motivate" him and get him "pumped up" for an upcoming game. Yet another person noted that her romantic partner hurt her early on in their relationship to "test" her and to determine what she would "put up with" (see Baxter & Wilmot, 1984). These examples and others not only underscore the importance of collecting dyadic data, but also suggest that hurtful messages may have positive relational consequences.

If hurtful messages are sometimes associated with positive relational outcomes, partners must have (or develop) ways to minimize their feelings of hurt. Some research has been conducted examining the ways in which relational partners deal with aggressive behavior (e.g., Ohbuchi, Kameda, & Agarie, 1989; Wagner, 1980). Individuals may offer apologies, ignore the behavior, or attempt to directly confront their aggressor. Such coping strategies are selected, in part, as a means for the recipients of extremely hurtful behavior to defend themselves. When hurtful messages have positive relational outcomes, coping with hurt may not require individuals to protect themselves from harm. Instead, partners may find themselves jointly negotiating an account for why the hurt was necessary, why it was worth the pain, or why it was relatively unimportant when compared to the ultimate outcome. Whether and how partners engage in such joint negotiations will likely depend on the nature of their relationship—how intimate they are, how satisfied they are, and how open they are with one another about emotional issues.

In sum, the findings of this research suggest that the old adage concerning "sticks and stones" requires, at the very least, a lengthy addendum. Hurt is a socially elicited emotion (de Rivera, 1977)—people feel hurt because of the interpersonal behavior of others. Because feelings of hurt are elicited through social interaction, words can "hurt"—both individuals and relationships.

ACKNOWLEDGMENTS

The author would like to thank Bill Cupach, Steve Duck, Robert Hopper, Mark Knapp, and Brian Spitzberg for their contributions to this chapter.

REFERENCES

Andrews, B. (1992). Attribution processes in victims of marital violence: Who do women blame and why? In J. H. Harvey, T. L. Orbuch, & A. L. Weber (Eds.), *Attributions, accounts, and close relationships* (pp. 176–193). New York: Springer-Verlag.

Austin, J. L. (1975). *How to do things with words* (2nd ed., J. O. Urmson & M. Sbisa, Eds.). Cambridge, MA: Harvard University Press.

Averill, J. R. (1980). A constructivist view of emotion. In R. Plutchik & H. Kellerman (Eds.), *Theories of emotion* (Vol. 1, pp. 305–339). New York: Academic Press.

Baxter, L. A., & Wilmot, W. W. (1984). "Secret tests": Social strategies for acquiring information about the state of the relationship. *Human Communication Research, 11*, 171–201.

Berscheid, E. (1983). Emotion. In H. H. Kelley, E. Berscheid, A. Christensen, J. H. Harvey, T. L. Huston, G. Levinger, E. McClintock, L. A. Peplau, & D. R. Peterson (Eds.), *Close relationships* (pp. 110–168). Beverly Hills, CA: Sage.

Berscheid, E., & Walster, E. (1974). A little bit about love. In T. L. Huston (Ed.), *Foundations of interpersonal attraction* (pp. 355–381). New York: Academic Press.

Booth, A. (Ed.). (1991). *Contemporary families: Looking forward, looking back*. Minneapolis: National Council on Family Relations.

Bowers, J. W. (1989). Introduction. In J. Bradac (Ed.), *Message effects in communication science* (pp. 10–23). Newbury Park, CA: Sage.

Bowers, J. W., Metts, S. M., & Duncanson, W. T. (1985). Emotion and interpersonal communication. In M. L. Knapp & G. R. Miller (Eds.), *Handbook of interpersonal communication* (pp. 500–550). Beverly Hills, CA: Sage.

Bradac, J. J., Hopper, R., & Wiemann, J. M. (1989). Message effects: Retrospect and prospect. In J. Bradac (Ed.), *Message effects in communication science* (pp. 294–317). Newbury Park, CA: Sage.

Brown, P., & Levinson, S. (1978). *Politeness: Some universals in language usage*. Cambridge: Cambridge University Press.

Bryant, F. B., & Veroff, J. (1982). The structure of psychological well-being: A sociohistorical analysis. *Journal of Personality and Social Psychology, 43*, 653–673.

Bulmer, M. (1979). Concepts in the analysis of qualitative data. *Sociological Review, 27*, 651–677.

Burgoon, J. K., & Walther, J. (1990). Nonverbal expectancies and the evaluative consequences of violations. *Human Communication Research, 17*, 232–265.

Buss, D. M. (1989). Conflict between the sexes: Strategic interference and the evocation of anger and upset. *Journal of Personality and Social Psychology, 56*, 735–747.

Cate, R. M., Henton, J. M., Koval, J., Christopher, F. S., & Lloyd, S. (1982). Premarital abuse: A social psychological perspective. *Journal of Family Issues, 3*, 79–90.

Cody, M. J., & McLaughlin, M. L. (1988). Accounts on trial: Oral arguments in traffic court. In C. Antaki (Ed.), *Analysing everyday explanation: A casebook of methods* (pp. 113–126). London: Sage.

Cuber, J., & Harroff, P. (1965). *The significant Americans*. New York: Van Rees.

de Rivera, J. (1977). *A structural theory of the emotions*. New York: International Universities Press.

de Rivera, J., & Grinkis, C. (1986). Emotions in social relationships. *Motivation and Emotion, 10*, 351–369.

Doherty, W. J. (1981). Cognitive processes in intimate conflict: I. Extending attribution theory. *The American Journal of Family Therapy, 9*, 1–13.

Doherty, W. J. (1982). Attribution style and negative problem solving in marriage. *Family Relations, 317*, 23–27.

Duck, S. (1990). Relationships as unfinished business: Out of the frying pan and into the 1990s. *Journal of Social and Personal Relationships, 7*, 5–28.

Duck, S., & Pond, K. (1989). Friends Romans countrymen, lend me your retrospections: Rhetoric and reality in personal relationships. In C. Hendrick (Ed.), *Review of social behavior and personality, Vol. 10: Close relationships* (pp. 17–38). Newbury Park, CA: Sage.

Fincham, F. D. (1985). Attributions in close relationships. In J. Harvey & G. Weary (Eds.), *Attribution: Basic issues and applications* (pp. 203–234). New York: Academic Press.

Fincham, F. D., Beach, S., & Nelson, G. (1987). Attribution processes in distressed and non-distressed couples: III. Causal and responsibility attributions for spouse behavior. *Cognitive Therapy and Research, 11*, 71–86.

Fincham, F. D., Bradbury, T. N., & Scott, C. K. (1990). Cognition in marriage. In F. D. Fincham & T. N. Bradbury (Eds.), *The psychology of marriage* (pp. 118–149). New York: Guilford Press.

Fincham, F. D., & Jaspers, J. M. (1980). Attribution of responsibility: From man the scientist to man as lawyer. In L. Berkowitz (Ed.), *Advances in experimental social psychology* (Vol. 13, pp. 82–139). New York: Academic Press.

Fincham, F. D., & O'Leary, K. D., (1983). Causal inferences for spouse behavior in maritally distressed and nondistressed couples. *Journal of Social and Clinical Psychology, 1*, 42–57.

Folkes, V. S. (1982). Communicating the causes of social rejection. *Journal of Experimental Social Psychology, 18*, 235–252.

Galvin, K. M., & Brommel, B. J. (1986). *Family communication: Cohesion and change* (2nd ed.). Glenview, IL: Scott, Foresman.

Galvin, K. M., & Cooper, P. J. (1990, May). *Development of involuntary relationships: The stepparent-stepchild relationship*. Paper presented at the annual meeting of the International Communication Association, Dublin, Ireland.

Garfinkel, H. (1967). *Studies in ethnomethodology*. Englewood Cliffs, NJ: Prentice-Hall.

Goffman, E. (1967). *Interaction ritual: Essays on face-to-face behavior*. Garden City, NY: Doubleday.

Graham, S., Doubleday, C., & Guarino, P. A. (1984). The development of relations between perceived controllability and the emotions of pity, anger, and guilt. *Child Development, 55*, 561–565.

Grice, H. P. (1975). Logic and conversation. In P. Cole & J. Morgan (Eds.), *Syntax and semantics* (Vol. 3, pp. 41–58). New York: Academic Press.

Harvey, J. H., Weber, A. L., & Orbuch, T. L. (1990). *Interpersonal accounts*. Oxford: Blackwell.

Heider, F. (1958). *The psychology of interpersonal relations*. New York: Wiley.

Hendrick, C., & Hendrick, S. S. (1986). A theory and method of love. *Journal of Personality and Social Psychology, 50*, 392–402.

Hendrick, C., & Hendrick, S. S. (1988). Lovers wear rose colored glasses. *Journal of Social and Personal Relationships, 5*, 161–183.

Henton, J. M., Cate, R. M., Koval, J., Lloyd, S., & Christopher, F. S. (1983). Romance and violence in dating relationships. *Journal of Family Issues, 4*, 467–482.

Herbert, T. B., Silver, R. C., & Ellard, J. H. (1991). Coping with an abusive relationship: I. How and why do women stay? *Journal of Marriage and the Family, 53*, 311–325.

Hilton, D. J. (1990). Conversational processes and causal explanation. *Psychological Bulletin, 107*, 65–81.

Holtzworth-Munroe, A. (1992). Attributions and maritally violent men: The role of cognitions in marital violence. In J. H. Harvey, T. L. Orbuch, & A. L. Weber (Eds.), *Attributions, accounts, and close relationships* (pp. 165–175). New York: Springer-Verlag.

Holtzworth-Munroe, A., & Jacobson, N. S. (1985). Causal attributions of married couples. When do they search for causes? What do they conclude when they do? *Journal of Personality and Social Psychology, 48*, 1398–1412.

Infante, D. A., Riddle, B. L., Horvath, C. L., & Tumlin, S. A. (1992). Verbal aggressiveness: Messages and reasons. *Communication Quarterly, 40*, 116–126.

Kelley, H. H. (1973). The process of causal attribution. *American Psychologist, 28*, 107–128.

Kelley, H. H. (1983). The situational origins of human tendencies: A further reason for the formal analysis of structures. *Personality and Social Psychology Bulletin, 9*, 8–30.

Kelley, H. H., Berscheid, E., Christensen, A., Harvey, J. H., Huston, T. L., Levinger, G., McClintock, E., Peplau, L. A., & Peterson, D. R. (1983). *Close relationships.* New York: Freeman.

Knapp, M. L. (1984). *Interpersonal communication and human relationships.* Boston: Allyn & Bacon.

Knapp, M. L., Ellis, D., & Williams, B. A. (1980). Perceptions of communication behavior associated with relationship terms. *Communication Monographs, 47*, 262–278.

Knapp, M. L., Stafford, L., & Daly, J. A. (1986). Regrettable messages: Things people wish they hadn't said. *Journal of Communication, 36*, 40–58.

Lazarus, R. S., Kanner, A. D., & Folkman, S. (1980). Emotions: A cognitive-phenomenological analysis. In R. Plutchik & H. Kellerman (Eds.), *Emotion: Theory, research, and experience* (pp. 189–217). New York: Academic Press.

Leffler, A. (1988). *Verbal abuse and psychological unavailability scales and relationship to self-esteem.* Paper presented at the annual meeting of the American Psychological Association, Atlanta, GA.

Mandler, G. (1975). *Mind and emotion.* New York: Wiley.

Marston, P. J., Hecht, M. L., & Roberts, T. (1987). "True love ways": The subjective experience and communication of romantic love. *Journal of Social and Personal Relationships, 4*, 387–408.

Martin, M. M., & Horvath, C. L. (1992, November). *Messages that hurt: What people think and feel about verbally aggressive messages.* Paper presented at the annual meeting of the Speech Communication Association, Chicago, IL.

McLaughlin, M. L. (1984). *Conversation: How talk is organized.* Beverly Hills, CA: Sage.

McLaughlin, M. L., Cody, M. J., & French, K. (1990). Account-giving and the attribution of responsibility: Impressions of traffic offenders. In M. J. Cody & M. L. McLaughlin (Eds.), *The psychology of tactical communication* (pp. 244–267). Clevedon, England: Multilingual Matters.

Metts, S., & Cupach, W. R. (1989). Situational influence on the use of remedial strategies in embarrassing predicaments. *Communication Monographs, 56*, 151–162.

Montgomery, B. M. (1988). Quality communication in personal relationships. In S. W. Duck (Ed.), *Handbook of personal relationships* (pp. 343–359). New York: Wiley.

Newman, H. (1981). Communication within ongoing intimate relationships: An attributional perspective. *Personality and Social Psychology Bulletin, 7*, 59–70.

Nisbett, R., & Ross, L. (1980). *Human inference: Strategies and shortcomings of social judgment.* Englewood Cliffs, NJ: Prentice-Hall.

Noller, P. (1984). *Nonverbal communication and marital interaction.* Oxford: Pergamon.

Noller, P., & Fitzpatrick, M. A. (1990). Marital communication in the eighties. *Journal of Marriage and the Family, 52,* 832–843.

Ohbuchi, K., Kameda, M., & Agarie, N. (1989). Apology as aggression control: Its role in mediating appraisal of and response to harm. *Journal of Personality and Social Psychology, 56,* 219–227.

Orvis, B. R., Kelley, H. H., & Butler, D. (1976). Attributional conflict in young couples. In J. H. Harvey, W. J. Ickes, & R. Kidd (Eds.), *New directions in attribution research* (Vol. 1, pp. 353–386). Hillsdale, NJ: Lawrence Erlbaum Associates.

Passer, M. W., Kelley, H. H., & Michela, J. L. (1978). Multidimensional scaling of the causes for negative interpersonal behavior. *Journal of Personality and Social Psychology, 36,* 951–962.

Planalp, S., & Honeycutt, J. M. (1985). Events that increase uncertainty in personal relationships. *Human Communication Research, 11,* 593–604.

Roscoe, B., & Kelsey, T. (1986). Dating violence among high school students. *Psychology, 23,* 53–59.

Ross, L. (1977). The intuitive psychologist and his shortcomings: Distortions in the attribution process. In L. Berkowitz (Ed.), *Advances in experimental social psychology* (Vol. 10, pp. 173–220). New York: Academic Press.

Schegloff, E. A., Jefferson, G., & Sacks, H. (1977). The preference for self-correction in the organization of repair in conversation. *Language, 53,* 361–382.

Scherer, K. R., Wallbott, H. G., & Summerfield, A. B. (1986). *Experiencing emotion: A cross-cultural study.* Cambridge: Cambridge University Press.

Semin, G. R., & Manstead, A. S. R. (1982). The social implications of embarrassment displays and restitution behavior. *European Journal of Social Psychology, 12,* 367–377.

Sharkey, W. F., & Stafford, L. (1990). Responses to embarrassment. *Human Communication Research, 17,* 315–342.

Shimanoff, S. B. (1985). Rules governing the verbal expression of emotion between married couples. *Western Journal of Speech Communication, 49,* 147–165.

Shimanoff, S. B. (1987). Types of emotional disclosures and request compliance between spouses. *Communication Monographs, 54,* 85–100.

Sillars, A. L. (1980). Attributions and communication in roommate conflicts. *Communication Monographs, 47,* 180–200.

Sillars, A. L., & Scott, M. D. (1983). Interpersonal perception between intimates: An integrative view. *Human Communication Research, 10,* 153–176.

Stamp, G. H., & Knapp, M. L. (1990). The construct of intent in interpersonal communication. *Quarterly Journal of Speech, 76,* 282–299.

Taylor, S. E. (1989). *Positive illusions: Creative self-deception and the healthy mind.* New York: Basic Books.

Vangelisti, A. L. (1989, November). *Messages that hurt: Perceptions of and reactions to hurtful messages in relationships.* Paper presented at the meeting of the Speech Communication Association, San Francisco, CA.

Vangelisti, A. L., Daly, J. A., & Rudnick, J. R. (1991). Making people feel guilty in conversations: Techniques and correlates. *Human Communication Research, 18,* 3–39.

Vissing, Y. M., Straus, M. A., Gelles, R. J., & Harrop, J. W. (1991). Verbal aggression by parents and psychosocial problems of children. *Child Abuse and Neglect, 15,* 223–238.

Wagner, J. (1980). Strategies of dismissal: Ways and means of avoiding personal abuse. *Human Relations, 33,* 603–622.

Weber, D. J., & Vangelisti, A. L. (1991). "Because I love you": The use of tactical attributions in conversation. *Human Communication Research, 17,* 606–624.

Weiner, B., (1986). *An attributional theory of motivation and emotion.* New York: Springer-Verlag.

Weiner, B., Amirkhan, J., Folkes, V. S., & Verette, J. A. (1987). An attributional analysis of excuse giving: Studies of a naive theory of emotion. *Journal of Personality and Social Psychology, 52*, 316–324.

Weiner, B., Graham, S., & Chandler, C. C. (1982). Pity, anger, and guilt: An attributional analysis. *Personality and Social Psychology Bulletin, 8*, 226–232.

Weiner, B., & Handel, S. (1985). Anticipated emotional consequences of causal communications and reported communication strategy. *Developmental Psychology, 18*, 278–286.

Weiner, B., Russell, D., & Lerman, D. (1978). Affective consequences of causal ascriptions. In J. H. Harvey, W. J. Ickes, & R. F. Kidd (Eds.), *New directions in attribution research* (Vol. 2, pp. 59–88). Hillsdale, NJ: Lawrence Erlbaum Associates.

Weiner, B., Russell, D., & Lerman, D. (1979). The cognition-emotion process in achievement-related contexts. *Journal of Personality and Social Psychology, 37*, 1211–1220.

Wicker, F. W., Payne, G. C., & Morgan, R. D. (1983). Participant descriptions of guilt and shame. *Motivation and Emotion, 7*, 25–39.

Yelsma, P. (1992, July). *Affective orientations associated with couples' verbal abusiveness.* Paper presented at the bi-annual meeting of the International Society for the Study of Personal Relationships, Orono, ME.

4

PATTERNS OF
INTERACTIONAL PARADOXES

Carol Wilder
Sue Collins
San Francisco State University

In formal logic a contradiction is the sign of defeat: but in the evolution of real knowledge it marks the first step in progress towards victory.
—Alfred North Whitehead, 1948

Although the best of all possible worlds may be free from contradiction and paradox, the highly probabilistic world of human behavior offers little such luxury. Long gone are the days when simple linear cause–effect determinism offered the hope of guiding construction of an adequate view of human communication, behavior, and change. New metaphors are needed, new methods, new ways of seeing.

One alternative construct that has received increasing attention in recent years is that of "paradox," an idea that has charmed and challenged generations of philosophers. Whereas current interest in paradox as a term of description for human interaction can be traced largely to the work of Bateson and his 1950s research team which formulated the double-bind theory of schizophrenia (Bateson, 1955; Bateson, Jackson, Haley, & Weakland, 1956), the concept has much richer roots and broader implications.

This chapter casts the net widely in exploring the idea of paradox in philosophy, logic, psychotherapy, and rhetoric with the end of laying some groundwork for the use of paradox as a form of description to illuminate a variety of communicational and interactional patterns. Far from positioning paradox on the "dark side" of interpersonal communication, we argue instead that paradoxical communication in the broadest sense is central to

83

human communication and is most appropriately viewed as normative rather than deviant behavior.

PARADOX: CHARMS AND CHALLENGES

Oscar Wilde captured the charm of the paradox when he reputedly quipped that "a paradox is a truth standing on its head to attract attention." It is probably unnecessary to expound here on the charm of the paradox (see Falletta, 1983, Hofstadter, 1979; Hughes & Brecht, 1975). Moreover, it is likely impossible, with any didactic attempt destined for the same tedium as explaining a joke. Rather, the challenge of paradox for communication theory, research, and teaching is more to the point, for attention to interactional paradoxes challenges at least four assumptions of conventional wisdom.

First is the assumption that ideas are to be judged by a binary truth criterion: Ideas are either true or false (given some probability factor), and certainly not true *and* false. But here we run into the first problem with paradox, for as Bateson (cited in Brand, 1974, p. 31) remarked, "a paradox is an argument in which you take sides—both sides," and as Watzlawick, Beavin, and Jackson (1967, p. 188) more formally suggested, "Paradox may be defined as a contradiction that follows correct deduction from consistent premises." The fact remains, as Alan Watts (1957) pointed out, that Western thinking is predominantly true/false and either/or rather than both/and. Binary thinking sets the stage for paradox by denying the validity of contradiction as a legitimate form of thought. From this perspective, paradoxical statements always represent something to be overcome, rather than standing for a peculiar form of truth in their own right. The "both/and" sort of logic said to characterize Eastern thought helps to explain why paradox as we conceive it is not problematic in Eastern philosophy, although the Western mind "finds," for instance, the discipline of Zen rife with paradox, especially in the teaching device of the Koans. Actually, there is no concept in Chinese or Japanese that even approximates the Western notion of paradox, although the Chinese character meaning *mujun* (*mu* = the spear that can pierce anything; *jun* = the shield that can deflect anything) conveys a similar notion of confusion.

A second challenge paradox presents is to the deep-rooted assumption that "man is a rational being." The "good man speaking well" in rhetorical theory has always been a creature of eminent *logos*, given to appeals of unreason (the classical *pathos*) only with some reluctance. This is not to suggest that reason is an inappropriate model of behavior, but rather to suggest in good company that at least syllogistic reason may be a grossly inadequate model of interpersonal logic. Paradox appeals to other than the common opinion, while paradoxically and often unnervingly making a sort of "uncommon sense." As Slaatte (1968, p. 6) argued, the "paradox of the paradox per se" refers to "two opposite properties of the paradox itself: its sheer impertinence to reason, on the one hand, and its profounder pertinence to reason, on the other." Paradox by definition counters prevailing opinion, thus if judged by extant standards of reason it inevitably is "non-sense." But here it can be shown that the "rational human" criterion misses the point: Paradox at its best is creative unreason, giving a profound glimpse of uncommon sense.

A third convention challenged by paradox is the stubborn persistence in much psychotherapy and interpersonal communication training of what Pearce (1977) termed the "Humanistic Celebration" approach. The assumptions of this model privilege behaviors related to self-disclosure, feedback, openness, trust, and self-actualization. It has taken some years for the full limits of these utopian assumptions to be recognized for the problem-engendering premises they contain (see Bochner, 1982; Parks, 1982). As Watzlawick, Weakland, and Fisch (1974, p. 61) pointed out, "it is the premise that things *should be* a certain way which is the problem and which requires change, and not the way things *are*. Without the utopian premise, the actuality of the situation might be quite bearable." How does paradox counter this trend? By striking at the heart of the matter and suggesting that perhaps human behavior is characteristically and endemically contradictory, perplexing, and even perverse. Life is complicated, and so are human relationships, and no simplistic utopian reductionism can even suggest the right questions, let alone provide eternal bliss through a few basic rules. To view paradox as normative in human communication can greatly increase one's understanding and tolerance for ambiguity, a hallmark of intelligence and maturity. Finally, paradox presents a strong challenge to the limits of prevailing research methods. Interactional paradoxes are multileveled, diachronic, context dependent, and transactional in nature. It is very difficult to capture any one of these qualities in a rigorous and systematic fashion, let alone all of them. In particular, the double-bind construct violates the assumption of traditional experimental design that all independent variables operate at equivalent levels of abstraction (Abeles, 1976).

Now that the challenges posed by the study of interactional paradoxes have been sketched, we can review how paradox has been conceptualized as a general idea and within the domains of philosophy, logic, psychotherapy, and rhetoric before suggesting what might be construed as critical dimensions of interactional paradoxes.

PARADOX IN GENERAL

From its earliest use in Western thought, the idea of paradox has had two meanings: first, a broad general sense, and second, the special sense posed by the logical paradoxes of Zeno of Elea. Both are legitimate, albeit within different domains, and confusion between paradox in a general sense and paradox as a technical term in logic remains today.

Paradoxos in the Greek combines two roots: *para*, which can mean variously beside, by, with, beyond, past, against, or contrary to; and *doxos*, which means "that which is generally thought or believed," the "common opinion" as contrasted to *episteme*, which is the ("higher") knowledge of scientific understanding. Thus, paradox is that which is "contrary to expectation" or "incredible" (as opposed to the orthodox "correct" opinion) (Liddell & Scott, 1968, p. 1309). Paradox is an anomaly that does not "fit" into one's system of premises and probabilities. Paradox "breaks frame," which may account for why it was also used in Attic Greek as a term for distinguished athletes, musicians, and artists. Paradox in this sense is the agent of learning, creativity, and change.

Two important elements at work here are *contrariety* and *surprise*. Paradox makes the sort of sense that is immediately apprehended but seldom anticipated and difficult to explain. Once the matter is resolved by a shift in one's premises such that the paradox becomes incorporated into the system of probabilities, it vanishes! This is the slippery part of the idea; the "now you see it now you don't" character of paradox. A joke is seldom funny upon second hearing; and there is nothing "incredible" about the second artist to make a giant soup can or the second runner of the 4-minute mile.

Paradox is time and context dependent. The doctrine that the earth revolves around the sun was once called the "Copernican paradox," anomalous as the belief was to the prevailing Ptolemaic cosmology. If one chooses to engage a paradox rather than ignore it, a certain law of diminishing novelty operates until the once incredible apprehension becomes yet another invisible premise of one's belief system. Thus, Quine (1976, pp. 9, 12) was led to remark that one man's paradox becomes another man's platitude, give or take a couple of thousand years.

PARADOX IN PHILOSOPHY

If one takes the study of paradox to be roughly synonymous with the study of contradiction and opposition, then much of Western philosophy is to the point. Slaatte (1968, p. 4) offered a capable synthesis of the pertinence of paradox to philosophy, suggesting that problems of unity and plurality, subject vs. object, freedom vs. necessity, permanence and change, form and matter, identity amidst diversity, Being vs. Nonbeing, and the coincidence of opposites pondered by the likes of Heraclitus, Plato, and Aristotle onward through Kant, Hegel, and Sartre are best captured through a dialectical model of paradox. From this view, "paradox is an idea involving two opposing thoughts or propositions which however contradictory, are equally necessary to convey a more imposing, illuminating, life-related or provocative insight into truth than either factor can muster in its own right." Here, then:

> paradox is a dialectical model of communication intrinsic to the existential perspective in contrast to the neutral, speculative, and objective approaches. Truth is seen in vital relation to the self in his existence-as-he-experiences-it; it is not related as though one object is thrust upon another. If truth is to be known, it must be something in which we are perennially involved as knowing subjects and from which, as persons, we are never exempt. (Slaatte, 1968, p. 33)

Slaatte views paradox as central to issues of existence, rather than taking the more typical philosophical stance that treats paradox as something to be neutralized.

Because paradox generally involves a sort of contradiction, perhaps most ideas could be generated as "paradoxical" by juxtaposing them to that which they are not. Master symbolist Burke (1969, p. 35) takes this approach in describing the "paradox of the absolute" (God as an "absolute" person would be *im*personal—the negation of personality) and the "paradox of substance":

> The word "substance," used to designate what a thing *is*, derives from a word designating something a thing *is not*. That is, though used to designate something *within* the thing, *intrinsic* to it, the word etymologically refers to something *outside* the thing, *extrinsic* to it. Or otherwise put: the word in its etymological origins would refer to an attribute of the thing's *context*, since that which supports or underlies a thing would be part of a thing's context. And a thing's context, being outside or beyond the thing, would be something that the thing *is not*. (p. 23)

Such "antimonies of definition" depend both on semantic manipulation and the either/or choice of a two-valued logic and are characteristic of philosophical treatments of paradox. More to the point is the special way in which paradox has been construed in formal logic, for we are then a step closer to the domain of interactional paradoxes.

PARADOX IN LOGIC

The various sorts of paradox common to studies in logic and mathematics always arise from a problem posed and found to be unsolvable within the frame of given axiomatic systems. Thus, logical paradoxes, like paradox in general, are fundamentally contrary to opinion—hence, incredible. The most common logical paradoxes are paradoxes of the infinite and paradoxes of self-reference.

Paradoxes of the infinite were first posed by Zeno of Elea (circa 390 B.C.) and reported in Aristotle's *Physics*. Zeno "proved," for instance, that motion is impossible by arguing that when a race is run, the runner must first run one-half the distance, and before that one-half of that, and before that one-half of that, and because the sequence of runs he or she must complete has the form of a regression ($\frac{1}{16}$, $\frac{1}{8}$, $\frac{1}{4}$, $\frac{1}{2}$), it has no first number, and thus the runner cannot even start. Common empirics say, of course, that such a conclusion is nonsense, but it was not until the invention of the theory of convergent series, according to which an infinite series can have a finite limit, that the logical problem posed was ameliorated by expanding the theoretical frame to account for Zeno's anomaly. The apparent triviality of Zeno's problems notwithstanding, they have engaged some of philosophy's finest minds (e.g., Grunbaum, 1967; Hofstadter, 1979; Salmon, 1970). As Salmon (1970, p. 43) put it, "Zeno's paradoxes have an onion-like quality: as one peels away outer layers disposing of the more superficial difficulties, new and more profound problems are revealed." However, the nature of Zeno's problems, which are all complex variations of the "contrary to common opinion" genre of paradox, are distinct from the more formally described paradoxes of self-reference.

Paradoxes of self-reference are typically assigned three necessary terms of description: self-reference, contradiction, and vicious circularity (Hughes & Brecht, 1975, p. 2).

Self-reference is a necessary but not sufficient condition for the generation of paradox. For instance, the sentence "I am apologizing" is self-referential, but trivial. "This sentence has thirty-one letters" is also self-referential (and true of itself), but not at all paradoxical. Branham and Pearce (1985, p. 23) called this form a "charmed loop."

Now, when contradiction is combined with self-reference, something puzzling begins to appear. "I'm sorry that I am apologizing" is self-referential and untrue, hence contradictory, as is "I never speak for myself," and "This sentence has thirty letters." Contradictory self-referential statements which begin to appear nontrivial and hence problematic, such as "Ignore this statement," or "All rules have exceptions," are called "subversive loops" by Branham and Pearce (1985, p. 24) and "circular contradictions"—"almost paradoxes" by Hughes and Brecht (1975, p. 2) because they lack vicious circularity. These contradictions, Hughes and Brecht (1975, p. 2) suggested, "do go round in a circle, but they do not go round and round. One might say that they are paradoxical, but that they are not paradoxes."

When the condition of vicious circularity is added to self-reference and contradiction, a full logical paradox can emerge, as in the classic "I am lying" paradox: If I am lying, I am telling the truth, and if I am telling the truth, I am lying (see also examples by Hofstadter, 1979, Quine, 1976). (Note how this depends upon a true/false logic.) Russell's classic question—"Is the set of all sets which are not members of themselves a member of itself?"—better meets the conditions of self-reference, contradiction, and vicious circularity. If they are not members, they are members, and if they are members, they are not members, ad infinitum in perpetual oscillation.

How does one untangle such knots? Ignoring the problem or not viewing such contradiction as problematic in the first place are two roads less traveled. More typically, some sort of bracketing and/or reframing is introduced in order to neutralize paradox (e.g., Brown, 1972; Korzybski, 1948; Quine, 1976; Whitehead & Russell, 1910).

In common to most of these attempts to "solve" the problem of paradox is a realignment of one's world view (semantic theory, etc.) in order to construct a frame large enough to accommodate the "problem" of paradox. Only Brown (1972, p. xi) renders paradox "unproblematic," claming that "the implications of this in the fields of logic, philosophy, mathematics, and even physics, are profound."

The problem with the "problem" of paradox is that by definition what is paradoxical is what is "contrary to opinion," thus there is no end to the progression of new paradoxes that challenge older solutions to former paradoxes. Paradox is always that which one cannot conventionally account for; whatever can be accounted for by the Theory of Types, or multiordinality of terms, or convergent series, or imaginary numbers, is no longer, by definition, paradoxical. Thus, "paradox," suggested G. K. Chesterton's interpreter, "might be called the science of gaps" (Kenner, 1947, p. 17). And once the gap is accounted for in some fashion, we are led back to Quine's suggestion that one person's paradox is another person's platitude, given time. It is for this reason that any attempt to establish a final and formal definition, taxonomy, typology, or whatever of paradox is bound to crumble after a short while as new anomalies arise to challenge—in the spirit of paradox— any taxonomy of paradox itself.

FROM PARADOX TO DOUBLE BIND

Bateson and his colleagues first fully explored the potential of paradox as what he called an "epistemological matrix" for the description of behavioral sequences (cited in Wilder, 1979, p. 178), although the term had been previously used by Frankl (1960) in a more limited sense, and the "spirit" of paradox is evident in earlier writers (e.g., Dunlap, 1928; Rosen, 1953). Bateson (1972, p. 202) gave Haley credit "for recognizing that the symptoms of schizophrenia are suggestive of an inability to discriminate the Logical Types," an observation which led directly to Bateson's formulation of the "double-bind" hypothesis. Specifically, Bateson (1972, p. 208) offered the general characteristics of a double-bind situation:

1. When the individual is involved in an intense relationship, that is, a relationship in which one feels it is vitally important that he or she discriminate accurately what sort of message is being communicated so that he or she may respond appropriately.
2. When the individual is caught in a situation in which the other person in the relationship is expressing two orders of message and one of these denies the other.
3. When the individual is unable to comment on the messages being expressed to correct his or her discrimination of what order of message to respond to, that is, one cannot make a metacommunicative statement.

The inability to metacommunicate about the conflicting levels of messages is what distinguishes double binds from mixed messages. One is in a bind only if one cannot escape. A binding interaction may result from repeated patterns from infancy, attempts by one interactant to control the other, fear of losing the relationship, and so on, which also warn in someway, "Do not talk about this." Bateson (1972, p. 217) provided the classic example to illustrate the double bind:

> A young man who had fairly well recovered from an acute schizophrenic episode was visited in the hospital by his mother. He was glad to see her and impulsively put his arm around her shoulder, whereupon she stiffened. He withdrew his arm and she asked, "Don't you love me any more?" He then blushed, and she said, "Dear, you must not be so easily embarrassed and afraid of your feelings." The patient was able to stay with her only a few minutes more and following her departure he assaulted an aide and was put in the tubs.

Bateson argued that if the man had been able to comment on his mother's difficulty with receiving affection, he might not have behaved violently after the episode. Instead, "the schizophrenic patient doesn't have this possibility open to him. His intense dependency and training prevents him from commenting upon his mother's communicative behavior, though she comments on his and forces him to accept and to attempt to deal with the complicated sequence" (Bateson, 1972, p. 217).

Or, consider the paradoxical injunction when a mother says to her son, "You are free to go son. Don't worry if I start crying." The two contradictory messages are operating on two levels which essentially control the son no matter if he stays or goes; he is in a "no win" situation because he cannot comment on the conflicting messages, and he will experience guilt if he goes and anger at his submission if he stays (Riordan, Severinsen, Martin, & Martin, 1986). If conditions for a double bind persist, an individual can begin to perceive his or her world in double-bind patterns, responding to any part of the pattern with behavior that is characteristic of schizophrenia. In this sense, paradoxical communication is pathological.

The double-bind hypothesis has provoked an enormous body of clinical and research literature (see, for instance, Berger, 1978; Sluzki & Ransom, 1976). Further, the double-bind hypothesis has been examined within a rich variety of contexts across many disciplines. Its principles have been critically applied in essays such as Watzlawick et al.'s (1967) analysis of *Who's Afraid of Virginia Woolf?*, Benson's study of double binds in Wiseman's film *High School* (in Benson & Anderson, 1989), Chesebro's (1980) study of paradoxical views of homosexuality in social science literature, Mechling's (1988) examination of Heller's *Catch-22*, Wilkins's (1989) interpretation of the Fool as an "unsuccessful medieval psychotherapist" in Shakespeare's *King Lear*, and Wilder's (1989, 1991) studies of the rhetoric of the Vietnam Veterans Memorial and portrayals of Vietnam veterans in film. The double-bind concept has been used to analyze mass conversions into a religious group (Edwards, 1981), the withdrawal and denial of responsibility in an organizational setting (Soldow, 1981), and the context for women caught between conflicting demands of their roles at work, at home, and within their culture (Camden & Witt, 1983; Gonzalez, 1988; Heriot, 1983; Moore & Twombly, 1990; Reohr, 1981).

From this range of studies it is evident that although paradox and double-bind are stubbornly resistant to experimental codification, they offer a metaphoric gold mine for critical and analytic thinking.

PARADOX IN THERAPY

The preponderance of double-bind studies come from research and practice in psychotherapy. In addition to positing schizophrenic behavior as a reaction to communicative context, Bateson and his team suggested that paradoxical forms can be activated within a different environment—that of therapy—to conversely "drive people sane" by posing a sort of paradoxical "double-blessing"—"blessed-if-you-do-blessed-if-you-don't"—in which the patient improves no matter which choice is pursued within a frame constructed by the therapist.

After Haley's (1963) seminal work, numerous researchers and clinicians incorporated paradoxical strategies into therapeutic practice. Most notable, the therapeutic domain has been explored by Selvini-Palazzoli, Boscolo, Checchin, and Prata (1978), Watzlawick et al. (1967), Watzlawick, Weakland, and Fisch (1974), and Weeks and L'Abate (1979, 1982). All of these researchers are less concerned with technical issues of paradox than with the practical task of discovering and explaining what works to change people. And, it appears, paradox is a suitable metaphor for describing the structure of a range of potent strategies.

During the late 1970s and 1980s, paradoxical strategies spread like wildfire through the family therapy literature, accompanied by much discussion and debate regarding how, where, when, and by whom such interventions should be considered. Of the many approaches to paradoxical intervention compared in several reviews (Bogdan, 1982; Massey, 1986; Mozdzierz, Lisiecki, & Macchitelli, 1989: Riordan et al., 1986; Rohrbaugh et al., 1977; Soper & L'Abate, 1980; West & Zarski, 1983), the most typical types are termed prescribing the symptom, positioning, restraining, and ordeal (Hirschmann & Sprenkle, 1989). In prescribing the symptom, the patient is told to maintain or exaggerate the behavior he or she seeks to change, with the end result giving the patient a sense of control over the symptom. In positioning strategies, the therapist takes a more extreme position about the problem than the patient ("I have overestimated your abilities to change your behavior, so we need to discuss how you're going to live with your problem"), using the patient's resistance to produce change. Restraining involves a "go slow" approach in which the patient is instructed either not to change or to think about the dangers of improvement. Ordeal intervention involves instructing the patient to perform an unpleasant task whenever the symptom "spontaneously" occurs, so that the symptom is preempted by a worse alternative and thus discouraged.

These paradoxical interventions are used to rupture individual patterns of behavior or behavior of a family system. From a communication perspective, it is interesting to note how each intervention operates from paradoxical assumptions. The patient is told, respectively: in order to lose the condition, keep it; in order to get better, get worse; in order to change, remain the same; and to get rid of the symptom, exchange it for a worse symptom.

One more intervention that is frequently discussed in the literature is reframing and relabeling of behavior (Haley, 1963; Watzlawick et al., 1974). This involves substituting the view of problematic behavior as negative with a view of it as positive and functional. For example, rather than treating a teenager's propensity toward deviance as a threat to family stability, the family could reframe the behavior as an opportunity to expand its capacity for accepting and incorporating change. Teismann (1979) suggested relabeling jealousy with words that accent the positive aspects of jealousy such as romantic, passionate, loyal, and so on, and to instruct couples to engage in what he calls "serious playfulness." Haley (1963), using relabeling as a synonym for reframing, pointed out that relabeling problematic behavior in couples can make continuing the behavior more of an ordeal than changing. Selvini-Palazzoli et al.'s (1978) Milan Group has become especially identified with the reframing strategy of "positive connotation," which frames all behavior as functional. What makes these reframing moves paradox like is their counterintuitive quality—their "uncommon sense."

The problem-solving model of the Brief Therapy Center at the Mental Research Institute in Palo Alto engages paradox at an even more general level. During the initial interview, once the presented problem and its attempted solution are identified to the satisfaction of the therapist, an intervention is designed to interdict the problem-engendering solution rather than the "problem" itself. This is done in the belief that the attempted solution itself is responsible for maintaining the problem. In this case the "solution" has become the "problem," through a bit of semantic wizardry. But this slight twist in perspective and framing, paradoxical indeed in the sense of "contrary to common opinion," produces some extraordinary interventions that "orthodox" approaches lead one to overlook (Weakland, Fisch, Watzlawick, & Bodin, 1974).

The general popularity and repeated success of paradoxical interventions can be attributed to several factors (Soper & L'Abate, 1980). Most practitioners do not recommend a paradoxical maneuver until more conventional approaches have been exhausted. In this case, paradox appeals to a sense of novelty. Because the approach is unexpected, it stands a chance of being heard and thus stimulates a potential for change. Further, after securing the patient's trust and agreement to comply, the "nonsensical" aspect of paradox places the patient in a position of not possibly being able to comply with the directive to not change. All the while the therapist plays dumb in order to facilitate patient compliance. Also, as the most widely agreed on explanation, paradox works because people enter into therapy seeking help but are often resistant to treatment, as well as often intent on proving therapy as a failure. Instructing the patient to not change suggests any resistance will promote change.

Lest one begins to accept paradoxical interventions as a panacea for transforming destructive interactional behavior, it must be noted that paradoxical techniques are not without their criticisms. There is controversy over what is to be regarded as a paradoxical intervention (Dell, 1986), how or if they should be used (Mozdzierz et al., 1989; Schwartz & Perrotta, 1985; Treacher, 1988; Wilkins, 1989), and whether ethical considerations have been fully addressed (Henderson, 1987).

Now, how does "paradox" as a descriptive metaphor for therapy map onto "paradox" as an idea in philosophy and logic? It depends. If one defines paradox in the most general sense as something unexpected that is contrary to opinion (i.e., incredible), then almost any clever and surprising therapeutic intervention can truly be termed "paradoxical."

If, however, one maps therapeutic paradoxes onto the more structured logical terms of description introduced earlier—self-reference, contradiction, and vicious circularity—the domain of what one may legitimately term an interactional or therapeutic paradox becomes more restricted. And it becomes more restricted yet if we add a fourth term of description for interactional paradoxes—proscription of conventional choice. For instance, self-reference—so critical to logical paradoxes—becomes a quiet attribute in most interactional paradoxes; descriptive, but seldom critically so. On the other hand, contradiction, vicious circularity, and proscription of choice are much easier to identify in terms of actual behavior: An assertion perpetually accompanied by its denial gets people stuck going round and round through the same routine, circle, pattern, script, and so forth.

The fundamental point in such mapping is that the domains of logic and philosophy and the domain of human behavior in relationships are different in important ways. Reading a paradox in a book and observing a paradoxical interaction in someone else's relationship and experiencing the direct effect of a paradox in one's own relationship are essentially different experiences. This is at least part of the reason why determination of the criteria for the transforms of a construct taken from the world of logic and mapped onto the far fuzzier world of human behavior present such a challenge (see, for example, Cronen, Johnson, & Lannamann, 1982).

FROM DOUBLE BINDS TO DOUBLE BLESSINGS

So far we have discussed some behavioral effects of paradoxical communication and the double bind. As Watzlawick et al. (1967) point out, a person caught in a double bind may exhibit behavior characteristic of the schizophrenic by either desperately searching for clues to give meaning to the messages being communicated, complying with illogical injunctions literally, or withdrawing from human interaction altogether. Although such reactions may be a product of long-term double-bind patterns, short-term paradoxical messages may also produce confusion and uncertainty in daily communication (Bowers & Sanders, 1974). Some typical paradox like contexts in so-called normative communication include irony (Kaufer, 1981; Weick & Browning, 1986), strategic ambiguity (Eisenberg, 1984), disqualification or equivocal communication (Bavelas, 1983; Bavelas, Black, Chovil, & Mullett, 1990; Chovil, this volume), constructive dilemmas (Wishbow, 1987), and humor (Koestler, 1964; Paulos, 1980).

Several studies have been conducted specifically related to speech pedagogy and persuasion. Worthington, Tipton, Cromley, Richards, and Janke (1984) found that paradoxical injunctions to instruct students to practice being anxious were not significant in reducing speech anxiety. Reframing, however, appears to be a teachable self-help skill for solving interpersonal problems (Miller & Osmunson, 1989). Swann, Pelham, and Chidester (1988) used a paradoxical strategy to test persuasion in opinion change, finding that people changed their beliefs because they were resisting questions reflecting more extreme positions than their own.

There also appears to be a strong relationship between double binds and creativity. Bateson's (1969) work with porpoises led him to believe that double-bind situations can produce entirely new behavior. Colligan (1983, p. 41) expanded on this hypothesis in arguing that "all creative acts will be the result of double bind sequences." Likewise, Peterson and Langellier (1982, p. 242) suggested that the "creative double bind" is instrumental in managing the situational constraints of "genuine pretense" in dramatic performance.

One of the most powerful and intriguing benevolent paradoxical contexts is created for the student of Zen Buddhism through practice of the Koans, paradox like statements such as "What is the sound of one hand clapping?" or "Don't think about a monkey." Jichaku, Fujita, and Shapiro (1984) suggested that the practice of Koan Zen as a path to enlightenment is a double-bind situation of the "Be Spontaneous" type. Students must resolve the Koan to attain enlightenment—reaching an understanding of the dualistic nature of the world as form (phenomenal existence) and emptiness (essential existence)—"form as emptiness and emptiness as form" (Aitken, 1982, quoted in Jichaku et al., p. 213). In the process of becoming enlightened, the student passes through the double bind because "enlightenment cannot be attained and deepened upon demand. Enlightenment is a spontaneous experience, and the very preoccupation with eliciting enlightenment, and with deepening it, is what obstructs it" (p. 215). Paradoxically, Zen masters instruct students to give up striving for what they are striving for and to become all absorbed with only the Koan.

Bateson et al. (1956, p. 208) first suggested that while the Zen master uses paradox to bring enlightenment to his pupil, in another context it might produce schizophrenia:

> One of the things he does is to hold a stick over the pupil's head and say fiercely, "If you say this stick is real, I will strike you with it. If you say this stick is not real, I will strike you with it. If you do not say anything, I will strike you with it." We feel that the schizophrenic finds himself continually in the same situation as the pupil, but he achieves something like disorientation rather than enlightenment. The Zen pupil might reach up and take the stick away from the master—who might accept this response, but the schizophrenic has no such choice since with him there is no not caring about the relationship, and his mother's aims and awareness are not like the master's.

Jichaku et al. (1984) asserted that the interpersonal context for practicing Zen is benevolent, because it involves a successful resolution to the double bind through a competent Zen instructor, the essential attitudes of Great Faith, Great Doubt, and Great Determination for students in Zen training, and a supportive Zen community; conditions very unlike the familial environment of the schizophrenic.

PERSPECTIVES ON INTERACTIONAL PARADOXES

If we have taken the long way around to come to the point of interactional paradoxes, it is because we believe that only through some appreciation of the richness and complexity of the idea of paradox (and we have but skimmed the surface) can one exercise due caution in attempts to reduce the notion to more "manageable" operational formalisms. Something is inevitably lost in that process, but if we employ wisely our economies of reduction, perhaps we need not lose everything, or at least what is essential. Before sketching the critical patterns of interactional paradoxes that must be accounted for in any formalism, several preliminary points are in order.

Paradox Is ("Just") an Idea

The truth lurking behind this banality is overlooked by those who attribute moral value to paradox, by those who rush to reify the construct, and by those who would give it the rank of an emergent *grande idee*.

In the medieval Church, paradox was associated with heresy, thus it was a devil term of sorts. Hobbes (1841, p. 304) wrote that "the Bishop speaks often of paradoxes with such scorn or detestation that a simple reader would take a paradox either for felony or some other heinous crime." Paradox was no less odious to Russell, who attempted to exorcise it from logic. Conversely, paradox has come to be regarded by some therapists as a sort of god term for therapeutic interventions. Such judgments miss the point, for there is nothing within the structure of paradox per se to indicate whether it is a double bind or double blessing; whether it will precipitate madness or art (or both).

And paradox is not some "thing" which is "in" a situation that can be counted like so many phonemes. Paradox is in the eye of the beholder, a term that can be used to describe a pattern of interaction. Paradox is a qualitative concept, exceedingly difficult to quantify because of its diachronic multilevel nature, as most double-bind researchers have discovered. Paradox is a way of looking at or framing communication and behavior, it is not immanent in the behavior itself. When incorporating any new idea, there is a tendency to "see it everywhere" for a while. But an idea that explains everything explains nothing at all very usefully. On the other hand, to insist on strict operationalism may deprive the concept of paradox of the heuristic power and charm which attracts us to it in the first place. The task of delineating patterns of interactional paradoxes must proceed with care if the idea is to be useful in research while preserving its conceptual integrity.

Interactional Paradoxes Should Be Defined Interactionally

It is ironic, given the widespread lip service paid to interactional/trans-actional/systemic views of communication, that research vocabulary is still so heavily lineal and monadic. The tendency to view paradox as something that a parent does to a child or therapist does to a patient is thus natural and very strong. After all, it is easier to model lineal causality than circular causality; systemic definitions are exponentially complex. The structure of interactional paradoxes is appropriately viewed as more enthymemic (where the terms that comprise the paradoxical pattern are distributed throughout the relationship) than syllogistic (where the pattern is unilaterally imposed by one person on another).

For instance, if contradiction is considered to be a critical dimension of interactional paradoxes, the contradiction does not reside "within" the messages that one person conveys to another, but rather is the result of the interaction between messages of often very different sorts within a given context. If a mixed message is not interpreted and responded to as mixed, for interactional purposes it is not mixed at all. The pattern of paradox is a relational pattern; a crude "epistemological matrix" that stands as a proto-typical interactional form. However fuzzy this form may appear under the scrutiny of scientific standards, it offers a glimpse of the shape that interactional concepts may take.

Patterns of Interactional Paradoxes

Any formalism presuming to model interactional paradoxes must account for the better part of at least three interdependent levels of patterns: structural patterns of logical description, relational patterns that frame the enactment of structural patterns, and contextual patterns that frame both relational and structural levels, while in turn being created by them.

Structural Patterns. The terms of description for logical paradoxes (self-reference, contradiction, vicious circularity, and proscription of conventional choice) can be mapped onto interactional paradoxes only if considered functionally within relational and contextual frames. There is nothing within the structure of paradox itself that suggests anything about its pragmatic consequences, although this is no reason to abandon logical terms of description altogether in favor of defining paradox only in the broadest sense as something "contrary to opinion." Optimally, any middle-level theory of interactional paradox will retain relatively rigorous terms of description while tying these inescapably to relational matters.

Relational Patterns.   Interactional paradoxes occur (or, more accurately, are observed to occur) within the context of a relationship. The patterns of logical paradox take on pragmatic meaning only within this matrix. Consideration of interactional paradoxes must take into account at the very least relationship intensity, relational control and power patterns, the relative salience and persistence of a given message exchange within the relationship, and the metacommunicative skill and tolerance for ambiguity of the interactants. All messages may be equal to an interactional coder, but surely in "real life" some messages are more equal than others.

On the one hand, if one can imagine a highly salient paradoxical message frequently repeated within a high-intensity relationship in which power is unequal and metacommunicative (reframing) ability and tolerance for ambiguity are limited, one has the classic conditions for a double bind. However, the same paradoxical message (from a logical point of view) might have no effect whatever as a low-salience, low-frequency message in a low-intensity relationship in which power is distributed equally and metacommunicative ability and tolerance for ambiguity are high. A "perfect" logical paradox may not even have any pragmatic effect as a high-salience message in a high-intensity relationship if metacommunicative ability and tolerance for ambiguity are high.

Take the following example of a variation on the "Be Spontaneous" paradox theme:

Wife: Tell me I'm not getting old and dowdy.

Husband: You're not getting old and dowdy.

Wife: You're just saying that.

Logically, this is a fairly strong paradox (or at least fairly strongly "paradoxical"), but relational cues suggest that the pragmatic effect will not be great, probably because it is not framed as an especially salient message within the relationship (although, of course, we cannot know), and power is likely to be evenly distributed.

However, consider this structurally identical paradox:

Parent: Tell me that you love me.

Child: I love you.

Parent: You're just saying that.

Given even the few relational inferences we may confidently make from such limited information, this paradoxical exchange is likely to have far stronger pragmatic consequences, for we know that power is unequal, the relationship is intense, love messages are usually very salient, and reframing ability—

at least on the part of the child—is probably limited. Of course, we do not "know" any of this in either hypothetical case, but that is not quite the point. The point is that structurally identical paradoxes according to any terms of logical description are pragmatically meaningless (or at least undecidable) unless framed within larger patterns of relationships.

Contextual Patterns. Relational patterns, in turn, are framed by larger patterns of time, social context, and one's observational stance. The context of research, the context of education, the context of therapy, the context of politics, and one's point of view within each context create the varied meanings and practical outcomes of otherwise isomorphic relational patterns.

Contextually imbedded rules and norms often conceal implicit premises that serve as the ground for the figure of an interactional paradox. For instance, in observing a therapist who employs a series of paradoxical restraining strategies such as "I doubt if I can do much for this problem," "I'd be skeptical of any improvement," or "You're improving too rapidly," the paradoxical nature of the message is lost unless it is understood that implicit within the context of therapy is a premise something like "the therapist is an expert problem solver who will support your efforts to change as quickly as possible." Now it is possible to see the contradiction of restraining strategies that suggest that the therapist will help by not helping and will promote change by discouraging it.

Although it is neither probable nor desirable to know everything about a context, certainly something must be known in order to render action comprehensible. Strict "behavioral" approaches to research that discourage more than minimal inferences from data surely suffer by denying the inevitability of the interpretative processes of the observer.

The scholar is the inventor of the context of research, charged with creating the most plausible and humane fictions from among the intricate plots of frequently competing story lines. Do the properties of this observer enter into the description of his observations? Howe and VonFoerster (1975, p. 1) wrote that:

> The logic of our Western industrial corporate society (with limited liability) is unidirectional, deductive, competitive, and hierarchical, and the keystones of its paradigm are the Claim to Objectivity and the Theory of Types, which exclude in principle the autonomy of paradox and of the individual. In the scientific revolution that we now create and experience, however, we perceive a shift from causal unidirectional to mutualistic systemic thinking, from a preoccupation with the properties of the observed to the study of the properties of the observer.

Part of any contemporary consideration of contextual patterns must begin to address issues of the observer, allowing that there is more to the research enterprise than clinical detachment.

Now, in considering this interdependent web of structural, relational, and contextual patterns of interactional paradoxes, what implications for further study emerge? The pressure to produce "results" in research (especially quantifiable results) is strong, and any possibility of operational formalism is sure to be exploited. This is the path of conventional revisionism in social and behavioral science, and crowded as the path may be with bodies of bright ideas led down it ("credibility," "cognitive dissonance," "self-disclosure," "ego-involvement," "communication apprehension," etc.), it is the way that most know best. There is a certain ephemeral security in being able to "tie an idea down" even knowing, as did Wordsworth, "we murder to dissect." But paradox will put up a good fight. For those who choose to tangle in this fashion, their work is cut out (albeit in the form of a Mobius strip).

Alternatively, in resisting the temptations of operational monism one can use paradox in one way as an early crude model for the shape that interactional concepts might take, moving then laterally to develop similarly rich metaphors in an aformalistic spirit of discovery. Or one might move to enlarge, rather than reduce, the idea by exploring its descriptive power at many different levels over a wide range of contexts.

Whatever the case, an idea that has endured for 2,500 years in philosophy is likely to survive whether relegated to the dark side of interpersonal communication or viewed more properly held up to the light.

REFERENCES

Abeles, G. (1976). Researching the unresearchable: Experimentation on the double bind. In C. E. Sluzki & D. C. Ransom (Eds.), *Double bind: The foundation of the communicational approach to the family* (pp. 113–149). New York: Grune & Stratton.

Bateson, G. (1955). A theory of play and fantasy. *Psychiatric Research Reports, 2,* 39–51. (Reprinted in G. Bateson, 1972, *Steps to an ecology of mind* [pp. 177–193]. New York: Ballantine.)

Bateson, G. (1969, August). *Double bind, 1969.* Symposium presented at the Annual Meeting of the American Psychological Association, Washington D.C. (Reprinted in G. Bateson, 1972, *Steps to an ecology of mind* [pp. 271–278]. New York: Ballantine.)

Bateson, G. (1972). *Steps to an ecology of mind.* New York: Ballantine.

Bateson, G., Jackson, D. D., Haley, J., & Weakland, J. H. (1956). Toward a theory of schizophrenia. *Behavioral Science, 1,* 251–264. (Reprinted in G. Bateson, 1972, *Steps to an ecology of mind* [pp. 201–227]. New York: Ballantine.)

Bavelas, J. B. (1983). Situations that lead to disqualification. *Human Communication Research, 9,* 130–145.

Bavelas, J. B., Black, A., Chovil, N., & Mullett, J. (1990). *Equivocal communication.* Newbury Park, CA: Sage.

Benson, T., & Anderson, C. (1989). *Reality fictions: The films of Frederick Wiseman.* Carbondale, IL: Southern Illinois University Press.

Berger, M. (Ed.). (1978). *Beyond the double bind: Communication and family systems, theories, and techniques with schizophrenics.* New York: Brunner/Mazel.

Bochner, A. P. (1982). On the efficacy of openness in close relationships. In M. Burgoon (Ed.), *Communication yearbook 5* (pp. 109–124). New Brunswick, NJ: Transaction.

Bogdan, J. L. (1982). Paradoxical communication as interpersonal influence. *Family Process, 21*, 443–452.

Bowers, J. W., & Sanders, R. E. (1974). Paradox as a rhetorical strategy. In W. R. Fisher (Ed.), *Rhetoric: A tradition in transition* (pp. 300–315). East Lansing: Michigan State University Press.

Brand, S. (1974). *II Cybernetic frontiers*. New York: Random House.

Branham, R. J., & Pearce, W. B. (1985). Between text and context: Toward a rhetoric of contextual reconstruction. *Quarterly Journal of Speech, 71*, 19–36.

Brown, G. S. (1972). *Laws of form*. New York: Julian Press.

Burke, K. (1969). *A grammar of motives*. Berkeley: University of California Press.

Camden, C., & Witt, J. (1983). Manager communicative style and productivity: A study of female and male managers. *International Journal of Women's Studies, 6*, 258–269.

Chesebro, J. W. (1980). Paradoxical views of "homosexuality" in the rhetoric of social scientists: A fantasy theme analysis. *Quarterly Journal of Speech, 66*, 127–139.

Colligan, J. (1983). Musical creativity and social rules in four cultures. *The Creative Child and Adult Quarterly, XIII*, 39–47.

Cronen, V. E., Johnson, K. M., & Lannamann, M. A. (1982). Paradoxes, double binds, and reflexive loops: An alternative theoretical perspective. *Family Process, 21*, 91–112.

Dell, P. F. (1986). Why do we still call them "paradoxes"? *Family Process, 25*, 223–234.

Dunlap, K. (1928). A revision of the fundamental law of habit formation. *Science, 57*, 360–362.

Edwards, C. (1981). The dynamics of mass conversion. *Marriage & Family Review, 4*, 31–40.

Eisenberg, E. M. (1984). Ambiguity as strategy in organizational communication. *Communication Monographs, 51*, 227–241.

Falletta, N. L. (1983). *The paradoxicon*. Garden City, NY: Doubleday.

Frankl, V. E. (1960). Paradoxical intention. *American Journal of Psychotherapy, 14*, 520–535.

Gonzalez, J. T. (1988). Dilemmas of the high-achieving Chicana: The double-bind factor in male/female relationships. *Sex Roles, 18*, 367–380.

Grunbaum, A. (1967). *Modern science and Zeno's paradoxes*. Middletown, CT: Wesleyan University Press.

Haley, J. (1963). *Strategies of psychotherapy*. New York: Grune & Stratton.

Henderson, M. C. (1987). Paradoxical process and ethical consciousness. *Family Therapy, 14*(3), 187–193.

Heriot, J. (1983). The double bind: Healing the split. *Women and Therapy, 2* (2–3), 11–28.

Hirschmann, M. J., & Sprenkle, D. H. (1989). The use of therapeutic paradox among members of the American association for marriage and family therapy. *The American Journal of Family Therapy, 17*, 348–358.

Hobbes, T. (1841). *The questions concerning liberty, necessity, and chance, clearly stated and debated between Dr. Bramhall, Bishop of Derry and Thomas Hobbes of Malmesbury*. London: Charles Richards.

Hofstadter, D. R. (1979). *Godel, Escher, Bach: An eternal golden braid*. New York: Basic Books.

Howe, H., & VonFoerster, H. (1975). Introductory comments to Francisco Varela's calculus for self-reference. *International Journal of General Systems, 2*, 1–3.

Hughes, P., & Brecht, G. (1975). *Vicious circles and infinity: A panoply of paradoxes*. New York: Doubleday.

Jichaku, P., Fujita, G. Y., & Shapiro, S. I. (1984). The double bind and Koan Zen. *The Journal of Mind and Behavior, 5*, 211–221.

Kaufer, D. S. (1981). Ironic evaluations. *Communication Monographs, 48*, 25–38.

Kenner, H. (1947). *Paradox in Chesterton*. New York: Sheed & Ward.

Koestler, A. (1964). *The art of creation*. London: Hutchison.

Korzybski, A. (1948). *Science and sanity*. Lakeville, CT: The International Non-Aristotelian Library Publishing Company.

Liddell, H., & Scott, R. (1968). *A Greek-English lexicon*. Oxford: Clarendon Press.

Massey, R. F. (1986). Paradox, double binding, and counterparadox: A transactional analysis perspective (a response to Price). *Transactional Analysis Journal, 16,* 24–46.

Mechling, J. (1988). Play and madness in Joseph Heller's *Catch-22. Play and Culture, 1,* 226–238.

Miller, L. D., & Osmunson, S. (1989). Reframing. *Journal of Human Behavior and Learning, 6,* 32–38.

Moore, K. M., & Twombly, S. B. (1990). Administrative careers and the marketplace. *New Directions for Higher Education, 72,* 89–98.

Mozdzierz, G. J., Lisiecki, J., & Macchitelli, F. J. (1989). The mandala of psychotherapy: The universal use of paradox—new understanding and more confusion. *Psychotherapy, 26,* 383–388.

Parks, M. R. (1982). Ideology in interpersonal communication: Off the couch and into the world. In M. Burgoon (Ed.), *Communication yearbook 5* (pp. 79–108). New Brunswick, NJ: Transaction.

Paulos, J. A. (1980). *Mathematics and humor.* Chicago: University of Chicago Press.

Pearce, W. B. (1977). Teaching interpersonal communication as a humane science: A comparative analysis. *Communication Education, 26,* 104–112.

Peterson, E. E., & Langellier, K. M. (1982). Creative double bind in oral interpretation. *The Western Journal of Speech Communication, 46,* 242–252.

Quine, W. V. (1976). *The ways of paradox.* Cambridge, MA: Harvard University Press.

Reohr, J. R. (1981, March). *Work and female identity.* Paper presented at the Annual Convention of the Association for Women in Psychology, Boston, MA.

Riordan, A., Severinsen, N., Martin, D., & Martin, M. (1986). Understanding the use of paradox in counseling. *Family Therapy, 13,* 239–248.

Rohrbaugh, M., Tennen, H., Press, S., White, L., Raskin, P., & Pickering, M. (1977, August). *Paradoxical strategies in psychotherapy.* Symposium presented at the Annual Meeting of the American Psychological Association, San Francisco, CA.

Rosen, J. (1953). *Direct psychoanalysis.* New York: Grune & Stratton.

Salmon, W. (1970). *Zeno's paradoxes.* Indianapolis: Bobbs-Merrill.

Schwartz, R., & Perrotta, P. (1985). Let us sell no intervention before its time. *Networker, 9,* 18–25.

Selvini-Palazzoli, M., Boscolo, L., Checchin, G., & Prata, G. (1978). *Paradox and counter-paradox.* New York: Brunner/Mazel.

Slaatte, H. (1968). *The pertinence of the paradox: The dialectics of reason-in-existence.* New York: Humanities Press.

Sluzki, C., & Ransom, D. (1976). *Double bind: The foundation of the communicational approach to the family.* New York: Grune & Stratton.

Soldow, G. F. (1981). Change in the organization: The detriment and benefit of the double bind. *Group & Organization Studies, 6,* 500–513.

Soper, P. H., & L'Abate, L. (1980). Paradox as a therapeutic technique: A review. *Family Psychotherapy, 2,* 369–384.

Swann, W. B., Pelham, B. W., & Chidester, T. R. (1988). Change through paradox: Using self-verification to alter beliefs. *Journal of Personality and Social Psychology, 54,* 268–273.

Teismann, M. W. (1979). Jealousy: Systematic, problem-solving therapy with couples. *Family Process, 18,* 151–160.

Treacher, A. (1988). The Milan method—a preliminary critique. *Journal of Family Therapy, 10,* 1–8.

Watts, A. W. (1957). *The way of Zen.* New York: Random House.

Watzlawick, P., Beavin, J., & Jackson, D. D. (1967). *Pragmatics of human communication.* New York: Norton.

Watzlawick, P., Weakland, J., & Fisch, R. (1974). *Change.* New York: Norton.

Weakland, J., Fisch, R., Watzlawick, P., & Bodin, A. (1974). Brief therapy: Focused problem resolution. *Family Process, 13,* 141–168.

Weeks, G., & L'Abate, L. (1979). A compilation of paradoxical methods. *American Journal of Family Therapy, 7,* 61–76.

Weeks, G., & L'Abate, L. (1982). *Paradoxical psychotherapy: Theory and practice with individuals, couples, and families.* New York: Brunner/Mazel.

Weick, K. E., & Browning, L. D. (1986). Argument and narration in organizational communication. *Journal of Management, 12*, 243–259.

West, J. D., & Zarski, J. J. (1983). Paradoxical interventions used during system family therapy: Considerations for practitioners. *Family Therapy, 10*, 125–134.

Whitehead, A. N. (1948). *Science and the modern world.* New York: New American Library.

Whitehead, A. N., & Russell, B. (1910). *Principia mathematica.* Cambridge, UK: Cambridge University Press.

Wilder, C. (1979). The Palo Alto group: Difficulties and directions of the interactional view for human communication research. *Human Communication Research, 5*, 171–186.

Wilder, C. (1989). Up against the wall: The Vietnam veteran's memorial and the paradox of remembrance. In A. A. Berger (Ed.), *Political culture and public opinion* (pp. 133–149). New Brunswick, NJ: Transaction.

Wilder, C. (1991). Wounded warriors and the revisionist myth. In A. A. Berger (Ed.)., *Media USA: Process and effect* (pp. 197–206). New York: Longman.

Wilkins, R. (1989). The king and his fool. *Journal of Family Therapy, 11*, 181–195.

Wishbow, N. (1987). Applying the concept of the double bind to communication organizations. In S. Thomas (Ed.), *Studies in communication* (Vol. 3, pp. 114–157). Norwood, NJ: Ablex.

Worthington, E. L., Tipton, R. M., Cromley, J. S., Richards, T., & Janke, R. H. (1984). Speech and coping skill training and paradox as treatment for college students anxious about public speaking. *Perceptual and Motor Skills, 59*, 394.

5

EQUIVOCATION AS AN INTERACTIONAL EVENT

Nicole Chovil
University of British Columbia

There is an assumption shared by many professionals and lay persons that communication should be clear, direct, and complete. Rhetoricians such as Aristotle have advised public speakers to strive for clarity and avoid ambiguity. Speech courses also emphasize the need for a straightforward manner of speaking. According to Grice (1975), even ordinary conversation generally proceeds by the "cooperative principle." Conversants expect speakers to contribute messages that are relevant to the purpose or direction of the talk, to say no more or less than is required for the understood purpose, be truthful, and avoid obscurity and ambiguity.

Although much of our discourse with others generally appears to follow this principle, there are many instances when our communication with others violates linguistic standards. Of particular interest here are equivocal messages: unclear or nonstraightforward messages that may, at best, be only tangentially related to the preceding talk.

Psychologists have often attempted to account for inadequate communication by turning to sources within the individual. Unclear or nonstraightforward messages are often viewed as the result of individual error, inadequate verbal skills, deliberate attempts to be deceptive, or disordered thought processes (e.g., symptoms of mental illness). Although individual differences in verbal skills undoubtedly exist, these explanations ignore the context in which these messages are produced.

Other scholars have suggested that explanations of these messages can be found by closely examining the interpersonal situation in which they occur. This approach is consistent with the increasing evidence that social and contextual factors also shape our communications (e.g., Brown & Levinson, 1978; Clark & Wilkes-Gibbs, 1986; Ochs, 1979). Communication, whether it be face-to-face dialogue, a telephone conversation, or a written message is as much an interpersonal act as it is cognitive.

In this chapter equivocation is examined as an interactional event. The approach taken is based on the assumption that equivocation, like other communicative processes, can best be understood by examining messages within their social context. The first section begins with a discussion of how equivocation has been conceptualized and how it is distinguished from three closely related phenomena: double bind situations, disconfirmation, and deceptive communication. The types of equivocal messages that have been observed as well as a quantitative method for measuring equivocation are also presented. The second half of this chapter focuses on four general communicative situations that elicit equivocation. Analysis of these situations reveals that equivocation is an effective communicative strategy rather than faulty communication.

EQUIVOCATION

Equivocation as Systematic Ambiguity

Over the years, both clinicians and communication researchers have taken interest in understanding why individuals sometimes produce messages that are unclear or ambiguous in meaning. This ambiguity may result from features of the message itself or in terms of its responsiveness to a preceding utterance. Equivocation then includes messages that are ambiguous, indirect, contradictory, or evasive.

The Palo Alto group (Bateson, Jackson, Haley, & Weakland, 1956; Sluzki, Beavin, Tarnopolsky, & Veron, 1967; Watzlawick, Beavin, & Jackson, 1967) took interest in the nonstraightforward communication that occurred in families of schizophrenics. These communications were termed "disqualifications" and included a variety of messages that contained contradictions or inconsistencies, subject switches, tangentializations, incongruence between levels of messages, and incongruent messages (see Bavelas & Smith, 1982, for a more complete list of definitions offered by early clinical researchers).

Although early writings have focused on disqualified messages that occurred within a disordered family system, there has been a continuing theme that disqualified messages also occur in normal communication (e.g., Cissna & Sieburg, 1981; Sluzki et al., 1967; Weakland & Fry, 1962). Equivocation has also been studied in communication among normal individuals. Williams and Goss (1975) assessed the effect of ambiguous political messages on the audience's ratings of the speaker. Eisenberg (1984) argued that ambiguity can be an effective communicational strategy in meeting multiple situational requirements of organizations. Putnam and Sorenson (1982) examined the process by which ambiguous messages are processed with an organizational setting. Indirect speech acts and the processes by which they are understood have also received considerable attention (Bowers, Elliott, & Desmond, 1977; Nofsinger, 1976; Searle, 1975). Our research team (Bavelas, Black, Chovil, & Mullett, 1990a) has developed a method by which equivocation can be measured quantitatively as well as a situational theory of equivocal messages.[1]

Types of Equivocal Messages

Equivocation can manifest itself in messages in a variety of ways. Sluzki et al. (1967) offered several examples of disqualification. Bowers et al. (1977) identified three kinds of indirect responses to a yes–no question. Brown and Levinson (1978) described several politeness strategies. Dillon (1990) suggested several strategies of responding in interviews. Our research group (Bavelas et al., 1990a) has found that the different forms of equivocal messages can be organized using Haley's (1959) observation that messages consist of four formal elements: content, sender, receiver, and context.

Ambiguity in the Meaning

Equivocal messages are often unclear in the content or meaning being conveyed. Ambiguity in meaning can result from inherently ambiguous words or phrases that make it difficult to interpret any specific meaning. For example, phrases such as "It was okay" or "It's fairly fine" are ambiguous as there is no precise definition of "okay" or "fairly fine." They could mean that it was not as good as it could have been or it is somewhere in between good and bad.

As Eisenberg (1984) noted, equivocal messages sometimes contained words or phrases with double meanings. These messages leave it up to the receiver regarding how to interpret the message. Some of our subjects also used this strategy in responding to questions. In one of our experiments subjects were asked to write a message to a friend who had sent a gift that was so bizarre that it was not clear whether the gift was serious or meant to be a joke. In

---

[1]Space limitations restrict the amount of detail that can be given here. Readers who are interested in learning more about our approach to studying equivocation are referred to Bavelas et al., *Equivocal Communication* (1990a), which presents a more detailed description of this 10-year project. There are also several published articles available (Bavelas, 1983, 1985; Bavelas, Black, Bryson, & Mullet, 1988; Bavelas, Black, Chovil, & Mullett, 1990b; Bavelas & Chovil, 1986; Bavelas & Smith, 1982).

the example below, the message is sufficiently vague to cover both possibilities:

I got a kick out of your gift. It was what I would have expected from you.

Examination of disqualified messages produced in families of schizophrenics (Watzlawick, Beavin, & Jackson, 1967) as well equivocal messages produced in our experiments revealed that equivocal messages sometimes contained contradictions within them. Consider the following examples:

It was okay, but sometimes I wasn't sure what you were getting at.

It's a great but a little strange.

In both cases the messages begin with a positive phrase followed by a criticism of the topic. These contradictions render the overall meaning of the message unclear. Brown and Levinson (1978) discussed the use of contradictions as a politeness strategy in conveying a complaint or criticism.

Ambiguity in meaning can also be created by using metaphors, incomplete sentences, or contradictions between verbal and nonverbal elements in a message (Bavelas & Smith, 1982).

Ambiguity in the Sender of the Message

Equivocal messages in this group are characterized by ambiguity in who is responsible for the ideas being expressed. A person can deny responsibility for the ideas being expressed by prefacing the message with "They believe . . ." or "It would appear . . ." These messages imply that the speaker is not the sender or source of the message, although he or she is obviously saying the message. This duality renders it unclear as to whether the speaker also agrees with the idea or is merely expressing what others believe. Haley (1959) proposed that communication of schizophrenics that claim God or an alien being is talking through them renders unclear the sender element of the message.

In many situations we are asked for our opinion on some object or event. One way to equivocate is to respond with an answer that focuses on someone else's opinion. This strategy is sometimes used by politicians who state the opinion of an investigative committee or summarize the conclusions of studies. This leaves it unclear as to whether the politician also agrees with these opinions.

A more subtle equivocation of opinion that we observed were messages that avoided the use of "I" or "I thought." Omitting these words rendered the response unclear as to whose opinion was being given:

Not too bad—but you could have done more work on it!

Notice that this opinion could reflect a general opinion or the speaker's opinion.

Ambiguity in the Receiver of the Message

Messages in this category equivocate by leaving it unclear as to who the message is being sent to. Equivocation with respect to the receiver element of messages has been observed in messages given by schizophrenic patients. For example, one son sent his mother a Mother's Day card that contained the inscription "For someone who has been like a mother to me" (Haley, 1959, p. 359). Haley also noted that schizophrenics could also disqualify on this element by talking to himself or herself or by insisting that the other person is someone else.

In our experiments, subjects sometimes equivocated on this element by qualifying the audience to which the message was being directed. In the following example, there is a suggestion that only certain individuals should consider purchasing the car.

FOR SALE 1966 VOLKSWAGEN. VERY CHEAP.
PERSON WHO LIKES WORKING ON CARS WOULD
BE WISE TO BUY THIS CAR.

It is likely that individuals may also equivocate on this element in face-to-face interaction by nonverbal means such as avoiding eye contact with the receiver. In a group situation the speaker may equivocate by not indicating verbally or nonverbally specifically who is being addressed.

Incongruity Between Message and Content

Within this category are a variety of responses that are incongruent with the context (defined as the preceding statement). Several scholars have observed that equivocal responses sometimes take the form of indirect answers to questions (e.g., Dillon, 1990; Washburn, 1969). Bowers et al. (1977) propositional implication ("I always go to the pub when Leslie's waiting tables"), relational implication (It's a good night to celebrate"), and transparent question ("Is the Pope Catholic?") are also types of indirect responses. We also found that equivocal messages produced in our experiments were often indirect responses to the question. The common feature is that although the responses are not totally unconnected to the preceding statement, all require the receiver to make an inference in order to know the answer to the question.

Sluzki et al. (1967) observed a second type of equivocal message: those that involve a change of subject. A related group were sleight-of-hand messages (messages that involved a change of subject but were labeled as an answer). We found that equivocal messages produced by normal individuals sometimes involved a subtle but distinct change in the referent. For example, in response to the question "How did I do on my presentation?", some subjects replied about the presentation ("It was . . .") instead of the person's performance ("You did . . .").

Dillon (1990) observed that interview responses sometimes answer a slightly different question than the one asked. Examine carefully the following question–answer sequence:

Q: Now first of all that criticism I quoted from Mr. Q. that these patients had actually had to be readmitted to hospital because they weren't treated properly, what do you say to that?

A: These patients are being discharged as part of an overall national, and regional policy, which says, on the best, expert advice. (Dillon, 1990, p. 98)

Close inspection of this reply reveals that it deals more with why patients are being discharged than whether they were readmitted because of improper treatment. Note though that the response is not totally unrelated to the topic of the talk.

Other equivocal messages completely avoid answering a question. Asking for clarification of the question (e.g., Well that depends on what you mean by a good employee) can, at the very least, postpone having to answer the question. Another strategy is to repeat the question back. For example, the response, "Well, how do *you* think you did?", does not provide an answer but instead forces the other person to now answer the question himself or herself. This also may enable the respondent to postpone answering the question or, as Washburn (1969) suggested, it may draw the other person away from the topic. Sluzki et al. (1967) also observed responses that consisted of redundant questions.

Washburn (1969) also suggested the strategy of managing the question: "If he asks about Tuesday night, start in by saying: Well, Monday we had gone . . . He waits, thinking you will get to Tuesday, but you never do" (p. 304).

Finally, we found that some participants avoided answering the question by giving messages that postponed the bad news. For example, when asked about the quality of a presentation, one participant offered to explain more fully during the lunch break and another suggested discussing the presentation over coffee after class.

Measuring Degree of Equivocation

In order to test our theory of equivocation it was first necessary to develop a reliable and valid measurement of equivocation. This method was based on the assumption that equivocation is a property on which messages can vary. In other words, some messages are more equivocal than others. We translated the four elements of a message (based on Haley's, 1959, article) into four questions. These questions formed the rating scales for measuring equivocation:

1. Content. How clear is the message, in terms of what is being said?
2. Sender. To what extent is this message the person's own opinion?
3. Receiver. To what extent is the message addressed to the other person?
4. Context. To what extent is the message a direct answer to the question?

Naive raters read (or listened to) each message, one at a time, and then indicated on rating scales how clear the content of the message was, the degree to which it was clearly the sender's own opinion, and so on.[2] After the raters had scaled a set of messages on the four dimensions, the numbers were standardized and averaged across the set of judges. This scaling procedure gives an equivocation value for each of the four dimensions (Content, Sender, Receiver, and Context) as well as a total sum. The reliability of this procedure has been consistently high; intraclass correlations for eight separate groups of judges have ranged from .90 to 1.00. This measure has enabled us to identify degree of equivocation, regardless of how it appears in messages.

Disqualification, Double Bind, and Disconfirmation

Disqualification has been closely linked with two other interactional patterns: double bind and disconfirmation. Although disqualification was seen as one form of double-bind communication (Sluzki et al., 1967), disqualification refers to the incongruency of messages, whereas double bind refers to a more general interactional pattern of communication that includes incongruent messages and the response by the recipient. As Sluzki et al. (1967) pointed out, "if the incongruent messages are neutralized by the response, there is no bind" (p. 496).

Bateson et al. (1956) proposed that the strange and often bizarre communication observed in schizophrenics might be explicable in the context of

---

[2]For example, the first dimension was concerned with clarity of content and consisted of a line that was labeled "Completely clear" at one end and "Completely unclear" at the other end. Judges had to decide how easily they could understand what was being conveyed and then to indicate how clear the content of the message was by placing a card that represented the message somewhere between the two endpoints. For example, the message "It was okay" would typically be placed close to the unclear end of the scale for the Content dimension as the statement is ambiguous in terms of the referent ("it") and the evaluation ("okay"). A complete description of the procedure can be found in Bavelas and Smith (1982) and Bavelas et al. (1990a).

the family's interaction patterns. The term *double bind* was used to refer to a pattern of interaction in which one party is subjected to a message consisting of two mutually incongruent assertions imposed at different levels. For example, a statement may contain a request to perform a certain action and a second assertion that this action is to occur without being a response to the request. As Watzlawick et al. (1967) noted, "double binds are not simply contradictory injunctions but true paradoxes" (p. 215). Double-bind situations also included a third injunction that prohibits the individual from commenting on the message itself or leaving the situation. This inability to comment or escape places the individual in an impossible situation. Metaphorical or other types of disqualified responses by the schizophrenic enabled the person to respond while at the same time denying that he or she is responding.

Disconfirmation is another disturbance of communication that was observed in families of schizophrenics. Watzlawick et al. (1967) proposed that in interpersonal communication individuals convey messages at two levels: content and relationship. In other words, individuals not only convey information in their messages, but at the same time offer definitions of their relationship (i.e., "This is how I see myself in relation to you in this situation"; p. 84). Responses to relationship messages can take one of three forms: they may confirm or accept the other's definition of self, reject the other person's definition, or disconfirm by negating the reality of the other as a source of the definition. Disconfirmation, then, implies a relational message "You do not exist." As Cissna and Sieburg (1981) noted, examples of disconfirmation include instances of misinterpretation of the other's point of view, denial of self-attributes or self-experience, and even total unawareness of the other person. Disqualification, indifference, and imperviousness have been identified as the three general types of responses that may lead to interpersonal disconfirmation (Cissna & Sieburg, 1981).

Equivocal Messages Versus Deceptive Messages

In recent years, the topic of lying has attracted the attention of many psychologists and communication researchers. Camden, Motley, and Wilson (1984), Hample (1980), and Turner, Edgely, and Olmstead (1975) examined the frequency and motivations underlying "white" lies. Other researchers have attempted to delineate the cues by which lies can be detected (e.g., DePaulo & Rosenthal, 1979; DePaulo, Zuckerman, & Rosenthal, 1980; Ekman, 1985; Zuckerman, DeFrank, Hall, Larrance, & Rosenthal (1979).

Attempts to define deceptive communication have resulted in a tendency to regard any message that is not "the whole truth" as deceptive communication. For example, Camden et al. (1984) described the use of a tactful remark as a form of "white lies." Vagueness and indirectness have been postulated as two characteristics of deceptive communication (Knapp, Hart, & Dennis, 1974). Thus, equivocal messages often have been included as a form of deceptive communication.

Knapp and Comadena (1979), however, noted one problem in the way deceptive communication has been defined. They pointed out that most studies conceptually define lying as the deliberate falsification of information but also include "treatment of information—adding or subtracting from the perceived truth" (p. 271). Knapp and Comadena argued that this component is problematic because information treatment does not always distinguish between lies and truths.

Other researchers have also questioned whether equivocation is a form of lying. Williams and Goss (1975) warned against equating ambiguity with untruthfulness. Our work on equivocation led us to explore this issue in more detail (Bavelas et al., 1990a, 1990b). We proposed that messages can be analyzed in terms of what is said (truthfulness) and how it is said (clarity). Separating these two dimensions of messages enabled us to test whether equivocal messages mislead the receiver.

We defined a truthful message as any message that provided the receiver with an accurate representation of reality (or as the sender believes it to be). Our measure of truthfulness was based on how far the interpreted meaning of any message is from the actual state of affairs. To test whether equivocal messages were deceptive we asked people to rate the meaning of the messages obtained in our experiments, all of which had been previously scaled for equivocation. Independent raters who were unaware of our interest in equivocation were asked to indicate on a scale what each message was saying. The scale consisted of a line with two endpoints. The endpoints for each set of messages corresponded exactly to descriptions given in the experimental instructions originally used to elicit that particular set of messages. For example, one set of messages was obtained in response to a hypothetical class presentation given by a fellow student. The presentation was described in one condition as "well organized and well delivered" and in another condition as "poorly organized and badly delivered." These two descriptions formed the endpoints of the scale. Raters were told to read the messages and then rate the quality of the class presentation described in the message. Messages that described a class presentation that was well organized and well delivered were to be placed at the left end, whereas messages describing a class presentation that was poorly organized and badly delivered were to be scaled at the right end. For example, the message "It was okay, but sometimes I wasn't sure what you were getting at" was typically interpreted as indicating that the presentation was not very good and thus rated toward the right endpoint (poorly organized and badly delivered). In contrast, the message "You did very well" was seen as saying that the presentation was good and rated more toward the left endpoint (well organized and well delivered).

The decoded meaning of messages was then compared to the actual state of affairs (i.e., what the speaker or writer had been told in the experimental instructions). The results supported our hypothesis that equivocal messages conveyed information that was consistent with the actual state of affairs. In other words, equivocal messages produced in our experiments did not convey false information. In a later study (Bavelas et al., 1990a), we further confirmed our hypothesis by demonstrating that equivocal messages and lies are produced in different communicative settings. (See the section on empirical evidence that equivocation is produced in avoidance–avoidance conflict for a description of how lies were elicited.)

Our measure of truthfulness also enabled us to check on whether equivocal messages were "lies of omission" (i.e., responses that do not answer the question). An example would be a message that repeated the question. We found only a few instances of nonanswers, and there was no difference in their frequency between clear messages and equivocal messages.

The results of our studies support our position that equivocal messages and lies are different types of messages. Equivocal messages are decoded as truthful representations of reality. They are, however, less direct ways of conveying the truth. Falsehoods, on the other hand, were not completely clear, but they were clearer than equivocal messages. More importantly, they were perceived as conveying information that in actuality misrepresented the state of affairs.

Although the work by our research team demonstrated that equivocal responses are decoded by naive raters as conveying accurate information, there have not been any attempts to systematically explore conversants' responses to equivocal messages and the conditions under which they are perceived as deceptive communication. It is possible that some types of equivocal messages are perceived by receivers as attempts to be deceptive. For example, hesitancy in responding may be perceived as an indicator of deceptive intent, even though the message itself is not a falsehood. Answers that are only tangentially related to the question might also be perceived as dishonest communications. It is quite likely that investigations that focus on the responses to equivocal messages may uncover other conditions in which equivocal responses are perceived as deceptive communication.

SITUATIONS THAT ELICIT EQUIVOCATION

Earlier in this chapter it was noted that the cause of equivocation has sometimes been ascribed to the individuals who produce unclear messages. In this section, four situations in which equivocation has been observed was examined. In each case certain features of communicative situations have been identified as leading to equivocal communication.

Avoidance–Avoidance Conflicts

Bavelas (1983) proposed a situational theory of equivocation which posits that equivocal responses are elicited by situations that proscribe direct communication but still require a response. This theory was adapted from Lewin's (1938) conflict model and begins by viewing communicative situations as metaphorical fields with particular paths. These paths are the possible messages that can occur in the situation. Some messages are more direct "routes" than others, that is, they are straightforward and clear. Others are less direct routes (i.e., equivocal). To account for why people may choose a more equivocal message over a straightforward one, this theory includes a second Lewinian concept—each path has a positive or negative valence. In other words, messages have social consequences, and these consequences can be positive or negative.[3] For example, most people feel that it is good to give a compliment to another and bad to say something that is unkind. Bavelas proposed that discourse is shaped in large part by its potential interpersonal consequences.

In many communicative situations there is at least one positive alternative among the possible direct message choices. In these situations individuals will choose a direct message. It is easy though to think of other situations in which all direct message choices have negative consequences. People are often faced with avoidance–avoidance conflicts. In many cases the direct message options center on a choice between telling a truth or lying. For example, probably all of us have received an awful gift from a dear relative we care deeply about. Often we are asked how we liked the gift. There are at least two direct message options in the situation: one could be truthful and tell the person that the gift was awful, or one could lie and say the gift was wonderful. Both of these options have negative consequences. The first option conveys a message that one does not care about the other person's feelings, and the second option (lying) may go against our personal values and runs the risk of detection. Equivocation is a solution to this difficult social dilemma; it is a way of avoiding any of the direct alternatives while at the same time enabling the speaker to respond in the situation. In this example, one could equivocate by saying "You are so thoughtful."

Equivocal messages are also found in situations in which direct truthful messages have negative consequences for the writer or speaker. For example, in one experiment we asked subjects to write a car ad for a car that they had to sell because they desperately needed money. The dilemma was that the car was old and in poor condition. In this case, telling the truth about

---

[3]Messages often have positive and negative consequences attached to them. We are proposing that when there are negative *social* consequences attached to direct messages, individuals will choose an equivocal way of responding.

the condition of the car would go against the self-interests of the writer. Lying about the condition of the car would also be ineffective as the condition of the car would be obvious to anyone who saw the car.

Avoidance–avoidance conflicts are not limited to truth/lie dilemmas. Responsibility to two different groups may also create conflict for individuals. For example, a store clerk is asked about some meat on sale that is old and of poor quality. In this case, the clerk has responsibility to two groups: the customers and the company he or she works for. The dilemma faced by the clerk is whether to lie to customers about the quality of the meat or to tell the truth and risk losing sales.

Another common dilemma is being caught between offending either of two groups who demand opposite replies. Politicians face this conflict when constituents are divided with respect to controversial political issues (e.g., pro-life vs. right to abortion). Direct replies supporting or criticizing either position will offend a substantial number of voters. Conflicts may also arise when the policy of the party is at odds with the interest of the constituency, for example, when the candidate's party favors a cut in military spending but this source of funds is an important part of the local economy. In these situations the politician is faced with a choice of direct messages that will either offend the party or the constituency.

This discussion of avoidance–avoidance conflicts has so far focused on equivocation as a way of avoiding negative consequences of direct messages. One can also look at the consequences of responding with an equivocal message. In many instances there are positive consequences for responding equivocally. For example, Eisenberg (1984) argued that equivocation can be useful for facilitating change within organizations. In addition, Eisenberg and other researchers have noted the positive effects equivocation can have on relationships with others.

Eisenberg (1984) discussed several ways in which strategic ambiguity can be used to facilitate relational development. One way results from the multiple interpretations of ambiguous messages. This flexibility enables individuals to interpret these messages in a way that is consistent with their own beliefs. In doing so, listeners may perceive a similarity between themselves and the speaker. This similarity can lead to increased attractiveness and development of a positive relationship. Second, as noted earlier, ambiguous communication can be useful in maintaining a positive relationship with two groups of individuals who have disparate views. Third, strategic ambiguity can be useful in situations involving the communication of abstract company goals or policies. Ambiguous statements regarding organizational goals can unite group members to a common abstract goal while at the same time enable individuals to interpret the policy statements in terms of what they believe is important. Finally, Eisenberg suggested ambiguity can also promote ingroupness—those who can interpret the messages share something that outsiders do not have access to.

Equivocation can also help to preserve a harmonious relationship between two individuals. As our work and others have found, an equivocal message provides a way of responding that is both truthful and tactful. In many interpersonal situations, direct messages may be truthful and clear in terms of information transmission, but they are "relationship lies" (Turner et al., 1975). In other words, a direct negative message conveys an implicit message that the speaker has no regard for the receiver's feelings. Thus, equivocal messages enable the speaker to be both tactful and responsive to the other person.

For the most part, relational consequences of equivocation have not been empirically studied. Williams and Goss (1975) found that the effect of equivocation on audiences was positive. Equivocal messages elicited more agreement and higher attractiveness ratings for the presumed authors than clear messages. The authors suggested that the effect of equivocation may depend on whether the listener detects the vagueness and attributes an underlying motive to the message.

The effects of equivocal messages on relationships between two individuals may depend on whether it is perceived as a cooperative or noncooperative response. Receivers may simply follow the cooperative principle and automatically interpret the answer. When a message is perceived as a noncooperative response, individuals may pursue a better answer to their question. Receivers may also realize that their partner is in a difficult situation and in these situations perceive the equivocal message as a tactful response. Mura (1983) explored how interactants mark apparent violations of Grice's maxims of conversations by use of qualifiers and other phrases. Her analysis showed that marking contributions as violations can function to legitimize the contribution while at the same time implicitly acknowledge the cooperative principle. Although she did not extend her analysis to include responses of the conversational partner, marking of violations did appear to facilitate smooth progression of the conversation. This suggests that conversants may perceive nonstraightforward or indirect responses as cooperative contributions.

Avoidance–Avoidance Conflicts as Sources of Equivocation

Our research program was aimed at testing a situational conflict theory of equivocation. We used a variety of scenarios as well as various formats for eliciting responses: forced choice, written, spoken, and face to face. Our procedure consisted of asking participants to respond to a question in hypothetical communicative situations. For each situation we created two experimental conditions: a control (nonconflict) condition in which there is no conflict, and a conflict condition in which the participant is faced with an avoidance–

avoidance conflict. For example, in one experiment subjects were asked to imagine that a friend had just given a class presentation. In the nonconflict condition, participants were told that the presentation was well organized and well delivered. In the conflict condition, the participants were told that the presentation was poorly organized and badly delivered. The question posed to the participants in both conditions was "How did I do on my class presentation?"

In the nonconflict (control) condition, participants produced written messages such as "You did very well," or "I think your presentation was well thought-up and delivered." In the conflict version, participants replied with messages such as "It was okay but there were some things that could be improved," and "Better than I probably would have done."

Our experiments have consistently shown that messages produced in the conflict condition were significantly more equivocal on one or more of the four dimensions (content, sender, receiver, or context) than messages given in the nonconflict condition.

We have found that truths, equivocations, and lies can be elicited by systematically varying the valences associated with truths and lies. The basic scenario centered around a local performance of the musical *Cats*. We created three different conditions. To elicit truths subjects were told to imagine that they had gone to see the play and it was wonderful. They were simply told that a friend was coming by and wanted to know how they liked the play. In this situation, a direct message has positive consequences. Equivocal responses were elicited by presenting the same information as in the nonconflict (truth) condition and adding that the friend was dating the director of the play. In this case, telling a direct truth would hurt the friend's feelings. To elicit nontruthful responses, subjects were told that "your favorite cousin's birthday is on Saturday, and you decided this would make a great surprise party."[4] In this situation, a truthful response would spoil the event, whereas a nontruthful message preserves the surprise and may even add to the fun later. The same question (How did you like the play?) was used in all three conditions. The results supported our hypotheses that messages would systematically vary as a result of the valences attached to the message options.

Situations that Involve Interactional Uncertainty

Equivocation has also been observed to occur in three situations involving uncertainty. Sharrock and Turner's (1978) work on complaint formulations

---

[4]This design had several advantages over much of the deception research: We did not mention anything about deception, nor did we tell subjects what to say, but rather left it up to their own devices as to how to respond.

revealed indefiniteness in the nature of the event as another type of problematic situation that led to equivocation. These researchers analyzed citizen phone calls to a metropolitan police station. They noted that citizen calls to the police are usually made in order to obtain some remedial action to rectify a troublesome situation. The best route to this goal is to provide a clear and direct description of the facts so that the police can act on them. One subset of calls fit this model of complaint giving. These calls were straightforward and to the point. They immediately revealed the trouble and what the caller expected of the police. The rest of the calls "struck [the authors] as rambling, packed with excessive detail, and unfocused" (p. 173).

Sharrock and Turner suggested that this difference in complaint formulation can be explained by examining the types of complaint situations that citizens face. Some cases, such as stolen articles or violence, are clearly police business. There is no need to explain why the situation requires police attention. Other situations are more problematic such as an event that might be construed as police business or as personal troubles. For example, troubles that involve neighbors could be perceived as legitimate complaints (i.e., the neighbors are breaking the law) or as attempts to settle private scores (i.e., reporting them to the police as a way of getting even with disliked neighbors). Sharrock and Turner found that calls about these more ambiguous "troubles" deviated in several ways from the direct, clear model of complaint giving. In many cases, extra information was included. Some callers prefaced their complaint with phrases such as "I have a complaint" before describing the complaint. Descriptions of the troubles often included extraneous information about individuals such as "they seem awfully nice an' everything but I don't know" or descriptions of parties that might be involved in the troubles: "Well not exactly hippie element but-eh bordering on it; and-eh an awful lot of people in an' out of the place."

These details appeared on the surface to be unimportant or irrelevant, however, when examined more closely, they help to legitimize the event as one requiring police attention.

In all cases, the extra information and narrative details provided by the caller had the effect of making the complaint less focused and harder to follow. It was successful, though, in assuring the legitimacy of a complaint. Thus, one finds that although the communication failed to meet standards of clearness and directness, it was successful in defining the trouble as legitimate police business.

Rummelhart (1983) described two other situations that proscribed direct communication. She examined the responses of mentally handicapped clients to interview questions and found several instances of evasive responses. Although poor communication of mentally handicapped individuals tends to be viewed a a language deficiency, there is evidence that context also affects the types of messages sent. For example, Angrosino (1989) pointed out, mentally handicapped individuals "know how to vary their response to the same question, depending on the setting—the more clinical the setting, the more correct or deferential the answer" (p. 86). Similary, Kelly, Farina, and Mosher (1971) found that schizophrenic women were very capable of following instructions to create a likable or unlikable impression on interviewers. Rummelhart also observed that mentally handicapped individuals who appear to lack social skills in an interview setting were remarkably fluent and capable in their communication with peers. All of these observations suggest that communication by mentally handicapped clients is affected by features of communicative situations.

Rummelhart found that clients were sometimes put into situations in which they were unsure that they understood the content or the context of the interaction but felt compelled to participate. This situation made it difficult for them to respond directly. If they revealed their lack of knowledge or uncertainty, it would be further confirmation of their limitations. If they misinterpreted the purpose of the interaction (e.g., desire to become friends rather than an attempt to find out about misconduct), they might reveal an action that was a violation of the rules. The consequence in this case would be punishment.

When faced with uncertainty about the content of the talk, clients employed "offensive" strategies, that is, they responded in a way that transformed the context into one in which they controlled the topic. This strategy included: (a) changing the topic to a more secure one, one that the participant had knowledge about; (b) saying something that sounds right—using jargon learned in clinical and therapy sessions; and (c) providing excessive detail in the answer.

Rummelhart observed that clients employed "defensive" strategies when they were uncertain as to the purpose of the interaction. These strategies consisted of minimal contributions that enabled the client to participate without really revealing any information. They included (a) minimal or vague responses that enabled the participant to provide a contribution without adding significant content, (b) turning the question back to the interviewer, (c) use of stock phrases (e.g., "That's a good question"), and (d) answering the literal question rather than the intended meaning of the question. Rummelhart noted that many professionals may be tempted to interpret this last response as a symptom of mental retardation (i.e., concrete thinking). She suggested that it also can be seen as a "conservative answer." She argued that although it may not be responsive to the intended interpretation of the question, it is a better answer than if the individual responded to a more abstract but incorrect interpretation.

Rummelhart noted that client's equivocal responses often had an effect on how the interviewer proceeded with the questioning. For example, answering in a literal way led one questioner to reformulate his question in an attempt to make it clearer to the client. When this did not seem to work, he switched to another example, and this change helped to clarify the purpose behind asking the questions.

In summary, these investigations revealed that equivocal messages are produced in situations in which individuals are confronted by features that make it difficult for them to respond adequately with clear, direct messages. The first class of situations were ones in which direct message choices had negative consequences for the participants involved. Equivocal responses not only enable a person to avoid the negative consequences of direct message options, but in many situations they can help in the establishment and facilitation of relationships.

In the case of calls to the police, ambiguity in the nature of the troubles resulted in formulations that deviated from the more straightforward style of complaint giving. The detailed narrations and reluctance to give names helped to define the troubles as legitimate police business. Equivocal responses by mentally handicapped clients in interview situations also enabled them to respond when they were unsure of the content or purpose of the dialogue. Together these findings provide support to the general proposition that non-straightforward messages arise as a result of features within the communicative situation and not simply because of individual error or deficiency.

CONCLUSIONS

Equivocal messages appear on the surface to be faulty communication. Examining equivocal messages in their interpersonal context however reveals how ambiguity can be a useful means to communicate effectively in problematic communicative situations. The study of equivocation demonstrates the necessity to look beyond the speech event itself to the broader context in order to fully understand messages produced in discourse. Communication between individuals is an interactive process; individuals solicit responses to their communications as well as respond to the messages of others. Whenever we communicate with others, we must decide what information to convey and how best to convey it. Formulation of messages involves taking into consideration not only the purpose of communicating but the receiver and general situation as well. In situations in which it is crucial that precise information be communicated and there are positive consequences attached to direct messages, senders will formulate messages that are direct and clearly encoded. In other situations though, equivocal messages may be more successful in terms of meeting the informational and social requirements of the situation.

Examination of the situations in which equivocation occurs reveals a number of features that lead to equivocal messages. Social consequences of messages, the uncertain nature of events, and unsureness as to the content or purpose of the talk are four features of situations that lead individuals to respond equivocally. It is also likely that individuals may sometimes evade questions for personal gains that may involve a cost to others. The research presented in this chapter suggests though that many equivocal messages that occur in day-to-day interactions are attempts to avoid difficulties and unsuccessful communication that might arise from direct messages. Nonetheless, there may be some readers who remain convinced that equivocation is something undesirable. We suggest to these readers that before they judge an equivocal message as poor communication, they take a closer look at the purpose behind the question asked, the consequences a direct message would have for the interactants, and whether they are prepared to give an unpleasant but direct truth to someone about whom they care deeply.

REFERENCES

Angrosino, M. V. (1989). *Documents of interaction: Biography, autobiography, and life history in social science perspective.* Gainsville: University of Florida.

Aristotle. (1952). Rhetoric. In *Britannica great books* (Vol. 9), W. R. Roberts (Trans.), Chicago: Encyclopedia Britannica.

Bateson, G., Jackson, D. D., Haley, J., & Weakland, J. (1956). Toward a theory of schizophrenia. *Behavioral Science, 1,* 251–264.

Bavelas, J. B. (1983). Situations that lead to disqualification. *Human Communication Research, 9,* 130–145.

Bavelas, J. B. (1985). A situational theory of disqualification: Using language to "leave the field." In J. P. Forgas (Ed.), *Language and social situations* (pp. 189–211). New York: Springer-Verlag.

Bavelas, J. B., & Chovil, N. (1986). How people disqualify: Experimental studies of spontaneous written disqualification. *Communication Monographs, 53,* 70–74.

Bavelas, J. B., Black, A., Bryson, L., & Mullett, J. (1988). Political equivocation: A situational explanation. *Journal of Language and Social Psychology, 7,* 137–145.

Bavelas, J. B., Black, A., Chovil, N., & Mullett, J. (1990a). *Equivocal communication.* Newbury Park, CA: Sage.

Bavelas, J. B., Black, A., Chovil, N., & Mullett, J. (1990b). Truths, lies, and equivocations: The effect of conflicting goals on discourse. *Journal of Language and Social Psychology, 9,* 135–161.

Bavelas, J. B., & Smith, B. J. (1982). A method for scaling verbal disqualification. *Human Communication Research, 8,* 214–227.

Bowers, J. W., Elliott, N. D., & Desmond, R. J. (1977). Exploiting pragmatic rules: Devious messages. *Human Communication Research, 3,* 235–242.

Brown, P., & Levinson, S. (1978). Universals in language usage. In E. N. Goody (Ed.), *Questions and politeness: Strategies in social interaction* (pp. 56–289). Cambridge, UK: Cambridge University Press.

Camden, C., Motley, M. T., & Wilson, A. (1984). White lies in interpersonal communication: A taxonomy and preliminary investigation of social motivations. *Western Journal of Speech Communication, 48,* 309–325.

Cissna, K. N. L., & Sieburg, E. (1981). Patterns of interactional confirmation and disconfirmation. In C. Wilder-Mott & J. H. Weakland (Eds.), *Rigor and imagination: Essays from the legacy of Gregory Bateson* (pp. 253–282). New York: Praeger.

Clark, H. H., & Wilkes-Gibbs, D. (1986). Referring as a collaborative process. *Cognition, 22,* 1–39.

DePaulo, B. M., & Rosenthal, R. (1979). Telling lies. *Journal of Personality and Social Psychology, 37,* 1713–1722.

DePaulo, B. M., Zuckerman, M., & Rosenthal, R. (1980). Humans as lie detectors. *Journal of Communication, 30,* 129–139.

Dillon, J. T. (1990). *The practice of questioning.* London: Routledge.

Eisenberg, E. M. (1984). Ambiguity as strategy in organizational communication. *Communication Monographs, 51,* 227–242.

Ekman, P. (1985). *Telling Lies.* New York: Berkley Books.

Grice, H. P. (1975). Logic and conversations. In P. Cole & J. L. Morgan (Eds.), *Syntax and semantics* (Vol. 3, pp. 41–58). New York: Academic Press.

Haley, J. (1959). An interactional description of schizophrenia. *Psychiatry, 22,* 321–332.

Hample, D. (1980). Purposes and effects of lying. *Southern Speech Communication Journal, 46,* 33–47.

Kelly, F. S., Farina, A., & Mosher, D. L. (1971). Ability of schizophrenic women to create a favorable or unfavorable impression on an interviewer. *Journal of Consulting and Clinical Psychology, 36,* 404–409.

Knapp, M. L., & Comadena, M. E. (1979). Telling it like it isn't: A review of theory and research on deceptive communications. *Human Communication Research, 5,* 270–285.

Knapp, M. L., Hart, R. P., & Dennis, H. S. (1974). An exploration of deception as a communication construct. *Human Communication Research, 1,* 15–29.

Lewin, K. (1938). The conceptual representation and measurement of psychological forces. *Contributions to Psychological Theory, 1* (4, Serial No. 4).

Mura, S. S. (1983). Licensing violations: Legitimate violations of Grice's conversational principle. In E. T. Craig & K. Tracy (Eds.), *Conversational coherence: Form, structure, and strategy* (pp. 101–115). Beverly Hills, CA: Sage.

Nofsinger, R. E., Jr. (1976). On answering questions indirectly: Some rules in the grammar of doing conversation. *Human Communication Research, 2,* 172–181.

Ochs, E. (1979). Social foundations of language. In R. Freedle (Ed.), *New directions in discourse processing* (pp. 207–221). Norwood, NJ: Ablex.

Putnam, L. L., & Sorenson, R. L. (1982). Equivocal messages in organizations. *Human Communication Research, 8,* 114–132.

Rummelhart, M. A. (1983). When in doubt: Strategies used in response to interactional uncertainty. *Discourse Processes, 6,* 377–402.

Searle, J. R. (1975). Indirect speech acts. In P. Cole & J. L. Morgan (Eds.), *Syntax and semantics* (Vol. 3, pp. 59–82). New York: Academic Press.

Sharrock, W. W., & Turner, R. (1978). On a conversational environment for equivocality. In J. Schenkein (Ed.), *Studies in the organization of conversational interaction* (pp. 173–197). New York: Academic Press.

Sluzki, C. E., Beavin, J., Tarnopolsky, A., & Veron, E. (1967). Transactional disqualification: Research on the double bind. *Archives of General Psychiatry, 16,* 494–504.

Turner, K. E., Edgley, C., & Olmstead, G. (1975). Information control in conversations: Honesty is not always the best policy. *Kansas Journal of Sociology, 11,* 69–89.

Washburn, C. (1969). Retortmanship: How to avoid answering questions. *Etc, 26,* 69–75.

Watzlawick, P., Beavin, J., & Jackson, D. D. (1967). *Pragmatics of human communication: A study of interactional patterns, pathologies, and paradoxes.* New York: Norton.

Weakland, J. H., & Fry, W. F., Jr. (1962). Letters of mothers of schizophrenics. *American Journal of Orthopsychiatry, 32,* 604–623.

Williams, M. L., & Goss, B. (1975). Equivocation: Character insurance. *Human Communication Research, 1,* 265–270.

Zuckerman, M., DeFrank, R. S., Hall, J. A., Larrance, D. T., & Rosenthal, R. (1979). Facial and vocal cues of deception and honesty. *Journal of Experimental Social Psychology, 15,* 378–396.

THE FACE BENEATH
THE MASKS

6

CONVERSATIONAL DILEMMAS

John A. Daly, Carol A. Diesel, and David Weber
University of Texas at Austin

This chapter is about difficult communication encounters—encounters in which people feel that no matter what they say, they are almost always bound to lose. These encounters create, for lack of another term, conversational dilemmas; they create difficult challenges for communicators. Although conversational dilemmas are not necessarily everyday occurrences, almost everyone has been caught in them. The notion that people face conversational dilemmas was brought to the fore by an excerpt in Beck (1988, p. 215):

Tom: Why are you moping around?

Sally: You told me I was stupid.

Tom: I really didn't mean it. I was angry at the time.

Sally: I *know* you really do think I am stupid.

Tom: That just isn't true. I was angry.

Sally: You always say that when people are angry they express their true thoughts.

At this point, Tom is in a difficult bind. No matter what he says, he has a problem. Denying he was angry contradicts what he just said. Suggesting that he was wrong about what he said before again contradicts what he has previously argued. Saying that Sally misunderstood what he meant can easily be construed by Sally as an attack. In short, Tom is trapped in a conversational dilemma.

Although dilemmas of this sort may not be common, they offer some interesting avenues for communication scholarship. Better understanding the pragmatic structure of these dilemmas may give some valuable insights into the nature and structure of a particular class of discourse. Communication scholars have spent little time examining situations when communication is difficult, even though all of us have had such experiences. Being at a loss for words, having to give bad news, coping with interpersonal crises, and so on represent very important, but seldom examined, arenas for communication scholarship. Conversational dilemmas fit within this genre of scholarly inquiry. Furthermore, studies of conversational dilemmas may provide some useful information about communication competence. In many disciplines a distinction is drawn between typical performance competence and maximal performance competence. Typical performance is what one usually does, whereas maximal performance is what one is theoretically capable of doing. Most paper-and-pencil measures of communication competence are self-reports, which indicate people's perceptions of how well they do in communication encounters. They do not actually challenge an individual to demonstrate any degree of competence. Yet one could argue that people differ in how "smart" or "savvy" they are about social interactions (Daly, Vangelisti, & Daughton, 1987). Tapping these differences in a subtle fashion might provide a useful way of identifying a person's maximal competence, at least cognitively, as it relates to communication expertise (Daly, 1992). Two issues, then, drove this research: We were interested in better understanding a particular genre of difficult communication encounters, as well as determining whether people's capability to resolve dilemmas is related to their communication competence.

RELATED RESEARCH

Although there is no research on conversational dilemmas per se, there is some relevant literature and theory that suggests interesting avenues for potential study. By briefly explicating three of these, Bateson's double-bind hypothesis, Bavelas, Black, Chovil, and Mullett's (1990a) concept of equivocal communication, and Newell and Stutman's (1988) social confrontation episode, what we mean by a conversational dilemma will be clarified.

One relevant area of research comes from the relational communication tradition and, more specifically, Bateson, Jackson, Haley, and Weakland's (1956) concept of the double bind. In their research on schizophrenics, Bateson et al. proposed a social cause for schizophrenia, theorizing that significant others in the schizophrenic's early life sent contradictory verbal and nonverbal messages. The result was that the child felt trapped in terms of how to respond to those messages. Bateson et al. provide as an example the case of a mother giving a verbal message asking the child to display affection toward her, while nonverbally indicating feelings of coldness and withdrawal. The child faces a dilemma: If he or she responds to the verbal messages encouraging closeness, he or she is ignoring the nonverbal indicators. But, if the child responds to the nonverbal messages, the mother may accuse the child of ignoring her verbal request.

Conversational dilemmas represent a similar kind of "Catch-22" in social interaction because, as the aforementioned example of Tom and Sally demonstrates, an undesirable outcome is likely to result for each response. Unlike double binds, however, there is often a wide repertoire of available responses to a conversational dilemma, many of which are undesirable. Moreover, the dilemma is not so much a matter of choosing whether to react to the verbal or nonverbal level of another person's message, but of choosing from a number of different verbal and nonverbal strategies to extricate oneself from the dilemma.

In recent research, Bavelas et al. (1990a) referred to double binds as "avoidance–avoidance conflicts." In these types of situations a direct response to another's message is always negative. One example they provide is the following: "You have received a gift from someone you really like a lot, but the gift is awful, and you don't like it at all. Now you have to write a thank you note to that person (who lives in another province)." If one tells the friend that he or she dislikes the gift, it can lead to hurt feelings. If one tells the friend he or she does like the gift, then one is lying. Furthermore, a friend may expect to see the gift in use when visiting, creating further difficulty. Bavelas and her colleagues have thoroughly examined how people cope with this sort of conflict. Avoidance–avoidance conflicts resemble conversational dilemmas, but our notion of the conversational dilemma is much broader than the Bavelas et al. (1990a) problem set, as we discuss later.

Newell and Stutman's (1988) research on social confrontation episodes is another related strand of research. They define a social confrontation episode as "a particular kind of communication episode initiated when one actor signals to another actor that his or her behavior has violated, or is violating, a rule or expectation for appropriate conduct within the relationship or situation" (p. 271). Newell and Stutman provide the following example: "Terry and Marty are roommates. Terry has discovered that Marty has been spreading rumors about him/her. Alone in the apartment with Marty, Terry decides to confront Marty." One can see how social confrontation episodes might represent a kind of conversational dilemma for Marty: If Marty admits to spreading rumors about Terry, Terry might think Marty is malicious or petty. If Marty denies that he spread rumors, Terry will know Marty is lying. Marty is trapped. Newell and Stutman (1988) carefully delineated how people deal with situations in which one person is confronted by another about a presumed violation of a norm or expectation.

Newell and Stutman's notion, however, is unnecessarily restrictive within the context of what we perceive as conversational dilemmas. A conversational dilemma is not limited to situations in which one's own behavior violates a norm. It can also result when another person violates a norm, placing one in an awkward situation. For example, many people have been in situations in which someone violates their privacy by asking questions that are too personal or makes other unreasonable demands. Often people trapped in these situations wish to refuse the request while simultaneously leaving social relationships intact. Further, unlike social confrontation episodes, conversational dilemmas can occur in the absence of an explicit rule violation, such as when a person asks another for his or her honest opinion, but the opinion, if honestly given, might hurt the requestor's feelings (e.g., your friend asks you what you think of her or his new outfit, and you hate it), or when one's gain might be someone else's loss (e.g., a person you are attracted to asks whether he or she should ask out your friend, and you want to tell that person to take you out instead).

One important characteristic of being caught in a conversational dilemma is the negative feelings often associated with being trapped in one. In examining available literature, two negative reactions seem especially likely when people are unlucky enough to be faced with a conversational dilemma from which they are unable to extricate themselves: embarrassment and defensiveness.

Perhaps one of the most common reactions to being caught in a dilemma is to experience embarrassment. Consider the definitional characteristics of embarrassment as identified by Cupach and Metts (1990): embarrassment arises in a situation in which (a) there is a rule violation or action inconsistent with the embarrassed person's image, (b) the embarrassed person is aware that the act occurred, (c) the consequences of the act are unintentional, and (d) the embarrassed person believes the act is, or will be, observed by one or more other people. All of these can arise in conversational dilemmas. Moreover, embarrassment can aggravate feelings of being trapped. For example, many people have at some point said something uncomplimentary about a person and suddenly realized that the person was listening. When people are already embarrassed and feel that nothing they say can reduce that embarrassment, they are trapped in a kind of conversational dilemma. But conversational dilemmas need not be limited to embarrassing situations. In the aforementioned example of Tom and Sally, Tom is more likely to be frustrated, rather than embarrassed, by his futile attempts to reassure Sally. That frustration often leads to defensiveness.

Defensiveness as a concept originated with Gibb (1961). It has been elaborated on by many communication scholars, most recently Stamp, Vangelisti, and Daly (1992), who characterized defensiveness as a situation consisting of the following elements: (a) a self-perceived flaw which the individual refuses to admit, (b) a sensitivity to that flaw, (c) an attack by another person, which (d) focuses on that flaw. Some conversational dilemmas involve defensiveness on the part of one, or both, of the interactants. The dilemma might be to extricate oneself from another's defensive reactions that one has inadvertently caused without appearing insincere by merely taking back what was said or producing even more defensiveness by saying something else wrong. Or dilemmas could arise when one is feeling defensive about what was said by another. In these situations, the dilemma involves the potentially negative consequences of expressing one's anger versus the potentially negative consequences of holding it in.

Research on embarrassment and defensiveness as well as double binds and social confrontation contain some elements common to conversational dilemmas and aid in understanding the nature and structure of conversational dilemmas. But none of that research focuses on the conversational dilemma as a unique communication phenomenon that cuts across various interpersonal situations and contains the definitive element of feeling trapped in a no-win conversation. What distinguishes a conversational dilemma from other problematic interactions is that the person trapped in a conversational dilemma is faced with a number of alternative responses, each varying in sophistication, and each containing some drawbacks in terms of the social consequences that may ensue if that response is selected.

IDENTIFYING DILEMMAS

One major goal of the current research was to identify the nature of conversational dilemmas. What is the universe of dilemmas people face in social interaction? Can they be organized into a coherent scheme? The first step in probing this concern was to collect a number of instances of conversational dilemmas. A large number of undergraduate students enrolled in communication courses as well as working adults enrolled in a management education program were asked to describe conversational dilemmas they had faced. We introduced the project with the following instructions:

> For this project, we'd like you to think of a time when you were stuck in a conversation—when no matter what you said you knew it was either going to be wrong or get you in trouble . . . just describe a situation where you felt there was "no way out" in a conversation.

Respondents wrote descriptions of their dilemmas, and these descriptions were then closely examined for overlap. From the excerpts eight clusters of conversational dilemmas were identified. The clustering was accomplished by having six graduate students in communication sort the descriptions into categories. Across the six, the average agreement was greater than 90%. What follows is a brief explication of the eight clusters.

Caught in a Lie

This category contains dilemmas in which people are caught blatantly lying to others and are then confronted about it in a conversation. Consider the example one individual provided:

> I called my boss at work to tell him that I wouldn't be in because I was sick, when the truth was that I really wanted to go to a party. When I got to the party, I ran into my boss, who said "I'm really disappointed. I trusted you, and paid extra to get temporary help, and you went out partying."

In such cases people are trapped in a conversational dilemma insofar as if they continue to lie, they only get themselves in deeper, but if they tell the truth, they potentially destroy any basis of trust they have previously established with that person.

Self Versus Other Needs

This category represents dilemmas involving people's desire to get what they want versus the obligation to attend to the other's needs by being polite or tactful in a particular situation, and in this sense it is more of a proactive dilemma than a reactive one. For example:

> This guy I really liked asked if he should go out with one of my friends. I really wanted him to ask me out, but I didn't want to hurt my friend.

This situation represents a dilemma because if she tells the person the truth, she is not only putting herself on the line, but also potentially betraying her friend. If she chooses not to tell, she could be giving up something she really wants.

Moral Dilemma

These dilemmas involve situations in which people witness a wrongdoing or a violation of a rule by someone they like. For example:

> My best friend and I worked together for the same company. One day I saw him do something wrong. My boss suspected him, and asked me whether he did it.

In this situation, one is faced with a tough decision: whether to turn in a friend or to let the moral violation occur. If one turns in the friend, he or she is liable to lose that friend. If one lets the violation occur, he or she could cause harm to others, and possibly oneself.

Foot in Mouth

These are situations in which people either "let the cat out of the bag" by revealing a secret that was not supposed to be revealed, are overheard saying something that was not intended for the overhearer's ears, or otherwise say something that they should not have. One respondent provided the following example:

> My friend and I were in the lunch line talking about how another friend of ours, Michelle, is really gaining weight. I said that she has become so obese that she looks disgusting, because her clothes no longer fit. After I got my food, we both turned around and found that Michelle was standing right behind us in line.

This is an obvious dilemma because Michelle was present during the conversation. The speaker cannot simply ignore Michelle, as this would most likely appear rude. The speaker cannot deny what she said (Michelle will know that she is lying). But by not denying it, she will alienate Michelle.

Can Never Please

These are dilemmas in which, no matter what people say, their words are not acceptable to another person. For example:

> My mom and I weren't getting along. My parents told me that I had to make some changes in my behavior because my mom couldn't handle me anymore. They asked me what I was going to change, and I made some offers. They told me that the offers I made weren't good enough. They told me to do such and such a thing, I did it, and they still said that's not good enough.

This category represents one of the most difficult types of dilemmas. In this example, literally anything that comes out of the person's mouth appears unacceptable to the parents. No matter what that person says, it is the wrong thing.

Ultimatums/Pressure From Others

Unlike the "can never please" category, this category represents dilemmas in which people are indeed able to please the other person(s), but only by doing something that they do not want to do. For example:

> My friends called me to go out tonight, but I didn't want to go. I tried "I don't feel like it," "I feel sick," "I have a lot of work to do," "I don't have any money," and "I don't like the club you're going to," but they wouldn't take any of my excuses, and kept hounding me to go with them.

The key problem in this dilemma is the relentless pressure of a person who is attempting to get the respondent to do something that he or she does not want to do, and in this sense it is a reactive dilemma rather than a proactive one, like the "Self Versus Other Needs" category. In these situations, one must either surrender to the other person and do what one does not want to do or else refuse the person's request and possibly end up alienating or angering him or her or hurting his or her feelings. Neither alternative is desirable.

Choosing Sides

These are situations in which people find themselves torn between two people they like. The two are involved in a conflict and ask the respondent to intervene, in effect, to side with one against the other. For example:

> Two of my friends were arguing about something in my presence. Each one strongly believed in their position and both really believed a friend ought to support their side. One of them finally turned to me and said "well, what do you think?"

The dilemma is obvious. If the respondent sided with one person he would alienate the other. If he did not side with either of them, he was likely to upset both people.

Tact Versus Truth

These are dilemmas involving a choice between being tactful and polite versus telling someone the truth, even if it hurts. For example:

> I picked up my best friend to go to a party, and she was wearing clothes that would look better on a dog. She was proud of her outfit, and asked me how she looked. If I told the truth, she might have time to change before the party, but on the other hand, might get her feelings hurt.

If the respondent tells the truth in this situation, she loses because she is likely to hurt her friend's feelings, especially since her friend is so proud of the outfit. But if she does not tell her friend, she also loses because her friend could embarrass herself. Furthermore, if her friend finds out that she was lying, her friend might later be angry at her for not being honest.

In tabulating and clustering the different examples respondents provided, we discovered the most common clusters were ultimatums ($N = 65$, 29.5%), choosing sides ($N = 43$, 19.6%), foot in mouth ($N = 27$, 12.3%), never pleasing ($N = 27$, 12.3%), and tact versus truth ($N = 24$, 10.9%). The least common clusters were moral dilemmas ($N = 6$, 2.7%), self versus other needs ($N = 9$, 4.1%), and being caught in a lie ($N = 19$, 8.6%).

RESOLVING DILEMMAS

Extricating oneself from conversational dilemmas is an age-old concern. In ancient Persia, military messengers who ran from battlefield to palace faced perhaps the ultimate conversational dilemma. If they brought news of a military success, all sorts of honors befell them; if they brought instead news of a military loss, they were executed (Cialdini, Finch, & De Nicholas, 1990). Therefore, a military loss presented the messenger with a grave conversational dilemma. In today's parlance, people sometimes kill the messenger of bad news. The research on this phenomenon demonstrates that when people are put in the position of communicating bad news, even when they are not responsible for what the news communicates, they are liked less than when they communicate positive information (Manis, Cornell, & Moore, 1974). This leads to a tendency to prefer communicating positive information and avoid communicating negative information (the "MUM" effect) (Bond & Anderson, 1987; Tesser & Rosen, 1975).

Yet conversational dilemmas are particularly difficult because extrication by avoidance is almost impossible. People are already in the conversation, they cannot simply not be there. Instead, they have to find a way of "getting out" of the dilemma, conversationally, while preserving both their own and the other person's "face." Optimally, they try to come up with responses that allow them to resolve the difficult situation with limited face loss for all involved. At the very least, they need to respond. This led to the following research question: Given that conversational dilemmas occur and that people experiencing conversational dilemmas are probably motivated to extricate themselves from them, how do they do so? Research on related conversational phenomena such as politeness, social confrontations, and embarrassment provides some clues.

Politeness is a key notion when discussing how people often cope with dilemmas. People, we would hypothesize, will attempt to be polite when verbally extricating themselves from a conversational dilemma. The literature on politeness and related concepts such as "face saving" is extensive (e.g., Brown & Levinson, 1987; Lim & Bowers, 1991) and need not be reviewed here. Suffice to say that when people are in conversational dilemmas, they are likely to want to insure that the "face" of all is protected, as much as possible.

Politeness may be reflected in the degree of directness of a person's response. In dilemmas in which one is at fault due to his or her own behavior (e.g., being caught talking about a person behind his or her back), a more direct strategy of resolving the dilemma seems appropriate. Attempts to lie or deny the behavior would probably make the situation worse rather than better. In contrast, if there is some confusion as to whether or not the person actually performed the undesirable behavior, there may be room for both more indirect and/or dishonest strategies for resolving the dilemma, such as denial, deception, or ambiguity. Turner, Edgely, and Olmstead (1975) pointed out that in some cases honesty may not be the best relational policy.

Beyond attempting to maintain politeness, interactants still have a number of alternatives in difficult situations. Consider the cases of social confrontation and embarrassment. Newell and Stutman (1988) suggested that in social confrontations, people may offer a remedy (ceasing the behavior, stating regret, offering compensation, and/or punishment), a reaffirmation (acknowledging the mistake and promising to follow the presumed rule in the future), legislation (clarifying the violated rule for future reference), or remediation (amending the original expectation or rule) when dealing with events such as dilemmas. Similarly, Cupach and Metts (1990) discussed a number of remedial strategies which can reduce the damage caused by embarrassing predicaments. Some of the remedial strategies available to the person who becomes embarrassed include apology, remediation (repairing the damage in some concrete way), accounts (excuses and justifications), avoidance (escape), humor, or aggression. The choice depends on the nature of the embarrassing predicament and who bears responsibility for its occurrence. For instance, Cupach and Metts found that the use of humor and avoidance were more common than accounts, possibly because these strategies serve to reduce the embarrassment without having to address it directly, which could create face-threatening results. Aggression (physical or verbal), however, was a commonly used strategy when the actor is not responsible for his or her own embarrassment (e.g., when another attempts to embarrass a person by teasing him or her in front of others).

Conceptually, then, people in dilemmas have a variety of potential alternative strategies they might use. Watzlawick, Beavin, and Jackson (1967) suggested a number of verbal responses people might use when faced with something akin to a dilemma (in this case, when a person initiates a conversation with another who is uninterested in participating). One response by the interested party, they suggested, was disqualification—communicating in ways that invalidate communication. Behaviorally, disqualification might be exhibited by responses such as engaging in self-contradictions, using an obscure language style, being inconsistent, switching subjects, moving to a tangential topic, not finishing their sentences, appearing to misunderstand, or going for the literal interpretation of a metaphorical remark or a metaphorical interpretation of a literal remark. Questioning might be another verbal alternative. McLaughlin and Cody (1982) found that conversants, after experiencing an awkward silence (something that may, in some cases, indicate a dilemma), were significantly more likely to engage in question and answer sequences; they speculate that questions provide for more conversational possibilities because they are more open ended than other forms of talk.

Although there is a wide variety of research on strategies and conversational moves people may make in difficult communication encounters, the most relevant work on conversational dilemmas is the use of vagueness, more commonly known as equivocal communication (Bavelas et al., 1990a) or strategic ambiguity (Eisenberg, 1984). Strategic ambiguity is the purposeful use of ambiguity in conversation to accomplish social goals. Eisenberg argues that in certain situations, people use ambiguity to preserve social relations and facilitate change at the same time. Similarly, Cunningham and Wilcox (1984), Rushing (1962–1963), and Stein (1967) noted that when nursing personnel are caught in a bind with a physician they tend to use indirect communication strategies. For instance, nurses prefer indirect responses when physicians order medications that might, in the nurses' opinions, have negative effects on patients. Direct approaches (e.g., "Doctor, I recommend a change to order Z . . .") threaten the status relationship that exists between nurse and physician. Directness by nurses increases, however, when there is a perceived substantial risk to the patient and there is a positive relationship between nurse and physician.

Bavelas et al. (1990a) argued that equivocal communication serves positive goals in social interaction. Definitionally, "the specific element of a situation that causes equivocation is an avoidance-avoidance conflict, where the direct response would be negative" (p. 23). In other words, when people try to avoid saying anything critical or uncomplimentary and simultaneously try to avoid lying, they use vague responses which can be interpreted in more than one way. Bavelas and her colleagues presented people with situations in which telling the truth could create negative feelings on the part of the recipient of the truthful message. For example:

> Someone you work with arrives at a staff meeting, where she is going to present a report. She is wearing a new dress and also has a new hair style. Both are awful—she looks really bad. She sits down next to you and passes you a note: "How do I look"?

In such situations, people preferred equivocal responses (e.g., "Don't worry— you'll do fine.") over the others (e.g., "Your dress doesn't suit you" and "Your hair doesn't look good that way."). This research suggests that when an individual is "caught between two or more incompatible aspects of the situation, and furthermore, still required to communicate" (Bavelas, 1983, p. 132), the person prefers indirect moves over other types of moves (e.g., deception, blunt honesty). In another study, Bavelas (1983) found that when people are presented with two negative options (a hurtful truth or a false message) or an equivocal one, more than 90% opted for the equivocal message over direct truth or falsehood. Bavelas presented undergraduates with several different scenarios that were similar to one type of conversational dilemma. For each she examined the degree to which undergraduates engaged in disqualification, defined as a conversational move that renders some aspect of the exchange unclear. Disqualification might occur in terms of content (making the response unclear), sender (communicator's own opinion is not given), receiver (message not clearly addressed to receiver), and/or context (message does not directly answer the implicit or explicit question raised in the event). She found that in avoidance–avoidance conflict situations (Lewin, 1938) interactants preferred a disqualification move—a "communicative equivalent of leaving the field" (p. 139).

One element distinguishing the present research from the extensive research by Bavelas and her colleagues is the typology of dilemmas previously described. Their focus has emphasized the responses one makes to a dilemma with relatively little attention to the nature of situations that create dilemmas. Furthermore, Bavelas (1983) dismissed the role of personality in the act of disqualification when people are in conversational binds: "Disqualifications are not a function of the communicator; they are a product of the interpersonal situation in which the communicator finds him/herself" (p. 144). A close reading of her study, however, does not demonstrate this. She never directly explored systematic differences among communicators. One might suggest that, in some situations, certain individual differences relevant to communication might affect the choices individuals make in responding to conversational dilemmas. We demonstrate support for this assertion later in the chapter.

Finally, all of the studies done by Bavelas (1983) and Bavelas et al. (1990a) contained scenarios that could be classified in our category system as "tact versus truth" dilemmas. In these dilemmas, it is easier for one to equivocate because the other person does not yet know what the real truth is. But what about other types of dilemmas in which the truth is obvious (e.g., someone catches you saying mean things behind his or her back, or someone catches you at a party after you've called in sick to work)? We examine a more varied array of dilemmas.

To gather some initial information about response strategies we randomly selected 22 different dilemmas falling into the 8 aforementioned categories. The dilemmas were selected from those collected in the first study. They are listed in Table 6.1 with the category each dilemma represents.

TABLE 6.1
Selected Dilemmas

CATEGORY/*Topic Dilemma*

ULTIMATUMS

Abortion   You're arguing with a friend about abortion, when the conversation boils down to "the women's life" versus "the baby's life." You can tell the discussion isn't going to get any further, but your friend doesn't seem to want to let go until you admit that he/she is right. You don't want to give in, but you don't want to keep arguing either.

Hounding   (see example in text)

Sex   You're talking with someone you consider to be a friend about your relationship. All of a sudden, he/she asks you, "Well, are the two of you having sex?" You feel the question is too intimate. You don't want to be rude, but you don't want to answer the question either.

Recruit   Recruiting new employees is a part of your job, and your roommate knows it. He/she asks you for a job during Christmas, which is the busiest time of the year for your store. People working at your store must be extremely patient with customers. You know from your roommate's stories about a former job that he/she is impatient with waiting on customers, particularly when they are rude or have trouble making up their minds, which your customers tend to do at Christmas. You like your roommate, and you know that he/she really needs the job, but you also know he/she is not right for it. More importantly, you know that if you hire poorly, your boss will think badly of you and may decide not to promote you. Your roommate comes to you one day and says, "Well, when can I start?"

B vs. C   You and your friend B have decided to go to a party on a particular night. That day you invite C, who doesn't have many social skills and isn't very popular, to go along. With C in the room, you call B to confirm arrangements for that night, and B gets upset on the other end of the line; he/she says, "I don't like C, and don't want him/her to go to the party with us."

Politics   You've been talking with person B, a very good friend of your parents, and your dad's boss, for about 15 minutes at a party, when the conversation turns to politics. All of the sudden, the friendly chat you were having gets heated, and B vehemently disagrees with everything you believe. B keeps insisting that you agree with him/her. You keep trying to change the topic, but B won't let you.

FOOT IN MOUTH

Secret   A friend of yours has given you some confidential information about your boyfriend/girlfriend. In the heat of an argument one day, you use that information, and your boyfriend/girlfriend is clearly upset that you know about it. He/she asks, "Who told you that?"

Michelle   Two of you are in the lunch line talking about how a friend of yours, Michelle, is really gaining weight. You go on to say that she has become so obese that she looks disgusting because her clothes no longer fit. After you get your food, you both turn around and find that Michelle was standing right behind you two in line.

Dislike   You are telling someone how much you dislike another person—about how you can't stand being around the person or even talking to him/her. The person you are talking to turns out to be best friends with the person you are complaining about.

(Continued)

TABLE 6.1

(Continued)

CATEGORY/Topic Dilemma

Lunch	You've been dating B for several months. One day you have lunch with A, but don't tell B about it, because you're afraid that B will be jealous, the way he/she often is when you go out with other people. Then, on a date with B, you bring up a story you thought he/she had told, then realize that you had heard it from A at lunch. B accuses you of getting him/her confused with someone else.

CAUGHT IN LIE

Sick	You called your boss at work to tell him/her you wouldn't be in because you were sick, when the truth is that you wanted to go to a party. When you get to the party, you run into your boss, who says, "I'm really disappointed. I trusted you, and paid extra to get temporary help, and you went out partying."
Promise	You promised your boyfriend/girlfriend that you wouldn't go out tonight because he/she has to write a paper and can't go with you. But a couple of your high school friends want to see the local action, so you take them. The next day, in front of your boyfriend/girlfriend, one of your high school pals asks you, "What was the name of that band we saw last night?"
Astroworld	Some friends ask you to go to Astroworld with them. You say, "Sure." Two days before the planned trip, one of your friends calls and asks you if you can drive. You didn't want to drive so you say "My car is in really bad shape." So the trip is canceled. A day later some family members call and you decide to go with them to Astroworld. Only your car is available, so you drive. It turns out that your friends picked the same day to go, and you run into them at the park.

SELF/OTHER

Likes Friend	A person of the opposite gender you really like asks whether he/she should go out with another one of your friends. You really want him/her to ask you out, but you don't want to hurt your friend.
Weekend	You go to a party on a weeknight where all the guys/gals are trying to find dates for an upcoming party. You see a wonderful looking guy/gal across the room who you would really love to go to the party with. As you are looking at him/her, another guy/gal comes up and starts talking. He/she isn't very good-looking; he/she is short, kind of overweight, and not too bright. He/she asks you to go to the party. You say, "Well, I really can't. I'm busy that night and I can't go to the party." At that point the guy/gal you had seen across the room comes up with one of your friends. Your friend whispers that he/she is planning to ask you to the party. You know that he/she has just overheard you telling the other one that you weren't going to be able to go. Both of them are standing there. You desperately want to go to the party with the good-looking one.

MORAL DILEMMA

B goofed	You and your best friend B work together for the same company. You saw B do something wrong. Your boss suspects and asks you whether B did it. If you say yes, B is in trouble. If you say no, your job may be in jeopardy, and you need the job.

(Continued)

TABLE 6.1
(Continued)

CATEGORY/Topic Dilemma

CAN NEVER PLEASE

Moping   (see example in text, p. 127)
Mom   (see example in text, p. 133)

CHOOSING SIDES

Arguing   (see example in text, p. 134)
Friend   A friend and his/her mom were in a fight because she/he wanted to go out. Her/his mother said no and wouldn't explain why. Your friend was going to go anyway and the mother asks you: "Would *you* disobey *your* mother?"

TACT VS. TRUTH

Sister   You think your sister's kids are unruly brats, and that your sister isn't doing a very good job of raising them. You're worried about the kids, and think they may get into serious trouble if your sister doesn't discipline them more strictly, but you've never been able to find the opportunity to raise the issue. One day when the two of you are talking about your futures, she tells you she hopes you have kids just like hers, and says, "I think I've raised them perfectly, don't you?" If you lie, you've missed an opportunity to make a real difference in the kids' lives. If you tell the truth, your sister may be hurt.
Clothes   You pick up your best friend to go to a party, and he/she is wearing clothes that would look better on a dog. He/she is clearly proud of him/herself, and asks you how he/she looks. If you tell the truth, he/she will have time to change before the party, but may have hurt feelings.

The dilemmas were presented to a large group of undergraduates who were asked to write down, for each dilemma, how they would handle the situation. Their answers were then content analyzed to identify typical responses to each dilemma. Our experience in categorizing these answers was interesting. First, there was notable variability in the sophistication of the responses. Some people were quite creative in their responses, offering solutions to dilemmas that were extraordinarily savvy. For example, in response to the dilemma in which B does not want C to go to the party with A and B, one respondent wrote:

> You tell B you'll call him back because you have company. Later you tell B that C needs to get some exposure. You also tell B that C needs B's help to meet people and gain acceptance. Besides it's only for one evening.

Others offered responses that were far less sophisticated. For example, in answer to the dilemma in which a person inquires about the respondent's sex life, one undergraduate said she would "tell that person off" in a blunt and obscene manner.

Second, there was a wide variety of responses to each dilemma, ranging from polite to blunt, flexible to unyielding. In attempting to understand the nature of these responses, a 16-category system was created that incorporated virtually every response across dilemmas. The 16 categories fell into 6 broader categories (see Table 6.2). The first category, entitled "Directness," contained strategies that were generally open and honest in nature, whether that honesty was exhibited in a tactful face-saving way or in a more blunt and straightforward manner. Of all of the responses to dilemmas, 41.2% fell into this category. One example of a tactful strategy was in response to the dilemma in which one's sister's kids are unruly brats: "I'm glad this came up; I love your kids, and I know you want what is best for them. But if you want to know the truth, sometimes I worry that because you love them so much, maybe you aren't as strict as you should be with them." An example of a more blunt response to the same dilemma was "To tell you the truth, I hope my kids are nothing like yours; I plan on raising my kids much more strictly, so they won't turn into brats, like yours are." Although the responses in this category varied in terms of the degree to which they were face saving, they were all in a sense honest and straightforward, making no attempt to avoid or deny the truth, in contrast to the next two categories.

The responses in the "Indirectness" category (6.1% of the responses fell into this category) involved strategic ambiguity, vagueness, or subtlety used to avoid stating the truth directly, but not through explicit deception. Often the respondent would indicate that the other was out of line by using humor,

TABLE 6.2
A Typology of Responses to Conversational Dilemmas

DIRECT
  1. directness/bluntness/backlash
  2. tactful but honest
INDIRECT
  3. subtle hints/sarcasm
  4. humor
  5. dismissing/vague/ambiguous
  6. topic shift/avoidance
DECEPTION
  7. cover-up/lying
IMPRESSION MANAGEMENT
  8. excuse/disclaimer/account
  9. massage ego/agree/reassurance
 10. apology/self-deprecation
 11. diplomacy/riding the fence
PLEASE OTHER
 13. compromise/reparations/concessions
 14. give up/give in
SOLICIT OTHER'S HELP
 15. mediate/persuade other to do something
 16. try to get more info.

sarcasm, hints, or nonverbal cues rather than directly informing that person. For example, in the case of the dilemma in which the respondent is pressured to reveal whether or not he or she is sleeping with his or her boyfriend or girlfriend, one response was to "say sarcastically, 'yeah, every chance we get.'" Another response to this same dilemma was "give him/her a look that says he/she should drop the matter." When one's own behavior was out of line, some respondents used indirect strategies to avoid addressing their own behavior explicitly, such as changing the topic or giving a vague answer to a question. For example, in response to the dilemma in which the person is accused of confusing something person B said with something that was said by person A during a secret lunch date, one indirect response to the confrontation was "Oh, one of my friends probably said it. How's that sandwich?" Another indirect response involved the use of humor as a way to avoid seriously addressing the issue: "Don't you remember telling me that, at the party where you were really drunk and stoned?"

At times, respondents attempted to lie their way out of a situation, such as when asked for an honest opinion when an honest opinion would be negative or when they did not want to get caught and rebuked for a behavior they had performed. These instances comprised the "Deception" category, involving a direct misrepresentation of the truth. Eighteen percent of the responses fell into this category. For example, in response to the dilemma in which one's best friend is wearing clothes that would look better on a dog and is asked for an honest opinion, some respondents indicated that they would simply lie and say the person looked great in the outfit. In the dilemma in which one is caught by one's boss at a party after calling in sick, one respondent reported that he or she would answer, "I was sick, but I started feeling better about an hour ago, so I came to the party," and another responded, "I'm here looking for my sister; it's a family emergency."

The category entitled "Impression Management," containing 18.4% of the responses, included any number of moves such as apologies, excuses, accounts, and reassurances to manage one's own impressions in a potentially face-threatening situation. For example, in response to the dilemma in which one is discovered breaking a promise to a boyfriend or girlfriend to go out with friends, one respondent wrote, "I took them out because they haven't seen Austin before and they didn't know where to go or what to do. I didn't want to leave them stranded so I offered to be their tour guide." Another wrote, "I'm sorry, I'm sorry, I'm sorry! Please don't be mad. They dragged me out, and I felt like I had no choice."

Sometimes when trapped in a conversational dilemma, the only way out is to do what the other wants, even if one does not want to do it. Responses in the "please other" category, which contained 10.3% of the responses, involved an attempt to satisfy the other's needs by compromising or by giving in, in order to avoid further awkwardness or conflict. For example, in response to the dilemma in which one is caught at a party by one's boss after calling in sick, one respondent said that he or she would offer to come in early all next week. In response to the dilemma in which one is hounded by one's friends to go out, one respondent answered, "I'll go if y'all buy the first round of drinks."

In 5.9% of the situations, the respondent tried to get the other to help him or her resolve the dilemma. Responses in the category entitled "Solicit Other's Help" involved asking for more information in order to resolve the dilemma or asking the other's cooperation in the resolution effort, such as when the respondent acted as a mediator between disputing parties. For instance, in response to the dilemma in which one is discovered criticizing another's best friend, one person responded, "why do you like him/her?" In response to the dilemma in which one cannot please his or her parents, one person wrote, "What do you want from me? Tell me what I can do to make you happy!"

The observation that there were some consistent patterns in people's responses led us to wonder whether people's reactions to the dilemmas might be related to people's sophistication about conversational processes. The notion was that for any communicative event there are more and less optimal responses available to communicators and that people might systematically differ in their preferences. These differences might be related to people's conversational sophistication.

Of course, what determines optimality is a complex issue that demands consideration of such things as the others involved in an exchange, the context within which the exchange occurs, and the goals of each interactant. With some people one response is preferred over another; in some settings one response is more appropriate than another; and sometimes it is important to a person to be sophisticated, and sometimes it is not. All of these issues need to be considered in any formulation of conversational decision making and sophistication. In addition, people's level of social skills, communication competence, and interpersonal sensitivity may be related to their response choices. It is this last issue that was of interest to us: Were people's responses to conversational dilemmas systematically related to their conversational competence?

CONVERSATIONAL COMPETENCE
AND DILEMMA RESPONSES

For each of the 22 dilemmas described previously, potential responses to the situation were identified that represented those suggested by respondents and that appeared reasonably different in the level of social sophistication they implied. There were more response alternatives for some dilemmas than for others, due to the fact that the dilemmas were of different types and represented a wide variety of settings. The number of alternatives for each dilemma ranged from 3 to 10.

A sample of the dilemmas and a listing of potential responses for each were then presented to groups of undergraduates along with some personality measures described later, which tap various aspects of communicative sophistication. Each student responded to 11 randomly selected dilemmas (this procedure insured that nearly an equal number of respondents received each dilemma but that no two respondents received the exact same pattern of dilemmas). For each dilemma students were asked to imagine they were in the situation and to rate each potential response on a scale indicating how likely they would be to use that alternative in the situation. The ratings were not mutually exclusive; respondents were allowed to indicate that they would be very likely to use each of the responses, or conversely, that none of the responses was preferable. Tables 6.3 through 6.10 display the brief alternative responses for each dilemma that was provided to the respondents as well as the mean response for each alternative.

There were noticeable patterns of preferences. Some alternatives were clearly more desirable than others. An inspection across dilemmas suggested that the ones that were ranked as more preferable were generally far more sophisticated than those less preferred. People seem to recognize that there are better and worse moves they might make in a conversational dilemma. Nevertheless, no single alternative provided for any dilemma was consistently unpopular. For every alternative there were at least some respondents who indicated that they would be at least somewhat likely to use that particular response. Why would people differ in their preferences? It may be that, as we noted previously, participants in the project perceived different goals, different meanings, or different contexts when responding to the dilemmas. These varying perceptions may have led them to rate the alternatives differently. In addition, though, individual differences in respondents' sophistication about social interactions might have had some impact on participants' responses: People who are more sophisticated about social interaction might rate alternatives differently than people who are less so. The communication literature is filled with projects that argue that people systematically differ in their sophistication about social interaction under broad rubrics such as communication competence (Wiemann, 1977) and interpersonal competence (Spitzberg, & Cupach, 1989) as well as narrower concerns such as conversational sensitivity (Daly et al., 1987) and conversational complexity (Daly, Bell, Glenn, & Lawrence, 1985). Given that people vary in their preferences for different alternatives to the dilemmas, the question that emerged was whether those differences might be related to varying levels of social sophistication.

To examine this, the response preferences of the undergraduate sample described earlier were compared to the preferences of "experts." The experts were individuals who were nominated by the faculty of a department

TABLE 6.3
Alternatives for Ultimatum Dilemmas

Dilemma	Alternatives	Mean	(SD)
ABORTION	"You're not going to persuade me, so give it up already! Off my back!"	5.91	(3.03)
	"OK, you win; you're right."	1.89	(2.05)
	"How about let's talk about something else? How's your history class going?"	6.17	(2.82)
	Walk off and don't say anything.	3.11	(2.66)
	"I guess we just have different ways of looking at it. It would be strange if everybody agreed on everything but I still respect you as a friend and I hope you respect me too."	8.57	(2.21)
POLITICS	"I'm sorry we don't see things in the same way, but everyone is entitled to his/her own beliefs. It's a free country." Then walk away.	5.45	(2.65)
	"I think I need to visit the restroom. Would you excuse me?"	6.43	(2.56)
	"You have some very good points, and I respect your opinion; I guess I just don't agree with everything you're saying, for the reasons I mentioned earlier. I guess we just see it differently."	7.96	(2.23)
	"You're right. I guess I was wrong."	2.36	(2.32)
	"You are a jerk! I can't believe a member of my family would work for you!"	1.77	(1.89)
HOUNDING	I'm absolutely not going out tonight and if you keep bugging me about it, I'm going to get really pissed off!	3.16	(2.61)
	I'll go if you all buy the first round of drinks.	4.20	(3.01)
	Okay, I'll go if you'll leave me alone.	3.57	(2.14)
	I appreciate the fact that you all want to spend time with me, but really I feel like staying home tonight. I hope you'll understand.	7.96	(2.30)
	Hang up on them.	1.63	(1.76)
	Guys, I'm sorry, but truthfully I would just like to hang out at home today. Maybe we can go out tomorrow night. You guys go out and have fun.	9.08	(1.29)
RECRUIT	Explain the situation to your boss, and ask your boss if she/he could interview your roommate.	6.44	(2.72)
	Tell your roommate that your boss wants to fill positions from current applications first, and then if there are any positions left over, you will give him/her an application.	7.17	(2.58)
	Tell him/her that since you two live together, from your experience it would be better if you did not also work at the same place; your friendship is more important and you don't want to put a strain on it.	4.94	(2.69)
	Lie and say there are no openings.	4.98	(3.23)
	Say, "Hold on a sec; we spend every afternoon with each other, live together, eat together, etcetera. I NEED MY SPACE."	2.52	(1.93)

(Continued)

TABLE 6.3
(Continued)

Dilemma	Alternatives	Mean	(SD)
	Say, "Okay, I'll get you the job but you have to remember that my job is on the line; you have to act polite to the customers, and don't be impatient. If you screw this up, I'll be very upset."	4.83	(2.68)
	Say, "I don't think you'd like this job. How about I try to help you get a job somewhere else?"	5.48	(2.74)
SEX	Say, "Why do you want to know?"	6.43	(2.69)
	Say sarcastically, "Yeah, every chance we get."	5.30	(3.53)
	Say, "My girl/boyfriend doesn't like me to talk about our personal life with anyone, and I promised him/her I wouldn't."	3.54	(2.61)
	Say, "Well, you know how it is."	3.72	(2.52)
	Say, "That's really none of your business!"	5.64	(2.96)
	Say, "Whether we're sleeping together or not isn't really important."	5.64	(3.18)
	Say, "I don't mean to be rude, but I really don't feel comfortable discussing my sex life right now."	6.57	(2.98)
	Tell the truth.	5.92	(3.28)
	Change the subject.	5.49	(3.10)
	Give him/her a look that says he/she should drop the matter.	6.28	(2.87)
B VS. C	Say to B, "Well, I'm sure the party will be a lot of fun. There will be lots of people. We might get separated, but C and I can always make arrangements to meet up with you later in the evening and drive home together."	6.33	(2.72)
	Say to B, "Yeah, C is here right now, and he/she can't wait!"	5.59	(2.90)
	Say, "I don't care if you want C to go or not; C's coming!"	2.85	(2.38)
	Ask C to bring you something from another room, and then lay it on the line with B and ask him/her to cooperate.	6.40	(2.73)
	Say, "It's no big deal! See you in a little while."	5.77	(2.68)

TABLE 6.4
Alternatives for Choosing Sides

Dilemma	Alternatives	Mean	(SD)
ARGUING	Calmly state what you really feel about the issue, then tell whoever you disagree with that it is nothing personal and it doesn't mean you don't respect his/her opinions; it's just how you happen to feel about the issue.	7.93	(2.24)
	Ignore them.	2.81	(2.60)
	Say, "There are really no easy answers to this issue which is why I'm not going to get involved in this discussion."	6.24	(2.71)
	Say, "Hey, you guys, let's not argue about this anymore. How about let's go out and get a beer and talk about something else?"	6.37	(3.20)
	Say, "You guys are being stupid and immature. Shut up!"	3.29	(2.55)

(Continued)

TABLE 6.4
(Continued)

Dilemma	Alternatives	Mean	(SD)
FRIEND	"*My* mom wouldn't say no without giving me a reason why."	3.20	(2.70)
	"Of course not; I'm a good kid!"	3.53	(2.59)
	"I guess if the evening had already been planned and was very important to me, I would go, and hope my mom would understand but that's just me."	6.29	(2.95)
	Change the subject.	4.87	(2.86)
	"I refuse to answer that question."	3.40	(2.94)
	"You probably both have good points; that's a tough one; I probably shouldn't get involved."	7.42	(2.41)
	"You're right; mothers know best. She/he should have more respect!" (Then tell your friend later that you really disagree with the mother, but were afraid to say so.)	2.98	(2.45)
	"That would depend on a lot of things, such as how important the date was and, of course, the *reasons* my mother had."	6.93	(2.94)

TABLE 6.5
Alternatives for Self vs. Other Needs

Dilemma	Alternatives	Mean	(SD)
LIKES FRIEND	"Well, I guess; I mean if you really want to go out with her/him. She/he is really nice . . . I guess."	5.10	(2.58)
	"I hope it works out, what ever you decide to do. I must say, I envy her/him a little."	5.06	(2.70)
	"Sure, go for it."	5.98	(2.74)
	"There's a lot of people that like him/her. You might have a lot of competition."	3.84	(2.24)
	"I refuse to discuss this subject."	2.25	(1.95)
	"I don't know if that would be a good idea."	3.20	(2.51)
	"Let me take you out instead!"	2.37	(1.72)
	Hint around that he/she should take you out instead. If that doesn't work, set them up and forget about it.	4.80	(2.76)
WEEKEND	Tell the one you like that you can't go to the party, so the first one doesn't find out and get his/her feelings hurt.	5.64	(2.87)
	Tell the one you like that you can't go but thanks for asking and maybe some other time. Then pull him/her aside privately before he/she leaves the party and explain the situation completely. Let him/her know that you would love to go out another time soon.	7.40	(2.85)
	Tell the unattractive one that you would really like to go to the party with someone else, and then smile at the good-looking one.	3.29	(2.71)

TABLE 6.6
Alternatives for Caught in a Lie

Dilemma	Alternatives	Mean	(SD)
ASTROWORLD	"I got my car fixed, but I thought it would be too late to call you. My family wanted to go and I got drafted to drive."	5.82	(2.83)
	"Hi, how are you guys? Who did you come with? Isn't it a great day? Not a cloud in sight!"	4.16	(2.90)
	"My car was the only one available, so my family asked me to drive; I didn't have a choice."	6.90	(2.99)
	"I'm here with my family. I'm glad I came with them and not you; at least they didn't use me just for the ride. Later!"	1.64	(1.82)
	"I wasn't going to Astroworld but I hadn't spent time with my family in a while, and I thought it would be nice. It's nothing personal; I hope you understand."	5.40	(3.28)
	Pretend you don't see the friends.	4.02	(3.29)
SICK	Offer to come in early all next week.	6.18	(2.80)
	Say, "I'm sorry! I feel awful. It will never happen again, I promise."	7.70	(2.14)
	Say, "I don't need to be hassled by you outside work: I quit!"	1.58	(1.49)
	Say, "I had to come pick up my friend here; his sister is in the hospital and might not make it through the night. It was an emergency, otherwise I would have stayed in bed myself."	3.61	(3.00)
	Say, "I'm sorry, but I've been working so hard and I really needed a break."	5.67	(2.84)
	Say, "I'm really sorry. Please don't be mad at me. How about I buy you a drink?"	3.61	(2.71)
PROMISE	"I know I promised you that I wouldn't go out last night, but I made an exception in this case. I thought you'd understand. I wish you could have been with us!"	7.81	(2.39)
	"Yes, I went out with them; what's the problem? You're not my ball and chain, and it's unfair for you to ask me to stay home just because *you* have to."	3.46	(3.01)
	"I took them out because they haven't seen Austin before and they didn't know where to go or what to do. I didn't want to leave them stranded so I offered to be their tour guide."	7.71	(2.47)
	"I'm sorry, I'm sorry, I'm sorry! Please don't be mad. They dragged me out, and I felt like I had no choice."	3.42	(2.91)
	"Look, I'm sorry I broke my promise, I really am; but you have to learn not to be so jealous and possessive."	4.90	(3.20)
	Answer the friends' question and change the subject. Hope the boyfriend/girlfriend doesn't question you about it later.	4.29	(3.21)

TABLE 6.7
Alternatives for Can Never Please

Dilemma	Alternatives	Mean	(SD)
MOM	"Fine, I'm outta here! Good riddance!"	4.45	(3.26)
	"Nothing I do seems to be good enough: I think you want me to move out because you don't really love me."	5.43	(3.11)
	"What more do you want me to do? I don't understand. Why are you so mad, and what do you expect of me? Please explain!"	8.51	(2.23)
	"Please try to recognize my point of view. I have tried everything you suggested and nothing works. What would you do if you were me?"	8.36	(2.20)
MOPING	"No, you're not stupid; you're just not as bright as me. Seriously, let's go grab a beer and forget it."	2.92	(2.37)
	"B, I honestly didn't mean it! You are one of the smartest people I know! I wouldn't hang around you if I didn't think so."	5.15	(2.96)
	"Yes, they do, but when people get angry they also might say untrue things to make other people mad, which is what I did. I'm sorry."	8.25	(1.89)
	"You're right; you are stupid."	1.92	(1.75)
	"I refuse to discuss this anymore."	3.39	(2.87)

TABLE 6.8
Alternatives for Moral Dilemmas

Dilemma	Alternatives	Mean	(SD)
B GOOFED	Lie and say "I don't know."	6.16	(3.13)
	Say, "Maybe you should ask B yourself rather than asking me."	7.28	(2.82)
	Tell your boss "Yes, B did it."	3.94	(2.67)
	Say "B might have done it, but if he/she did, it was probably just an honest mistake."	6.04	(2.61)
	Say "No, B didn't do it; he/she would never do such a thing."	2.43	(1.95)
	Say "I did it; not B."	1.88	(1.79)

TABLE 6.9
Alternatives for Tact Versus Truth

Dilemma	Alternatives	Mean	(SD)
CLOTHES	"You should wear whatever makes you feel comfortable, and not worry about anyone else's opinion."	5.51	(2.84)
	"To be quite honest, you look tacky."	3.33	(2.51)
	"It looks great."	3.41	(2.65)
	Be silent and don't answer the question, hoping she/he will get the message.	3.74	(2.81)
	"I don't think the clothes you're wearing do justice to your best features."	5.76	(3.04)
	"It's okay, but I like what you wore last week a lot better; it looks really good on you and it will probably be better for this party. Why don't you put the other thing on? There is still time; I don't mind waiting."	8.29	(2.17)

(Continued)

TABLE 6.9
(Continued)

Dilemma	Alternatives	Mean	(SD)
SISTER	"I'm glad this came up; I love your kids, and I know you want what is best for them. But if you want to know the truth, sometimes I worry that because you love them so much, maybe you aren't as strict as you should be with them."	8.56	(1.90)
	"To tell you the truth, I hope my kids are nothing like yours; I plan on raising my kids much more strictly, so they won't turn into brats like yours are."	2.50	(2.27)
	"They're great. I love them. You've raised them perfectly."	2.27	(2.01)
	"There are some things I would do differently, but if you're happy with the way you've raised them, I guess I won't argue."	4.85	(2.61)

TABLE 6.10
Alternatives for Foot in Mouth

Dilemma	Alternatives	Mean	(SD)
LUNCH	"Stop being silly. I had lunch with A, and that's all it was. If you weren't so jealous, I could have told you earlier about this. So, just deal with it."	4.67	(2.79)
	"Don't you remember telling me that at the party where you were really drunk and stoned?"	3.31	(2.76)
	"Oh one of my friends probably said it. How's that sandwich?"	6.29	(2.82)
	"I guess I heard it from my friend A. We had lunch once, just as friends. I probably thought I heard it from you because it sounded like something you'd say."	6.98	(2.49)
SECRET	"I can't tell because I can't get that person in trouble."	5.88	(2.60)
	"That's not the issue."	7.74	(2.44)
	Don't answer the question; change the subject.	4.57	(2.79)
	"I heard some people discussing you in the elevator once. I didn't see who they were because they were standing behind me and it was too crowded to turn around."	2.63	(2.07)
	"I think you know who I heard it from; you better not get mad at him/her; it's your own fault! I'm glad he/she told!"	4.86	(2.93)
	"Actually, I heard it from a mutual friend. Maybe he/she should not have told me; but on the other hand, I feel I had a right to know."	6.74	(2.52)
MICHELLE	"Hi Michelle, how's it going? I was just looking for you; I wanted to see if you wanted to go to the library with me tomorrow night."	2.93	(2.75)
	"I'm sorry Michelle, I didn't know you were standing there. I'm sorry if I offended you. I was just concerned about you."	6.65	(2.72)
	"I'm sorry you heard that, Michelle. But I really think you do need to lose weight."	3.81	(2.81)

(Continued)

TABLE 6.10
(Continued)

Dilemma	Alternatives	Mean	(SD)
	"Michelle, everything I said was true. You do need to lose weight. Why don't you come with me to aerobics next week? It will really get you in shape, and it's good for your health!"	4.30	(2.84)
	"Michelle, I'm glad you heard that. I was going to tell you anyway; you're a cow."	1.88	(2.14)
DISLIKE	"I'm sorry I said that; I should try to keep my opinions to myself."	6.84	(2.52)
	"Sorry, but everyone has a right to their own opinions. And this is mine; I hate her."	3.25	(2.23)
	Change the subject.	5.39	(2.70)
	"I'm sorry for talking about your friend like that; it's just that we don't get along very well; she is probably nicer to you because you know each other better."	7.98	(2.16)
	"Why do you like him/her?"	3.36	(2.41)
	"You're right; he/she isn't all that bad."	4.51	(2.68)

of communication. Faculty members were asked to identify colleagues within the department that they perceived as "highly competent communicators, people who have a way of communicating that make others like them, who are both sensitive and savvy about talk, and who are diplomatic and yet highly effective at achieving their communicative goals." There was strong agreement among nominators on those individuals who were particularly competent. Six of the most frequently nominated people were asked to participate in this project. They, as "experts," completed the entire 22-scenario questionnaire. They were asked to read each dilemma and then rate (using the same scale the undergraduates used) each alternative response. The instructions they received were identical to those the undergraduate respondents received.

The responses of the "experts" to the alternatives for each scenario were then tabulated, and the means were calculated. These mean responses served as expert ratings. Undergraduates' responses were then compared to the mean expert rating, creating a difference score for each alternative, for each scenario, and for each undergraduate respondent. The average discrepancy within a scenario was then calculated for every subject. Thus, for each undergraduate respondent, there were 11 potential difference scores.

Those scores were then related to three personality measures that the undergraduate subjects were asked to fill out as part of the project. The scales assessed individual difference variables related to conversational sophistication: self-monitoring, conversational sensitivity, and communication apprehension. The three are typical of the many measures available that tap related aspects of people's propensities to exhibit more or less sophisticated social interaction skills. The self-monitoring scale (Snyder, 1974) measures the degree to which an individual adapts his or her behavior to the social situation. The scale contains three dimensions: extroversion, other directedness, and acting (Briggs, Cheek, & Buss, 1980). The conversational sensitivity scale (Daly et al., 1987) taps people's views of their perceptiveness about what goes on in conversations in terms of affinity, power relationships, and the like. It also measures a person's self-perceived memory for conversations, diplomacy in conversations, and tendency to manipulate and play with words. In this project, the measure was treated as unidimensional. The communication apprehension scale was developed by McCroskey (1978). It assesses the degree to which people avoid or enjoy social interaction. Taken together, the three measures provide a collection of indices related to conversational sophistication. A sophisticated conversationalist, in terms of these measures, ought to be high in conversational sensitivity, low in communication apprehension, and high in acting, other directedness, and extroversion.

High and low groups on each personality measure were created by using a mean split. People falling above the mean were considered high in the particular dimension (e.g., high apprehension, high extroversion); people scoring low were considered low (e.g., low apprehension, low acting ability). A series of simple sign tests were computed using the 22 different scenarios to determine which group, high or low, differed more from the "experts" for each of the personality variables. In other words, for each of the scenarios, the question was asked: For example, is the mean difference score for high apprehensiveness or low other involvement larger than the mean difference score for low apprehensiveness or higher other involvement?

The results were consistent with expectations. For communication apprehension the pattern was as expected: High apprehensives displayed larger differences from the "experts" in 20 of the 22 scenarios ($p < .001$) than low apprehensives. The same pattern appeared for the extroversion component of the self-monitoring measure (17 vs. 5, $p < .008$), whereas the opposite pattern appeared for the other-oriented component (3 vs. 19, $p < .002$). The patterns for conversational sensitivity and acting measures were not significant. To summarize, it appears that people with a high degree of communication apprehension or a high degree of introversion prefer responses that are less sophisticated and/or effective, and that other-oriented individuals tend to choose the more sophisticated and effective responses, ones that more closely matched those of the panel of communication experts.

This final investigation is an important one. It demonstrates that communication competence, measured in terms of certain personality dispositions, is positively related to people's abilities to use more socially effective solutions to conversational dilemmas. The implication of this is that when we speak of competence one aspect may well be the ability to solve complex social dilemmas. People who are conversationally sophisticated are able to successfully extricate themselves from social dilemmas with aplomb. Just as important, the technique of having people resolve dilemmas masks the obviousness of many self-reports of communication competence. The dilemma approach serves as a test of people's maximal skills in resolving difficult communication in a way that is not transparent. Of course, the procedures used in this study limit the strength of these findings. First, the measures of competence were personality indices that are commonly associated with conversational competence. But they do not directly measure competence. Second, people were given options to rate rather than being presented open-ended opportunities to describe what they might do in each dilemma. Although rating responses is a far easier procedure, the open-ended method might have provided participants with a better chance to evidence their optimal solutions. Finally, the task was not an interactive one. It may be that some highly competent communicators are better at structuring interactive situations than they are in rating responses.

DISCUSSION

Most conversations are relatively easy social events. We do them without much thinking, and we seem to more often than not accomplish most of our goals. But sometimes, often when we least expect it, we find ourselves in difficult communication encounters—dilemmas of social interaction in which there appears, at first, no way of extricating oneself from the exchange while maintaining positive relationships with the others involved in the interaction. This chapter represents a first investigation into these dilemmas.

To summarize briefly, we first introduced the concept of conversational dilemmas. We then created a typology of dilemmas that people face in social interaction. For a sample of these dilemmas we identified a series of responses that ranged from very sophisticated to very simplistic and ineffective. Undergraduates, varying in a number of personality traits related to communication competence, then rated their likelihood of using each alternative for each dilemma. Their ratings were compared to those of a "known" group of experts. We found that people who scored higher on the measures tied to competence also more closely resembled expert communicators' scores on the dilemmas questionnaire.

This chapter makes some important contributions to the communication literature. First, the notion of conversational dilemmas is an important one. There are traps people can fall into as they converse, and understanding their nature is an important challenge for communication scholarship. This chapter only takes a first look at this phenomena. It advances our knowledge in three ways. First, we present a preliminary typology of conversational dilemmas. The eight categories, although obviously having some degree of overlap, provide a parsimonious catalog of dilemma types. Future scholarship will need to examine the generality of the typology: Are there other categories? Which categories occur with what frequencies in different sorts of relationships? Do dilemmas within some of the categories present more difficult problems to communicators than dilemmas in other categories? Second, we identify a number of different ways people cope with conversational dilemmas. Again, future work will need to explore the six broad response categories along with the more specific responses falling within each category. Which responses work "best" in social interactions? Which responses are most preferred by others? Why do people select the responses they do? Third, we propose that dilemmas might serve as an integrative framework for a variety of difficult communication issues ranging from social confrontations to equivocal communication. Research on topics such as these might, when tied with the notion of dilemmas, offer a broader rubric for scholarship in the area of difficult communication. Future scholarship will need to examine the structure of these traps in a more formal fashion.

Second, the notion that these dilemmas might serve as a subtle index of people's communication competence offers some important potential directions for scholarship. In previous literature, with few exceptions, measures of competence that are not behaviorally based suffer from two interrelated problems: they are palpably obvious in their concern, and they focus on general self-evaluations. You are asked if you are a good or bad communicator, whether you pay attention in social interactions or not. As a field we lack good measures of cognitive competence—how smart people are about social interaction. When studying cognitive competence one might take a number of different avenues. One would be to test individuals' knowledge about communication based on knowledge claims proffered by communication scholarship. It is surprising that we do not have agreed upon tests of people's knowledge about social interaction after more than 30 years of systematic study. We have a number of knowledge claims that people should know about communication. Yet, measures do not exist that tap that knowledge. The dilemmas approach, described in this chapter, is another avenue—people in this procedure are challenged to find optimal solutions to difficult communication encounters. The material presented in this chapter is a first step. If research could devise a collection of dilemmas, along with scoring guides for the potential responses people might make to the dilemmas, we could well be on our way to developing such a measure. Within the frame of existing work, the notion of scoring people in relationship to their responses to dilemmas fits nicely with other scholarship exploring what it is to be a "savvy" or "smart" communicator. In addition to demonstrating sensitivity in complex ways, good communicators also are successful at extricating themselves from conversational dilemmas in ways that maintain positive face for both self and other.

There are clear limitations to the projects described in this chapter. For instance, everything reported is based on people's written responses to questionnaires. Although useful as a first probe of the concept, we are missing the critical interactive data that are necessary for a full explication of the concept. Social interaction involves two people both contributing and reacting to one another in the give and take of conversation. What one person says is a function of both people within a particular context. Future scholarship on conversational dilemmas needs to structure carefully situations so that there is true interactivity present. It would be both useful and interesting to create social events in which dilemmas naturally emerged. Examining how people in those interactive situations cope with the dilemmas, both as a victim and as a causal agent, would be fascinating.

Second, most actual conversational dilemmas occur, we would guess, among well-acquainted individuals. In the studies presented in this chapter, there was no relational information. It may well be that among friends, relatives, and significant others, the manner in which dilemmas are created and resolved are very different.

Third, in the studies described in this chapter, respondents were never given any goals when asked to generate instances of dilemmas or offer responses to dilemmas. Yet, social goals define what is appropriate, what should be done, and what should be avoided in conversation. Respondents might, given different goal states, offer very different responses to the scenarios they were asked to create or imagine. For example, in some settings, it matters to be polite. In other situations, politeness is far less important. Our general presumption has been that the resolutions of dilemmas are typically designed to save face for all involved. The more sophisticated move helps the interaction and relationship continue. In most cases, this is probably true. But there are instances in which more blunt, unsophisticated responses might be seen as desirable. For instance, interactants may create interpersonal dilemmas for the purposes of testing their relationship. I put you in a dilemma to see how you react. If you react in a way favorable to me, then great, but if you act in a more neutral or unfavorable manner, then you must not be my true friend. Similarly, if one has no desire to continue a relationship, or one feels terribly imposed on by another, even harshly negative responses might be appropriate.

Although both of these limitations need to be considered carefully in any discussion of competency, they may not affect in any substantive way the basic typology of dilemmas nor the typology of responses. Nevertheless, future scholarship may revise these presumptions. Understanding the unusual, the difficult, in conversation can offer special insights into the ways people communicate.

REFERENCES

Bateson, G., Jackson, D., Haley, J., & Weakland, J. H. (1956). Toward a theory of schizophrenia. *Behavioral Science, 1,* 251–264.

Bavelas, J. B. (1983). Situations that lead to disqualification. *Human Communication Research, 9,* 130–145.

Bavelas, J. B., Black, A., Chovil, N., & Mullet, J. (1990a). *Equivocal communication.* Newbury Park, CA: Sage.

Bavelas, J. B., Black, A., Chovil, N., & Mullett, J. (1990b). Truths, lies, and equivocations: The effects of conflicting goals on discourse. *Journal of Language and Social Psychology, 9,* 135–161.

Beck, A. (1988). *Love is never enough.* New York: Harper & Row.

Bond, C. F., & Anderson, E. L. (1987). The reluctance to transmit bad news: Private discomfort or public display. *Journal of Experimental Social Psychology, 23,* 176–187.

Briggs, S., Cheek, J., & Buss, A. (1980). An analysis of the self-monitoring scale. *Journal of Personality and Social Psychology, 38,* 679–686.

Brown, P., & Levinson, S. C. (1987). *Politeness: some universals in language use.* Cambridge, MA: Cambridge University Press.

Cialdini, R. B., Finch, J. F., & De Nicholas, M. E. (1990). Strategic self-presentation: The indirect route. In M. J. Cody & M. L. McLaughlin (Eds.), *The psychology of tactical communication* (pp. 194–206). Clevedon: Multilingual Matters.

Cunningham, M. A., & Wilcox, J. R. (1984). When an M.D. gives an R.N. a harmful order: Modifying a bind. In R. N. Bostrom (Ed.), *Communication yearbook 8* (pp. 764–778). Beverly Hills, CA: Sage.

Cupach, W. R., & Metts, S. (1990). Remedial processes in embarrassing predicaments. In J. Anderson (Ed.), *Communication yearbook 13* (pp. 323–352). Newbury Park, CA: Sage.

Daly, J. A. (1992). *Designing a national assessment of communication.* Paper completed for the U. S. Department of Education, National Center for Educational Statistics.

Daly, J. A., Bell, R., Glenn, P., & Lawrence, S. (1985). Conceptualizing communication complexity. *Human Communication Research, 12,* 30–53.

Daly, J. A., Vangelisti, A. L., & Daughton, S. M. (1987). The nature and correlates of conversational sensitivity. *Human Communication Research, 14,* 167–202.

Eisenberg, E. M. (1984). Ambiguity as strategy in organizational communication. *Communication Monographs, 51,* 227–242.

Gibb, J. R. (1961). Defensive and supportive communication. *Journal of Communication, 11,* 141–148.

Lewin, K. (1938). The conceptual representation and the measurement of psychological forces. *Contributions to Psychological Theory, 1*(4, Serial No. 4).

Lim, T., & Bowers, J. W. (1991). Facework: Solidarity, approbation, and tact. *Human Communication Research, 17,* 415–450.

Manis, M., Cornell, S. D., & Moore, J. C. (1974). Transmission of attitude-relevant information through a communication chain. *Journal of Personality and Social Psychology, 30,* 81–94.

McCroskey, J. C. (1978). Validity of the PRCA as an index of oral communication apprehension. *Communication Monographs, 25,* 192–203.

McLaughlin, M. L., & Cody, M. J. (1982). Awkward silences: Behavioral antecedents and consequences of the conversational lapse. *Human Communication Research, 8,* 299–316.

Newell, S. E., & Stutman, R. K. (1988). The social confrontation episode. *Communication Monographs, 55,* 266–285.

Rushing, W. A. (1962–1963). Social influences and the social-psychological function of deference. *Social Forces, 41,* 142–148.

Snyder, M. (1974). The self-monitoring of expressive behavior. *Journal of Personality and Social Psychology, 30,* 526–537.

Spitzberg, B. H., & Cupach, W. R. (1989). *Handbook of interpersonal competence research.* New York: Springer-Verlag.

Stamp, G. H., Vangelisti, A. L., & Daly, J. A. (1992). The creation of defensiveness in social interaction. *Communication Quarterly, 40*(2), 177–190.

Stein, L. I. (1967). The doctor–nurse game. *Archives of General Psychiatry, 16,* 699–703.

Tesser, A., & Rosen, S. (1975). The reluctance to transmit bad news. In L. Berkowitz (Ed.), *Advances in experimental social psychology* (Vol. 8, pp. 193–232). New York: Academic Press.

Turner, R., Edgely, C., & Olmstead, G. (1975). Information control in conversations: Honesty is not always the best policy. *Kansas Journal of Sociology, 11,* 69–89.

Watzlawick, P., Beavin, J., & Jackson, G. (1967). *Pragmatics of human communication: A study of interactional patterns, pathologies, and paradoxes.* New York: Norton.

Wiemann, J. (1977). Explication and test of a model of communication competence. *Human Communication Research, 3,* 195–213.

7

SOCIAL PREDICAMENTS

William R. Cupach
Illinois State University

This chapter examines a pervasive dark side of everyday social interaction—predicaments. Most individuals are capable of performing adequately in routine social interactions. Inevitably, however, we are faced with more challenging situations in which social performances are botched, expectations are disconfirmed, identities are threatened, interactions are disrupted, and persons are held accountable. Communication competence entails the ability of a social actor to avoid the pitfalls and pratfalls of social encounters to the extent possible and to gracefully repair problematic situations when they occur. The purpose of this chapter is to explicate the nature of social predicaments and the means by which communicators effectively manage such encounters.

PREDICAMENTS: WHEN DARKNESS FALLS

Predicaments are problematic situations characterized by awkwardness or difficulty. They occur when individuals are perceived to have acted incompetently, such as when behavior is judged to be inappropriate, ineffective, or foolish. Social predicaments engender "undesirable implications for the identity-relevant images actors have claimed or desire to claim in front of real or imagined audiences" (Schlenker, 1980, p. 125). Thus, in Goffman's (1967) terminology, predicaments produce symbolic implications that are face threatening. They are face threatening for the individual caught in the predicament because an unwanted image of the self has been projected to others (or at least the individual *thinks* an unwanted image has been portrayed). Predicaments are potentially face threatening to others to the extent they have been imposed on, and/or the events are seen to reflect badly on their own self-images.

The Structure of Predicament Episodes

A number of different labels have been employed to depict the variety of social predicaments. The most common approach is to identify precipitating circumstances or a trigger event. These have been referred to as faux pas (Harris, 1984), failure events (Cody & McLaughlin, 1985; Schönbach, 1980), incidents (Goffman, 1967), offenses (Blumstein et al., 1974), embarrassing circumstances (Miller, 1992), regrettable messages (Knapp, Stafford, & Daly, 1986), and face-threatening acts (Brown & Levinson, 1987). Adopting a more macroscopic approach, some scholars have discussed the structure of problematic situations under the rubrics of social confrontation episodes (Newell & Stutman, 1988), account episodes (Schönbach, 1980), rule-breaking episodes (Argyle, Furnham, & Graham, 1981), remedial episodes (Morris, 1985), and remedial interchanges (Goffman, 1971; Owen, 1983). Goffman (1967) described the familiar corrective interchange (also referred to as the remedial interchange; Goffman, 1971) as consisting of a sequence of moves following an "event" or "incident." These moves consist of: (a) challenge—calling attention to misconduct; (b) offering—"whereby a participant, typically the offender, is given a chance to correct for the offense and re-establish the expressive order" (p. 20); (c) acceptance—whereby the recipient of an offering indicates that it is satisfactory, and (d) thanks—in which "the forgiven person conveys a sign of gratitude" (p. 22).

Schönbach's (1980) depiction of the "account episode" is quite similar to Goffman's remedial interchange. It consists of four sequential phases: offense, reproach, account, and evaluation. These phases respectively correspond rather closely to Goffman's incident, challenge, offering, and acceptance moves. These sequential elements provide a useful and convenient framework for describing and studying predicaments; consequently, this chapter is roughly organized around these elements. However, it will become apparent that predicaments do not always conform to these lock-step phases (Buttny, 1985, 1987; Goffman, 1967; Newell & Stutman, 1988).

Types of Predicaments

Schönbach (1990) lamented the lack of a full-blown taxonomy for classifying predicaments. Nevertheless, research on a large subclass of predicaments, such as embarrassing situations, offers considerable insight into the nature and content of predicaments in general. Several researchers have developed category schemes to characterize the types of circumstances giving rise to embarrassing predicaments (Buss, 1980; Edelmann, 1987; Gross & Stone, 1964; Modigliani, 1968; Sattler, 1965; Sharkey & Stafford, 1990; Weinberg, 1968). Two recent, inductively derived classifications have been proposed by Cupach and Metts (1990) and Miller (1992).

Cupach and Metts (1990) presented a taxonomy that distinguishes predicaments caused by an actor versus those created by an observer. Predicaments are created by actors when they fail to maintain any one of three aspects of their social image. First, actors are motivated to show an Idealized Social Self, in which they follow social rules and exhibit dignity and poise during social interaction. Second, as part of their identity, actors are Accomplished Role Performers. This means that they are able to demonstrate certain skills and abilities, and that they are capable of meeting obligations and responsibilities associated with social roles. Third, individuals are expected to display their Idealized Self-Image. The positive image and reputation that one portrays for a certain audience currently and historically over time is expected to be upheld.

When individuals fail to maintain any of the three aspects of desired identity, they appear incompetent and fall into a predicament. Thus, predicaments arise when one violates rules due to forgetfulness, misinterpretation, or ignorance, as well as when one loses comportment (e.g., tripping, spilling, farting), because such behavior is incongruent with the idealized social self. When an actor fails to demonstrate an expected skill or fails to meet obligations and responsibilities (e.g., missing an appointment), he or she has failed as a role performer. When an actor gets caught lying or cheating, a predicament occurs because his or her behavior contradicts an idealized self-image.

In classifying embarrassing predicaments caused by another, Cupach and Metts (1990) distinguished between direct and indirect involvement of the embarrassed actor. Direct forms of involvement occur "when the embarrassed person is targeted explicitly as the recipient of the embarrassing act" (p. 345). Two categories of direct involvement are Individualization and Causing to Look Unpoised. Individualization includes receiving recognition or praise, being criticized or corrected, or being teased. Causing to Look Unpoised occurs when another intentionally or unintentionally makes an actor look foolish or discombobulated (such as by spilling a drink on the actor).

Indirect involvement in embarrassing situations can arise in three ways. Embarrassment by Association "occurs when the embarrassed person feels embarrassed because he or she is associated with someone who is enacting untoward behavior and assumes that negative attributions will be generalized to him or her from those actions" (p. 346). Empathic embarrassment occurs when one feels abashment for another's untoward behavior (see Miller, 1987). Privacy Violations result when personal, secret information is revealed to another. Recent empirical studies of embarrassing predicaments have evidenced the utility and generality of this taxonomy (Cupach & Metts, 1992; McPherson & Kearney, 1992).

A categorization of embarrassing circumstances reported by Miller (1992) exhibits considerable overlap with the Cupach and Metts (1990) scheme. Miller describes four general categories: Individual Behavior, Interactive Behavior, Audience Provocation, and Bystander Behavior. *Individual Behavior* includes normative public deficiencies such as physical pratfalls and inept performance, cognitive shortcomings such as forgetfulness, loss of control over possessions or body, and failures of privacy regulation. Also included in this general category are causing harm to others and conspicuousness. The category of *Interactive Behavior* includes two varieties. "Awkward interaction" involves circumstances in which an individual experiences a loss of script regarding how to proceed in an ongoing interaction or feels uncomfortable as a result of possessing guilty knowledge of a past incident. "Team embarrassment" is equivalent to Cupach and Metts's (1990) category of Association, in which the embarrassed individual is a member of a dyad or group that is responsible for a transgression.

Miller (1992) identifies two forms of *Audience Provocation*. This category includes events in which an audience publicizes one's past transgressions ("real transgressions"), as well as incidents in which others tease or badger a target in the absence of any real deficiency ("no real transgressions"). Finally, the third general category of *Bystander Behavior* consists of embarrassed feelings resulting from the actions of another which do not implicate the embarrassed actor, such as "empathic embarrassment."

Although these and other classification schemes for embarrassing situations offer considerable information about predicaments, additional research is needed to verify that the complete domain of all types of predicaments is represented. Moreover, obtaining actors' and observers' perceptions of relevant situational dimensions of predicaments would offer information to supplement the typical classification of events. Although his own preliminary taxonomic efforts were abandoned, Schönbach (1990) reported that his initial efforts included the following dimensions: "(1) type and degree of normative consensus, (2) type and degree of norm violations, (3) type and severity of consequences for victims and (4) type and degree of actors' involvement" (p. 183). Similarly, Edelmann (1987) has called for more elaborate classifications of embarrassing predicaments. He indicates that "orthogonal dimensions of rules known—rules not known; intentional action—accidental action; actor responsible—observer responsible; could provide a useful starting point" (p. 53).

Predicament Severity: How Dark Is It?

Clearly, one of the most important dimensions of a predicament is its severity. Predicaments vary considerably in degrees of complexity and severity, ranging from a minor faux pas to a serious moral breach. The relative severity of a predicament is based on two principal factors: the undesirability of the event, and the actor's apparent responsibility for the event (Schlenker, 1980; Snyder, 1985). The greater the undesirability and the greater the attributed responsibility, the more severe the predicament. These two factors parallel the fundamental dimensions that people use to appraise behavior, such as the valence of an act and the actor's linkage to the act (Snyder & Higgins, 1990).

The negative repercussions of a predicament occur in two primary domains. First, undesirability of an action can be judged in terms of the emotional effects on the actor. The affective consequences of predicaments range from amusement to anger, from mild and fleeting chagrin to intense and enduring shame or guilt. The state most frequently associated with predicaments (at least in the literature) is embarrassment (Cupach & Metts, 1990; Edelmann, 1987; Miller, 1992). The more personally distressing a predicament is for a person, the more severe it is.

Imahori and Cupach (1991) asked respondents in the United States and Japan to describe the feelings experienced during self-reported face-threatening predicaments. The emotions reported included: (a) awkward (clumsy, uncomfortable), (b) embarrassed, (c) stupid (unintelligent, ignorant, foolish, idiot), (d) ashamed (humiliated, loss of pride, loss of face), (e) guilty, (f) uncertain (tentative), (g) scared (worried, petrified, afraid), (h) regretful (sorry, awful, bad), (i) shocked (surprised, stunned), and (j) impatient. Interestingly, in the comparison between cultures, Japanese more frequently reported the emotions of shame and uncertainty, whereas Americans more frequently reported feelings of embarrassment and stupidity.

The aversive nature of predicaments stems principally from the negative attributions ascribed to an actor who has behaved inappropriately. Getting caught in a predicament potentially casts aspersions on one's character or social competence. Thus, an actor's reaction to a predicament is intimately tied to the perceived expectations and exhibited reactions of observers (e.g., Argyle et al., 1981).

Undesirability is also judged with respect to the impact of the predicament on others. As the negative consequences for others intensify, so does the severity of the predicament. Thus, causing embarrassment, inconvenience, annoyance, aggravation, or offensiveness for others exacerbates severity of the predicament for the actor.

Both actual and attributed responsibility for predicaments varies considerably. Goffman (1967) noted that some incidents are innocent and unwitting, others are incidental in that the transgression is anticipated but not spiteful, still other events entail malicious and spiteful intent. In classifying reasons for committing rule violations, Argyle et al. (1981) similarly suggest that some transgressions are deliberate (i.e., personal gain, trying to be funny), some "reflect inability on the part of the rule-breaker to recognize the applicability of the rule or to perform behaviors reflective of it," and some reflect "ignorance of the rule or of the conditions for its application" (p. 140). Whatever the actual responsibility, as an actor's perceived linkage to an untoward act increases, so does the severity of the predicament for the actor.

Engineering Predicaments

Although predicaments are generally to be avoided, individuals sometimes intentionally perpetrate predicaments. Consistent with the curvilinear relationship between competence and many functional behaviors (see Spitzberg, this volume), showing some weakness can make one appear human in the eyes of others and can enhance one's attractiveness under certain circumstances (Aronson, Willerman, & Floyd, 1966; Helmreich, Aronson, & LeFan, 1970). Employed as a form of self-handicapping, predicaments may reduce the performance expectations held by others. Creating mild predicaments for oneself can be used to elicit sympathy as well as to demonstrate one's ability to handle adversity.

Creating predicaments for others is also done intentionally. Sharkey (1991) found that individuals report a number of explicit goals for intentionally embarrassing another person, including showing solidarity, negatively sanctioning unwanted behavior, exercising power, discrediting another, and obtaining self-gratification. These same goals were attributed (by victims) to perpetrators of embarrassment in a study of college students who reported on incidents in which they were embarrassed by a teacher (McPherson & Kearney, 1992).

FINDING FAULT: ("WHO TURNED OUT THE LIGHTS!?")

Subsequent to the circumstances creating a predicament, there may or may not be explicit fault finding. The absence of a reproach or challenge does not deny the occurrence of a predicament. Sometimes a reproach, by virtue of the context, is superfluous. "In some settings (medical interviews, traffic court, explanations to parole boards, complaint departments), reproaches are not needed simply because the fundamental *purpose* of the communication exchange is to hear and evaluate accounts" (Cody & Braaten, 1992, p. 228).

On other occasions finding fault may be unnecessary because the offending party reproaches himself or herself. Offering an apology or engaging in self-castigation may obviate the need for others to call untoward actions into question. Similarly, disclaimers (Hewitt & Stokes, 1975), requests (Goffman, 1967), or politeness (Brown & Levinson, 1987) presented by a transgressor may soften a violation sufficiently to obviate the need for a reproach.

There also are situations in which an untoward or unexpected event occurs, but observers deem that offering a reproach may be unwise or inappropriate. If the predicament is one that embarrasses the actor but is not face threatening to others, then strategic inattention to the event may be warranted because calling attention to it may complicate matters for all concerned. It is not uncommon for an individual whose zipper is undone to remain uninformed about the mistake. If the predicament was intentionally staged in an effort to be amusing or humorous, then fault finding may be irrelevant, unless it is part of the staged performance. Alternatively, sanctioning of a transgression may be forfeited when the transgressor possesses higher social status, when administering a sanction may be more costly than it is worth, or there is a superseding rule that renders sanctioning inappropriate (Shimanoff, 1980).

When a reproach or sanction is given, it is typically motivated by one or more of the following factors: (a) to repair the transgression and restore equilibrium to social relations, (b) to obtain revenge or retribution for an unjustified transgression, and (c) to deter future transgressions. Comments following a transgression can be directed toward the actor's conduct during the failure event (i.e., criticizing the behavior, ascribing guilt, expressing disappointment, issuing a warning) and/or the actor's liability for the consequences of the event (i.e., making demands or threats, administering sanctions, forecasting dire predictions) (Schönbach, 1990).

McLaughlin, Cody, and O'Hair (1983) identified six forms of reproach: (a) silence, (b) behavioral cues such as looks of disgust, (c) projected concessions (e.g., "Aren't you sorry you did it?"), (d) projected excuses (e.g., "Were you stuck in traffic?"), (e) projected justifications (e.g., "Did you have something more important to do?"), and (f) projected refusals to account (e.g., "Don't try to pretend you didn't see me"). These reproach types function as solicitations of remedial responses from the offending actor.

Responses to a predicament can be located theoretically on a continuum of aggravation-mitigation (Cody & McLaughlin, 1985; Labov & Fanshel, 1977). Aggravating behaviors are aggressive, challenging, inflammatory, and generally escalate or exacerbate a face threat to the hearer. Mitigating moves are relatively more deferential, conciliatory, and generally attempt to minimize a face threat to the hearer. With respect to reproach forms, Cody and McLaughlin (1985) maintain that projected concessions and projected excuses are relatively mitigating, whereas silence and projected refusals are relatively aggravating. In a subsequent section, we shall see that observers to a predicament may offer supportive remedial strategies of their own instead of a reproach. In this broader context, all reproaches would be considered relatively more aggravating compared to protective remedial behavior.

Determinants of Reproaches and Sanctions

The issuance of a reproach or sanction depends on a number of factors. The most obvious and perhaps the most potent factor is the degree of offensiveness stemming from the predicament. The greater the offensiveness of a violation, the more appropriate and legitimate a reproach is perceived to be (Blumstein et al., 1974). As one's right to reproach is increasingly justified, the reproach itself is more likely to be direct, aggravating, and face threatening (e.g., Lim & Bowers, 1991). Not surprisingly, research demonstrates that the severity of offense typically is positively associated with the severity of reproach or sanction (Schönbach, 1990; Young & Cupach, 1991). Minor breaches typically elicit a simple correction, whereas a severe offense usually draws commensurate punishment.

The likelihood and degree of sanctioning for a transgression is moderated by the competence, reputation, and status of a transgressor. Hollander's (1960) work on group influence suggests that an individual who has displayed a history of conformity and competence acquires increasing status. Such status reflects an accretion of positive impressions regarding the individual, referred to as "idiosyncracy credits." The accumulating fund of these status credits eventually allows the individual to deviate from the norm with greater impunity. Consistent with this theory, Young and Cupach (1991) found, for example, that workers perceived to be generally competent at their jobs were sanctioned less severely for rule violations than were workers perceived to be less competent. This is consistent with evidence that the evaluation of accounts is affected by the prior reputation of a transgressor (Darby & Schlenker, 1989; Morris & Coursey, 1989). Similarly, the higher the status of a transgressor vis-à-vis the offended party, the more reluctant are those with lesser status to challenge a transgressor.

Beyond Reproach

Morris (1988) noted that there are other forms of fault finding besides reproaching or soliciting an account. He argues that the fault-finding process "is not typically to request clarification, merely disagree, or identify palpable faults, but rather to construct an interpretation that what someone did was problematic" (p. 4). According to preliminary research by Morris, the time focus of fault finding distinguishes methods for dealing with problematic behavior. Fault finding for past incidents typically involves determining whether or not a situation can be defined as problematic. This is followed by a negotiation of precisely what behavior was problematic, how it occurred, and who performed the behavior. "For presently occurring faults, the usual formula is for the fault finder to 'stop' the action and explain why he or she has done so" (p. 8). In order to prevent the potential future occurrence of a fault, an advisory or warning is issued.

Ambiguity surrounding the interpretation of an apparent predicament often stimulates discussion that logically precedes or even replaces a sanction. Newell and Stutman (1988, 1991) delineated the potential issues of disagreement in these so-called "social confrontation" episodes:

1. Is the implied rule mutually acceptable as legitimate?
2. Is this a "special" situation? That is, does some higher order rule take precedence over the implied rule?
3. If invoked, is the superseding rule mutually acceptable as legitimate?
4. Did the accused actually perform the behavior in question?
5. Does the behavior constitute a violation of the rule?
6. Does the accused accept responsibility for the behavior?

Thus, when a transgression stems from the apparent violation of a rule or expectations, attempts may be made to discern whether the rule is known, understood, applicable, endorsed, and enforceable in the current situation. Such discussions clearly deviate in numerous possible ways from the canonical form depicted by the "remedial interchange" or the phases of "accounting episodes."

REMEDIAL RESPONSES
(TURNING DARKNESS INTO LIGHT)

The maintenance of face is a functional imperative in social interaction. Consequently, when predicaments arise and face is threatened, individuals are motivated to cope with the problematic nature of the situation and to save face (Goffman, 1967; Modigliani, 1971; Petronio, 1984). Face work directed at repairing predicaments consists of remedial responses. The impetus for repair is grounded in an actor's perception that something has gone awry. This perception may or may not be primed initially by the reactions of others.

Remedial responses to a predicament serve several useful functions. First, remedial behavior, such as offering accounts and apologies, can help an individual cope with anxiety and stress (Cupach & Metts, 1990; Harvey, Orbuch, & Weber, 1990). In addition to lessening the immediate discomfort surrounding the problematic event, the ability to make amends for predicaments seems to render beneficial effects on an individual's esteem and health (Snyder & Higgins, 1988, 1990; Weiner, Figueroa-Munoz, & Kakihara, 1991). Second, remedial behavior addresses the inconvenience, offensiveness, or harm perpetrated on others, whether unintentionally or deliberately. This has the effect of mitigating negative attributions ascribed by offended others (Cupach & Metts, 1990), not to mention mitigating their face loss, anger, and potentially aggressive retaliation (Folkes, 1982; Ohbuchi, Kameda, & Agarie, 1989; Weiner, Amirkham, Folkes, & Verette, 1987; Weiner & Handel, 1985; Yirmiya & Weiner, 1986). Third, remedial behavior counteracts the potential escalation of interpersonal conflict (Schönbach, 1990) and restores stability and normality to the ongoing social interaction (Goffman, 1967).

As Goffman (1967) indicated, remedial behavior may be "defensively" offered by the actor responsible for a predicament or may be "protectively" offered by others. Defensive responses may or may not be prompted by an overt reproach or subtle nonverbal cues from others that expectations have been violated. Similarly, protective responses may be offered because the actor caught in a predicament looks chagrined and is signaling the need for assistance, or observers may offer help because the offending party seems not to have "sufficient sense of shame or appreciation of the circumstances to blush on his own account" (Goffman, 1967, pp. 99–100).

Defensive Responses

Avoidance. A common class of responses to predicaments involves various forms of avoidance. The principle underlying the use of avoidance is that calling further attention to some types of predicaments is unnecessary (because others have not been inconvenienced or irritated) and unwise (because it would serve to exacerbate the predicament) (Cupach & Metts, 1990). Indeed, everyday interactions are replete with instances of social actors strategically glossing over their own and each other's boo-boos. This is accomplished by acting as if no predicament exists, changing the conversational topic, and so on. Gracefully continuing with social interaction following a minor predicament demonstrates an actor's poise and minimizes the extent to which others become embarrassed or annoyed. An extreme form of avoidance occurs when one physically flees from an embarrassing or shameful encounter (Cupach, Metts, & Hazleton, 1986).

Humor. Humor is frequently a response to predicaments, partly because some predicaments are intended to be comical (Argyle et al., 1981; Knapp et al., 1986; Sharkey, 1991), and some are inherently funny in their consequences. Argyle and colleagues (1981) found, for example, that rule-breaking episodes are characterized by a fundamental underlying dimension ranging from humorous to irritating. Similarly, affective reactions to rule-breaking episodes were characterized by the dimension of laughter versus anger. If the predicament involves a harmless accident or flub, then laughter allows the release of nervous tension and signals that the problematic circumstances need not be taken too seriously. Making a joke out of a predicament can show that the offending actor acknowledges blameworthiness (as with a simple excuse or apology), whereas also allowing the actor to demonstrate poise and social competence (Edelmann, 1985; Fink & Walker, 1977).

Concession/Apology.   Apologies admit blame and seek atonement for untoward behavior (Goffman, 1967; Schlenker, 1980; Tedeschi & Riess, 1981). The form of an apology can range from a perfunctory statement such as "I'm sorry" to more elaborate forms including one or more of the following elements: (a) expression of regret or remorse, (b) requests for forgiveness, (c) self-castigation, (d) promises not to repeat the transgression in the future, and (e) offers of restitution (Goffman, 1971; Schlenker & Darby, 1981).

The mere display of one's anxiety or discomfort can functionally serve as a form of apology insofar as it demonstrates to others that the offending actor acknowledges and regrets the impropriety of his or her own behavior (Castelfranchi & Poggi, 1990). Merely appearing to be chagrined (by blushing or grimacing) can show one's self-effacement and thereby mitigate negative attributions that might be ascribed by observers (Edelmann, 1982; Semin & Manstead, 1982).

Accounting.   Accounts are verbal explanations given to explain inappropriate or awkward behavior (Scott & Lyman, 1968). Two general classes of accounts are excuses and justifications. These types of statements correspond to the fundamental dimensions of predicament severity: responsibility and valence. Excuses attempt to minimize the actor's responsibility for a predicament ("I didn't mean it," "I couldn't help it," "It's not my fault"). Justifications reframe a transgression by downplaying its negative implications ("It's not so bad," "It's for your own good"). There are numerous varieties of excuses and justifications. Several authors have expanded and refined Scott and Lyman's (1968) original typology of accounts, including Schlenker (1980), Schönbach (1980, 1990), Semin and Manstead (1983), and Tedeschi and Riess (1981).

Refusals.   Schönbach (1990), among others, considers refusals to be a distinct category of accounting, though they could be considered an extreme form of excuse. Refusals include a refutation of the allegation that a failure event occurred or that the accused was involved in such an event.

Physical Remediation.   Physical remediation involves behavioral (nonverbal) correction or repair of damage attendant on a predicament. This includes such acts as zipping up one's pants, cleaning up a spill, fixing a broken toy, and so forth (Metts & Cupach, 1989; Semin & Manstead, 1982; Sharkey & Stafford, 1990).

Protective Responses

Due to the cooperative and interdependent nature of symbolic interaction, interlocutors are compelled to protect the face of others as well as self. As Goffman (1967) commented, heartless is the person who will "witness another's humiliation and unfeelingly retain a cool countenance" (pp. 10–11). Observers have a vested interest in assisting actors whose face has been threatened, lest the interaction becomes so disrupted that the observers experience discomfort and face threat.

Most of the strategies employed by actors caught in a predicament can be utilized as well by observers on the actor's behalf. It is not uncommon for observers to offer an excuse for the offending actor or assist in physical remediation. Humor is also a common strategy, although it entails some risk as the inferred line between laughing "with" the actor and laughing "at" the actor can be blurry (Cupach & Metts, 1990). Similarly, attempts to avoid calling attention to an untoward act are expected, particularly for minor infractions. However, such inattention can exacerbate discomfort on some occasions.

Observers also have unique remedial responses at their disposal that can be particularly effective in diminishing the abashment felt by the actor creating the predicament. In fact, one study found that observers were much more effective than actors in ameliorating the actor's embarrassment following a predicament (see Cupach & Metts, 1990). In particular, observers can offer help by expressing empathy, communicating to the distressed actor that his or her predicament is not unique or uncommon. They can also offer support by indications of positive regard in spite of the predicament. Metts and Cupach (1989) found that approximately half of all remedial responses offered by observers were such displays of empathy and support.

Schönbach (1990) presents a more general and elaborate taxonomy of opponent reactions during the phases of reproach and evaluation. This taxonomy includes macro-categories of comments on accounts, comments on failure events, comments on actor's personality, and comments on the relationship between actor and opponent. Particularly relevant are the subcategories for "positive" comments on failure events. These include variations on the following: (a) inability, unwillingness, or hesitation to comment on the event; (b) attribution of guilt or responsibility for the occurrence of the event to persons other than the actor; (c) positive comments on the actor's conduct during the failure event (exculpation, understanding, appeasement, friendly advice); and (d) positive comments on the actor's liability for the consequences of the failure event (exoneration, waiving of claims, pardon, compassion, offers of help).

It is difficult on an a priori basis to classify general remedial response categories on the aggravation–mitigation continuum. First, the assessment of remedial responses, including the relative politeness of such responses, is highly context bound. Certainly, some responses are more effective across contexts than others. Apologies and excuses seem to be generally mitigating and more consistently effective than justifications or denials (e.g., Cupach et al., 1986; Gonzales, 1992; Holtgraves, 1989; Riordan, Marlin, & Gidwani, 1988). But the relative level of aggravation or mitigation will be moderated by situational factors such as the reputation and status of the transgressor, the relationship between transgressor and victim, prior history of transgressions, and so on. Second, differences in the tactical instantiation of any remedial strategy are likely to produce differences in the consequences of the remedial behavior. The "quality" of an account influences its evaluation (Bies, Shapiro, & Cummings, 1988; Hale, 1987). The content of any particular type of remedial response can be quite variable; not all "excuses," for example, are created equal. Denial of intent seems to be a more effective excuse compared to other types (Cody & McLaughlin, 1988). Research has yet to untangle the complexities of which types of accounts are more or less efficacious. Third, the delivery of a remedial response, such as the nonverbal characteristics, can substantially alter or modify the evaluative consequences of remedial messages. Two different apologies containing precisely the same verbal message will be interpreted differently depending on how sarcastic, sincere, or genuine the apology "sounds." Repentance must evidence a ring of sincerity to merit forgiveness.

Factors Influencing Selection of Remedial Strategies

As predicaments become more severe, actors experience greater negative repercussions and are more motivated to engage actively in remedial behavior (Schlenker, 1980). Frequently, therefore, as the severity of a predicament increases, so too does the mitigating nature of remedial responses. As the actor's responsibility for an act and the negative nature of an act increase, offending actors are more likely to offer concessions, more explicit and elaborate apologies, and apologies that are accompanied by accounts (Cupach & Metts, 1992; Fraser, 1981; Knapp et al., 1986; McLaughlin, Cody, & O'Hair, 1983; Schlenker & Darby, 1981). These responses serve to counteract the negative evaluations made by others when consequences of the predicament are mild or moderate. However, when the severity of consequences stemming from a predicament is high, then defensive accounting behavior may follow (e.g., Felson & Ribner, 1981; Hupka, Jung, & Silverthorn, 1987;

Schönbach, 1990). Cody and Braaten (1992) also suggest that more defensive and aggravating responses are also likely when a "person is *wrongly* accused of a severe failure event, or a person is correctly accused of having caused a failure event, but the severity of the failure event has been exaggerated" (p. 240).

The nature of a reproach also affects the subsequent remedial response. Aggravating reproaches seem to intensify an already face-threatening situation. Aggravating reproaches tend to provoke aggravating accounts (Cody & McLaughlin, 1985). The more severe a reproach, generally the more defensive is the subsequent account (Schönbach & Kleibaumhuter, 1990). In synthesizing the findings from several studies (Cody & McLaughlin, 1985; McLaughlin et al., 1983; McLaughlin, Cody, & Rosenstein, 1983), Cody and Braaten (1992) explain:

> When an aggravating reproach form was used, the aggravating reproach form functioned as an interactional constraint that interfered with the account-giver's freedom to communicate an intended or preferred form of an account. Confronted with hostility, direct rebukes, expressions of moral superiority, projected refusals or reproaches that exaggerate the severity of the offense, account-givers became less conciliatory and more defensive. (p. 230)

Mitigating reproaches, however, are followed by a wider range of account types. In these situations, the conciliatory or defensive nature of an account is determined by such factors as perceived guilt and responsibility of the transgressor, severity of the offense, and the nature of the relationship between the reproacher and the reproached (Cody & McLaughlin, 1985).

Other situational factors surrounding a predicament also affect remedial responses. For example, predicaments perpetrated by others (such as being teased) are more likely to lead to aggravating responses (e.g., aggression) (Cupach & Metts, 1992; Metts & Cupach, 1989).

Strategies employed to cope with embarrassing predicaments are tailored to the nature and degree of face loss attendant on the situation. Sharkey and Stafford (1990) asked respondents to recall and describe three different embarrassing incidents: one in which they were highly embarrassed, one in which they were moderately embarrassed, and one in which they were mildly embarrassed. The researchers failed to discover differences in the use of remedial strategies across the three levels of embarrassment intensity. However, they did find differences in responses depending on the cause of the embarrassment. For example, embarrassed persons responded to criticism from others most often with hostility, whereas they responded to violations of privacy with remediation (such as closing the door, buttoning a blouse).

Metts and Cupach (1989) solicited recollections of highly embarrassing incidents and classified them into four types (see Weinberg, 1968): (a) faux pas (i.e., misinterpreting a situation, such as wearing informal attire to a formal function), (b) accidents (i.e., unintentional awkward acts such as tripping or belching), (c) mistakes (i.e., performing ineptly, such as forgetting one's checkbook to pay for groceries), and (d) recipient (i.e., being the victim of another's face-threatening act, such as being ridiculed by another, or another person invading the actor's privacy). Descriptive accounts of remedial strategies indicated that excuses were more likely to be offered in mistake situations, but less likely to be offered in recipient situations. Justifications were more likely in faux pas situations, whereas humor and remediation were more likely in accident situations. As would be expected, aggression was used by embarrassed actors who were recipients of the face-threatening behavior of another, such as being teased, ridiculed, or criticized. This corresponds to results reported by Sharkey and Stafford (1990) and Cupach and Metts (1992).

Cupach and Metts (1992) found that apologies were given by embarrassed actors more frequently in situations of rule violations and failed role performance. These types of incidents are more likely than other types (such as loss of comportment) to threaten the face of others and disrupt the social order. Hence, relatively mitigating remedial moves directed at others are clearly appropriate. Accounts were more likely to be offered in situations of damaged self-image. Because these events call into question the actor's face, it is logical that accounts be used to redefine the actor's role in the predicament and the severity of event. Humor was more likely to appear in situations in which the actor lost comportment, but less likely when the actor vicariously experienced the observed chagrin on another (i.e., empathic embarrassment).

EVALUATING REMEDIAL RESPONSES

Given that there are multiple goals in the enactment of remedial behavior, and there are multiple parties to a remedial episode, the relevant consequences are potentially numerous. Thus, the question of whether a remedial response is effective remains a complex and relative one.

In the final analysis, people are not judged strictly by their actions that create a predicament. The evidence suggests that "people do not react so much to what we do, but rather to the interpretation we provide for our acts" (Blumstein et al., 1974, p. 558). Thus, the remedial response to a predicament exerts a potent influence on the evaluations made about erring social actors.

In general, apologetic behavior seems important in minimizing negative repercussions for an actor who has committed a transgression. But apologies (and other remedial responses) must be legitimate; they should be commensurate with the seriousness of the offense (Scott & Lyman, 1968). As predicaments become more severe, apologies need to be more elaborate. More elaborate apologies produce less blame, more forgiveness, more liking, perceptions of greater remorse, and sometimes less punishment (Darby & Schlenker, 1982, 1989). Apologies, when seen as sincere, are almost always (at least partially) effective. "The apology-forgiveness sequence may be such a familiar script that its appearance automatically benefits the actor" (Darby & Schlenker, 1989, p. 362). On the other hand, as remedial responses become increasingly defensive, evaluations of the offender become more negative (Schönbach, 1990). Of course, contextual factors will influence judgments regarding how defensive a particular response is, as well as the relative appropriateness of such a response.

Although apologies consistently mitigate negative consequences of predicaments, complete confession of guilt may or may not work in favor of a confessor. Weiner and colleagues (Weiner, Graham, Peter, & Zmuidinas, 1991) conducted a series of studies to assess the effects of confession on forgiveness. They found that if an actor is perceived to have committed a transgression, confession was especially advantageous when given prior to being accused and when the causal attribution for the transgression is ambiguous. Additionally, they demonstrated that "evaluation must be determined by factors other than the outcome, particularly the perceived character of the accused, if the confession is to have positive effects for the confessor" (p. 309). Thus, confessing to a traffic violation will likely result in punishment, regardless of whether the violator is perceived as a "good" person. In this context, the evaluative response is based strictly on the attribution of fault.

The "honoring" of remedial responses to a predicament represents their "acceptance," and thereby signals the effective repair of the problematic situation. Remedial responses that are honored are not necessarily truthful, but they must at least be credible and comport with background knowledge (Scott & Lyman, 1968). Riordan, James, and Runzi (1989) explored the accounts given for a failure in a work context. Less than half of the time truthful accounts were proffered to explain the failure event. When contrived explanations were given, they were seen by the accounters as more believable than the truthful reasons. The contrived explanations were also perceived to be more commonly given by others as explanations, compared to the truthful explanations that were withheld. Other research indicates that believability, perceived sincerity, and adequacy of accounts are associated with less negative attributions about the character of a transgressor (Bies & Shapiro, 1987; Bies et al., 1988; Riordan, Marlin, & Kellogg, 1983). Thus, acceptability of an account to the audience is an important criterion when those caught in a predicament select a remedial response.

From an attributional framework, Weiner and his colleagues (Weiner & Handel, 1985; Weiner et al., 1987, 1991) offered some evidence regarding the content of normative (and hence effective) accounts (which they generically refer to as excuses). In general, "good" excuses that are given because they are seen as "acceptable" are those that identify external, uncontrollable, and unstable causes. "Bad" excuses, considered nonnormative and therefore typically withheld, are those that cite internal and controllable causes.

As alluded to previously, the perceived character and reputation of an actor can interact with remedial responses to affect evaluations of actors in a predicament. Tedeschi (1990) explained that remedial behaviors which are "intended to protect identities, are themselves made more or less effective by the identities of the actor" (p. 319). Particularly when ambiguity surrounds a predicament, an actor's good reputation can enhance impressions of an actor (Darby & Schlenker, 1989) as well as believability of an account (Morris & Coursey, 1989). Moreover, an actor who possesses a good reputation and expresses remorse may receive more lenient punishment (Darby & Schlenker, 1989).

It is worth noting that the honoring of an account in principle does not necessarily mitigate punishment. In some circumstances, an offender may inflict self-punishment and thereby obviate the need for others to do so. However, even under circumstances in which an account has successfully mitigated negative attributions of character and responsibility for the offensive act, recommendations for punishment may still be enforced due to the seriousness of the breach (e.g., Felson & Ribner, 1981; Riordan et al., 1983). Even when an apology is "accepted," some form of compensation for wrongdoing may be expected as well.

It should also be noted that the overt acceptance of remedial behavior is not tantamount to its "honorability" (Blumstein et al., 1974). An offended worker may be obligated to publicly honor an excuse or apology presented by his or her boss (e.g., for forgetting an important appointment), yet privately disbelieve the excuse and denigrate the moral worth of the boss. Public acceptance and private judgments of character and competence may differ, especially when constraining norms are present (e.g., against public criticism of others) (Schlenker, 1980; Tedeschi, 1990).

THINGS THAT GO BUMP IN THE NIGHT AREN'T ALL BAD

This chapter began with the premise that social predicaments represent a "dark" side of interaction. Certainly, the undesirable features of predicaments are fairly obvious. Predicaments create varying degrees of personal distress and are associated with a host of unpleasant emotions, including embarrassment, shame, guilt, humiliation, anger, contempt, regret, and sorrow. Interpersonally, predicaments disrupt interaction and often can escalate conflict between people. It is tempting to conclude, therefore, that predicaments are events that should be strictly prevented, hidden, or quickly fixed. But like other problematic areas of social interaction, the dark elements of predicaments tend to obscure some of the functional aspects of their occurrence.

Predicaments permit people to cope constructively with the imperfect fit between expectations and social performance that is often inevitable in social interaction. They play an important role in socializing actors regarding the inappropriateness of certain behaviors. The aversive nature of emotions associated with predicaments teaches us the existence of social norms, as well as the importance of maintaining our own dignity and showing respect to others. Predicaments therefore offer a social mechanism for regulating interpersonal behavior in a civil manner.

As well as facilitating interpersonal control, predicaments can foster affiliation between people. Getting caught in a predicament shows one's fallible side, which may ultimately facilitate attraction. Successfully repairing a predicament demonstrates one's interpersonal competence. An important byproduct of this competence is that individuals cooperate to help each other save face and thereby confirm their identities. Indeed, predicaments are not infrequently engineered by partners as a mechanism to foster solidarity in their relationship (Sharkey, 1993). In short, predicaments are endemic to social interaction. When they are managed competently, they allow people to save face, coordinate mutually shared meanings, and regulate interpersonal behavior.

REFERENCES

Argyle, M., Furnham, A., & Graham, J. A. (1981). *Social situations*. Cambridge: Cambridge University Press.

Aronson, E., Willerman, B., & Floyd, J. (1966). The effect of a pratfall on increasing interpersonal attractiveness. *Psychonomic Science, 4*, 227–228.

Bies, R. J., & Shapiro, D. L. (1987). Interactional fairness judgments: The influence of causal accounts. *Social Justice Research, 1*, 199–218.

Bies, R. J., Shapiro, D. L., & Cummings, L. L. (1988). Causal accounts and managing organizational conflict. *Communication Research, 15*, 381–399.

Blumstein, P. W., Carssow, K. G., Hall, J., Hawkins, B., Hoffman, R., Ishem, E., Maurer, C. P., Spens, D., Taylor, J., & Zimmerman, D. L. (1974). The honoring of accounts. *American Sociological Review, 39*, 551–566.

Brown, P., & Levinson, S. (1987). *Politeness: Some universals in language usage*. Cambridge: Cambridge University Press.

Buss, A. H. (1980). *Self-consciousness and social anxiety*. San Francisco: W. H. Freeman.

Buttny, R. (1985). Accounts as a reconstruction of an event's context. *Communication Monographs, 52*, 57–77.

Buttny, R. (1987). Sequence and practical reasoning in accounts episodes. *Communication Quarterly, 35*, 67–83.

Castelfranchi, C., & Poggi, I. (1990). Blushing as discourse: Was Darwin wrong? In W. R. Crozier (Ed.), *Shyness and embarrassment: Perspectives from social psychology* (pp. 230–251). Cambridge: Cambridge University Press.

Cody, M. J., & Braaten, D. O. (1992). The social-interactive aspects of account-giving. In M. L. McLaughlin, M. J. Cody, and S. J. Read (Eds.), *Explaining one's self to others: Reason-giving in a social context* (pp. 225–243). Hillsdale, NJ: Lawrence Erlbaum Associates.

Cody, M. J., & McLaughlin, M. L. (1985). Models for the sequential construction of accounting episodes: Situational and interactional constraints on message selection and evaluation. In R. L. Street & J. N. Cappella (Eds.), *Sequence and pattern in communicative behavior* (pp. 50–69). Baltimore: Edward Arnold.

Cody, M. J., & McLaughlin, M. L. (1988). Accounts on trial: Oral arguments in traffic court. In C. Antaki (Ed.), *Analyzing everyday explanation: A casebook of methods* (pp. 113–126). London: Sage.

Cupach, W. R., & Metts, S. (1990). Remedial processes in embarrassing predicaments. In J. A. Anderson (Ed.), *Communication yearbook 13* (pp. 323–352). Newbury Park, CA: Sage.

Cupach, W. R., & Metts, S. (1992). The effects of type of predicament and embarrassability on remedial responses to embarrassing situations. *Communication Quarterly, 40*, 149–161.

Cupach, W. R., Metts, S., & Hazleton, V. (1986). Coping with embarrassing predicaments: Remedial strategies and their perceived utility. *Journal of Language and Social Psychology, 5*, 181–200.

Darby, B. W., & Schlenker, B. R. (1982). Children's reactions to apologies. *Journal of Personality and Social Psychology, 43*, 742–753.

Darby, B. W., & Schlenker, B. R. (1989). Children's reactions to transgressions: Effects of the actor's apology, reputation and remorse. *British Journal of Social Psychology, 28*, 353–364.

Edelmann, R. J. (1982). The effect of embarrassed reactions upon others. *Australian Journal of Psychology, 34*, 359–367.

Edelmann, R. J. (1985). Social embarrassment: An analysis of the process. *Journal of Social and Personal Relationships, 2*, 195–213.

Edelmann, R. J. (1987). *The psychology of embarrassment.* Chichester, UK: John Wiley & Sons.

Felson, R. B., & Ribner, S. A. (1981). An attributional approach to accounts and sanctions for criminal violence. *Social Psychology Quarterly, 44*, 137–142.

Fink, E. L., & Walker, B. A. (1977). Humorous responses to embarrassment. *Psychological Reports, 40*, 475–485.

Folkes, V. S. (1982). Communicating the reasons for social rejection. *Journal of Experimental Social Psychology, 18*, 235–252.

Fraser, B. (1981). On apologizing. In F. Coulmas (Ed.), *Conversational routine: Explorations in standardized communication situations and prepatterned speech* (pp. 259–271). New York: Mouton Publishers.

Goffman, E. (1967). *Interaction ritual: Essays on face-to-face behavior.* New York: Pantheon Books.

Goffman, E. (1971). *Relations in public.* New York: Basic Books.

Gonzales, M. H. (1992). A thousand pardons: The effectiveness of verbal remedial tactics during account episodes. *Journal of Language and Social Psychology, 11*, 133–151.

Gross, F., & Stone, G. P. (1964). Embarrassment and the analysis of role requirements. *American Journal of Sociology, 70*, 1–15.

Hale, C. L. (1987). A comparison of accounts: When is a failure not a failure? *Journal of Language and Social Psychology, 6*, 117–132.

Harris, T. E. (1984). The "faux pas" in interpersonal communication. In S. Thomas (Ed.), *Communication theory and interpersonal interaction* (pp. 53–61). Norwood, NJ: Ablex.

Harvey, J. H., Orbuch, T. L., & Weber, A. L. (1990). A social psychological model of account-making in response to severe stress. *Journal of Language and Social Psychology, 9*, 191–207.

Helmreich, R., Aronson, E., & LeFan, J. (1970). To err is humanizing—sometimes: Effects of self-esteem, competence, and a pratfall on interpersonal attraction. *Journal of Personality and Social Psychology, 16*, 259–264.

Hewitt, J., & Stokes, R. (1975). Disclaimers. *American Sociological Review, 40*, 1–11.

Hollander, E. P. (1960). Competence and conformity in the acceptance of influence. *Journal of Abnormal and Social Psychology, 61*, 365–369.

Holtgraves, T. (1989). The form and function of remedial moves: Reported use, psychological reality and perceived effectiveness. *Journal of Language and Social Psychology, 8,* 1–16.

Hupka, R. B., Jung, J., & Silverthorn, K. (1987). Perceived acceptability of apologies, excuses and justifications in jealousy predicaments. *Journal of Social Behavior and Personality, 2,* 303–314.

Imahori, T. T., & Cupach, W. R. (1991, March). *A cross-cultural comparison of the interpretation and management of face: American and Japanese responses to embarrassing predicaments.* Paper presented at the Conference on Communication in Japan and the United States, California State University, Fullerton, CA.

Knapp, M. L., Stafford, L., & Daly, J. (1986). Regrettable messages: Things people wish they hadn't said. *Journal of Communication, 36,* 40–58.

Labov, W., & Fanshel, D. (1977). *Therapeutic discourse: Psychotherapy as conversation.* New York: Academic Press.

Lim, T. S., & Bowers, J. W. (1991). Facework: Solidarity, approbation, and tact. *Human Communication Research, 17,* 415–450.

McLaughlin, M. L., Cody, M. J., & O'Hair, H. D. (1983). The management of failure events: Some contextual determinants of accounting behavior. *Human Communication Research, 9,* 208–224.

McLaughlin, M. L., Cody, M. J., & Rosenstein, N. E. (1983). Account sequences in conversations between strangers. *Communication Monographs, 50,* 102–125.

McPherson, M. B., & Kearney, P. (1992, November). *Classroom embarrassment: Types, goals, and face saving strategies.* Paper presented at the Speech Communication Association convention, Chicago, IL.

Metts, S., & Cupach, W. R. (1989). Situational influence on the use of remedial strategies in embarrassing predicaments. *Communication Monographs, 56,* 151–162.

Miller, R. S. (1987). Empathic embarrassment: Situational and personal determinants of reactions to the embarrassment of another. *Journal of Personality and Social Psychology, 53,* 1061–1069.

Miller, R. S. (1992). The nature and severity of self-reported embarrassing circumstances. *Personality and Social Psychology Bulletin, 18,* 190–198.

Modigliani, A. (1968). Embarrassment and embarrassability. *Sociometry, 31,* 313–326.

Modigliani, A. (1971). Embarrassment, facework, and eye contact: Testing a theory of embarrassment. *Journal of Personality and Social Psychology, 17,* 15–24.

Morris, G. H. (1985). The remedial episode as a negotiation of rules. In R. L. Street, Jr. & J. N. Cappella (Eds.), *Sequence and pattern in communicative behaviour* (pp. 70–84). London: Edward Arnold.

Morris, G. H. (1988). Finding fault. *Journal of Language and Social Psychology, 7,* 1–25.

Morris, G. H., & Coursey, M. (1989). Negotiating the meaning of employees' conduct: How managers evaluate employees' accounts. *Southern Communication Journal, 54,* 185–205.

Newell, S. E., & Stutman, R. K. (1988). The social confrontation episode. *Communication Monographs, 55,* 266–285.

Newell, S. E., & Stutman, R. K. (1991). The episodic nature of social confrontation. In J. A. Anderson (Ed.), *Communication yearbook 14* (pp. 359–392). Newbury Park, CA.

Ohbuchi, K., Kameda, M., & Agarie, N. (1989). Apology as aggression control: Its role in mediating appraisal of and response to harm. *Journal of Personality and Social Psychology, 56,* 219–227.

Owen, M. (1983). *Apologies and remedial interchanges: A study of language use in social interaction.* Berlin: Mouton.

Petronio, S. (1984). Communication strategies to reduce embarrassment: Differences between men and women. *Western Journal of Speech Communication, 48,* 28–38.

Riordan, C. A., James, M. K., & Runzi, M. J. (1989). Explaining failures at work: An accounter's dilemma. *The Journal of General Psychology, 116,* 197–205.

Riordan, C. A., Marlin, N. A., & Gidwani, C. (1988). Accounts offered for unethical research practices: Effects on the evaluations of acts and actors. *Journal of Social Psychology, 128,* 495–505.

Riordan, C. A., Marlin, N. A., & Kellogg, R. T. (1983). The effectiveness of accounts following transgression. *Social Psychology Quarterly, 46,* 213–219.

Sattler, J. M. (1965). A theoretical, developmental, and clinical investigation of embarrassment. *Genetic Psychology Monographs, 71,* 19–59.

Schlenker, B. R. (1980). *Impression management: The self-concept, social identity, and interpersonal relations.* Monterey, CA: Brooks/Cole.

Schlenker, B. R., & Darby, B. W. (1981). The use of apologies in social predicaments. *Social Psychology Quarterly, 44,* 271–278.

Schönbach, P. (1980). A category system for account phases. *European Journal of Social Psychology, 10,* 195–200.

Schönbach, P. (1990). *Account episodes: The management or escalation of conflict.* Cambridge: Cambridge University Press.

Schönbach, P., & Kleibaumhuter, P. (1990). Severity of reproach and defensiveness of accounts. In M. J. Cody & M. L. McLaughlin (Eds.), *The psychology of tactical communication* (pp. 229–243). Clevedon, England: Multilingual Matters.

Scott, M. B., & Lyman, S. M. (1968). Accounts. *American Sociological Review, 33,* 46–62.

Semin, G. R., & Manstead, A. S. R. (1982). The social implications of embarrassment displays and restitution behavior. *European Journal of Social Psychology, 12,* 367–377.

Semin, G. R., & Manstead, A. S. R. (1983). *The accountability of conduct: A social psychological analysis.* London: Academic Press.

Sharkey, W. F. (1991). Intentional embarrassment: Goals, tactics, and consequences. In W. R. Cupach & S. Metts (Eds.), *Advances in interpersonal communication research, 1991* (pp. 105–128). (Proceedings of the Western States Communication Association Interpersonal Communication Interest Group.) Normal, IL: Personal Relationships Research Group, Illinois State University.

Sharkey, W. F. (1993). Who embarrasses whom? Relational and sex differences in the use of intentional embarrassment. In P. J. Kalbfleisch (Ed.), *Interpersonal communication: Evolving interpersonal relationships* (pp. 147–168). Hillsdale, NJ: Lawrence Erlbaum Associates.

Sharkey, W. F., & Stafford, L. (1990). Responses to embarrassment. *Human Communication Research, 17,* 315–342.

Shimanoff, S. B. (1980). *Communication rules: Theory and research.* Beverly Hills, CA: Sage.

Snyder, C. R. (1985). The excuse: An amazing grace? In B. R. Schlenker (Ed.), *The self and social life* (pp. 235–260). New York: McGraw-Hill.

Snyder, C. R., & Higgins, R. L. (1988). Excuses: Their effective role in the negotiation of reality. *Psychological Bulletin, 104,* 23–35.

Snyder, C. R., & Higgins, R. L. (1990). Reality negotiation and excuse-making: President Reagan's 4 March 1987 Iran arms scandal speech and other literature. In M. J. Cody & M. L. McLaughlin (Eds.), *The psychology of tactical communication* (pp. 207–228). Clevedon, England: Multilingual Matters.

Tedeschi, J. T. (1990). Self-presentation and social influence: An interactionist perspective. In M. J. Cody & M. L. McLaughlin (Eds.), *The psychology of tactical communication* (pp. 310–323). Clevedon, England: Multilingual Matters.

Tedeschi, J., & Riess, M. (1981). Verbal strategies in impression management. In C. Antaki (Ed.), *The psychology of ordinary explanations of social behavior* (pp. 271–309). New York: Academic Press.

Weinberg, M. S. (1968). Embarrassment: Its variable and invariable aspects. *Social Forces, 46,* 382–388.

Weiner, B., Amirkhan, J., Folkes, V. S., & Verette, J. A. (1987). An attributional analysis of excuse giving: Studies of a naive theory of emotion. *Journal of Personality and Social Psychology, 52,* 316–324.

Weiner, B., Figueroa-Munoz, A., & Kakihara, C. (1991). The goals of excuses and communication strategies related to causal perceptions. *Personality and Social Psychology Bulletin, 17,* 4–13.

Weiner, B., Graham, S., Peter, O., & Zmuidinas, M. (1991). Public confession and forgiveness. *Journal of Personality, 59,* 281–312.

Weiner, B., & Handel, S. (1985). Anticipated emotional consequences of causal communications and reported communication strategy. *Developmental Psychology, 21,* 102–107.

Weinberg, M. S. (1968). Embarrassment: Its variable and invariable aspects. *Social Forces, 46,* 382–388.

Yirmiya, N., & Weiner, B. (1986). Perceptions of controllability and anticipated anger. *Cognitive Development, 1,* 273–280.

Young, C. N., & Cupach, W. R. (1991, February). *Determinants of sanctions for organizational rule violations.* Paper presented at the Western States Communication Association convention, Phoenix, AZ.

8

DECEPTION

H. Dan O'Hair
Texas Tech University

Michael J. Cody
University of Southern California

An open society living by a rhetoric of deception cannot long endure.
—Wayne Booth, 1974

Keep your tongue from evil, And your lips from speaking deceit.
—Psalms 34, 13

One thing I want to tell you now and you can be sure of it. As your president, I will never tell you a lie.
—Jimmy Carter, 1976 presidential campaign

Deception is a message strategy much like other forms of communication in that it is purposeful, often goal directed, and frequently functions as a relational control device. Deceptive messages are distinct as communication strategies because they serve to produce the very results most communicators attempt to avoid: false impressions and erroneous assumptions. A chapter devoted to deception in a volume exploring the dark side of interpersonal communication presents a number of opportunities, not the least of which is a chance to proselytize about our personal views. In spite of the moralistic implications of the dark side label, we focused our efforts on a variety of research programs to provide a broad picture of deception as an interpersonal communication strategy.

THE NATURE AND SCOPE OF DECEPTION

What Is Deception?

Defining *deception* is not an easy task because the number of interpretations for this communication strategy are as varied as there are people using it. We are fortunate that a number of scholars have made attempts toward generalizing a conceptualization that could capture the dynamic properties of deceptive communication. Buller and Burgoon (in press, p. 3) define deception "as the intent to deceive a target by controlling information (e.g., transmitting verbal and nonverbal messages and/or manipulating situational cues) to alter the target's beliefs or understanding in a way which the deceiver knows is false." Implicit in their definition is intention to deceive and expected target misunderstanding as parameters to separate lesser forms of fabrication (e.g., transparent lies, mistaken lies, self-deception). This approach is compatible with Knapp and Comadena (1979, p. 271) who argue deception to be "the conscious alteration of information a person believes to be true in order to significantly change another's perceptions from what the deceiver thought they would be without the alteration." The foregoing discussion suggests, therefore, that deception must be a conscious and intentional act. A slightly different perspective was offered by Ekman (1985, p. 28) in his book *Telling Lies*: "In my definition of a lie or deceit, then, one person intends to mislead another, doing so deliberately, without prior notification of this purpose, and without having been explicitly asked to do so by the target."

These perspectives on deception focus more on message strategy than motives; in fact, with a few exceptions, most communication scholars elude the issue of ethics and morality when discussing deception. Obviously, it is easier to examine cognition and behavior associated with deceptive acts than render an opinion about the moralistic motivation of liars. A general assumption among communication and social psychology researchers is that deception is a communication strategy employed for specific purposes. Whether deception is reprehensible and therefore one of the dark sides of interpersonal communication is an issue yet to be addressed. We should note at this point that research on deception does not include compulsive liars who believe that what they are saying is the truth, when in fact it is not, nor do we include self-deception as the situation in which a person has reconstructed reality to appear innocent, blameless, a victim, and so on. We only consider communication episodes in which one communicator knowingly and purposefully fosters a false belief in another person.

Our definition varies from the other viewpoints in that we believe deception is a more broadly conceived communication strategy than simply altering a target's beliefs or understanding. Previous definitions seem to focus on one act of deception—lies. Although we do not view deception as broadly as some (Hopper & Bell, 1984), we do realize that deceptive acts can occur even in contexts in which the receiver may suspect deception but is willing to allow the deceiver the benefit of a doubt, or in contexts in which the deceiver may suspect deception, thereby not having his or her beliefs altered, but condones the use of strategy. Further, we do not construe deception exclusively as a complete and successful communication transaction. Attempted deception is still deception. Therefore, we define *deception* as the conscious attempt to create or perpetuate false impressions among other communicators.

How Prevalent Is Deception?

An important consideration of deception as a dark side of communication is the prevalence with which this strategy is employed in interpersonal relationships. There is some limited empirical data that point to a prevalent tendency for its use. Turner, Edgley, and Olmstead (1975) conducted a study that discovered approximately 62% of conversational statements made by subjects could be classified as deceptive. This translates into only 38% of communication acts as completely truthful. Venant (1991) reported survey research from several sources and concluded that deception is a widespread communication phenomenon. A nationwide survey of 5,700 people concluded that 97% of respondents had lied and nearly one-third of married respondents had cheated on their spouses. A decade earlier, *Psychology Today* polled its readership (24,000 returned questionnaires) and determined that 88% had told white lies in the past year and one-third deceived their best friend about something significant (Hassett, 1981).

Bok, a noted ethicist at Brandeis University, believes that based on the me-first attitude of the 1980s and the example of dishonesty set by businesspersons and politicians, most people feel little hesitation in distorting the truth (Venant, 1991). The popularity of deceptor extraordinaire Col. Oliver North painfully illustrates Professor Bok's claim. The following dialogue occurred between Lt. Col. Oliver North and George Van Cleve, minority counsel for the committee, during the Senate Iran-Contra Committee (Carlson, 1987, p. 34):

Van Cleve: You've admitted before this committee that you lied to representatives of the Iranians.

North: I lied every time I met the Iranians.

Van Cleve: And you admitted that you lied to General Secord with respect to conversations that you had with the president? Is that correct?

North: In order to encourage him to stay with the project, yes.

Van Cleve: And you admitted that you lied to the Congress. Is that correct?

North: I have.

Van Cleve: And you admitted that you lied in creating false chronologies of these events. Is that correct?

North: That is true.

Van Cleve: Can you assure this committee that you are not here now lying to protect your commander in chief?

North: I am not lying to protect anybody, counsel. I came here to tell the truth.

In an informal study conducted by these authors (see Table 8.4, later in this chapter), 59% of respondents indicated either deception was a prevalent communication strategy, or that it had its place in interpersonal communication. Considering the plethora of news coverage depicting business executives, politicians, and religious leaders as cheats and liars, it is little wonder that survey respondents possess such a cavalier attitude about lying and deception. There is a general consensus that deception, unethical acts, and cheating increased dramatically over the past several years. Unfortunately, only a few projects have been conducted concerning either the frequency by which people admit lying or the perceived acceptability of lies (see discussion later in the chapter). There are several alternative viewpoints regarding the proliferation of deception: Deception is becoming a fairly commonplace event, our society's definition of deception is broader today (including withholding, con games, etc.), or more people report or talk about deception today because it appears to be more commonplace and is less negatively evaluated, relative to several decades ago.

How Are Types of Deception Differentiated?

One of the areas that has received a great deal of attention in the deception area is the specification of categories, taxonomies, or classes of deceptive acts. One mentioned previously was developed by Turner et al. (1975). In a study of 130 subjects five categories of deception were found. Lies were communication acts that distorted the truth by providing contradictory information to what the agent (deceiver) knew to be the truth. The second category of deception was exaggerations and was depicted as a communication act that provided more information (quantity and quality) than what the truth called for. Half-truths were deceptive acts in which the agent controlled the level of information such that only part of the truth was revealed or that the agent modified or qualified the message in order to soften or minimize the impact of the truth. Subjects revealed a category of deception termed *secrets*, in which agents would remain silent when they in fact had information needed or requested by targets. The final category discovered by Turner et al. is *diversionary responses*, in which the agent will provide information that diverts the topic to a new area so that the agent will not have to tell the target either a lie or the truth (i.e., changes the subject). Turner et al. found that diversionary responses accounted for 32% of deceptive acts committed, followed by lies (30%), half-truths (29%), exaggerations (5%), and secrets (3%).

Ekman (1985) in his book *Telling Lies* specifies two categories of deception. *Concealment* is a type of lie in which one person withholds information from the other in order to perpetuate an erroneous assumption about facts or emotions. *Falsification*, like concealment, is a tactic used to conceal true information, but goes even further by deliberately conveying false information. Sometimes concealment is all a deceiver needs to accomplish goals (e.g., remaining silent about a crime), whereas falsification is necessary when confrontation or proactive behavior is required (e.g., manipulating a co-worker).

Metts and Chronis (1986) identified three forms of deceptive acts that occur in interpersonal relationships: falsifications, half-truths, and concealments (the latter two categories were broken down into separate affective and information areas). Metts and Chronis reported slightly different results from Turner et al. in that falsification accounted for almost half of deceptive acts (48%), followed by concealments (27%) and half-truths (23%).

Perhaps the most encompassing category of deception types was proposed by Hopper and Bell (1984) in an attempt to broaden this context. Their research led to a six-dimensional taxonomy that includes *fictions* (exaggeration, tall tale, white lie, make believe, irony, myth), *playings* (joke, tease, kidding, trick, bluff, hoax), *lies* (dishonesty, fib, lie, untruth, cheating), *crimes* (con, conspiracy, entrapment, spy, disguise counterfeit, cover-up, forgery), *masks* (hypocrisy, two-faced, back stabbing, evasion masking, concealment), and *unlies* (distortion, mislead, false implication, misrepresent). As one can observe, this system goes well beyond the normal contexts of interpersonal communication. However, it is a useful system, in that it provides a detailed description of most of the deception contexts that are likely.

An often cited treatise from the field of philosophy suggested eight different methods of deception (Chisholm & Feehan, 1977). These strategies were divided into two categories: deception by commission and deception by omission. *Deception by commission* is a group of four deception strategies in which the agent actively engages in communication to cause a target to be deceived. One strategy is when an agent causes a target to acquire a belief in deception. Another strategy involves the agent in causing the target to continue a belief in deception. A third strategy is when an agent causes a target to cease to believe in nondeception, whereas a fourth strategy is one in which the agent prevents a target from acquiring nondeception. *Deception by omission* consists of strategies in which the agent passively allows the target to be deceived. In the first case, an agent will allow a target to acquire a belief in deception from external sources without intervening to set the target straight. Another strategy of this type is when the agent will allow the target to continue a belief in deception. The third type of deception is somewhat different in that the agent will allow the target to cease to have a belief in nondeception. The final case is when the agent allows the target to continue without the belief in truth.

So far we have discussed deception as a unilateral action in which one person perpetrates a falsification on another. *Collaborative deception* is also common and involves communication that both agent and target recognize as deception but collude to carry out the act in a seemingly, mutually negotiated manner (Knapp & Comadena, 1979). Andersen (in press) suggested five types of collaborative deception. First, situations occur when lies are expected or anticipated. Negotiating the price of a house would qualify for this category (A: "I couldn't get a loan for that much money"; B: "I am taking a loss on the house as it is"). A second type of collaborative deception is when lies are used to mutually benefit the self-esteem of the participants. Participants involved in "bragging" sessions or gaming such as "playing the dozens" (insulting behavior) or one-upmanship ("Oh yeah, well I can top that . . .") would represent this category. Collaborative lies may also be used to minimize situational embarrassment. An agent may be put in a situation in which to tell the truth would create embarrassment for self or others. Instead, a lie that is recognized by a target may be sanctioned for the purpose of extricating the parties from an uncomfortable situation. Take the example of two couples out on a date, and one couple asks the other if they would like to go back to their house for a nightcap. The other couple knowing that the first couple wants to head straight for the bedroom, declines saying that they have early morning appointments (on Sunday?) the next day. Targets recognize such strategies as potential deception and collude to make it work.

Andersen mentions a fourth category of collaborative deception that has as its motive the avoidance of consequences of detecting the deception. There are many things in this world that people simply do not want to know about. Employers and teachers do not always want to know the motives behind absenteeism, parents are not always interested in their children's behavior so long as it does not harm them, college administrators do not always want to know where faculty are when they are not in their offices. The agent and the target collaborate to prevent unwanted information from entering into the relationship. In a similar vein, Andersen suggests a fifth category termed the requested lie. This type of deception occurs when the potential target requests that the agent deceive him or her in order to preserve feelings, the status quo, and so on. Students sometimes ask that professors not tell them when they are doing poorly in class. Spouses may ask that their counterparts not reveal their infidelities (Andersen, in press). Collaborative lies seem to be a special case of deception because agent and target work together to make the deceptive act successful. However, as we will see later, the long-term consequences of collaborative lies may not be significantly different than other types of lies.

It could be argued that collaborative lies do not qualify as deceptive acts because the target does not harbor any false belief. There are several reasons why collaboration should be considered a deceptive act. First, our definition of deception suggests that this form of communication is an attempt to create or perpetuate a false impression among communicators. Collaborative lies work to perpetuate false impressions, although communicators may understand the motives and deeper meaning involved in the interaction. Third parties may actually believe the fabrication. Second, it is quite possible that instances of collaborative deception are only "apparent" deceptions on the surface. An adulterous husband may lie to his wife about infidelities, thinking that she does not really want to know, when in fact the wife is a very trusting person. Third, collaborative lies may begin as a cooperative action, but rapidly transform into other types of deception. If requested lies become repeated and routine ("You don't mind if I'm a little overweight?"), the requester/target of deception may begin believing in the lie requiring the deceiver to engage in a more independent form of deception.

A concept similar to deception is that of equivocation. Bavelas, Black, Chovil, and Mullett (1989, p. 28) defined *equivocation* as "nonstraightforward communication; it appears ambiguous, contradictory, tangential, obscure, or even evasive." Some would argue that this could qualify as a definition of deception. According to Bavelas et al., equivocation is used when the truth may be too painful or create too much difficulty for those involved, but when deception or lying is not a viable communication strategy. A classic example often used to depict equivocal communication is when Person A asks Person B his or her opinion about A's new hairstyle. Even though B thinks the new hairstyle stinks, rather than lie and say it looks beautiful or tell the truth and say it is one of the worst, B would say "it is very interesting." B, therefore, is not committed to a valanced point of view and can extricate him- or herself from the situation without lying and without hurting A's feelings.

Bavelas et al. argue that, given a choice, an agent will equivocate truth rather than lie, that is, the agent will provide irrelevant information instead of misrepresenting information. We feel that this is an overgeneralization for several reasons. First, this is an empirical question yet to be addressed. Second, the numerous surveys and widespread anecdotal evidence reveals that lying and deception are very prevalent phenomenon. Third, equivocal truth may be more difficult to construct and less plausibly perceived than a lie. Bavelas et al.'s own work suggests that equivocation requires a longer response latency than lying, suggesting that it may be more cognitively difficult to communicate. Furthermore, equivocation may require subsequent messages that would lead to lies anyway ("interesting huh, in what ways?"). Fourth, this is a generalization that ignores and obscures certain parameters that are likely to predict strategy selection. Situational variables could make direct communication (truth, lies) more desirable than equivocation. The following list represents some of those situational variables likely to affect strategy selection:

Motives: self- vs. other benefits, avoiding punishment, avoid embarrassment, protect others, avoid conflict, status building, avoid interaction, protect self-esteem, acquire resources, etc.

Consequences: guilt, discovery/detection, loss of self-esteem, loss of trust/respect, sequential interaction [cover-up], punishment, hurt others, backfires, etc.

Target tolerance for equivocation: apathy toward topic/person = high tolerance; high tolerance = equivocation; low tolerance = choose truth/lie?

Confrontation potential: many targets will not confront liars but will confront equivocators, possibly requiring subsequent interaction

Consent of target: conspiracy theory, collaborative lies

Concern for success: equivocation = mixed message, if it is important that it be received positively, truth/lie might be best strategy

Types of lies: prepared—opportunity for rehearsal and contingency planning, spontaneous response may require different strategy

Intimacy: intimacy usually leads to an increase in relational goals

Dominance: dominant agents have a wider range of potential strategies, low dominance agents must also be concerned about image goals

Rights: extent to which agent believes actions are legitimate, warranted, and justified; superiors may perceive more rights (interactions with dominance) and use truth "your report was poor"

Situational apprehension: fear of failure, fear of success, etc.

We do not claim to review all of the taxonomies related to deceptive acts, nor are we interested in examining every viewpoint expressed in this area. Rather, the preceding discussion allows us an opportunity to synthesize deceptive acts into a taxonomy that captures the essence of strategies people use to prevaricate the truth. We have constructed a 5-level taxonomy of deceptive acts based on the research reviewed in this section. This taxonomy is more representative of interpersonal deception than Hopper and Bell, and more detailed than some of the others reported earlier (see Ekman, 1985; Metts & Chronis, 1986). Furthermore, by limiting ourselves to five categories, subsequent discussion will proceed more easily. As displayed in the taxonomy (see Fig. 8.1), varying levels of deception/truth are represented, allowing greater latitude in behavioral and moralistic attributions. *Lies* represent direct acts of fabrication intending to create a belief in the

Deceptive Act	Description	Supporting Research
Lies	Self-initiated; falsification; barefaced; deceive	Chisholm & Feehan; Ekman; Hopper & Bell; Metts & Chronis; Turner et al.
Evasion	Equivocation; other-initiated; fabrication; understatement; diversionary tactic	Bavelas et al, Chisholm & Feehan; Metts & Chronis; Turner et al.
Overstatement	Exaggeration; embellishment; self-promotion; fantasy	Hoppper & Bell; Turner et al.
Concealment	Masking, omission; facade; diguise; secrets	Chisholm & Feehan; Ekman; Hopper & Bell; Metts & Chronis; Turner et al.
Collusion	Cooperative; collaborative; mutual action	Andersen; Ekman; Knapp & Comadena; Rodriguez & Ryave

FIG. 8.1. Taxonomy of deceptive acts.

receiver contrary to the truth or facts. *Evasion* is a category encompassing those behaviors intended to sidestep or redirect communication away from sensitive topics. Equivocation is included among these behaviors. *Concealment* behaviors attempt to hide or mask true feelings or emotions, whereas *overstatements* are deceptive acts intended to exaggerate or magnify facts or data. Finally, *collusion* is a grouping of behaviors in which deceiver and target cooperate, at least initially, in allowing deception to succeed. Subsequent discussion takes advantage of the category system of deceptive acts outlined here.

What Are the Behavioral Forms of Deception?

A different way of conceptualizing acts of deception involves categorizing the verbal and nonverbal behaviors associated with deceptive acts. Extensive research has examined the behaviors that accompany deception, those involving conscious and intentional acts, and those that are unintentional and unmonitored. Space does not allow a detailed examination of behaviors observed in the hundreds of studies in this area, but category systems have been developed that summarize the behavior of deceivers (see Andersen, in press; Buller & Burgoon, in press; Zuckerman, DePaulo, & Rosenthal, 1981). We discuss three behavioral categories of deception that have appeared recently.

Buller and Burgoon (in press) summarized deceptive acts by utilizing a strategic approach. They identified seven relational message categories organized into two sets: intentional or strategic, and leakage or nonstrategic. Strategic behaviors are those manipulated by deceivers with the goal of presenting oneself behaviorally that portrays truthfulness and veracity. Because deceivers know that deception can produce detection cues, they will strategically attempt to form an honest impression through specific behaviors thought to be indicative of veracity. The strategic list of behaviors includes *uncertainty or vagueness* or behaviors used to demonstrate ambiguity or to send intentionally mixed messages. Specific behaviors included in this category include irrelevant information, conditional language, shorter responses, fewer references to self-experiences, more frequent hand shrugs, and fewer absolute verbs. A second strategic category identifies *nonimmediacy, reticence, and withdrawal* behaviors that are used as messages used in creating distance with others or withdrawing oneself from direct interaction. Behaviors in this group include shorter responses, verbal nonimmediacy, longer response latencies, less eye gaze, less forward lean, and greater proxemic distance. *Disassociation* was mentioned as the third strategic deception category and can be described as messages used to divert responsibility for a previous message or an attempt to remove self from the act of deception. Behaviors associated with disassociation include fewer self-references, fewer self-interest statements, more other references, and verbal nonimmediacy. The final strategic category was labeled *image and relationship protecting behavior*. These behaviors attempt to present oneself in a favorable light in hopes of diverting attention away from deception scrutiny. Behaviors such as nodding, smiling, refraining from interruptions, and suppression of leakage cues constitute this category.

Nonstrategic leakage cues differ from strategic behaviors in that deceivers are unaware of these cues revealing deception or are unable to control them in preventing deception detection. These behavioral cues are "leaked" out by the deceiver. The nonstrategic leakage list of behaviors includes three categories: *revealing arousal and nervousness, revealing negative affect*, and *incompetent communication performance*. Arousal and nervousness behaviors are typified by more blinking, higher pitch, vocal nervousness, more speech errors, longer response latencies, less gesturing, more leg and foot movements, and fewer facial changes. Negative affect can be observed from displeasurable facial expression, less positive feedback, reduced eye gaze, less pleasant vocal tone, and more negative statements. Finally, behaviors that demonstrate incompetent communication performance could include more speech errors, hesitations, word repetitions, rigidity, halting, brief messages, channel discrepancies and dissynchrony, exaggerated performances, lack of spontaneity, and departure from normal behavior.

Andersen (in press) proposed a behavioral category of deception in a different way. Based on previous research (Andersen, Andersen, & Landgraf, 1985; Shennum & Bugental, 1982), Andersen suggested that five types of deception can be displayed through facial expressions alone. The first type was labeled *simulation* which refers to a communicator expressing feelings and emotions when none are actually felt (feigning happiness when you have no emotion). Second, *intensification* is the act of exaggerating feelings (acting more happy than you actually are). *Inhibition* is the attempt to conceal completely your true feelings (not letting people know you are surprised), and *miniaturization* is reducing or softening the intensity of felt emotions or feelings (sick smile hiding how low you feel). Finally, *masking* refers to demonstrating a facial expression that is opposite or unrelated to true feelings (e.g., a nurse may smile at a burn victim in an emergency room in order to show support, although she may be repulsed at his appearance).

A third method of describing the behavioral production of liars (and truth tellers) was proposed by O'Hair, Cody, Goss, and Krayer (1988). Instead of employing a microanalytic approach to deception cues, the O'Hair et al. study utilized a macroanalytic technique. An honesty profile was developed based on evaluators' assessments of liar's and truth teller's communicator style (Norton, 1978, 1983). Evaluators found both liars and truth tellers to be more honest when they were perceived as more attentive, friendly, precise, and demonstrating a low dramatic style. The importance of this study centered on the willingness of honesty evaluators to make judgments of veracity based on macrobehaviors. Without baseline behavioral data to use as a benchmark, communicators may be judging honesty less on specific behaviors (eye contact, response latency, hand shrugs, etc.) and more on general communicator style.

The Buller and Burgoon, the Andersen et al., and the O'Hair et al. behavioral systems are helpful to our study of deception as a dark side of interpersonal communication for several reasons. First, these deception categories illuminate the various strategies that deceivers have at their disposal for manipulating information and emotions for specific purposes. The behavioral act of deception is quite complex. The Buller and Burgoon system allows greater explanatory power based on deceivers' decision and (in)ability to strategically control behavior. Second, it is obvious from these categories that the degree of reprehensibility could vary according to the behaviors involved (e.g., masking some behaviors may protect other's self-esteem). Moreover, behaviors (cues) may be leaked more openly if guilt or deception apprehension are present (Ekman, 1985). We discuss the relative valence of deception in a later section. Third, these categories allow numerous opportunities for comparing deceptive acts (see Fig. 8.1) with behavioral production. For example, future research might address how strategic behaviors are associated with evasion, or investigate the relationship between intensification behaviors and overstatement acts, or how animated liars are more likely to avoid collusion when accommodating behaviors by the target might be required.

THE FUNCTIONS OF DECEPTION

So far, our discussion depicts deception as a prevalent strategy among communicators, and that a diverse array of deceptive acts and behavioral cues have appeared in research reports. The pervasiveness of deception in interpersonal encounters suggests that well-meaning and generally honest people must find this tactic useful or functional in various situations. First, occupations often require deceptive acts in order to function properly. Police officers must lie to protect their undercover image, nurses or physicians lie to patients about their condition or the pain they will experience to build confidence and ensure compliance with treatment regimen, FBI agents deceive terrorists about their plight if they will release the hostages, and negotiators purvey an intimidating persona when negotiating major financial deals when in fact they are frightened of their adversary. Numerous other professions must create and maintain a certain public image that may be deceptive in order to serve the best interests of their employers and customers (e.g., airline attendants, customer service representatives, receptionists, etc.). A plethora of government officials have deceived agencies, congress, and constituencies in the public interest or in defense of national security.

Then there is the issue of politeness in conversation. Turner et al. (1975) found that most people do not want to voice direct interpersonal disagreement, rather they will be deceptively polite in order to go along with the flow of social interaction. Thus, a person might say *Batman Returns* is my favorite movie, and we politely say, "Gee, I liked it well enough. It had good scenery and special effects," when in fact, we hated the movie so much we left in the middle. The person who is brutally honest will be a very lonely person.

Collusion (collaborative lies) is another case when deception becomes a functional issue. Both people agree to accept one explanation for an event, when at least one of them knows that the explanation is false. Take, for example, postrelational breakup depression (see Canary & Cody, 1994, for a broader explanation). A man leaves his wife for another woman. The ex-wife confides in a friend about how awful she was treated and what a bad man the ex-husband was over the years. Part of the normal process of accounting for a traumatic event such as this is to tell stories (narratives) that pull together various aspects of the 10-year history of relational problems. When the ex-wife does this, she may place all the blame on the husband, exaggerate his faults, and accept no blame or responsibility for the failed marriage. As a friend, we hear the story and agree with her—although we know that she was a person who was difficult to live with and isn't completely free of responsibility. We collaborate about this lie so that the friend feels better about herself, and we feel we are helping her by agreeing with falsehoods. However, as the months pass, if our friend doesn't move past this phase and begin to cope realistically with her own role, our tolerance of, and collusion in agreeing with, an untrue narrative ceases to be functional. A true friend, at this stage of the game, would serve as a reality check for our friend's assessment and account of the breakup.

MORALITY AND DECEPTION?

Defining, describing, and typing deceptive acts provide a benchmark for recognizing what may constitute deception. By drawing on the descriptive level, we can better understand whether deception can be considered one of the dark sides of interpersonal communication, that is, how can determinations be made about the sanctionableness of deceptive acts? Prevailing opinion suggests that not all deception is dark and reprehensible (Andersen, in press; Buller & Burgoon, in press; Camden, Motley, & Wilson, 1984; Ekman, 1989; Hopper & Bell, 1984), rather, the valence of a particular lie depends on three factors: motives, consequences (Ekman, 1989; Goffman, 1974), and ethical considerations.

Motives

Goffman (1974) dichotomized the motives for deception along two lines that he termed benign and exploitive fabrications. *Benign fabrications* are "engineered in the interest of the person contained by them, or, if not quite in his interest and for his benefit, then at least not done against his interest" (p. 87). Conversely, *exploitive fabrications* serve the interests of the deceiver. In other words, if deception is communicated to meet the needs of others, then such acts are more innocuous in comparison to deception that is self-serving.

Buller and Burgoon (in press) are particularly insistent on a motives perspective to judging the acceptability of deception. Taking a strategic approach to deception they argue, "it is the motivations behind deception, not the deceptive act itself, whose morality should be judged. . . . We believe an amoral perspective on deception is more likely to encourage research and thinking about the broader process of deception" (p. 4). In other words, if a deceiver has good intentions and is motivated to serve the interests of others, deception is an acceptable form of communication. In concert with this notion, Spitzberg and Cupach (1984), in making a case for communication competency, suggest that if a lie is both appropriate and effective it may serve the best interests of the communicator. However, predicting the situational factors affecting appropriateness and effectiveness is not an easy task.

Hample (1980) conducted research into the reasons or motives behind deceptive behavior using several hundred subjects in a multistudy design. His results led him to construct a 4-part taxonomy of deception motives: lies that benefit the deceiver, lies that benefit the relationship that the deceiver is a member of, and lies that benefit the deceived. The fourth category was termed "other." The second and third types of lies could be considered benign deception using Goffman's terminology, whereas the first type may fall into the exploitive category. The results from Hample's sample indicated that two-thirds of all self-reported liars engaged in deception for selfish reasons. In a follow-up study, Camden et al. (1984) proposed a typology of motives that included four basic categories. Basic needs are lies that are told to acquire or protect resources (money, possessions, time, privacy, etc.). Lies are also told to enhance or decrease affiliation. Lies of this type are told in order to initiate, continue, or avoid interaction, avoid conflict, leave take, avoid self-disclosure, and redirect conversation. The third type of lie involves self-esteem needs. Liars may deceive in order to protect their image of competence, to enhance their image relating to taste, or to improve their status relating to social desirability. The final category of lies described by Camden et al. was termed "other" and includes three parts: dissonance reduction in which a liar may lie to her- or himself in order to reduce the discomfort associated with cognitive dissonance, practical jokes, and exaggeration for effect. Camden et al. labeled all of these deceptions white lies, or "socially somewhat accepted, capable of generating little or no negative consequences to the recipient, etc." (p. 309). As we examine these types of lies they do not appear any more "white" than those described by Hample.

A third and related study was conducted by Lippard (1988) who identified eight primary motivation categories for deception. These motivations for lying and their relative frequency were as follows: (a) resources (deception used to acquire or protect resources; 13%), (b) affiliation (deception used to manipulate interaction with others; 8%), (c) self-protection (deception used for protecting image or avoiding self-disclosure; 17%), (d) conflict avoidance (using deception to avoid confrontation, lectures, or questions of fidelity; 29%), (e) protection of others (preventing harm, worry, or discomfort for others; 18%), (f) manipulation of others (using deception to create guilt, sympathy, or attempting to control another's behavior; 4%), (g) obligation excuse (deception used to extricate oneself from a failure event; 10%), and (i) joke (tricking, teasing others; 2%). No doubt the reader recognized categories similar to those reported earlier. The noteworthy aspect to Lippard's study is relative frequency of deception in each of the categories. Respondents report more "self-defense" strategies than in other studies.

Ekman (1989), in conducting research for his book *Why Kids Lie*, interviewed 65 children in an attempt to confirm previous motivational categories for lying. He discovered that children lie to avoid punishment, acquire resources, protect friends, protect self or others from harm, win admiration, avoid awkward situations, avoid embarrassment, maintain privacy, and exert power over an authority. Although cast in slightly different terminology, the motives children use for deception are not dissimilar from those employed by adults.

By way of summarizing the various categories pertaining to motives for deception, we have developed a taxonomy representing what we feel are the purposes or reasons behind deceptive acts. The preceding discussion serves as a resource base for forming the categories involved in the taxonomy. It seems that deception motives can be classified into six categories that are determined by two dimensions: valence and target. Motives for deception have valence in that such acts pursue positive or negative goals. Motives also have a target for which deception is intended to affect most directly. Deception motives may be targeted to benefit or affect self, some other person, or a relationship. Figure 8.2 presents the taxonomy in tabular form.

Deception is often used to benefit self. *Egoism* is a self-directed motive employing deceptive strategies intended to protect, preserve, or promote the self-concept or self-esteem of the deceiver. It carries a positive valence because these deception tactics do not intend any harm to others, and positive benefits are expected for the deceiver. Deception with the intent of *exploitation* serves selfish motives with the purpose of gaining at the expense of other people. It is a negative, self-directed motive because deception strategies used in support manipulate or harm others. In a relevant study (Shippee, 1977), it was interesting to note that experimental participants reported that other people lie most often to prevent bad things from happening to them (egoism) instead of lying to make good things happen to them (exploitation).

Deceptive strategies are also employed for the purpose of helping, influencing, and manipulating others. Message strategies directed toward the advancement and security of others are termed *benevolence*. Included in this category would be acts with the goal of protecting or promoting the resources, self-worth, or safety of other people. *Malevolence* is a deception motive with the intent of hurting or harming others. Revenge, vindictiveness, retaliation, sadism, sabotage, and hatefulness would serve as examples of malevolent deception. Shippee's study discovered that people lie most often to hurt other people (malevolent) rather than to help them (benevolent).

Valence \ Motive	Self	Other	Relational
+	Egoism	Benevolence	Utility
−	Exploitation	Malevolence	Regress

FIG. 8.2. Taxonomy of motives for deception.

A third target for deception is interpersonal relationships. Again, we can point to the valence dimension and recognize positive and negative relational motives. Positive relational deception strategies are termed *utility* and usually focus on tactics intended to improve, enhance, escalate, and repair relationships. Other instances of the utility motive include avoiding conflict, promoting intimacy, and relational maintenance. *Regress* is a category depicting negative relational motives. Unlike the negative motives of exploitation and malevolence, regress has one goal in mind—damage or stagnation to a relational system. One individual may not necessarily want to hurt a relational partner but perceives conditions warranting a regress in the relationship itself. Attempts at relational deescalation, disintegration, disengagement, and even termination would be included in this category. For instance, one relational partner may tell another that she no longer feels any attraction for the relationship because she knows that she is becoming too deeply involved. In this case, the relational partner lies about her attraction level to avoid getting hurt in the relationship at a later time.

In this taxonomy, we have avoided a complicated system of motives that could easily become cumbersome and unwieldy as subsequent discussion of the entire deception process ensues (consequences, behavior, motives, etc.). Furthermore, we have intentionally ignored the possibility of a third level of valence—neutrality. Although theoretically conceivable, a neutral disposition toward deception is not likely to generate the same level of motivation as a positive or negative valence. As potential deceivers weigh the benefits and costs of deception, they are likely to find the costs of potential consequences disproportionate to the marginal benefits offered by deception with a neutral valence.

Consequences

There is less research to draw on when discussing the consequences of deceptive acts. Many deceptive acts may start with altruistic motives (to protect someone's feelings) but eventually lead to negative consequences (truth revealed in a compromising way). Consequences are difficult to judge because the latency period for such evaluation may be lengthy.

Different perspectives can be taken to judge the consequences of deception. One involves the relative success of the deceptive act. If detection can be avoided, negative consequences of the act can be minimized for the deceiver. The goals of the deceptive act do not stand much of a chance if detection occurs, or even if suspicion is aroused. The consequences of detection are problematic for the deceiver and for those who placed trust in him or her. Another perspective focuses on the consequences or effects of the deception on the deceived or third parties.

Trust, Suspicion, and Detection.   Having one's deceptive acts uncovered or detected can inflict great harm on the relationship. Normally, lie detection efforts occur as a result of one or more of the following elements, what we term *detection markers*: (a) contextual cues alert receivers to deception (e.g., "Jim doesn't normally feel that way about his parents"), (b) behavioral cues or profiles reveal dishonesty (verbal, nonverbal leakage, see earlier reviews), (c) implausibility of the message ("That's just too outlandish to believe") and (d) informant ("You'd better watch out for Dave, he can't be trusted"). Behavioral cues have received the greatest amount of attention from communication and social science research, and several conclusions can be drawn from that body of work. For instance, some behavioral cues are more reliable detection indicators than others (see Buller & Burgoon, in press; Zuckerman et al., 1981, for reviews), preparation and spontaneity of lies produce different behavioral cues (Cody, Marston, & Foster, 1983; Cody & O'Hair, 1983; Greene, O'Hair, Cody, & Yen, 1985; Miller, deTurck, & Kalbfleisch, 1983; O'Hair & Cody, 1987; O'Hair, Cody, & Behnke, 1987; O'Hair, Cody, & McLaughlin, 1981; O'Hair, Cody, Wang, & Chen, 1990), personality characteristics are not reliable predictors of deception cues (Exline, Thibaut, Hickey, & Gumpert, 1970; O'Hair et al., 1981, 1987), and gender differences may account for some variance in the production of and sensitivity to behavioral cues (Cody & O'Hair, 1983; O'Hair et al., 1988, 1990). Furthermore, some behavioral cues may change over the course of the interaction (Buller & Aune, 1987; Buller, Comstock, Aune, & Strzyzewski, 1989), sending mixed signals about the deceiver's intent.

Any one of the detection markers described (contextual cues, behavioral cues, implausibility, informant) can increase suspicion depending on factors related to the relationship between deceiver and deceived. Suspiciousness of deception can be viewed as a continuum with complete trustworthiness on one end and intense suspicion on the other. Put another way, suspicion can vary according to the truth bias or lie bias present in the relationship. "Lie bias" is conceptualized as the tendency to view one's relational partner as deceptive in many instances (Levine & McCornack, 1991; McCornack, 1988). Having a lie bias assumes that a relational partner is willing to distort the truth without much hesitation. Conversely, a "truth bias" is when a relational partner is assumed to be telling the truth in most instances (McCornack & Parks, 1986). Relational partners develop confidence in one another's veracity based on their knowledge and experience with the relationship. They expect and anticipate the truth from their relational partner. Truth bias works in favor of an honest relationship, in that suspicion is low and trust between relational partners remains high. It has adverse effects on relationships when one relational partner is dishonest, because an honesty predisposition clouds the potential for detection. Lie bias in relationships carries similar advantages and disadvantages. Lie bias may harm an honest relationship with unwavering suspiciousness, inhibiting any chance of trust and intimacy, whereas it works to a relational partner's advantage when suspiciousness is well founded. Obviously, a relationship can go from truth bias, to suspicion, to lie bias rather quickly when one of the detection markers surfaces, however, moving from lie bias to truth bias is not so easy. Once detected in a deceptive act, it is difficult to shake the label of "liar" for a long time.

Detection Consequences.   We have only discussed deception detection in a general way without examining the various consequences of discovery. There are two behavioral alternatives available to detectors of deception. They can *expose* the deceiver openly by accusation ("You're a damn liar"; "That's not true and you know it"), evidentiary proof ("You're misstating the facts, let me prove what the truth is"), or denial of claims ("You're lying, you know you love me!"). The other alternative available to detectors is to *suppress* knowledge of the detection. There are a number of motives a detector could have for suppressing knowledge of deception. First, a detector may not feel that the deception is worth exposure, thereby ignoring it ("It's just a little white lie, I'm not going to worry about it"). Second, they may actually attempt to deny that deception took place ("Oh, she couldn't really lie to me, I must be wrong"). Third, a detector may have empathy for the deceiver, allowing him or her the benefit of the doubt ("Well, in that situation, Jerry is justified in lying"). Or, a detector may suppress detection by becoming a post facto collaborator of the deceptive act by supporting the deceptive act. Additionally, detectors may suppress detection knowledge in order to allow time for analyzing and interpreting the deceiver motives and to provide lead time for developing responses to the deception.

Regardless of the detector's response (expose, suppress), the consequences of deception detection involve a number of implications for the deceiver, the detector, and their relationship. One of the more obvious costs of detection for the deceiver is a loss of trust and respect. Reestablishing one's credibility after deception detection is one of the most difficult and challenging communication strategies. Embarrassment or "loss of face" is a common consequence for those detected in deception as well. Negative consequences for the detector include hurt feelings, lowered self-esteem, bewilderment, and thoughts of retaliation. Relational consequences would include such costs as relational strain, conflict, aggression, and lingering suspicion and doubt.

Deception detection may also carry with it some positive consequences.[1] It could be argued that a deceiver might garner greater respect when his or her true motives are detected, if those motives are laudable or altruistic.

---

[1]The editors of this volume were instrumental in calling our attention to this important aspect of deception detection consequences.

Those who are exposed for giving other people credit for their own good deeds or competent performance not only benefit from an exposure of their altruistic intent, but also profit from getting credit when it is due. Moreover, detection might lead to positive long-term consequences involving self-concept and/or relational development. Take the example of the deceiver who subconsciously wants to get caught in a lie so that he can express his true feelings about being a substance abuser, or the wife and husband who reconcile and rejuvenate their relationship following the exposure and discussion of a perennial lie. Undoubtedly, there are numerous other positive consequences of deception that critical analysis and exploratory research could uncover.

Unwitting Participants and Innocent Bystanders. Deception also produces consequences or effects for both unwitting targets and innocent bystanders involved in the deceptive act. Assuming that deception goes undetected, the effects or negative consequences could still materialize for those affected by the duplicity. The boyfriend who is told by a friend that his girlfriend is being faithful when in fact she is having a love affair with someone else is suffering the consequences of (a) being used, and (b) a poor image among those who are privy to the affair. Even presuming the friend had good intentions for not revealing the truth, the effects of the lie could be judged negatively. A salesperson may lie to a customer about the price of a product because he knows the product is no longer available at a lower price. He feels that he is helping his customer get the products he needs. However, the customer might have looked for the product elsewhere had he known that the company used to sell at a lower price. A liar may tell his friend that he was working all night, when in fact he was out on a date with another woman. When asked by the liar's wife where her husband was that night, the unwitting friend unknowingly tells a lie to the friend's wife. Innocent bystanders are often implicated in deception by their mere presence. A prankster caught in the act while among a group of people may lie about his or her culpability, implicating everyone there with his or her denial.

Deception consequences for unwitting participants and innocent bystanders becomes even more dramatic and macabre when considering the issue of sexually transmitted diseases (STD). Two people become attracted to one another and consider the possibility of sexual intercourse. What are the consequences of lying about past sex partners? If one person carries STD, for instance, the HIV virus, and transits the disease to his or her partner, are they culpable for not disclosing this information? Most people would argue affirmatively, especially if the STD-negative receptor asks about the transmitter's disease status. Unfortunately, sexual partners will often use deception to achieve sexual experiences. A study reported in the *New England Journal of Medicine* (Cochran & Mays, 1990) indicates that a large percentage of sexually active individuals have lied in order to have sex, including deception about sexual history, sexual partners, results of HIV tests, and the existence of current sexual partners. From these results, it appears that deception becomes a communication strategy to ensure personal satisfaction at the expense of the deceived. What about the HIV carrier who does not know he or she is infected? Does this individual have a responsibility to determine their disease status in order to avoid perpetrating a potentially fatal, yet indirect form of deception? Although HIV carriers may become that way as a result of egoism, exploitation, or possibly utility, they unwittingly perpetuate deception on innocent bystanders (spouses, lovers).

Ethical Perspectives

To pose the question "Is deception a dark side of interpersonal communication" risks the eventual answer, "it depends on the situation." Our brief exploration of situational parameters was not unfounded. However, an ethical perspective to truth and deception would reject such a simplistic position. Certainly there has been ample thinking and writing on the issue of truth and deception by ethicists, although no fundamental theory has been embraced universally by any society or culture. In an attempt to shed some moralistic light on these issues, we propose three viewpoints based on some of the major ethical theories of truth and deception.

Deception as an Unethical Act. Kant (1981) advanced the categorical imperative, which states that for an action to be truly moral one could will that the maxim of his or her actions become universal law (that is, one's actions could be universally accepted). From this perspective, lying to protect others should be pursued in all circumstances. Therefore, lying to the police to protect your best friend, who just happens to be an ax murderer, would be ethically justified. Few people would hold this view. This is a difficult perspective for some people because it does not allow for situational flexibility.

Ethical purists would also argue that the ends do not justify the means. Deceivers often use this test to determine the morality of their acts. In their quest to accomplish some goal or satisfy a need, they justify their motives by arguing for the utility of the ends or that the consequences do not affect others. In opposition to this viewpoint, ethicists argue that not only do the ends not justify the means, but that the ends do not justify the intentions (motives) of the deceiver. One of the implications of this position is that immoral means are not justified, even if intentions and ends are altruistic.

A different perspective holds that harmless or white lies cannot be justified, even if the motives are unselfish and benevolent (Bok, 1979; Makau, 1991). First, it is impossible to predict all of the consequences emanating from a deceptive act. Smoothing over interpersonal disagreements with "white lies" may prevent unpleasantness in the short run but lead to erroneous assumptions in the long run. Consequences can take on a life of their own once deception has been communicated. Second, deception deprives the deceived from making an informed choice about the issues discussed. Liars circumvent the process of allowing receivers the opportunities to weigh evidence, alternatives, and options that are relevant to their circumstances. Interpersonal interaction therefore becomes an artificial system designed to portray facts and information from a biased and self-serving perspective. From a sociopolitical standpoint, deception abrogates an individual's freedom of choice.

Relatedly, deception is looked on by ethicists as an inherent obstruction to meaningful communication systems (Bok, 1979; Deetz, 1990; Kursh, 1971; Makau, 1991). Drawing on Gadamer (1975), Deetz (1990) argued for ethical communication—that which encourages responsiveness to the subject matter and facilitates the "conditions for future unrestrained formation of experience" (p. 232). Deetz feels that ethical communication allows for the building of a common meaning between interactants in which conjoint language and mutual experience are realized. Deception would obstruct common meaning by its very nature because communicators could not share mutual assumptions or factual information. Mutual understanding and shared meaning (terms often used to index communication outcomes) become subordinate goals when deception is mixed in with other message strategies. Only through veracity, fidelity, authenticity, and veridicality can an ethical communication system survive.

Deception as a Means of Survival. It seems that even those who reject, out of hand, an amoralistic stance on deception must confront the fact that some deception is justified and some is not. Where do these moral purveyors draw the line, and what criteria are used to determine a truthful or deceptive strategy? Bentham (1983) proposed an approach to ethics termed *hedonistic calculus*, which argues that those things (communication acts) that increase pleasure or decrease pain are morally justified. True to its name, the communicator views communication as a method to gain personally from people and situations. From a similar viewpoint, Nietzsche (1896/1967) held that all things that increase the power of man to control his surroundings are justified (the will to power). Because deception is a strategy to control one's environment, it becomes an ethical act of social influence. Kursh (1971) concurred with the general tone of this argument and goes further to suggest that deception is a singular strategy that allows dependents (or inferiors) to equalize the controlling nature of situations constructed and manipulated by dominant individuals. By controlling information dependents are able to exert some "countercontrol" over situations that are normally dominated by "superior" individuals.

Kursh points to two additional arguments justifying the use of deception.

First, occasional deception breeds skepticism, which in turn fosters independent thought among communicators. Ideal societies consisting of nothing other than veracity and truth prevent uncertainty and doubt, conditions that often lead to creative and critical communication processes. Assumptions of honesty can engender tendencies to accept information on face value without careful analysis. Paradoxically, deception keeps people honest. Another point advanced by Kursh involves the role of the receiver in the deception process. How responsible is the victim for any deception perpetrated on him or her? It is not a unique experience for targets to question the motives and intentions of their counterparts, although skepticism and suspicion escalate when context cues, markers, or content are discerned. It can be argued that communication is a transactional process requiring both parties to assume responsibility for shared meaning. Victims of deception could be held accountable for ignoring or denying the deception cues available for detection. What about those trusting victims with poor detection skills? How culpable is the gullible deception victim? Some might argue that such naiveté is inexcusable, and therefore responsibility should be shared between deceiver and victim. Alternatively, what are the responsibilities for those adept at deception detection cues? Exposure? Collaboration? Prevention? It is worth noting that victims may consider their own motives and consequences before making decisions about deceptive acts.

Situational Determination.   Few would sanction all instances of deception, for it is far too impractical to deal with widespread duplicity. In contrast to the moralistic stance espoused by Kant and others, a more deceiver-justified approach is readily available for those who view deception as a viable alternative. For example, a situational ethics perspective suggests that ethical and moral evaluation must be made while taking into account the situational parameters under which the action occurs. From this view, deception could be morally justified given circumstances in which deception is necessary. This perspective does not make deception categorically justified, just situationally sanctioned (children lying to strangers about their parents being at home; single women recording on their answering machines, "*we* are not home right now"). If, indeed, it is situational parameters that precipitate and determine strategy selection, how might we categorize or even prioritize situational criteria?

One perspective on situational ethics leaves the decision about deception entirely in the hands of the potential deceiver without regard to external moralistic values. Ethical relativism reflects a communication strategy based on the subjective and arbitrary impulses of actors (Makau, 1991). Consideration of the motives, consequences, and behavior associated with deception is left at the discretion of the deceiver. The ethics of the situation are relevant only insofar as they appear useful to the actor.

A different approach to situational ethics involves the ordering of deceptive acts according to the benefits and costs affecting actor and target. In an often cited study that focused on college students' perceptions of the ethical and moral evaluation of deception, Lindskold and Walters (1983) developed a hierarchy of "acceptability" for deceptive acts. Lies that prevented others from hurt, embarrassment, and shame were rated most permissible, followed by lies protecting oneself from punishment for a minor shortcoming in which no one was hurt, to telling lies to officials in which the deceiver would gain but no one would get hurt, to telling lies that would acquire resources that the deceiver is not actually entitled to. The most reprehensible categories were those that would harm others, while benefiting the deceiver. These results suggest that research subjects have definitive ideas about the ethics and morals of deceptive acts, as they are ordered on a hierarchical category system. Such a balancing of the rights and benefits of the deceiver with the costs for the deceived target is an argument supported earlier by Kursh (1971).

THE SOCIAL EVALUATION OF DECEPTION

We investigated some of the preceding issues by asking 72 students in a beginning interpersonal communication class to respond to 4 questions about the deception context. Tables 8.1–8.4 present descriptive statistics for the four questions posed in the questionnaire. In response to the first question ("What are the motives that people have for lying to someone else?"), participants reported that accomplishing goals, sparing others hurt feelings, avoiding trouble, and self-presentation are the most likely motives for lying. Other less frequently reported motives were protecting someone else, concealing personal information, avoiding embarrassment, self-preservation, and being able to fit in. It is fairly safe to conclude from this data that the majority of respondents has a self-serving motive behind the justification for lying to others, indicating that self-oriented motives (egoism, exploitation) were more prevalent than motives directed toward others (benevolence, malevolence) or relationships (utility, regress).

Question 2 asked, "What are the negative effects of lying to someone?" This question was intended to elicit information pertaining to the personal effects experienced by a deceptive act (although some respondents perceived this question as "consequences" of detection). Respondents mentioned most frequently loss of trust, having to tell more lies to cover up the first one, feeling guilty about the deception, getting caught, and lowering their self-esteem. Other negative effects mentioned were deception becomes habitual, it backfires, it gets others into trouble, it inhibits relational development, and anxiety produced about the deception being detected. Two individuals even feared "going to hell" as a result of lying. As in the first question,

TABLE 8.1
Motives People Have for Lying

Category	Frequency	Percent
Accomplish Goals	32	15.7
Spare Feelings	30	14.7
Avoid Trouble	26	12.7
Self-Presentation	25	12.3
Protect Someone	15	7.4
Conceal Personal Information	14	6.9
Avoid Embarrassment	10	4.9
Self-Preservation	7	3.4
To Fit In	5	2.5
Avoid Conflict	4	2.0
Exaggeration	4	2.0
Gain Control	4	2.0
Insecure About Self	4	2.0
To Hurt Others	4	2.0
Avoid Explanations	4	2.0
Maintain Confidences	3	1.5
Compulsive Liars	2	.9
Habit	2	.9
To Seduce	2	.9
To Get Information	1	.4
Reduce Tension	1	.4
Have Fun	1	.4
Test for Truth	1	.4
Avoid Responsibility	1	.4
Gain Sympathy	1	.4

Note. $N = 72$; Total responses $= 204$.

TABLE 8.2
Negative Effects of Lying

Category	Frequency	Percent
Loss of Trust	30	16.0
More Lies to Cover Up	25	13.3
Feel Guilty	24	12.8
Getting Caught	19	10.0
Lowers Self-Esteem	17	9.0
Becomes Habitual	11	5.9
Eventually Hurt Others	10	5.3
It Backfires	7	3.7
Get Others in Trouble	6	3.2
Inhibits Relational Development	5	2.7
Anxiety About Detection	5	2.7
Being Detected	4	2.1
Destroy Credibility	4	2.1
Start to Believe Lies	3	1.6

(Continued)

TABLE 8.2
(Continued)

Category	Frequency	Percent
Could Go to Hell	3	1.6
Lie is Ineffective	3	1.6
Worsens Situation	2	1.1
Delayed Truth Worse	2	1.1
Morally Wrong	2	1.1
Distrust Others	1	.5
Only Fooling Self	1	.5
Can't Help Problems	1	.5
Creates Confusion	1	.5
Avoid People Who Lie	1	.5
More Exciting	1	.5

Note. N = 72; Total responses = 188.

TABLE 8.3
Consequences of Being Detected in Deception

Category	Frequency	Percent
Loss of Trust/Respect	47	24.9
Lose Friends	35	18.5
Punishment	20	10.6
Embarrassment	19	10.1
Labeled as a Liar	13	6.9
More Lies to Cover Up	10	5.3
Guilty Conscience	10	5.3
Hurt Reputation	9	4.8
Loss $/Job	6	3.2
Hurt People	5	2.6
Looking Bad	5	2.6
Having to Admit Lie	4	2.1
Lose Objectives	2	1.0
Eternal Hell	1	.5
Increase Problems	1	.5
Retaliation	1	.5

Note. N = 72; Total responses = 189.

TABLE 8.4
Is Deception One of the Dark Sides of Interpersonal Communication

Category	Frequency	Percent
One Should Never Lie	15	20.8
Depends on Situation	12	16.7
Has Its Place in IPC	5	6.9
It's Not All Dark	4	5.6
It's a Fact of Life	4	5.6
Wrong, But All Do It	4	5.6
Hurts Relationships	3	4.2
Very Prevalent	3	4.2
Creates Interpersonal Distrust	3	4.2
Defeats Purpose of IPC	2	2.8
Inhibits Real IPC	2	2.8
Can't Help Myself	2	2.8
No, If Not Caught	1	1.4
It's Too Common	1	1.4
It's a Taboo Topic	1	1.4
Must Be Smart About It	1	1.4
Required for Good IPC	1	1.4
Need Better Detection	1	1.4
Situations Require It	1	1.4
Needed to Know What Truth Is	1	1.4
"White Lies" Are OK	1	1.4
Comes Back to Haunt You	1	1.4
A Side of Personality that Can't Be Shared	1	1.4
Prevents True Intimacy	1	1.4

Note. N = 72; Total responses = 72. IPC = Interpersonal Communication.

respondents took a self-centered perspective about the negative effects of deception.

Question 3 asked, "What are the consequences of getting caught in a deceptive act?" Loss of trust/respect, loss of friends or lovers, punishment, embarrassment, being labeled as a liar, having to tell more lies to cover up the first one, and experiencing a guilty conscience were reported most frequently by students. Once again, respondents were more likely to think of themselves when considering the consequences of deception detection.

Question 4 was interested in determining whether respondents felt that deception/lying was one of the dark sides of interpersonal communication. The single most frequent response concurred with this assumption and emphatically claimed that no one should ever lie. However, when combining categories, 59% of respondents indicated that deception was a prevalent communication strategy, or that it had its place in interpersonal communication. Others claimed that situations require it, white lies are fine, and it is required for good interpersonal communication. These data seem to indicate that college students do not view deception much differently than scholars/

researchers in the area. Suggestions of motives, consequences, and ethics permeate these respondents' views, with some mirroring the views expressed by experts who feel that deception is an inevitable communication act.

DECEPTION: DARK? GRAY? WHITE?

A cursory examination of the responses reported here, along with claims made by scholars in the area, suggests that some deceptive acts may be viewed as necessary and justifiable. Yet, as with any moral issue, determination of legitimate deceptive behavior ultimately rests with the deceiver, and the process engaged in making such a determination is directed by both affective and cognitive motives. Even motives that are altruistic in nature may produce consequences that foreshadow the good intentions of the deceiver. Actually, it is not the intent of this chapter to pose value judgments for determining the legitimacy of deception. Rather, the thoughts contained here are intended to raise issues that would lead to criteria for judging the appropriateness of deceptive acts. However, even at this formative stage, it is not too risky to state that some deceptive acts qualify as components of the dark side of interpersonal communication. Let's explore some possibilities by summarizing our discussion thus far.

Based on the empirical, anecdotal, and philosophical literature reviewed earlier, it is useful to conceive of deception as a process in which deceivers make decisions about lying (based on three factors), select a deception strategy, and produce behaviors they feel best serve the needs of the deceptive act. Figure 8.3 illustrates this process. Making a decision to deceive will likely involve a consideration of the motives, predicted consequences, and/or ethical and moral issues before selecting an eventual message strategy.

Only future research can determine if there is some superordinate category system among these factors. Determining the appropriate deceptive act will be based on many situational and relational variables not mentioned here, but it is safe to assume that strategy selection will be made with motives, consequences, and ethics in mind. How to successfully carry off the deceptive act depends on a deceiver's ability to avoid looking like a liar (strategic and leakage cues) and appearing truthful (conveying an honesty profile).

As we carefully consider the deception process presented here, it becomes obvious that the interplay among components is a most important determining factor. At a general level, potential deceivers might evaluate the overall morality and ethics of deception. Is deception ever ethical? Is it ever justifiable? A few of our respondents seem to assume this staunch moralistic stance. This perspective would argue that motives and consequences are irrelevant. If agents make a decision that some deception can be justified, how do they determine the ethical value of a particular act? Are motives and consequences

Critical/Ethical Analysis	Strategy Selection	Behavioral Production
Motives		
1. Exploitation		
2. Egoism		
3. Benevolence		**Strategic Deception**
4. Malevolence	**Deceptive Act**	
5. Utility		1. Behavioral Presentation
6. Regress	1. Lies	2. Leakage Control
	2. Evasion	
Predicted Consequences		
	3. Overstatement	
1. Detection Potential		
2. Harm to Target/3rd Party	4. Concealment	
3. Loss of Trust & Respect		**Honesty Profile**
4. Relational Costs	5. Collusion	
5. Positive Consequences		1. Friendliness
		2. Attentive
Ethical/Moral		3. Precise
Considerations		4. Low Drama
1. Deception is Unethical		
2. Means of Survival		
3. Situational Determination		

FIG. 8.3. Deception process.

the factors that tip the balance toward deceptive intent? Which factor plays the larger role? The means of deception (strategies) should play a role in this process because agents may feel that how deception is perpetrated affects not only their ability to avoid detection, but also their affective position toward the motives, consequences, and ethics of the situation. Likewise, behavioral production is influenced by the cognitive state of the deceiver (see Greene et al., 1985, Zuckerman et al., 1981, for reviews). If deceivers retain lingering doubts about the ethical, motivational, or consequential issues associated with their strategy selection, deception cues could be leaked and an honesty profile may give way to detection markers.

The deception process depicted here raises other issues worthy of consideration. How strong are the relationships among motives, consequences, ethics, and strategy selection? Is portraying an honesty profile directly influenced by one's motives? Is an exploitative liar with no regard for a target's feelings, communicating a lie with a convincing honesty profile, more reprehensible than someone using an evasion strategy constructed with relational motives, knowing that the ends justify the means? Can motives ever be evaluated in isolation, or must we know the situational parameters involved?

Returning to Goffman (1974) for the moment, when deception is dichotomized according to self-motivated versus other-motivated interests, we naturally infer that the former is reprehensible, while the latter is acceptable. However, this oversimplified view of motives does not reveal the deep structure embedded within the intentions of the deceiver, nor does it recognize the behaviors associated with the deceptive acts (as we have argued earlier). Seemingly self-centered acts of deception may actually be motivated by altruistic goals. For example, respondents in our survey most frequently reported accomplishing personal goals ("getting what I want") as a motive for deception, an apparently self-oriented objective. However, the motive to lie about immigration status may generate a job for the applicant (goal achievement), but also put food on the table for her family. On the other hand, whereas sparing other's feelings could readily be perceived as an other-oriented motive and therefore considered acceptable, the real intent behind this deception may be to protect self from adverse consequences (a self-motivation goal). The neat distinction between self and other-motivated goals is clouded by the complexity of one's motivational system and values structure.

As we argued earlier, relationships must also be considered as a component for determining the nature of the dark side. Do deceptive acts designed for developing, enhancing, protecting, or even dissolving relationships constitute acceptable or reprehensible behavior? Several of our respondents claimed that deception was useful for gaining control of the relationship. Others felt justified in using deception to conceal information that their relational partner did not need to know about ("it would only hurt our chances"). Still others were motivated to lie to avoid relational conflict. Presumably, all of these deceptive acts are motivated by a concern for the relationship, but at whose expense—deceiver or target?

Testing deception for motives behind such acts provides a limited framework for assessing the dark side. Determining the consequences of deception may reveal additional information for making a determination. The data reported in this study suggest that most consequences are usually perceived from a self-oriented perspective. Very few respondents identified consequences that could be attributed to others. Even fewer people responded that relational consequences were at stake with deceptive acts. If the consequences of deception are attributed primarily to self, which presumably guides decision making about engaging in this activity, is deception wrong? Is deception more justifiable if the consequences are attributed to others or the relationship? Again, the answers to these questions have to be guided by a more in-depth analysis of the situational constraints imposed by the context and by the complexity of the consequences (deception that is detected by a relational partner hurts self, other, and the relationship).

CONCLUSION

We make no apology for pursuing an inquisitive rather than a prescriptive treatment of deception as a dark side of interpersonal communication. Additional research is necessary to illuminate issues that would assist in understanding how individuals make moralistic judgments. We have attempted to argue that deceptive acts cannot be viewed in isolation. The deception process as we have described it (refer to Fig. 8.3) must be tested to discern potential relationships among component parts. There are a number of important questions to pose. Is evasion a more desirable strategy than concealment? Is it more moral to engage in evasion than to lie to someone else? The answers to questions such as these can only be posed after careful thought about the situational parameters inherent in the context.

Exploring potential situational variables should prove useful in constructing a decision framework for the selection of deception strategies. Take the example of evasion. Targets will have varying levels of tolerance for equivocation or evasion. Some individuals will be more satisfied with an ambiguous statement than others. If individuals are apathetic toward the topic, their tolerance for evasive messages may be high, and thus such a strategy would be received appropriately. On the other hand, those with a great deal at stake or those who view the topic in a salient manner may not accept equivocation and require a follow-up message. Similarly, agents must consider confrontation potential. Many targets will not confront liars because of the embarrassment and conflict involved, whereas they may confront an evasive communicator. Alternatively, what effect does suspiciousness and probing have on strategy selection (see Buller et al., 1989, for a review)?

This chapter raises more questions than it answers. The formative nature of the ideas contained here are due to the dearth of information related to the values associated with deception. Societal norms regarding the acceptability of interpersonal deception change with the times, often depending on how the media portrays society. Raising the issue of deception as a dark side of interpersonal communication is useful, if for no other reason than to search our motives for misrepresenting the truth. Do the means justify the ends? Is deception a worthy strategy for saving a relationship or sparing others' feelings? These issues will continue to obsess our thinking as we consider the dark side of interpersonal communication.

We were struck by comments from two of our respondents concerning the question, "How do you respond to the statement, 'Lying is the dark side of interpersonal communication'?" The examples illustrated here seem to characterize two broad and well-represented perspectives toward interpersonal deception. The first one takes a more cynical position that deceptive communication constitutes something of a quandary: Deception is wrong, but especially if you are detected:

Everybody lies. Baseball players, politicians, preachers, etc., are all susceptible to this supposed dark side. I believe this question puts me in a catch-22 position. I can say it's true and play the idealistic do-gooder whom I believe went the way of disco, or I can be self-centered, selfish, lying bastard by saying, "so what, it's bad for those who get caught, big deal." Either way, I lose out. I guess lying is bad because I'm no good at it. So I agree with lying being one of the dark sides of interpersonal communication.

The second perspective takes a more absolutist view, one that abhors deception for its deleterious affects on the interpersonal process:

Lying/deception is one of the dark sides of interpersonal communication because it "short circuits" the connection between the minds and spirits of the persons involved and is, therefore, a deterrent to true intimacy.

In both cases, it is the "consequences" of deception that influenced their respective viewpoints on deception as a dark side of interpersonal communication.

ACKNOWLEDGMENTS

The authors wish to thank Christopher Carver, Texas Tech University, for his insightful comments during the early stages of this chapter.

REFERENCES

Andersen, J. F., Andersen, P. A., & Landgraf, J. (1985, May). *The development of nonverbal communication competence in childhood.* Paper presented at the annual convention of the International Communication Association, Honolulu, HI.

Andersen, P. A. (in press). *Beside language: Nonverbal communication in interpersonal interaction.* Mayfield Press.

Bavelas, J. B., Black, A., Chovil, N., & Mullett, J. (1990). *Equivocal communication.* Newbury Park, CA: Sage Publications.

Bentham, J. (1983). *Deontology: Together with a table of the springs of action and the article on utilitarianism.* New York: Oxford University Press.

Bok, S. (1979). *Lying: Moral choice in public and private life.* New York: Vintage Books.

Booth, W. C. (1974). *Modern dogma and the rhetoric of assent.* Chicago: University of Chicago Press.

Buller, D. B., & Aune, R. K. (1987). Nonverbal cues to deception among intimates, friends, and strangers. *Journal of Nonverbal Behavior, 11,* 269–289.

Buller, D. B., & Burgoon, J. K. (in press). Deception. In J. A. Daly & J. M. Wiemann (Eds.), *Communicating strategically: Strategies in interpersonal communication.* Hillsdale, NJ: Lawrence Erlbaum Associates.

Buller, D. B., Comstock, J., Aune, R. K., & Strzyzewski, K. D. (1989). The effect of probing on deceivers and truthtellers. *Journal of Nonverbal Behavior, 13,* 155–169.

Camden, C., Motley, M. M., & Wilson, A. (1984). White lies in interpersonal communication: A taxonomy and preliminary investigation of social motivations. *The Western Journal of Speech Communication, 48,* 309–325.

Canary D., & Cody M. J., (1994). *Interpersonal communication: A goals approach.* New York: St. Martin's Press.

Carlson, P. (1987). The Academy Awards of untruth. *Washington Post Magazine*, p. 34.

Chisholm, R. M., & Feehan, T. D. (1977). The intent to deceive. *Journal of Philosophy, 74*, 143–159.

Cochran, S. D., & Mays, V. M. (1990). Sex, lies, and HIV. *New England Journal of Medicine, 322*, 774–775.

Cody, M., Marston, P. J., & Foster, M. (1983). Deception: Paralinguistic and verbal leakage. In R. Bostrom (Ed.), *Communication yearbook 8* (pp. 466–490). Newbury Park, CA: Sage.

Cody, M., & O'Hair, D. (1983). Nonverbal communication and deception: Differences in deception cues due to gender and communication dominance. *Communication Monographs, 50*, 175–192.

Deetz, S. (1990). Reclaiming the subject matter as a guide to mutual understanding: Effectiveness and ethics in interpersonal interaction. *Communication Quarterly, 38*, 226–243.

Ekman, P. (1985). *Telling Lies*. New York: Norton.

Ekman P. (1989). *Why kids lie: How parents can encourage truthfulness*. New York: Charles Scribner's Sons.

Exline, R. V., Thibaut, H., Hickey, C. B., & Gumpert, P. (1970). Visual interaction in relation to Machiavellianism and an unethical act. In R. Christie & F. L. Geis (Eds.), *Studies in Machiavellianism* (pp. 53–75). New York: Academic Press.

Gadamer, H. G. (1975). *Truth and method* (G. Barden & J. Cumming, Eds. & Trans.). New York: Seabury Press.

Goffman, E. (1974). *Frame analysis: An essay on the organization of experience*. New York: Harper & Row.

Greene, J., O'Hair, D., Cody, M., & Yen, C. (1985). Planning and control of behavior during deception. *Human Communication Research, 11*, 335–364.

Hample, D. (1980). Purposes and effects of lying. *The Southern Speech Communication Journal, 46*, 33–47.

Hassett, J. (1981, November). "But that would be wrong. . ." *Psychology Today*, pp. 34–53.

Hopper, R., & Bell, R. A. (1984). Broadening the deception construct. *Quarterly Journal of Speech, 70*, 288–300.

Kant, I. (1981). *Grounding for the metaphysics of morals*. Indianapolis: Hackett Publishing.

Knapp, M. L., & Comadena, M. E. (1979). Telling it like it isn't: A review of theory and research on deceptive communications. *Human Communication Research, 5*, 270–285.

Kursh, C. O. (1971). The benefits of poor communication. *Psychoanalytic Review, 58*, 189–208.

Levine, T. R., & McCornack, S. A. (1991). The dark side of trust: Conceptualizing and measuring types of communicative suspicion. *Communication Quarterly, 39*, 325–340.

Lindskold, S., & Walters, P. S. (1983). Categories for acceptability of lies. *Journal of Social Psychology, 120*, 129–136.

Lippard, P. V. (1988). "Ask me no questions, I'll tell you no lies": Situational exigencies for interpersonal deception. *Western Journal of Speech Communication, 52*, 91–103.

McCornack, S. A. (1988, May). *When lovers become leery: The lie-bias of suspicion*. Paper presented at the annual meeting of the International Communication Association, New Orleans, LA.

McCornack, S. A., & Parks, M. R. (1986). Deception detection and relationship development: The other side of trust. In M. L. McLaughlin (Ed.), *Communication yearbook 9* (pp. 377–389). Beverly Hills, CA: Sage.

Makau, J. M. (1991). The principles of fidelity and veracity: Guidelines for ethical communication. In K. J. Greenberg (Ed.), *Conversations on communication ethics* (pp. 111–120). Norwood, NJ: Ablex.

Metts, S., & Chronis, H. (1986, May). *An exploratory investigation of deception in close relationships*. Paper presented at the annual meeting of the International Communication Association, Montreal.

Miller, G. R., deTurck, M. A., & Kalbfleisch, P. J. (1983). Self-monitoring, rehearsal, and deceptive communication. *Human Communication Research, 10*, 97–117.

Nietzsche, F. (1967). *Thus spake zarathustra.* Norwood, MA: Norwood Press. (Original work published 1896)

Norton, R. (1978). Foundations of a communicator style construct. *Human Communication Research, 4,* 99–112.

Norton, R. W. (1983). *Communicator style.* Beverly Hills: Sage.

O'Hair, D., & Cody, M. (1987). Gender and vocal stress differences during truthful and deceptive information sequences. *Human Relations, 40,* 1–14.

O'Hair, D., Cody, M., & Behnke, R. (1987). Communication apprehensions and vocal stress as indices of deception. *The Western Journal of Speech Communication, 49,* 286–300.

O'Hair, D., Cody, M., Goss, B., & Krayer, K. (1988). The effect of gender, deceit orientation and communicator style on macro-assessments of honesty. *Communication Quarterly, 36,* 77–93.

O'Hair, D., Cody, M., & McLaughlin, M. (1981). Prepared lies, spontaneous lies, machiavellianism, and nonverbal communication. *Human Communication Research, 7,* 325–339.

O'Hair, D., Cody, M., Wang, X., & Chen, E. (1990). Vocal stress and deception detection among Chinese. *Communication Quarterly, 38,* 158–169.

Shennum, W. A., & Bugental, D. B. (1982). The development of control over affective expression in nonverbal behavior. In R. S. Feldman (Ed.), *Development of nonverbal behavior in children* (pp. 101–122). New York: Springer-Verlag.

Shippee, G. (1977). Perceived deception in everyday social relationships: A preliminary statement. *Psychology, 14,* 57–62.

Spitzberg, B. H., & Cupach, W. R. (1984). *Interpersonal communication competence.* Beverly Hills, CA: Sage.

Turner, R. E., Edgley, C., & Olmstead, G. (1975). Information control in conversations: Honesty is not always the best policy. *Kansas Journal of Sociology, 11*(1), 69–89.

Venant, E. (1991, December 10). Our cheating hearts. *Los Angeles Times,* pp. 1, 3.

Zuckerman, M., DePaulo, B. M., & Rosenthal, R. (1981). Verbal and nonverbal communication of deception. In L. Berkowitz (Ed.), *Advances in experimental social psychology* (Vol. 14, pp. 1–59). New York: Academic Press.

IV

RELATIONAL WEBS

9

RELATIONAL TRANSGRESSIONS

Sandra Metts
Illinois State University

Dear Abby: My husband and I were planning a 40th anniversary celebration, but I called it off three months ago when I learned from someone that my husband had had an affair with a young woman while he was stationed in Alameda, Calif., during World War II. The affair lasted about a year while he was waiting to be shipped out, but never was. When I confronted him with the facts, he admitted it, but said it was "nothing serious.". . . I am devastated. I feel betrayed, knowing I've spent the last 37 years living with a liar and a cheat. How can I ever trust him again? The bottom has fallen out of my world.

This letter is a poignant illustration of how a transgression can rock the very foundation of a relationship. In this case, the act of infidelity is only the first blow; the 37 years of omission is the second, and probably more devastating, hit. Moreover, although it is not likely that any account would be easily accepted by this wife, the statement that the affair was "nothing serious" is insufficient and does not address her feelings of betrayal.

Relational transgressions are not necessarily as traumatic as the one experienced by this letter writer. However, even comparatively minor offenses tend to disrupt the stability of a relationship because they involve violations of rules for appropriate relational conduct. Some rules have been explicitly established by the couple, whereas others have been taken-for-granted expectations that were not recognized until the moment of their violation. In either case, if the behavior is considered sufficiently untoward by the offended partner, the misconduct will be considered a relational transgression. The consequences to the relationship depend in large part on the ability of a couple to negotiate the meaning of the event, the legitimacy of the rule, and the implications of its violation.

The purpose of this chapter is to examine the revelation or discovery of relational transgressions as critical events in the life of a relationship and to propose a preliminary model of how such events might be managed with what type of consequences. The chapter is divided into three sections. The first is a discussion of relational transgressions as untoward acts that violate some explicit or taken-for-granted rule in the relationship. The second section reviews research on phenomena that fall logically within the domain of the transgression rubric, though they are not identified formally as relational transgressions. Gender differences in how these phenomena are evaluated are discussed as well. The final section considers the management of relational transgressions based on relevant models of predicaments and the social confrontation episode.

TRANSGRESSIONS AS RULE VIOLATIONS

Transgressions are a particular class of relational event which can be meaningfully distinguished from other forms of relationship stressors. Although transgressions very likely increase uncertainty in a relationship, many other occurrences that are not transgressions also increase uncertainty (Planalp & Honeycutt, 1985; Planalp, Rutherford, & Honeycutt, 1988). For example, discovering that one's partner was deceptive or had betrayed a confidence might increase uncertainty and constitute a rule violation, whereas partners realizing that they have grown apart or changed in terms of values might increase uncertainty without also entailing the violation of a rule. Similarly, transgressions often cause conflict, but so do issues not associated with transgressions.

In short, transgressions are a source of relational disruption that have certain characteristics. Among these are salience (transgressions are known to partners because they are observed, revealed, experienced, or discovered actions or events), focus (tied to particular standards or parameters of behavior—"How could you do X?"), and consequence (they require explanation or remediation sufficient enough to neutralize the emotions they evoke, e.g., betrayal, anger, shame). These characteristics all stem from the fact that transgressions are violations of relationally relevant rules.

Social Rules

Although this chapter is concerned with rule violations occurring in intimate relationships, it is important to explain briefly the function of rules in coordinating and sequencing more general social routines and episodes. Rules are the "musts," "oughts," and "shoulds" that guide an individual's behavioral choices and that shape the interpretations of and attributions assigned to the behavior of others. Rules are designed to operate in particular contexts or under certain sets of circumstances and in this respect have "scope conditions" under which they are applicable. For example, grabbing a man's ankles and throwing him to the ground is inappropriate on a city sidewalk, but acceptable on the football field. Moreover, because failure to adhere to rules disrupts social order and the smooth sequencing of interdependent social actions, rules carry prescriptive force. Thus, rules do not merely describe typical or normative behavior, they "prescribe" obligated, prohibited, and preferred behavior (Shimanoff, 1980). Adults who fail to demonstrate knowledge of rules, willingness to follow rules, or the skills necessary to enact rule-following behavior may elicit negative sanctions from observers.

Relational Rules

As part of the relationship formation process, friends and romantic couples test, create, and explore the expectations and behavioral parameters that will characterize their relationship. In other words, they infer, negotiate, assume, and specify the rules of conduct and relationship functioning that will coordinate their behaviors, standardize their goals, and define their relationship. Indeed, it would seem that one type of information being sought when partners employ "secret tests" (Baxter & Wilmot, 1984) or induce jealousy (White, 1980) is information indicative of whether relationship-specific rules exist or not. Increasing intimacy provides a specific scope condition which exempts partners from following certain types of social rules (e.g., Do not brag; Do not request favors), but obligates them to follow others (e.g., Provide emotional support; Be available in time of need). Through various types of secret tests, explorative partners can infer whether desired scope conditions (i.e., relationship definitions) exist by violating rules that should be operative in that scope condition and watching for sanctions. For example, if a couple had been dating only each other for several months, one partner might infer that the relationship was "exclusive" and that the partners were following the rule appropriate to that scope condition (e.g., Date only one's primary partner). However, on the outside chance that the dating pattern was merely rule consistent (and not necessarily rule following), the curious partner might accept a date with someone else to see if sanctions were expressed. If they are, he or she might then feel secure that partner's exclusive dating behavior was rule following and consistent with a relationship definition appropriate to such a rule.

Even after a relationship has become fully established, the importance of rules does not diminish. At one level, rules are essential for coordinating behaviors so that interdependence can be managed. This level of rule might be called "regulative," in the sense that Searle (1969) used the phrase (i.e., to refer to rules that guide an activity or episode once the activity has begun). Much like the rules that guide the performance of a game such as chess or basketball, regulative rules in a relationship specify how episodes and activities will be conducted. For example, a couple might agree that they should never go to bed with a conflict unresolved or that they should never voice a conflict in front of the children. Jones and Gallois (1989) identified several rules that married couples followed for communication in public and private marital conflicts: (a) be considerate, (b) be rational, (c) be specific, (d) try to resolve the dispute, and (e) keep the interaction positive.

A second level of rule in close relationships is akin to what Searle (1969) called "constitutive" rules. As expressed by Sanders and Martin (1975), these rules specify the behaviors that must occur if a particular activity is going to come into being or continue to exist. When constitutive rules are violated, the result is not merely poor coordination but incoherence. This seems to be the type of rule described by Ellis and Weinstein (1986) in their discussion of how rules function to sustain the cohesion of a relationship. The essence of Ellis and Weinstein's argument is that certain rules operationalize abstract sentiments such as attachment. They note that it is one thing to speak the words "I love you more than anyone else" but it is another thing to follow a rule of monogamy and thereby demonstrate trustworthiness to oneself and to others. Moreover, according to Ellis and Weinstein, it is not a particular set of rules that is important to relationship cohesion, but the fact of having rules that is important. "Being bound by rules, even if they are rooted only in the definition of one's own relationship, provides a source of cohesion for that relationship and protects the relationship bonds" (p. 344).

The centrality of rules, both regulative and constitutive, in maintaining the quality and cohesion of relationships has been demonstrated in a variety of empirical studies. In a study of dating couples, Baxter (1986) examined rule violations embedded in the accounts given to explain the end of a romantic relationship. Although some of the problems that led to the terminations are not rule violations (for example, becoming less similar to each other over time), others are clearly so (Baxter, 1986). Rules identified in the breakup accounts and percentage of total they represent include: (a) allow autonomy (37%), (b) show similarity (30%), (c) be supportive (27%), (d) be open (22%), (e) be loyal and faithful (17%), (f) share time (16%), (g) be equitable (12%), and (h) keep the "romance" (10%).

Rules are also critical in sustaining the quality of friendships. Argyle and Henderson (1984) found that adherence to certain rules distinguishes high-quality friendships from low-quality ones and viable friendships from lapsed ones. The rules most likely to be associated with the termination of a friendship were those prohibiting expression of jealousy about, criticism of, or lack of tolerance for third-party relationships, those prohibiting disclosing confidences to others, those obligating the volunteering of help when needed, those obligating the public expression of support (i.e., not criticizing one's friend publicly), and those obligating private expression of support as in the demonstration of trust and confiding, positive regard, and emotional support.

Finally, accounts of relationship termination indicate that rule violations are not merely an unintentional cause of termination, but in fact a strategy used to initiate the termination sequence. In her analysis of individuals' accounts of relationship termination, Vaughan (1986) noted that one of the indirect methods used for initiating termination is to violate a rule so important to one's partner that he or she will terminate the relationship. According to Vaughan, "The transgression is a breach of trust so great that the partner's self-concept is put in jeopardy; personal dignity is challenged to the extent that the partner cannot continue in the relationship without losing face" (p. 93). These rules might include those concerning kindness and respect shown to loved ones, rules about sexual intimacy with the partner, rules about sex with other people, rules about trust with partner's secrets, and rules against physical assault.

As is evident in the following section, the violations described by Vaughan's respondents are among the most common forms of behavior perceived by college students and other adults to be relational transgressions. Other actions, perhaps less vivid, have also been identified in the research. We turn now to a discussion of these typologies and the gender differences that they evidence.

What Counts as a Transgression (and Who's Counting)?

The research on relational transgressions reflects an orientation toward transgressions as behaviors occurring in relationships that are heterosexual and romantic. It should be noted, however, that relationship transgressions occur in families, same-gender relationships (both platonic and romantic), and among co-workers. In all circumstances in which violation of rules carries implications for the viability or integrity of the relationship, performance or nonperformance of certain behaviors may be considered a transgression by the members. For example, Jones and Burdette (1993) report data on betrayal that includes such instigators and targets as spouses, boy- or girlfriends, same-sex friends, opposite-sex friends, co-workers, mothers, fathers, children, and siblings.

The conventional research on relational transgressions is also dominated by a fairly narrow use of the term *transgression*. By far the most common reference is to third-party involvement outside of the primary romantic relationship. Thus, the sexual affair is a prototypical example of a relational transgression, even among couples who are not yet married (Lieberman, 1988). However, as defined in this chapter, the term *relational transgression* actually covers a broad range of behaviors and theoretical constructs that are referred to in various ways in the literature.

Even the prototypical transgression, the extrarelational affair, is perceived by laypersons as behavior that might include, but not be limited to, sexual involvement (Thompson, 1983). For example, Thompson (1984) asked respondents to evaluate three types of extrarelational involvement: sexual involvement only, emotional involvement only, and both. Respondents rated the combined emotional-sexual affair as the "most wrong" and "most detracting from the marriage." However, the emotional-only affairs were not consequently viewed favorably; they were merely considered less wrong and less detracting to the marriage relative to the other two types of affairs. This was true even for people who had had affairs themselves. Analysis of gender differences indicated that women perceived all types of affairs, especially the sexual only, to have more negative consequences for a primary relationship compared to men.

An even broader notion of infidelity emerged from a survey study of college students (*n* = 247) who were asked to describe behaviors that comprised "unfaithfulness" (Roscoe, Cavanaugh, & Kennedy, 1988). Interestingly, "dating/spending time with another" was listed more often (57%) than were "sexual intercourse" (42%) and "sexual interactions such as flirting, kissing, and necking" (40%). The list also included violations of informational privacy such as "keeping secrets from one's partner" (17%) and "betraying a confidence of partner" (3%). "Being emotionally involved with another" was associated with unfaithfulness by only 10% of the respondents. Gender differences revealed that women were more likely than men to cite dating/spending time with another and keeping secrets from partner as examples of infidelity. Men were more likely to cite sexual involvement than were women.

These responses are similar to a study (Metts, 1991) that asked college students to list behaviors, actions, or attitudes they would consider a transgression if it occurred in an intimate relationship. "Sexual intercourse outside of the primary relationship" was the most frequently listed behavior (17.9%), but "wanting to or dating others" was a close second (15.4%). "Deceiving partner" (11.7%) was the third most often listed behavior, and "flirting/necking/petting" was the fourth (10.3%). In addition, because the term *transgression* is broader than the term *unfaithfulness*, this sample also produced a variety of untoward acts not reported by respondents in the Roscoe et al. (1988) study. These are listed in Table 9.1.

It is interesting that among these additional acts are specific references to sexual or emotional involvement with a former partner. For these respondents, not only are relationship rules established, but the scope conditions under which certain rules are more strongly enforced or more severely sanc-

TABLE 9.1
Additional Transgressions Listed by Respondents

Violating a Confidence
Violating Privacy of Relationship to Network
Forgetting Plans and Special Occasions
Emotional Attachment to Former Partner
Sex with Former Partner
Nonreciprocal Expressivity (Failure to reciprocate sentiments of affection/love/commitment)
Not Trusting/Being Jealous
Breaking a Significant Promise
Changing Important Plans
Physically Abusive
Not There During a Time of Need
Not Fighting Fair (Bringing up past mistakes during arguments)
Unfair Comparisons (Of current relationship or partner to former)

---

*Mentioned by 5% to 10% of respondents

tioned are also established. The category of *nonreciprocal expressivity* is of interest because it implies that failure to return an expression of love or commitment is a violation of some more abstract rule, for example, that confirming relational ties should be mutual, or that nonreciprocity leaves the partner vulnerable and open to potential face threat.

Gender differences were reflected in several categories: Women were more likely to list violations of confidence, violations of privacy to the network, emotional attachment to former partner, violations of a significant promise, and not fighting fair. For women, compared to men, it appears that the specialness of "this" relationship (both emotional commitment and keeping it private) is an important rule, as is adherence to promises. Women also mentioned the category of physical abuse more often than men. However, this may simply reflect its greater salience to women, rather than men not thinking of it as a transgression.

Studies of related phenomena indicate similar patterns. Studies of betrayal, for instance, summarized by Jones and Burdette (1993) are consistent with the Roscoe et al. and Metts studies of transgressions noted previously. Jones and Burdette define betrayal as perceptions that follow when problems arise within the domains of relationship expectations, commitment, and trust. From the accounts of over 200 adults, nine types of betrayal were identified: extramarital affair, lies, betrayed confidence, two-timing, jilting, lack of support, ignoring/avoiding, criticism, and gossip.

Comparisons of male and female responses revealed that men were more likely to report instigating (38.6%) and experiencing an extramarital affair (36.2%) than were women (21.2% and 16.4%). But women were more likely to report betrayal through breaking confidences both as instigator (21.2%) and recipient (25.5%) than were men (9.1% and 6.2%).

In a study of reactions to discovered deception, Levine, McCornack, and Avery (1992) confirmed the relatively greater importance assigned to violations of "relational information" rules by women compared to men. College students were asked to recall a recent (within 1 month) occasion when they discovered that they had been lied to. Findings indicated that women viewed deception as a "much more profound relational transgression than men" based on lower ratings of the lie as "acceptable," higher ratings of "importance" for the act of telling the lie, and more "negative" and "intense" emotional reactions to being lied to.

Summary

Although few studies of relational transgressions broadly defined are present in the literature, studies of the related phenomena reviewed here suggest several conclusions. First, sexual involvement outside of the primary relationship is a frequently reported and prototypical example of a relational transgression, but other types of behaviors are also recognized as transgressions. At the risk of obscuring subtle differences, these various other behaviors can be sorted into five categories. One category that is prominent in respondents' reports is a "privacy/secrets" category. This category includes behaviors that misuse information, either by withholding true information from partner (deception) or by revealing private relational information to the network (betraying a confidence). A second category has to do with "commitments" made to partner but not fulfilled. This category includes breaking promises, changing plans, and so forth. A third category is more difficult to label but might be called "privileging the primary relationship." This category includes actions that disregard the symbolic confirmation of the relationship's importance (e.g., choosing to spend disposable time with another person) or for the specialness of the partner (e.g., not providing support, comparing partner to previous partners). A fourth category is "interaction management," including fighting fairly and nonabusively during conflict. And finally, a category that merits special attention might be labeled "appropriate emotions." Although, in reality, it is not feasible to order a partner to love us, it is nonetheless evident in the research that people expect love and affection to be reciprocated and expect that expressing their feelings will be positively received and returned. Not doing so in certain circumstances is considered a relational transgression.

A second conclusion that can be drawn from the existing literature is that although there is wide consensus about what counts as relational transgressions, men and women display different patterns of evaluation. Women seem to have a broader view of behaviors that count as transgressions. The only category of behavior that men are more likely to list than women is sexual involvement, though women rate these transgressions as more detrimental to the primary relationship than do men. Women are more likely than men to list categories dealing with privacy and secrets, commitments, privileging the relationship, and regulating the routines of interaction. These differences may lead to confusion or conflict in relationships in which rules have not been articulated explicitly. The next section elaborates the role of explicitness and other factors in determining the consequences for a couple when a transgression is confessed or discovered.

CONSEQUENCES OF A CONFESSED/DISCOVERED RELATIONAL TRANSGRESSION

Relational transgressions vary in the extent to which they affect the stability of a relationship. Some may be relatively easy to manage, and some very difficult; some may lead to enhanced understanding, and some to termination. Several factors contribute to these differences, particularly (a) the severity of the violation from the perspective of the offended partner, (b) the explicitness of the rule, (c) motivations and attributions for the behavior, and (d) the level of relationship understanding gained during the negotiation process.

Severity of Offense

Rule violations exist at various levels of significance to the "meaning" or identity of a relationship. Most couples would consider forgetting a birthday less reprehensible than having an affair. This was discussed earlier in terms of constitutive and regulative rules. Locating severity in the type of rule violated does not, of course, mean that all couples consider the same rules to be the most fundamental. In fact, it is more likely the case that couples adapt socially shared and conventional rule structures to the unique features in their relationship. Thus, for one couple, breaking a particular rule might be considered a severe violation, whereas for another couple breaking the same rule repeatedly might culminate in a severe violation.

In addition, violations that are "public" or known to members of the social network are usually considered more severe than those that involve only the couple. Goffman (1959) might say that the properties of the "backstage" region have been brought into public view. Vaughan (1986, p. 95) among others has noted the public embarrassment that often attends the private hurt when an affair is discovered or revealed. Similarly, the consequences of discovered deception is often exacerbated by the realization that one has been acting on assumptions that others in the network knew to be false. In a sense, the target of a deception realizes after the fact that he or she was "out of face" during previous interactions (Goffman, 1967), and the hurt of the deception is compounded by the embarrassment of face loss.

Explicitness

The ability of a couple to deal with, or at least talk about, a transgression is probably increased if the rule that was violated had been explicitly discussed previously during the development of the relationship. Of course, explicitness also increases the likelihood that the offended partner will attribute forethought or intentionality to the transgressor. This then puts a greater burden on the transgressor to generate an acceptable account for his or her behavior, because the offended partner is not likely to accept a plea of ignorance as an account.

Explicitness may also be indirectly related to severity. Rules that have not been explicitly discussed are often those so fundamental to the relationship or to one partner's relationship schemata that they have simply never come up. Friends do not often, for example, state to each other that they consider "talking about the other behind his or her back" to be a rule violation. It is generally taken-for-granted that such behavior would not be acceptable (Argyle & Henderson, 1985). To violate very basic rules would be seen as a serious infraction, and thereby be difficult to manage.

In addition, some rules that have not been made explicit are likely to remain implicit because they are inherently difficult to articulate. A case in point is provided by Hochschild's (1979) description of emotion rules that inform individuals of the type and intensity of emotions appropriate to feel in certain contexts and that prescribe the manner of display. Although many feeling rules are cultural, Hochschild argues that some are unique to a relationship: "Feeling rules also emerge from and become incorporated into the structure of specific personal relationships as the residue of interpersonal negotiations between couple members" (p. 349). Some feeling rules that function primarily as regulative (e.g., "Let's never show anger through a raised voice") may be negotiated easily. Other feeling rules, such as how to show love or passion, how to express guilt or hurt, and when to feel jealousy are not as easily negotiated because they are difficult to articulate.

Motivations and Attributions

To some extent, the factors motivating a transgression and the attributions assigned by the offended partner are negotiated outcomes. The transgressor will offer an explanation (motivation) that is a working compromise between the actual motivation and a proffered motivation that he or she assumes will be acceptable to the offended partner. The offended partner will attribute a motivation to the transgressor consistent with his or her relationship satisfaction, level of trust, knowledge of partner, knowledge of the present situation, and knowledge of past situations (Fincham & Bradbury, 1989; Holmes & Rempel, 1989).

Although no coherent body of literature has examined motivations for all types of transgressions, several studies have explored the motivations for extrarelational affairs in some detail. The study mentioned previously by Roscoe et al. (1988) asked the college student respondents to list reasons why a partner might be motivated to be "unfaithful." As this list indicates, some factors are associated with the attractiveness of the transgression (e.g., variety/experimentation, attraction to the other person), whereas some are factors associated with the unattractiveness of the primary relationship (e.g., dissatisfaction with the relationship and sexual incompatibility). Some are circumstantial and generally passive (e.g., boredom and partner geographically distant), whereas others are focused and active (e.g., revenge, anger, jealousy and testing the relationship). Table 9.2 lists the motivations reported by Roscoe et al.'s (1988) sample.

In an interview study of 40 married women who had had an affair, Atwater (1979) found that pull factors (attractions in the extrarelational involvement) such as satisfying curiosity, enjoying a new experience, and personal growth were more commonly described than were push factors (unattractive elements in the primary relationship) such as boredom, inattention, and lack of love. Consistent with these two orientations, Atwater found that the lover in the pull model tends to be a friend and companion, whereas in the push model, the lover tends to be passionate and not easily resisted. Interestingly, the push model is also characterized by greater feelings of guilt.

TABLE 9.2
Reasons for Unfaithfulness

Reason	Percent
Dissatisfaction with the reationship	43.5
Boredom	34.1
Revenge/anger/jealousy	25.6
Being insecure/unsure about relationship	20.3
Variety/experimentation	19.9
Immaturity/lack of commitment	15.4
Lack of communication/understanding	15.0
Attraction to another	11.8
Sexual incompatibility	10.2
Partner geograpically distant	8.1
Testing the relationship	6.9

From "Dating Infidelity: Behaviors, Reasons and Consequences," by B. Roscoe, E. Canavaugh. & D. R. Kennedy, *Adolescence, 23*, p. 39. Copyright © 1988 by Libra Publishers. Reprinted by permission.

The tendency for people to explain their own untoward behavior in ways different from how they explain their partner's behavior is well documented (e.g., Bradbury & Fincham, 1989; Fletcher & Fincham, 1991). This general tendency is reflected also in studies of relational transgressions. In addition, comparison of responses for men and women provide some evidence that his attributions may differ from her attributions.

Buunk (1987) compared a group of 44 men and women who had been sexually involved outside their primary relationships and subsequently broken up, with a matched control group of 44 people who had also been involved but had not broken up. The terminated group reported a higher level of relationship dissatisfaction, attributed their own and partner's motive to aggression and deprivation, and reported more conflict caused by the extrarelational involvements. Both men and women were more likely to say their partner's affair played a significant role in the breakup than to say their affair did. However, men were three times more likely to blame the breakup on their wives' affair than on their own. Women were more likely to report aspects of the relationship that had to do with feeling strain in the relationship and not getting attention; men did not report boredom for themselves, but attributed boredom in the primary relationship to their wives as a strong motivator.

Spanier and Margolis (1983) interviewed 205 people whose marriage was estranged or terminated following an extramarital sexual relationship. Most respondents said that their own extramarital involvement was an effect, not a cause, of marital problems, yet they reported that their spouse's infidelity was a cause of marital problems. Women reported more guilt for their affairs compared to men, and significantly more emotional involvement with their extramarital partner compared to men. For both, guilt was inversely related to satisfaction with the extramarital affair.

Understanding and Insight

In dealing with a transgression, a couple may begin to scrutinize rules that were previously implicit or taken for granted by one or both partners. As Morris and Hopper (1980) observed, "during problematic situations, rules become evident, salient, and vulnerable to analysis" (p. 268). The results may be a realization that the partners are operating on different fundamental assumptions about how the relationship should be conducted. This realization may result in positive revitalization of assumptions that were no longer viable. This realization may also, however, completely destabilize the relationship because assumptions that constituted the existence of the relationship and indirectly the partners' identities are not valid. To the extent that "presumed understanding" is a stronger predictor of relational satisfaction than is actual agreement (Sillars & Scott, 1983), realization that these presumptions are not accurate, at the worst, may reveal a serious rift in the foundation of the relationship or, at the least, may temporarily increase uncertainty (Planalp & Honeycutt, 1985; Planalp et al., 1988) as assumptions are reconsidered.

In sum, reevaluation of relationship rules may lead to a more cohesive relationship based on mutual understanding or may lead to lower levels of trust, commitment, and affection. In some cases, reevaluation will lead to relationship termination. The outcome of a confessed or discovered transgression depends in large measure on the way the transgression and the emotions it evokes are dealt with during remediation episodes.

MANAGING THE CONFESSION/DISCOVERY OF RELATIONAL TRANSGRESSIONS

Given the variability in the nature of relational transgression noted earlier, it is likely that different types of remedial processes will be required for different types of transgressions. Although this is true, it is also possible to explore common structures in transgression episodes by considering them to be one form of a problematic episode. Like other such predicaments, these episodes challenge partners to meet multiple goals, for example, information seeking, relationship repair, and impression management. Unlike many other types of predicaments, however, these episodes also include the need to understand whether rules were broken or not, whether the rules in question are central to the relationship or peripheral, whether the rules are legitimate or not, and so forth. In this regard, they also share features with the "social confrontation episode."

Predicaments

Both the general notion of predicaments and the more specific instantiation in the confrontation episode originate in the concept of face restoration described by Goffman (1967) as the "remedial interchange." The basic sequence includes a challenge, an offering, an acceptance, and sometimes an expression of appreciation (thanks) for a favorable evaluation. In the case of being confronted about a transgression, the challenge may be issued by the partner in the form of an accusation, a reproach, or an innuendo. The directness of the challenge depends on the degree of severity of the transgression and, perhaps, how certain the partner is that the rule was known and that the rule was broken. A challenge may, of course, by preempted by the confession of the offender.

Following the challenge is the need for an offering. The most common types of offerings are accounts and apologies. Accounts help (a) reframe the event and deny its pejorative nature (justifications), or (b) redefine the actor's responsibility in the event (excuses) (Scott & Lyman, 1968). Schlenker (1980) identified a third type of account, defense of innocence. One might defend one's innocence by saying that the event did not occur (defense of nonoccurrence) or by saying that he or she did not do it (defense of noncausation).

Apologies both accept responsibility for the untoward act and acknowledge its offensiveness. A fully formed apology can contain a number of elements directed toward restoring a damaged identity and realigning interaction: (a) express an appropriate emotional response for having committed the offense (guilt, remorse, sorrow, etc.), (b) indicate awareness of proper conduct and acknowledge that violations should be punished, (c) separate the social actor from his or her "bad self" through self-castigation, (d) promise proper behavior in the future, and (e) perform an act of penance and/or offer restitution (Goffman, 1967).

Although accounts and apologies are the preferred (and generally expected) response to a challenge, social actors can refuse to provide either (Fraser, 1981; Schönbach, 1980). Refusals may consist of a counterreproach, a silent turn, or a turn in which no reference is made to the act in question (McLaughlin, Cody, & O'Hair, 1983). Refusals may also be expressed as a denial: denial by the accused that he/she committed the act in question ("defense of innocence"), or denial that the accuser has the right to issue the challenge (Schönbach, 1980).

If during the initial episode, an acceptable offering is made (or negotiated) and the person who has been offended honors the account (or accepts the regret expressed in an apology), then the episode has been effectively managed. However, to the extent that "aggravating" moves prevail (e.g., refusing to provide an account or denying the right of the accuser to call for one), the episode may escalate to conflict.

In an attempt to determine whether the remedial interchange and the offerings that are typically described in the literature were sufficient to represent couples' actual experiences, Aune, Metts, and Ebesu (1991) asked 145 community adults to describe the episodes that unfolded when they or their partner was found to have been deceptive. Although findings were generally consistent with the predicament literature, some response categories were not represented in the literature. Moreover, some responses are more likely to be used after the initial interchange than during. This finding confirms the intuitive assumption that accounts provided by a relational partner during a single episode are likely to be augmented by other types of relational repair strategies over time.

As indicated in Table 9.3, the most common responses in the initial episode

TABLE 9.3
Strategies for Managing the Discovery of Relational Deception

Short Term	
Truth:	Telling the truth; continued honesty within the relationship ("I decided to be totally honest").
Apology:	Expressions of regret or self-castigation that accompany direct or indirect acceptance of responsibility for the deception ("I'm sorry, please forgive me"). May also include the promise of better behavior in the future ("I assured him that it would never happen again").
Excuse:	Statements that minimize the deceiver's responsibility for the deceptive act, both through appeal to inability ("I didn't know how to tell you") and through shifting the blame to other people, including the target ("I couldn't tell you because I knew you would get mad and make a scene").
Justification:	Statements that accept responsibility for the deceptive act but minimize the pejorative nature of the original event or of the decision to be deceptive ("I told him it was no big deal"; "I said that I was going to tell her later anyway so it wasn't really deception").
Refusal/Deny:	Verbal or nonverbal attempts to manage the extent of explicit revelation during discussions of the deceptive act. Refusals include such practices as failing to provide an account when challenged by the target (e.g., sit in silence), denying that a deception has occurred ("That's not what I said"), and intentionally omitting undiscovered aspects of the truth ("I did admit to seeing Doug, but I didn't reveal everything that happened").
Impression Management:	Statements or behaviors designed to repair or reestablish a threatened image or to create a situation-specific image ("I acted guilty"; "I acted innocent"; "I acted angry as though unjustly accused"). Statements or behaviors designed to arouse empathy, understanding, or forgiveness for deceiver ("I tried to get her to forgive me"; "I tried to get him to understand my position").
Relationship Invocation:	Statements or behaviors expressing attitudes or beliefs about the relationship or invoking qualities of the relationship in order to use it as a frame for interpreting the deceptive act ("We are strong enough to talk this out"; "If our relationship was important, this wouldn't be an issue").
Affective State/ Arousal:	References to an emotional state or leakage cue (e.g., crying) or references to a loss of control over verbal and/or nonverbal behavior (e.g., stuttering, stammering).
Long Term	
Avoidance/ Evasion:	Efforts to avoid references to or discussions of the deception and/or the confrontation episode. Implicit in these tactics is the belief that the consequences of the deceptive act can be minimized by allowing it to fade into relational history and conducting the business of the relationship as though nothing had happened ("I tried to avoid bringing it up"; "We just went on as though it had never happened").
Soothing:	Statements or behaviors intended to placate or ingratiate the target ("I complimented her more often"; "I tried to be more attentive to his needs"). Statements or behaviors that express empathy, sympathy, or validation for the other ("You have every right to be angry").
Relational Work:	Explicit efforts to reaffirm or strengthen the intensity or stability of the relational bonds ("We spent more time together"; "I called her more often"; "I told him I loved him a lot").
Relational Rituals:	Normative or ritualistic behavior directed toward appeasing the target or acknowledging the relationship (e.g., gifts, flowers, candy).
Metatalk:	Explicit discussion of the deception and its impact on the relationship ("We talked about it").

of the discovery of deception reflected several goals of a person in a predicament: (a) the need to control attributions about one's identity, both as a decent human being and as a dependable partner (reflected in the strategies of impression management, telling the truth, and providing an excuse); (b) the need to control the extent of involvement in the remedial interchange and avoid possible contributions to culpability (reflected in the strategy of refusal/deny); and (c) the need to control one's nonverbal displays (reflected in the strategy of affective state/arousal). These strategies together accounted for 72% of all strategies used in the immediate context.

By contrast, the cluster of strategies most often reported after the revelation event tended to represent concern for restoring, revitalizing, or reaffirming the relationship. Relationship-focused strategies included both fairly passive approaches to restoring the status quo (reflected in the strategy of avoidance/evasion) and more active or explicit approaches (reflected in the strategy of relationship work). There was also an increase in attention and solicitous behavior toward partner (reflected in the strategy of soothing). These strategies together accounted for 71% of all strategies used over time to repair the relationship.

Not only were some responses more likely to be used than others, but some were more effective than others in restoring relational stability. Specifically, respondents who reported the use of apology and impression management were more likely to restore trust to their relationship compared to respondents who did not use apology and impression management.

Similar patterns of strategy effectiveness, especially for apologies, have been found in studies of other types of transgression predicaments. For example, in a follow-up study with college students, transgressions were not limited to deception but were broadly defined to include any action identified by respondents as a relational transgression (Metts, 1991). Findings indicated that relationship qualities such as commitment and expressions of affection were affected by the type of remedial strategy used during the initial discussion of the transgression. Specifically, the use of justifications was associated with higher commitment, apologies were associated with increased expression of affection, and excuses were associated with decreased expression of affection. Finally, results supported the conventional view that sexual infidelity strikes to the core of the relationship's identity. Means for ratings of "specialness of the relationship" were significantly lower in cases of sexual infidelity than any other type of transgression.

Using vignettes rather than self-reported experiences, Hupka, Jung, and Silverthorn (1987) asked subjects to read jealousy-inducing vignettes (portraying flirting or sexual involvement with a rival) while imagining themselves as either the jealous partner or the offending partner. Subjects then rated 22 explanations for the errant behaviors that were provided. Factor analysis yielded three factors: justifications, excuses, and apologies. Results indicate that regardless of the participant's role, apologies were by far the preferred offering, followed by excuses and then justifications.

Interestingly, however, justifications were the preferred response if the source of jealousy was a hypothetical partner's sexual affair. This particular finding may underscore the desire of the offended partner to separate the "meaning" of the event from the act of violating a rule. Indeed, it might be speculated that in the case of infidelity (both emotional and sexual), it is imperative first to establish whether the rival is a serious threat to the existing relationship, then next to deal with the rule violation. For if the rival has become the preferred partner, the change in status may in effect neutralize the scope conditions that make a rule of faithfulness to the original partner valid.

This speculation suggests that managing a transgression is a particular type of dilemma, one that requires attention to the type of rule and the legitimacy of the rule that was violated (Morris, 1985). Newell and Stutman (1988, 1991) offered one such model to illuminate this process called the social confrontation episode.

The Social Confrontation Episode

As described by Newell and Stutman (1988), the social confrontation episode is the relatively bounded, functionally coherent span of talk that focuses on the assertion of one person that the other person's behavior "has (or is violating) a rule or expectation for appropriate conduct within the relationship or situation" (p. 271). The general function of the episode is to work through disagreement over behaviors (as opposed to ideas); the specific function of the episode is to negotiate rules and the conditions of their relevance.

According to Newell and Stutman (1991), the episode is initiated by acts that vary on two dimensions: focus and explicitness. Three tactics that focus on behavior and vary in level of explicitness are hinting, seeking confirmation, and blaming/accusing. Two tactics that focus on emotional state of the confronter and vary in level of explicitness are emotional display and emotional statement.

The episode unfolds through a series of decision points, like a decision tree with each fork representing a potential issue or area of controversy. The first choice in trajectory is based on the answer to the question, "Is the implied rule mutually acceptable as legitimate?" If the answer is no (nonlegitimacy), the couple will move directly to legislation, remedy, or nonresolution. If the answer is yes (legitimate), then the accused might (a) invoke a superseding rule to account for the behavior—a rule whose legitimacy has to then be negotiated, (b) admit that the behavior did occur, or (c) deny that the behavior occurred. If the behavior is denied, the couple will move directly to reaffirmation of the importance of the rule or to nonresolution. If the behavior in question is admitted to, the accused must then answer whether the behavior broke the rule or did not break the rule. If the accused denies that the behavior he or she committed broke the rule, then the couple will move directly to remediation. If the accused admits that the behavior broke the rule, then he or she must accept or deny responsibility. Each of these decisions leads to a set of endpoints: Remedy and reaffirmation will follow from acceptance of responsibility, whereas legislation, remediation, reaffirmation, remedy, or nonresolution will follow from denial of responsibility. Figure 9.1 illustrates the decision process (Newell & Stutman, 1988).

Each endpoint brings a particular type of closure to the episode and provides various levels of understanding about new rules or implementation of existing rules in the future. For example, remedies consist of such actions as stopping the behavior in question, expressing remorse, remediating damages, offering an account to redress face loss, and punishment. Thus, they provide resolution for the current situation, however, they do not necessarily provide a guide for future behavior. Endpoints that are more useful for guiding future interactions are legislation, remediation, and reaffirmation. Legislation centers on the "development of and agreement to a new rule" (Newell & Stutman, 1988, p. 278) or on some form of metarule specifying when the new rule should operate. Remediation centers on the clarification of existing rules and expectations. Reaffirmation signals mutual agreement that an existing rule is legitimate and that the offender agrees to follow the rule in the future.

Apologies, accounts, and refusals are incorporated in the confrontation model at various points. Apologies are clearly relevant and central to the concept of remedies, particularly in expressing regret for the behavior. Excuses can be used to reframe responsibility by claiming ignorance of the rule or "undermining the shared consensual validity" of the rule. Excuses for behavior when the rule is recognized as legitimate and explicit (known) can be traditional appeals to carelessness, oversight, forgetfulness, biological weakness, and so on.

Justifications can be used to reframe behavior by challenging the legitimacy of the rule or by calling on a superseding rule. Refusals can occur in several places in the decision tree, but most critically in denying the legitimacy of the rule, denying the alleged behavior ever occurred, and denying that the behavior broke the rule in question.

Although the confrontation episode model is a useful heuristic for the rule-relevant problematic episode, several additions are necessary to increase its explanatory power for the unfolding of episodes focused on relational transgressions. First, the initiating act is not necessarily the offended person's challenge. When a transgressor assumes responsibility for initiating the remedial episode, a confession (probably accompanied by an account) will initiate the episode. This confession may preempt the confrontation move or may

A. Is the implied rule mutually accepted as legitimate?
B. Is this a special situation?
C. If invoked, is the superseding rule mutually accepted as legitimate?
D. Did the accused actually perform the behavior in question?
E. Does the behavior constitute a violation of the rule?
F. Does the accused accept responsibility for the behavior?

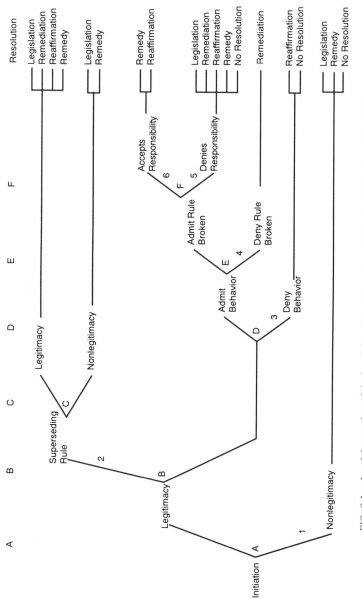

FIG. 9.1. An elaborated model of social confrontation. From "The Social Confrontation Episode," by S. E. Newell & R. K. Stutman, *Communication Monographs, 55*, p. 274. Copyright © 1988 by the Speech Communication Association. Reprinted by permission.

prompt the offended partner to confront with an emotional display or emotional statement. The extent to which these beginnings alter the sequence outlined by Newell and Stutman merits investigation.

Second, the nature of the rule in question, and thus the severity of its violation, must be considered. As noted previously, some rules are constitutive of the very identity of the relationship, whereas others regulate relationship processes. Recognition of the level of rule violation might be the first consideration in the possible trajectories of the episode. For example, it is less likely for the accused to argue that sexual exclusivity is a nonlegitimate rule than to argue that keeping a promise is nonlegitimate. It is also more difficult to call on a superseding rule in the former case than in the latter.

Recognition of the severity of rule violation is also related to the type of account and remedy that will likely follow. The literature reviewed previously indicated that justifications were preferred over excuses and apologies in cases of sexual affairs (Hupka et al., 1987) and were associated with degree of commitment in a relationship experiencing a transgression. This suggests that when a constitutive rule has been violated, the offender is expected to (and probably willing to) exert the effort to explain and reframe the event to minimize its negative implications for the viability of the relationship. Apologies are not only the preferred response to many types of transgressions, they are also more likely to be provided in relationships that are high in affection, and they are associated with increased levels of trust in relationships that previously experienced a transgression.

Third, description of the confrontation episode would also profit from consideration of emotional reactions, both of the partner and the transgressor. Although the research in this regard is scattered, a series of studies by McGraw (1987) suggests the promise of this direction. McGraw found that "harmdoers" feel less guilt after intentional transgressions than after accidental transgressions, but the victim feels greater anger in the same condition. McGraw hypothesizes that the harmdoer has had time to process guilt when a transgression was intentional, but is caught unprepared when the transgression is unintentional. The effect of this attributional pattern on decisions made in the confrontation model would provide interesting directions for future research. What may happen in the unfolding episode is that violations of explicit rules and violations that are confessed (rather than discovered) initiate sequences in which the transgressor is in somewhat more control than in situations in which he or she violated an implicit rule or in which the violation was discovered.

Perhaps more critical in the management of a relational transgression is the management of the affective response of the offended partner. Newell and Stutman's model may work well to map interactions in conditions of low arousal and low investment. (Although for a view less convinced of a prevailing norm of logic and order see Morris, 1991.) It is probably less descriptive in conditions of high arousal and high investment, particularly when the confronter is angry, hurt, and/or aggressive. When a relational transgression is being discussed, the influence of emotional arousal on the process and outcome cannot be ignored. Any model that will account for differences in normative patterns or for differences in outcomes needs to include a subroutine that deals with the offended person's affective response. At the very least, the transgressor must acknowledge and validate his or her partner's feelings to prevent escalation of arousal. This is similar to the function served by comforting messages in managing negative affect for distressed others who are feeling sad, lonely, and so on. Before social support can be maximally effective, emotional states must be validated (Burleson, 1994). Similarly, in managing relational transgressions, some indication of legitimacy of feelings must be expressed before rules are negotiated and accounts are offered.

CONCLUSION

The management of relational transgressions is a complicated issue for researchers and an exceedingly difficult process for intimate couples. Every attempt, and particularly the first attempt, to deal with the revelation, discovery, or experience of a transgression is a complicated matrix of interaction mandates. First, emotional damage must be contained to prevent escalating emotional entanglements. The typical emotional profile of anger and pain for the offended person and guilt, humiliation, and shame for the transgressor can easily become blurred as both parties become angry and accusatory. Second, the nature of the transgression must be clarified. Understanding of what the behavior (or lack of behavior) means (i.e., what rule was broken) not only influences emotional responses, but also the unfolding of the discussion episode. For couples in crisis, figuring out what rule was broken helps set parameters on appropriate emotional reactions and helps direct talk to the source of the problem. After all, some rules do require specification of scope conditions and what counts as rule-following behavior; some require negotiation because one person may not hold that a rule is legitimate; some rules even require articulation because they have never been expressed. But, of course, when explicit and nonnegotiable rules have been violated, discussion may give way to a solitary decision for the offended person to terminate the relationship or to forgive the transgressor. The accounts of the transgressor and the nature of the relationship play a critical role in this decision.

Further explication of this complicated process is worth the effort. Though it is certainly true that people can use transgressions as a catalyst to break up a relationship, or use them as a way to declare independence from perceived relational constraints, transgressions are more typically the unintended consequence of human fallibility and individual needs conflicting with relational needs. A transgression need not destroy an otherwise viable and satisfying relationship. The fact that it sometimes does is perhaps the clearest signal that additional research into the coping process is necessary.

REFERENCES

Argyle, M., & Henderson, M. (1984). The rules of friendship. *Journal of Social and Personal Relationships, 1*, 211–237.

Argyle, M., & Henderson, M. (1985). The rules of relationships. In S. Duck & D. Perlman (Eds.), *Understanding personal relationships* (pp. 63–85). London: Sage.

Atwater, L. (1979). Getting involved: Women's transition to first extramarital sex. *Alternative Lifestyles, 2*, 33–68.

Aune, R. K., Metts, S., & Ebesu, A. S. (1991, November). *Managing the outcomes of discovered deception.* Paper presented at the Speech Communication Association Convention, Atlanta, GA.

Baxter, L. A. (1986). Gender differences in the heterosexual relationship rules embedded in break-up accounts. *Journal of Social and Personal Relationships, 3*, 289–306.

Baxter, L. A., & Wilmot, W. (1984). Secret tests: Social strategies for acquiring information about the state of the relationship. *Human Communication Research, 11*, 171–201

Bradbury, T. N., & Fincham, F. D. (1989). Behavior and satisfaction in marriage: Prospective mediating processes. In C. Hendrick (Ed.), *Close relationships* (pp. 119–143). Newbury Park, CA: Sage.

Burleson, B. R. (1994). Comforting messages: Features, functions, and outcomes. In J. A. Daly & J. M. Wiemann (Eds.), *Strategic interpersonal communication* (pp. 135–161). Hillsdale, NJ: Lawrence Erlbaum Associates.

Buunk, B. (1987). Conditions that promote breakups as a consequence of extradyadic involvements. *Journal of Social and Clinical Psychology, 5*, 271–284.

Ellis, C., & Weinstein, E. (1986). Jealousy and the social psychology of emotional experience. *Journal of Social and Personal Relationships, 3*, 337–357.

Fincham, F. D., & Bradbury, T. (1989). Attribution of responsibility in close relationships: Egocentric bias or partner-centric bias? *Journal of Marriage & the Family, 51*, 27–35.

Fletcher, G. J. O., & Fincham, F. D. (1991). Attribution processes in close relationships. In G. J. O. Fletcher & F. D. Fincham (Eds.), *Cognition in close relationships* (pp. 7–35). Hillsdale, NJ: Lawrence Erlbaum Associates.

Fraser, B. (1981). On apologizing. In F. Coulmas (Ed.), *Conversational routine: Expectations in standardized communication situations and prepatterned speech* (pp. 259–271). New York: Mouton.

Goffman, E. (1959). *The presentation of self in everyday life.* Garden City, NY: Doubleday Anchor Books.

Goffman, E. (1967). *Interaction ritual.* Garden City, NY: Doubleday Anchor Books.

Hochschild, A. R. (1979). Emotion work, feeling rules, and social structure. *American Journal of Sociology, 85*, 551–575.

Holmes, J. G., & Rempel, J. K. (1989). Trust in close relationships. In C. Hendrick (Ed.), *Close relationships* (pp. 187–220). Newbury Park, CA: Sage.

Hupka, R. B., Jung, J., & Silverthorn, K. (1987). Perceived acceptability of apologies, excuses and justifications in jealousy predicaments. *Journal of Social Behavior and Personality, 2*, 303–313.

Jones, E., & Gallois, C. (1989). Spouses' impressions of rules for communication in public and private marital conflicts. *Journal of Marriage and the Family, 51*, 957–967.

Jones, W. H., & Burdette, M. P. (1993). Betrayal in close relationships. In A. L. Weber & J. Harvey (Eds.), *Perspectives on close relationships* (pp. 1–14). New York: Allyn & Bacon.

Levine, T. R., McCornack, S. A., & Avery, P. B. (1992). Sex differences in emotional reactions to discovered deception. *Communication Quarterly, 40,* 289–296.

Lieberman, B. (1988). Extrapremarital intercourse: Attitudes toward a neglected sexual behavior. *Journal of Sex Research, 24,* 291–299.

McGraw, K. M. (1987). Guilt following transgression: An attribution of responsibility approach. *Journal of Personality and Social Psychology, 53,* 247–256.

McLaughlin, M. L., Cody, M. M., & O'Hair, H. D. (1983). The management of failure events: Some contextual determinants of accounting behavior. *Human Communication Research, 9,* 208–224.

Metts, S. (1991, February). *The wicked things you say, the wicked things you do: A pilot study of relational transgressions.* Paper presented at the Western Speech Communication Association Convention, Phoenix, AZ.

Morris, G. H. (1985). The remedial episode as a negotiation of rules. In R. L. Street, Jr. & J. N. Capella (Eds.), *Sequence and pattern in communicative behavior* (pp. 70–84). Baltimore: Edward Arnold.

Morris, G. H. (1991). Alignment talk and social confrontation. In J. A. Anderson (Ed.), *Communication yearbook 14* (pp. 403–413). Newbury Park, CA: Sage.

Morris, G. H., & Hopper, R. (1980). Remediation and legislation in everyday talk: How communicators achieve consensus. *Quarterly Journal of Speech, 66,* 266–274.

Newell, S. E., & Stutman, R. K. (1988). The social confrontation episode. *Communication Monographs, 55,* 266–285.

Newell, S. E., & Stutman, R. K. (1991). The episodic nature of social confrontation. In J. A. Anderson (Ed.), *Communication yearbook 14* (pp. 359–392). Newbury Park, CA: Sage.

Planalp, S., & Honeycutt, J. M. (1985). Events that increase uncertainty in personal relationships. *Human Communication Research, 11,* 593–604.

Planalp, S., Rutherford, D. K., & Honeycutt, J. M. (1988). Events that increase uncertainty in personal relationships II: Replication and extension. *Human Communication Research, 14,* 516–547.

Roscoe, B., Cavanaugh, E., & Kennedy, D. R. (1988). Dating infidelity: Behaviors, reasons and consequences. *Adolescence, 23,* 35–43.

Sanders, R. E., & Martin, L. W. (1975). Grammatical rules and the explanation of behavior. *Inquiry, 18,* 65–82.

Schlenker, B. R. (1980). *Impression management: The self-concept, social identity, and interpersonal relations,* Monterey, CA: Brooks/Cole.

Schönbach, P. (1980). A category system for account phases. *European Journal of Social Psychology, 10,* 195–200.

Scott, M. B., & Lyman, S. M. (1968). Accounts. *American Psychological Review, 33,* 46–62.

Searle, J. R. (1969). *Speech acts: An essay in philosophy of language.* Cambridge: Cambridge University Press.

Shimanoff, S. B. (1980). *Communication rules: Theory and research.* Beverly Hills, CA: Sage.

Sillars, A. L., & Scott, M. D. (1983). Interpersonal perception between intimates: An integrative review. *Human Communication Research, 10,* 153–176.

Spanier, G. B., & Margolis, R. L. (1983). Marital separation and extramarital sexual behavior. *Journal of Sex Research, 19,* 23–48.

Thompson, A. P. (1983). Extramarital sex: A review of the research literature. *Journal of Sex Research, 19,* 1–22.

Thompson, A. P. (1984). Emotional and sexual components of extramarital relations. *Journal of Marriage and the Family, 46,* 35–42.

Vaughan, D. (1986). *Uncoupling: Turning points in intimate relationships.* New York: Oxford University.

White, G. L. (1980). Inducing jealousy: A power perspective. *Personality and Social Psychology Bulletin, 6,* 222–227.

10

PRIVACY BINDS IN FAMILY INTERACTIONS: THE CASE OF PARENTAL PRIVACY INVASION

Sandra Petronio
Arizona State University

To some, the notion of family privacy seems to be an oxymoron. But, as scholars like Berardo (1974) and Karpel (1980) have indicated, privacy provides important functions for family members. For example, privacy helps protect family members from outside scrutiny or gives the members a chance to try out arguments on each other without risk of humiliation. Clearly, knowing that information will be kept secure is comforting. Yet, there is more to the concept of family privacy than the issue of protection from outsiders. Understanding family privacy entails focusing on the way members manage privacy issues within the family as well as with nonfamily members. Within the family, members define territory, possessions, and information as belonging to them collectively, between certain members, or to individual members alone (Altman, 1975; Karpel, 1980). In order to maintain privacy within the family unit, ownership recognition of space, information, and possessions by the members is necessary (Petronio, 1991). One complicated task is determining when space, possessions, or information belongs to one or more of the members. For example, if information belongs to just one person, he or she has the right to protect the privacy of that information. If it belongs to more than one family member, those involved need to negotiate the rules for how the information is kept private or revealed. As families grow, communication increases about who has the right to control certain space, possessions, and information (Wolfe & Laufer, 1974). These interactions are an attempt to manage privacy rights internally within the family structure.

For the most part, the attempts to manage privacy within the family are beneficial to the members (Karpel, 1980). But, there are times when conflict may arise because the boundaries drawn by one member compromise another family member's definition of privacy. When this happens, the conflict may be useful for the family, but there are instances in which this boundary conflict results in problems for its members. The present chapter focuses on an example of boundary conflict that represents the darker side of family privacy.

This chapter presents a series of studies based on the theoretical proposal of Communication Boundary Management (Petronio, 1991), which examines the dynamics of parental privacy invasion for college-aged children. First, Communication Boundary Management is introduced as a theoretical underpinning applied to the study of parent privacy invasion. In the next part of the chapter, findings from four studies conducted to investigate this issue are presented. In the remainder of the chapter, the implications for privacy regulation and parent–child relationships are discussed in depth.

THEORETICAL UNDERPINNING

In relationships with others, individuals often face paradoxical demands regarding privacy (Baxter & Wilmot, 1984; Petronio, 1991). For example, individuals want to be close to family members, but also want to maintain a sense of autonomy that ensures independence. One way to balance separateness with closeness is through regulating privacy. Managing privacy, for example, allows openness about personal matters when desired or keeps information from others when individuals do not wish to disclose. The notion of privacy regulation was initially presented by Altman (1975) and later developed by Altman, Vinsel, and Brown (1981). Derlega and Chaikin (1977) contributed to this thesis of privacy regulation by applying the conceptualization to disclosure. More currently, Petronio (1991) extended the notion of boundary regulation, focusing on the communicative aspects of the proposal, suggesting a communication boundary management model.

Using a boundary metaphor more clearly illustrates the individual's use of a privacy territory to mark ownership of space, possessions, and information. In identifying boundaries around privacy, individuals also assume that they will have a measure of control over the space, possessions, and information considered their own. This sense of control is necessary to minimize the individual's feelings of risk to privacy (Petronio, 1991). When the risk of vulnerability is great, individuals tend to control their boundaries more tightly, protecting privacy. When people perceive less risk, they grant more access and regulate their boundaries more loosely. Boundary control is used to protect feelings of vulnerability and manage the risks to autonomy and independence. The privacy regulation process is based on criteria or rules that people use to achieve the level of desired access to information, space, and possessions. The criteria may be behaviorally understood when a person acts in a particular way that is recognized as a rule for privacy maintenance. The criteria may be verbally communicated as a rule for privacy regulation, or the criteria may be developed through a decision process in which two or more individuals enter into a negotiation.

Individuals tend to manage their boundaries proactively by deciding how, when, and who might occupy their space and use their possessions or by controlling the flow of information going out to others. Managing boundaries proactively may also involve protecting privacy when an individual anticipates possible invasion from others. Thus, people may proactively control privacy boundaries by implementing rules for when they open up space, allow others to use possessions, and disclose private information. Individuals also proactively control boundaries when they anticipate potential violations of space, possessions, and information. However, there are times when proactive control is not possible and individuals may not be able to protect their privacy. In these cases, individuals may retroactively reconstruct their boundaries (Petronio & Braithwaite, 1987). The most common example of retroactive boundary control is seen when a person violates another's privacy. After the invasion of privacy, individuals may feel the need to restore a sense of protection and equilibrium to their territory (Lyman & Scott, 1970). Essentially, people reclaim their space, possessions, or information in a way that allows them to regain a level of control. This process is enacted because invasion brings into question the assumptions about a person's ownership rights. When invasion occurs, the person works to restore a protective boundary shield to safeguard privacy once again. In both proactive and retroactive boundary control individuals act in ways that defend their territories. Thus, these defensive actions provide a way of maintaining or regulating boundaries around privacy for the individual.

On an individual level, this description of privacy regulation is relatively straightforward. But, examining the process in a family setting is more complicated because there needs to be some consideration of the way, for example, parents and children differentially define ownership and boundary control. Often parents and children do not see eye to eye on where the boundary lines should be drawn. When the lines are different for parents and children they may experience boundary conflict.

Boundary conflict develops when there are inconsistencies between the way family members define ownership of space, possessions, and information. For example, between parents and children, the parents may believe that they have ownership rights to their children's bedroom space, and the children may define that space as their own. In this example, the boundary lines are not consistently drawn by either the parents or the children. The parents, defining the space as belonging to them, may act on their definition and insist that the room remain clean. The children, defining the bedroom as their own, may insist that it can be left in any condition they desire. The differences in definition of boundaries may lead to conflict over whose point of view will prevail. Yet, part of individuation for children is their development and understanding of privacy rights (Wolfe & Laufer, 1974).

Often a way of differentiation for children is to define something private and have the right to exercise control apart from their parents. But, parents are also in a learning process during this time. They are trying to understand that space, possessions, and information which were once accessible to them may no longer be defined in the same way by their children (Coleman & Hendry, 1990). New boundary lines are being drawn by children during the period of individuation. To aid them in their development, it is useful when parents recognize the change in status (Wolfe & Laufer, 1974). But, drawing new boundary lines is difficult for children, and it is often as difficult for parents to clearly recognize and acknowledge the change in ownership. Perhaps the dissimilarity in boundary definition between parents and children becomes most clear when there is privacy invasion. When a violation of privacy takes place, it underscores the disaccord in ownership definition that often results in boundary conflict. Parents or children may invade each other's privacy. But, parents' invasion may be somewhat more problematic because they are looked up to for guidance and are responsible for granting independence to their children (Parke & Sawin, 1979).

Parental privacy invasion appears to occur at various times during adolescent development (Wolfe & Laufer, 1974). But, the college period is of particular interest because there are more opportunities for mixed messages regarding parents granting personal control over privacy needs. When children are away at college, they are expected to be independent and take responsibility for their actions. Yet, when children are home or interact with their parents, the parents may contradict these expectations by invading their children's privacy boundaries. The confusion and frustration may lie in the inconsistency of expectations. Embedded in this problem is a fundamental divergence between perceived privacy rights granted or obtained by college-aged children and the way parents enact their own definition of the children's privacy boundaries. Hence, in many ways, when invasion occurs, parents are not fully conceding to their children's independence. Parents are attempting to retain control through their actions. In this way it appears to the children that their parents are defining the ownership issues of privacy rights differently from their own view.

For parents, the reasons for these inconsistencies in definition may stem from a sense of confusion about changing roles. As Coleman and Hendry (1990) point out,

> Parents themselves usually hold conflicting attitudes toward their teenage children. On one hand they may wish young people to be independent, to make

their own decisions, and to cease making childish demands, whilst, on the other, they may at the same time be frightened of the consequences of independence (especially the sexual consequences), and sometimes [are] jealous of the opportunities and idealism of youth. (p. 84)

Inevitably, invasion of privacy by the parents may send a message to college-aged children that indicates the reluctance of parents to let go. This parental reluctance may be viewed by college-aged children as an unwillingness to acknowledge their attempts to define a privacy boundary independent of their parents. As such, college-aged children may feel frustration and resentment toward their parents. These feelings ultimately may lead to problems in the parent–child relationship (Callan & Noller, 1986; Campbell, Adams, & Dobson, 1984; McGoldrick & Carter, 1982).

We know that children give a wide berth to their parents regarding the limits of privacy invasion (Burgoon et al., 1989). From research by Burgoon et al. (1989), in general, adolescents are willing to grant their parents a greater latitude concerning privacy violations in comparison to nonfamily members. But, as Petronio and McDaniel (1992a) point out, given that leeway, "when children do feel that violations have occurred, they may react more negatively toward their parents than under other circumstances" (p. 8). Acknowledging parental invasion of privacy may lead to college-aged children having confusing feelings about their parents.

Invading privacy, thus, becomes an excellent issue in which to understand this paradoxical time for parents and college students. The college students define these controlling behaviors as invasive to their privacy and as inconsistent with their own boundary definitions. Regardless of the parents' reasons for these actions, the children may perceive invasions of privacy in a less positive way. Because these violations often contradict the children's assumptions about their own independence, they may act defensively. As defensive moves, the college-aged children may try to proactively or retroactively cope with these invasions. As noted earlier, when there is a threat of invasion, individuals work to proactively protect their privacy boundaries. If unable to predict invasion and violations do occur, people tend to restore their boundaries after privacy invasion (Petronio & Braithwaite, 1987). Defensive actions as a way to contend with parental invasion may take many forms; however, the strategies may be idiosyncratic to the invasion situation (Petronio & Braithwaite, 1987). The extent to which college-aged children are successful at protection or restoration may influence their feelings about their parents. Further, the combination of particular types of invasion tactics in conjunction with the defensive actions of the children may influence the way children see their relationship with the parent as well.

There are four studies reported in this chapter. The first study focuses on determining the way parents invade their children's privacy and the tactics children use as defensive actions to proactively protect or retroactively restore invaded boundaries. The second study, using a larger population, refines the categories found in Study One for invasion tactics and defensive actions. The third study assesses the relationship between the kind of invasions used by the parents and the defensive action enacted by the college-aged children. The fourth and last study reports an analysis of the interrelationship between the kinds of parental invasion tactics used, the defensive actions enacted, and the impact on the parent–child relationship from the college children's perspective.

STUDY ONE: IDENTIFYING PARENTAL INVASION AND DEFENSIVE ACTIONS

In the first study conducted by Petronio and Harriman (1989), a number of parental invasion tactics were identified. This was a preliminary study to discover forms of parental privacy invasion and defensive actions, as well as to confirm that college-aged children experience parental invasion. Seventy-five respondents of college age ($M = 19$) reported 10 different kinds of parental privacy invasion derived from a content analysis. Using an open-ended format, the respondents were asked to indicate the ways their parents currently invade their privacy. Interestingly, only 3% of the respondents did not identify a type of invasion, suggesting that parental invasion for these college children was not unusual. The categories included parents who: (a) enter the children's bedrooms without knocking, (b) listen to telephone conversations, (c) ask personal questions, (d) open the children's mail, (e) infringe on the children's personal time, (f) give unsolicited advice, (g) make demands, (h) go through the children's personal belongings, (i) enter the bathroom without knocking, and (j) eavesdrop on children's conversations with others.

These categories show a wide range of activities that represent parental invasions. This thesis suggests that when boundaries maintaining privacy are breached, or there is an anticipation that they will be breached, individuals tend to proactively protect or retroactively restore their boundaries. In response, college children enact a variety of behaviors to protect or restore their boundaries regarding privacy.

From the same study, a content analysis was performed on open-ended responses which asked college students to identify the ways they cope with their parents' privacy invasion. The analysis of these data revealed 14 different kinds of defensive action tactics suggested by these college students: (a) locking or closing the bedroom/bathroom doors, (b) making private phone calls outside of the home, (c) hiding personal belongings, (d) confronting parents with evidence of invasion, (e) using signs such as "keep out," (f) withholding personal information, (g) making their parents feel guilty, (h) giving their parents the silent treatment, (i) asking their parents to stop, (j) indicating their disappointment in their parents, (k) leaving out details when answering questions, (l) having meetings with friends outside of the home, (m) convincing their parents that they do not want them to know about their private lives, and (n) leaving notes showing knowledge of invasion.

In total, 70% of these respondents reported that their parents typically entered their bedrooms without knocking, listened to telephone conversations, asked personal questions, and opened their mail. The remaining 30% was distributed among the other five categories. In response to these violations, 62% of the respondents reported that they hid personal belongings, used signs, made phone calls outside the home, and locked their doors. These data suggest that there are certain types of parental invasions and child defensive action tactics that were more frequently reported by college-aged children. However, these data were preliminary. Although categories had been identified, they were developed from a small population of college-aged children. In an effort to refine these types of invasion tactics and defensive actions to parental privacy violations, a second, more extensive study was conducted using a survey questionnaire format.

STUDY TWO: REFINING MEASURES
OF PARENTAL INVASION AND DEFENSIVE ACTIONS

In the second study (Petronio & McDaniel, 1992a), a survey questionnaire was developed using the categories found in Study One for parental invasion and boundary defensive actions. A total of 286 college students in communication classes were asked to report how invasive (6 = very invasive; 1 = not invasive at all) parental use of the 10 types of privacy invasion found in Study One was for them. The college students were also asked to report their perceptions of how frequently (6 = very frequently; 1 = not frequently at all) they used the 14 defensive tactics also found in Study One. The rationale for the choice of frequency response categories was based on the fact that certain categories were used more often than others in Study One for defensive tactics. Hence, the authors reasoned that frequency for defensive actions seemed to be a critical indicator. Although, the concept of frequency was also noted for the parental invasion tactics, using the Burgoon et al. study as a base, the authors reasoned that the intensity of invasion for the parents' invasion actions was a more viable indicator for this concept.

To refine the categories identified in Study One for both the parental invasion and the defensive actions, two separate principal components factor analyses were conducted using these survey data. The analysis for the parental privacy identified two main types of tactics: (a) subversive invasion, and (b) direct invasion tactics. The factor analysis for the defensive actions also identified two tactics used as responses to parental violations of privacy by the college-aged children: (a) confrontational tactics, and (b) evasive tactics.

Parents' use of *subversive invasion* tactics refers to such acts as going through personal belongings without permission, eavesdropping on conversations, and listening to a telephone conversation on an extension without permission. Parents' use of *direct invasion* tactics refers to such acts as asking for personal information, making unsolicited remarks about the child's personal life, and giving advice.

In response, the college-aged children in this study used *confrontational* tactics, such as a sign telling the parents to "keep out" of their room, asking the parents to stop, and locking their room. These tactics are more representative of retroactive control strategies for boundary maintenance. College-aged children may also use *evasive* tactics in response to parental invasion, such as making phone calls outside of the home and hiding personal belongings. The evasive tactics reflect a proactive form of controlling privacy boundaries. Thus, from this study, it seems in a general way that parents are perceived to use both direct and indirect invasion tactics, and children respond by using direct and indirect reaction tactics.

The first two studies gave us firm footing regarding the way college children contend with their parents' invasion through certain kinds of defensive actions and the kind of boundary violations parents are typically perceived to use. The next study helped the authors understand if there were any interconnections between parental invasion, the children's defensive actions, and assess the nature of that relationship from the perspective of the children. As discussed earlier, there is some reason to believe that a link exists between the way parents invade and college-aged children respond to those privacy violations. For example, if the parents are direct about the way they violate privacy, the college-aged children may be able to anticipate the invasions and proactively protect boundary lines. Thus, the defensive actions on the part of the children may be related, in part, to the type of invasion tactic the parents use.

STUDY THREE: RELATIONSHIP BETWEEN PARENTAL INVASION AND DEFENSIVE ACTIONS

In order to examine the relationship between the type of parental invasion and the defensive actions of college-aged children, a third study was conducted on this issue (Petronio & McDaniel, 1992a). Using the data collected in Study Two, including the parental tactics of *subversive and direct* invasion found in the factor analysis and the defensive actions of *confrontation and evasion* used by children, Petronio and McDaniel (1992a) analyzed the relationship of parental invasion and defensive actions by children.

When examining the degree of invasiveness of the subversive and direct invasion tactics by parents, the more invasive the direct style is perceived to be by college students, the more frequently they use both confrontational and evasive defenses. Thus, the way these college-aged children contend with direct, highly invasive parental violations, such as parents asking personal questions, is to frequently confront them by telling them to stop or evade the direct violation by using a pay phone and having meetings outside of the home with friends. Boundary control is exercised by either or both means to counterbalance these explicit violations of privacy used by the parents.

When parents use more subversive tactics, such as listening on a telephone extension, eavesdropping, opening mail without permission, and so on, college-aged children respond by confronting their parents. In a covert way, the parents have compromised the children's ability to claim control over their privacy. This may make the college-aged children feel frustrated and leave them with few options to regain control over the situation. When parents are direct, and therefore obvious about the invasions, children are better able to make proactive moves in anticipation of the violations. Hence, the children are able to hide personal belongings or use a pay phone outside of the home. If the parents are more subversive in their invasions, the children may be less able to predict when these violations will happen. Therefore, the children may be less able to take control when invasions occur. With subversive tactics, the children must first rely on discovery, thereby limiting them to confrontational responses rather than evasive actions to defend privacy.

As these data indicate, there is a connection between parental privacy invasion and college-aged children's defensive actions. The privacy boundary is either being proactively protected by the children or retroactively restored, depending on the type of invasion tactics used by the parents. Although college-aged children are capable of protecting and restoring their privacy boundaries regarding invasion by their parents, there may be a toll on the parent–child relationship as a result. The last study examines the interrelationship between parental privacy invasion tactics, defensive actions by the children, and the impact on the parent–child relationship.

STUDY 4: IMPACT ON THE PARENT–CHILD RELATIONSHIP

As pointed out earlier, granting privacy control by the parents is a critical factor in the children's ability to develop a sense of independence from the family and be able to explore their own identity (Parke & Sawin, 1979). But, as this chapter also points out, there are times when the parents feel compelled to invade their children's privacy. The actions that violate children's feelings of separateness from their parents appear to negatively affect the parent–child relationship. As Noller and Callan (1991) note, "it seems clear that close supervision and other manifestations of parental control provoke negative attitudes and behavior in adolescents" (p. 68).

The kind of relationship children have with their parents often depends on the extent to which the children feel in control of their lives (Noller & Callan, 1991). Youniss and Smollar (1985) suggest that "adolescents gain independence from parental authority when they are allowed to act outside their parents' den and without their parents' intervention" (p. 73). When parents are able to renegotiate the structure of unilateral authority, such as excluding themselves from involvement, the parent–child relationship appears to benefit (Youniss & Smollar, 1985). Children move away from being dependent on the parents, but they still need to maintain a level of connectedness. However, the connectedness needs to shift from parental authority to mutual respect for each other in order to be successful (Youniss & Smollar, 1985).

Grotevant and Cooper (1986) refer to the dual process of connectedness and separation as individuation. One of the primary indicators of individuation is "the limited contact with parents and possession of private lives apart from the family" (Youniss & Smollar, 1985, p. 77). As children grow older, they spend more time away from the control of parents so as not to be monitored. Children also maintain control over their privacy by limiting or withholding information from their parents. The parents that tend to grant the increasing sense of personal control help foster the development of their adolescents. Conversely, those parents who are unable to resolve their differences in boundary definitions may make it more difficult for their children to advance successfully into adulthood.

The last study focuses on the interrelationship between parental invasion tactics, defensive actions by the college-aged children, and the impact on the parent–child relationship from the perspective of the children (Petronio & McDaniel, 1992b). In a final data collection, 298 college students were administered a survey questionnaire that again asked questions about the invasiveness of parental privacy invasion tactics, frequency of defensive actions enacted by children in response or anticipation, and added questions about their assessment of parent–child trust, communication satisfaction, relational quality, and openness. The questions representing these four parent–child relationship issues were based on existing measures. A LISREL analysis was conducted to determine the interrelationships among parental privacy invasion tactics, defensive actions by the children, and the impact on the four parent–child relationship measures.

The data analysis from Study Four shows that the invasions and defensive actions in combination impact the parent–child relationship. The results show that as parents select a particular method of privacy violation that is perceived to be highly invasive, the tactics children use in response to defend their boundaries has an impact on the children's perceptions of the parent–child relationship. When college children use confrontational tactics in response to direct and subversive parental invasions of their privacy, there is a negative effect on trust and relational quality and a positive impact on parent–child openness. But when children use an evasive tactic in response to direct parental invasion methods, only a negative impact on trust and relational quality is found.

When college children defend their boundaries against either a direct or subversive parental invasion tactic that is considered highly invasive with confrontation, they see trust and relational quality declining. But they also report that openness increases. Confrontation by college children appears to be a pivotal issue in opening lines of communication between them and their parents. Yet, the type of openness described seems more adversarial than that which fosters a positive relationship. This is evidenced in the declining levels of trust and relational quality.

The confrontational approach to boundary defense is an open form of communication in its own right. When using this method, college children outwardly show disappointment, ask parents to stop invading their privacy, make parents feel guilty, or show parents evidence of invasion. The children seem to be sending a message about their disapproval. Although this defense style enhances a type of parent–child openness, the response is seen as confrontational. Perhaps this behavior on the part of the children is helpful to clear the air and provides a vehicle for them to regain boundary control. But, these actions by parents are perceived by their children to weaken a sense of trust and erode feelings of relational quality. The tension between parents and children results in a paradoxical outcome. Children believe they have a type of openness, but they also see a decline in trust and relational quality.

When college children use an evasive boundary defense in response to a direct invasion, there is also a negative impact on trust and parent–child relational quality. By responding to the direct invasion method through evasive tactics college children perceive that trust is diminished, as is the quality of the relationship with their parents. Openness, in this instance, is not affected.

Frequently having to hide personal belongings, make phone calls outside the home, and have meetings with friends away from their house tend to make children feel more distrustful and suspicious of their parents. The children want to protect their boundaries but seem to be put into a position of taking actions that work against a positive parent–child relationship. For example, one respondent from the open-ended questions in Study One stated:

> These invasions still happen to me and I'm 20 years old and 1200 miles away from home! To protect my privacy I usually lock or hide anything of particular value to me. When I am in the bathroom the door is locked. If I am having

private phone conversations, I will go and make calls at my older sister's home. Mail is a big taboo. I *hate* and resent it when it comes to me in a "new" envelope. Usually this means that it has been inspected. To take care of this problem, all of my mail is now automatically forwarded to school whenever possible.

These findings complement the literature, in that, adolescents and college-aged children who are most able to achieve autonomy and differentiation from their parents have a better relationship with their parents overall (Murphey, Silber, Coelho, Hamburg, & Greenberg, 1963; Walsh, 1982). These data suggest that interfering with this process by invading children's privacy may result in negative outcomes for the parent–child relationship, at least from the perspective of college students.

Even when openness is achieved through confrontational reactions by the children, trust and the quality of the relationship are disrupted. Evasive actions appear to be problematic to trust and quality as well. Evasiveness on the part of children may reflect a sense of suspicion about the parents. When the children's suspicion is acted upon by implementing tactics to counterbalance the expected or enacted invasion, they are attempting to regain control over their privacy boundaries.

Thus, when examining boundary conflict from the children's point of view, invasion by parents may be seen as a marker for inconsistency in the way privacy rights are defined for parents and college-aged children. To understand the way this inconsistency influences the parent–child relationship, it seems necessary to consider not only the parent's actions but the reactions of the children.

IMPLICATIONS

There are several issues that these studies raise in regard to both learning about privacy for college-age children and the parent–child relationship in general. This discussion also suggests some implications for understanding the dynamics of openness and privacy as well.

The examination of parental privacy invasion found in this chapter seems most appropriate for a book on the dark side of interpersonal communication. Given children are willing to grant a wide latitude of acceptance to their parents concerning privacy invasion (Burgoon et al., 1989), by focusing on the intensity of invasiveness, these studies examined the perceived extremes of privacy violations. These studies did not tap into the ordinary or typical kinds of invasions that are of less consequence. Instead, this research focused on the magnitude of the invasion. Thus, the emphasis was on actions of privacy violation that have a certain degree of significance to the college-age child. As such, this chapter presents a darker side to the way college-age children view invasive actions of their parents.

In the most general terms, it has been argued that understanding the meaning of privacy for college-aged children is tied to the issues of separation and autonomy from their parents (Wolfe & Laufer, 1974). The clearest signs of granting separation by parents is the reduction of direct control and freedom from monitoring. The ability of parents to give college-aged children room to explore their own values and ideas helps facilitate advancement into adulthood (Youniss & Smollar, 1985). As Youniss and Smollar state, "hence, it is clear that separation occurs through the license that parents grant adolescents to have private lives and through the activities that adolescents undertake when they are apart from their families" (p. 77).

Yet, separation and the quest for autonomy are often pursued in conjunction with the need for a continued connection with parents (Moore, 1984). Youniss and Smollar (1985) point out that "even after emancipation has begun, adolescents still appear to seek parental endorsement for their ideas" (p. 161). Given this dialectical process of needing to establish autonomy through privacy and also wanting a continued relationship with parents, the perceived magnitude of parental privacy invasion seems to jeopardize these dual needs.

Parents tend to communicate mixed messages about their college-aged children's ability to act independently when they invade their privacy. College students, no doubt, restrict information and may be generally wary of talking to their parents about certain things that might upset them. But, college-aged children are learning how to manage face presentation to their parents. Their parents' opinions are important to them, yet, they may be exploring principles, values, and ideas that are contrary to those held by their parents (Campbell et al., 1984).

College-aged children seem to need time apart from parents to determine which values of their parents they will keep and which they will discard (Parke & Sawin, 1979). The goals of this balancing process are to maintain connections with their parents while establishing their own turf. Through privacy violations, parents often compromise the freedom of this exploration and their children's ability to manage how they want to present themselves to their parents. Even though parents may not define privacy invasion as problematic, when information is exposed and possessions and space are taken over, children seem to perceive a decline in the parent–child relationship. Hence, children may not be as inclined to trust their parents and reveal their feelings.

Research has shown that parents who are nurturing and supportive are more frequently told private information by their children (Doster & Strickland, 1969; Komarovsky, 1974). Perhaps, when violations are considered very invasive, in which children are coerced into disclosure, this may result in a sense of face loss or embarrassment and diminished feelings of autonomy. Children may not define highly invasive actions as nurturing. As these data show, privacy invasion tends to make them act defensively toward their parents. Rather than providing a more productive balance between connectedness and autonomy, parental privacy invasion appears to obligate the children into being more adamant about protecting their boundaries rather than opening them up to parents. The result of boundary conflict stemming from parental privacy invasion may lead children to alternative ways of exploring privacy management. Thus, children may depend even more on friends to examine feelings or disclose private information because the parental relationship has become problematic. Rather than being forced to expose feelings, as with parental invasion, college-aged children might find that their friends accord them more personal control over information, space, and possessions they call their own.

For example, research shows that adolescents typically talk to friends more than parents about self-doubts and sexual issues (Youniss & Smollar, 1985). As parental privacy violations are perceived to be highly invasive, children may seek out their friends more often than they would ordinarily. By violating private domains, parents may be hindering their children's choice of deciding in whom to confide. Instead, children may turn more frequently to their friends. In the process, the ability to develop feelings of connectedness with their parents is jeopardized by their parents' invasive actions.

Although the rules for the parent–child relationship are similar to those held for friendships with regard to privacy (Youniss & Smollar, 1985), the defensive responses by children appear more varied with regard to their parents. As suggested by Youniss and Smollar (1985), the rules include: "keeping promises, not disclosing privileged information, being attentive, being sensitive to . . . needs, not being insulting, not lying, not intruding . . . respecting property, acting in a self-respecting way, not acting selfishly, and not becoming overdemanding" (p. 153). When these rules are violated for friendships, adolescents confront the friend and expect remedial action to be taken (Youniss & Smollar, 1985). From these data, when parents violate privacy rules, boundary defense includes both confrontations (as with their friends) as well as evasive actions. While some children are able to openly confront their parents, others find it difficult to question the authority of their parents and appear to use evasive ways of protecting their privacy boundaries.

As these data also suggest, when parents use either highly invasive direct ways of privacy invasion or subversive tactics, children respond by confronting their parents. Openness is perceived to increase; however, trust and relational quality are weakened. This finding appears to have some implications for the nature of openness in general. Many researchers regard openness as mostly positive and with good justification (e.g., Chelune, 1979; Jourard, 1971; Pennebaker, 1989). But, from these studies, openness may have an alternative dimension, that is, openness resulting from confrontation. Confrontational openness seems to extend beyond the general notions of valence.

This conceptualization of openness appears to be somewhat different from the research on valence of disclosure (Gilbert & Whiteneck, 1976; Hendrick, 1987). In the studies examining valence, the focus is on the person choosing to reveal private information to others in seemingly unprovoked ways. As both Gilbert and Whiteneck (1976) and Hendrick (1987) suggest, valence refers to positive or negative information about the self that the person is willing to disclose. The concept discussed in this chapter concentrates on recipients of invasive acts who are protecting or restoring their boundaries by open confrontation in response to invasion of their privacy. Thus, it is not so much the good or bad things individuals tell others about themselves; it is the willingness to challenge the appropriateness of actions taken by others.

Confrontational openness is not enacted by taking into account the "likelihood of candor" for another (Rawlins, 1983). In these studies, college-age children do not seem to necessarily care if they hurt their parents' feelings by open confrontation. Children may feel betrayed by their parents' actions of invasion, and the defensive response is to openly tell their parents how they feel about their behavior. In speculation, the positive side may be that children feel within their rights to openly challenge their parents with the knowledge that they have acted contrary to the children's expectations. But, the negative side is that the children perceive diminished parent–child trust and quality.

Yet, open confrontation in reaction to parental invasions contributes to perceptions of openness by children. They feel they are taking control over the situation by indicating their disapproval. For example, one respondent stated, "I would confront them as to what they are doing, tell them it is wrong and that they should respect me and my personal things. I respect them, therefore I should get the same treatment." Another respondent concurs with this attitude, "My first reaction [to invasion by parents] would be to confront them and let them know I know that they have invaded my privacy, I would also let them know to what degree it has upset me. Hopefully I would make them feel bad and they won't do it again." Even though children see this tactic as a way to regain control over their privacy, and there is a type of openness with their parents, they also feel that other aspects of the relationship with their parents have been jeopardized. One might wonder whether this kind of openness gained outweighs the reduction in trust and quality.

These perceptions of privacy invasion may also be very different from the perspective of the parents. They may view the willingness of their children to stand up for their rights as a useful exercise. Although it is communicated in the form of confrontation, parents may find that children are learning ways of coping with difficult situations. On the other hand, parents might find contending with these kinds of conflicts demanding because they have not defined parental privacy invasion in the same way as their children. They may consider acts of invasion as their right to keep informed about their children. Perhaps, parents may even conceive of invasions as necessary in being "good" parents. From this view, the kinds of reactions discussed in this chapter may perplex these parents. This type of speculation is beyond the current chapter, but to form a more complete picture of family privacy binds, it seems important to compare the parents' perspective with the college-age children's point of view.

Regardless of the parents' orientation to privacy violations of their children, the point remains that from these data, college-age children believe that invasions comprise the parent–child relationship in meaningful ways. As Youniss and Smollar (1985) point out, "individuality, which is probably a primary issue between parents and adolescents, develops gradually through a series of accommodations. . . . The parents retain authority by giving more freedom to adolescents by recognizing their personal needs and capabilities" (pp. 158, 162).

REFERENCES

Altman, I. (1975). *Environmental and social behavior: Privacy, personal space, territory, and crowding.* Monterey, CA: Brooks/Cole.

Altman, I., Vinsel, A., & Brown, B. (1981). Dialectic conceptions in social psychology: An application to social penetration and privacy regulation. In L. Berkowitz (Ed.), *Advances in experimental social psychology* (Vol. 14, pp. 108–160). New York: Academic Press.

Baxter, L., & Wilmot, W. (1984). Secret tests: Strategies for acquiring information about the state of the relationship. *Human Communication Research, 5,* 264–272.

Berardo, F. M. (1974). Family invisibility and family privacy. In S. Margulis (Ed.), *Privacy* (pp. 55–72). Stony Brook, NY: Environmental Design Research Association.

Burgoon, J., Parrot, R., Le Poire, B., Kelley, D., Walther, J., & Perry, D. (1989). Maintaining and restoring privacy through communication in different types of relationships. *Journal of Social and Personal Relationships, 6,* 131–158.

Callan, V., & Noller, P. (1986). Perceptions of communicative relationships in families with adolescents. *Journal of Marriage and the Family, 48,* 813–820.

Campbell, E., Adams, G., & Dobson, W. (1984). Familial correlates of identity formation in late adolescence: A study of the predictive utility of connectedness and individuality in family relations. *Journal of Youth and Adolescence, 13,* 509–525.

Chelune, G. (1979). *Self-disclosure.* San Francisco, Jossey-Bass.

Coleman, J., & Hendry, L. (1990). *The nature of adolescence.* London: Routledge.

Derlega, V., & Chaikin, A. (1977). Privacy and self-disclosure in social relationships. *Journal of Social Issues, 33,* 102–115.

Doster, J., & Strickland, B. (1969). Perceived childrearing practices and self-disclosure patterns. *Journal of Consulting and Clinical Psychology, 33,* 382.

Gilbert, S., & Whiteneck, G. (1976). Toward a multidimensional approach to the study of self-disclosure. *Human Communication Research, 3,* 347–355.

Grotevant, H., & Cooper, C. (1986). Individuation in family relationships: A perspective on individual differences in development of identity and role-taking skill in adolescence. *Human Development, 29,* 82–100.

Hendrick, S. (1987). Counseling and self-disclosure. In V. Derlega & J. Berg (Eds.), *Self-disclosure: Theory, research and therapy* (pp. 303–324). New York: Plenum.

Jourard, S. (1971). *Transparent self.* New York: Van Nostrand.

Karpel, M. A. (1980). Family secrets: I. Conceptual and ethical issues in the relational context; II. Ethical and practical considerations in therapeutic management. *Family Process, 19,* 295–306.

Komarovsky, M. (1974). Patterns of self-disclosure of male undergraduates. *Journal of Marriage and the Family, 36,* 677–686.

Lyman, S. M., & Scott, M. B. (1970). Territoriality: A neglected sociological dimension. In G. Stone & H. A. Farberman (Eds.), *Social psychology through symbolic interaction* (pp. 214–226). Waltham, MA: Xerox College Publishing.

McGoldrick, M., & Carter, E. (1982). The family life cycle. In F. Walsh (Ed.), *Normal family processes* (pp. 167–195). New York: Guilford.

Moore, D. (1984). Parent-adolescent separation: Intrafamilial perceptions and difficulty separating from parents. *Personality and Social Psychology Bulletin, 10,* 611–619.

Murphey, E., Silber, E., Coelho, G., Hamburg, D., & Greenberg, I. (1963). Development of autonomy and parent–child interaction in late adolescence. *American Journal of Orthopsychiatry, 33,* 643–652.

Noller, P., & Callan, V. (1991). *The adolescent in the family.* London: Routledge.

Parke, R., & Sawin, D. (1979). Children's privacy in the home: Developmental, ecological, and child-rearing determinants. *Environment and Behavior, 11,* 87–104.

Pennebaker, J. W. (1989). Confessions, inhibitions, and disease. In L. Berkowitz (Ed.), *Advances in experimental social psychology* (Vol. 22, pp. 211–244). San Diego, CA: Academic Press.

Petronio, S. (1991). Communication boundary management: A theoretical model of managing disclosure of private information between marital couples. *Communication Theory, 1,* 311–335.

Petronio, S., & Braithwaite, D. (1987). I'd rather not say: The role of personal privacy in small groups. In M. Mayer & N. Dollar (Eds.), *Issues in group communication* (pp. 67–79). Scottsdale, AZ: Gorsuch Scarisbrick.

Petronio, S., & Harriman, S. (1989). *Parental privacy invasion I: Tactics and reactions to encroachment.* Paper presented at the Speech Communication Association Convention, Chicago, IL.

Petronio, S., & McDaniel, S. (1992a). *Parental privacy invasion II & III: The effect of parental method on the parent–child relationship.* Unpublished paper, Arizona State University, Tempe, AZ.

Petronio, S., & McDaniel, S. (1992b). *Parental privacy invasion IV: Reactions of college children and the effect on parent–child relationships.* Unpublished paper, Arizona State University, Tempe, AZ.

Rawlins, W. K. (1983). Openness as problematic in ongoing friendships: Two conversational dilemmas. *Communication Monographs, 50,* 1–13.

Walsh, F. (1982). Conceptualizations of normal family functioning. In F. Walsh (Ed.), *Normal family processes* (pp. 3–42). New York: Guilford.

Wolfe, M., & Laufer, R. (1974). The concept of privacy in childhood and adolescence. In S. Margulis (Ed.), *Privacy* (pp. 29–54). Stony Brook, NY: Environmental Design Research Association.

Youniss, J., & Smollar, J. (1985). *Adolescent relations with mothers, fathers, and friends.* Chicago: University of Chicago Press.

11

THE DARK SIDE
OF "NORMAL" FAMILY INTERACTION

Laura Stafford
Marianne Dainton
The Ohio State University

Despite the cozy family photographs in the album and all those family picnics and Christmas parties, there is also a dark side to families. Partly this is because we spend most of our time there, but it is also because of the intensities of emotion, both positive and negative, that are learned and experienced there.

—Duck, 1992, p. 104

Although the mere mention of the dark side of family interaction conjures images of abused spouses and children and clinically disturbed families, there are darker elements of "normal" family interaction as well. However, when normal families are considered in research and popular culture, a positivity bias exists. Conjointly, the foci on the negative elements of dysfunctional families and the positive aspects of normal families have served to conceal the dark side of normal families. The purpose of this chapter is to illuminate some of the negative interactions of ordinary families. In so doing, we briefly consider some myths surrounding American families. Next, we center on potentially harmful interaction patterns within the family. Finally, we entertain the argument of the family as a subversive institution.

Before proceeding it is necessary to review what "normal" means. There are variations as to what constitutes normalcy (see Walsh, 1982). The most common use of the term *normal* references family health. Usually, a family is considered normal if pathology is absent from all members. Such families are often referred to as nonclinical or nonlabeled families.

A second view of normal permeates the American culture: normality as utopia. This ideal view is sometimes equated with health, as exemplified by Curran's (1983) 15 traits of "healthy" families. According to Curran, healthy families communicate, listen, share leisure time, and have a strong religious core. Moreover, all family members respect, trust, support, and value all others. In other words, a normal family resembles the situation comedy families of the 1950s. When this notion of normality is embraced, however, normality does not exist; such optimal functioning is "seldom, if ever, seen in flesh and blood" (Offer & Sabshin, 1966, p. 104).

A third view of normality refers to statistical averages. By this definition, a family is normal if it is like most other families. That is, an optimal or ideal family is as abnormal, if not more so, than a clinical family. "Normal families are not necessarily asymptomatic. If most families are found to have occasional problems, the presence of a problem does not in itself imply that a family is not normal" (Walsh, 1982, p. 6).

This last version of normal comports to our belief. From a dialogical point of view, the positive and the negative co-exist in social behavior (Duck, 1990). Duck (1990), extending the work of Billig (1987), argues that individuals face the fundamental dilemma of continuously negotiating and contemplating these opposite poles within the context of their relationships. Similarly, we contend that normal family interaction is a paradox of conflicting messages of support and hurt. More specifically, all families occasionally manifest communication patterns that are not only less than optimal, they may be damaging. Yet, this dark side is seldom brought to light unless some problem becomes serious enough to require intervention. Although we are all too aware of the staggering statistics on family violence, adolescent substance abuse, juvenile delinquency, and a host of other family disorders, such clinical issues are beyond our scope. Rather, we focus on negative interactions that the average family experiences.

MYTHS ABOUT THE FAMILY

The American culture is filled with myths concerning what the family is and should be. The most pervasive myth is that there is such a thing as a normal family.[1] This normal family takes the form of a white, middle-class group consisting of a first—and only—time legally married, heterosexual couple, 1.8 children, and (of course) a family pet, all of whom interact in the

---

[1]Definitions of family are quite diverse, and there remains no single accepted definition (Galvin & Brommel, 1991; Trost, 1990). Historically, families have been conceived as kinship groups who live together, the primary function of which is the socialization of children (Fitzpatrick & Badzinski, 1985). Galvin and Brommel (1991) note that today the definitions of family may be much broader. Nevertheless, a lay conceptualization of the family is sufficient for the purposes of this chapter.

idealistic manner of utopian normalcy. This view is highly skewed in several ways.

First, numerous family structures currently exist. Single-parent, step-, cohabiting, homosexual, and co-parental families are common family forms. In fact, the traditional nuclear family is certainly not typical. For example, estimates indicate that by the year 2000 stepfamilies will outnumber all other family forms (Beer, 1989).

Another way in which this view of normalcy is skewed is in the impact of such a mythical standard on both researchers and families. Researchers typically have considered alternative structures and co-cultural variations deviant or pathological (Adams, 1988). Recently, however, variations in structures and co-cultural interaction patterns have received some recognition as equally functional and normal, representing an emergent as opposed to a deviant model (see McKenry, Everett, Ramseur, & Carter, 1989). Still, it remains questionable as to the extent to which scholarly acceptance is occurring. Ganong, Coleman, and Mapes (1990) conclude that the traditional nuclear family remains the standard against which other family forms are judged.

Scholarly opinions aside, family members themselves reference prevailing cultural ideologies in evaluating their own family (see McCall, 1988). For example, co-cultural family members often internalize the values of the White, middle-class ideal and evaluate their own families as lacking (Adams, 1988; Engram, 1982). Furthermore, it is quite likely that White middle-class family members also gauge their families against the supposedly optimal model and hence perceive their families as deficient as well.

A second widely accepted myth about the family is that there was once a golden age of family relations. During this fictitious utopian era, divorce was unheard of, children respected their elders and knew right from wrong, multiple generations dwelled blissfully in the same home, and family members spent their abundant leisure time together engaged in wholesome activities such as eating stone-ground bread that had been baked in their own ovens from plates they made themselves at their joint pottery class.[2] In short, once upon a time there was a period of great family solidarity that provided a "haven in a heartless world" (Lasch, 1977, p. 6). Family historians, however, have been unable to find any era in American history that approaches this idyll (see Elder, 1974; Hareven, 1982).

The truth behind the myth is that the golden age of family interaction is ultimately nothing more than a nostalgic construction. Accordingly, the "new family history group" is making significant inroads in reconstructing the history of the family apart from the mythic historical accounts of families (Adams, 1988). Nevertheless, the pervasive myth of the golden age of the family fosters

---

[2]We thank Steve Duck for suggesting this mocking example of a wholesome family leisure activity.

a tension between the ideal and real family experience. Indeed, "nostalgia for a lost family tradition that in fact never existed prejudices understanding of the conditions of families in contemporary society" (Hareven, 1982, p. 460).

THE DARK COUNTENANCE
OF FAMILY COMMUNICATION

Increasingly, scholars have argued that routine interactions constitute the substance of marital relationships (see Duck, 1992). In a similar vein, a fundamental assumption here is that routine interaction is the mainstay of family life. Though by no means are we discounting the consequences of turning points, traumatic events, or chaotic junctures, routine interaction also may have long-standing and equally profound effects on family members. Indeed, the mundane or day-to-day communication between spouses, between parents and children, and between siblings is likely the mucky, murky playing field of the dark elements of family interaction. Nevertheless, whether messages are part of the mundane daily interaction or traumatic turning points, we live with the messages of our families throughout our lives and carry with us the consequences; our insecurities, neuroses, and even dislike of vegetables may well be rooted in family interaction.

In examining family interaction, we adopt a systemic view, that is, we believe that all members of a family influence all other members in some way (see Minuchin, 1985). Further, all relationships between family members affect all other family members and their relationships with each other (see Hinde & Stevenson-Hinde, 1988). Hence, examples are offered to illustrate that adverse interaction permeates routine family interaction at all levels: the marital relationship, the parent–child relationship, the sibling relationship, and the family as a whole.

Marital Relationships

Although people may marry due to love and romantic images, marriage is not all hearts and flowers. Even individuals who consider themselves to be happily married find they are not immune from unpleasant everyday interactions (Kirchler, 1988). Marriage is characterized by a dearth of companionate talk, an abundance of conflict, and a general failure to engage in "good" communication skills. Spouses seldom meet the "requirements" touted by skills enthusiasts in terms of active listening, self-disclosure and openness, or even basic politeness. This section discusses the gap between the utopian ideal and real marital interaction, specifically in terms of relationship "work," conflict, and generally poor communication.

Over 90% of all Americans marry at some time in their life (see Skolnick & Skolnick, 1989). Clearly, the vast majority of American adults view marriage as desirable. Apparently, in this culture, most people get married because they love their partner and wish to achieve and maintain intimacy (Bellah, Madsen, Sullivan, Swidler, & Tipton, 1985; Schaefer & Olson, 1981). Ironically, however, feelings of love and behaviors associated with intimacy (such as demonstrations of affection) decrease almost immediately after a couple marries (e.g., Huston, McHale, & Crouter, 1986). However, the number of negative interactions remains constant (Huston & Vangelisti, 1991). This may be because, as Bochner (1984) contends, once day-to-day interaction occurs the realities of married life set in and the romantic ideals fostered by cultural ideals are difficult to sustain. Because of cultural expectations for intimacy in marriage (see Bellah, et al., 1985), a gap may be widening between inflated marital expectations and "normal" marital interaction.

> People usually marry out of an emotional attraction: love, sex, romance, companionship, and other idealized experiences that a couple look forward to. Once into the marriage, though, they experience the hard material realities of family life. The home, after all, turns out to be an economic unit. . . . Every home is a combination of hotel, restaurant, laundry, and often a child-care and entertainment center. Each of these activities takes work, work that is often invisible when one is merely the recipient of these services. (Collins, 1988, pp. 281–282)

In brief, most people recognize that relationships take "work," but they often fail to recognize the form and extent that work will take. Relational work may have less to do with striving to maintain intimacy and more to do with accomplishing instrumental tasks. For instance, Dainton and Stafford (1993) found that the routine relational maintenance behavior most frequently mentioned by married couples was sharing tasks. Discouragingly, a program of research indicates that the use of sharing tasks as a relational maintenance strategy adds relatively little predictive value to relational characteristics such as love, liking, control mutuality, commitment, or satisfaction (although there were some exceptions to this general trend; see Canary & Stafford, 1992; Dainton, Stafford, & Canary, 1991; Stafford & Canary, 1991).

As depressing as these results are, most research imparts even more depressing news for women. When it comes to home-related tasks, women labor far more than men. On average, wives spend between 50 and 60 hours a week on housework and child care, whereas husbands spend approximately 22 hours per week on these tasks (Berk, 1985). Moreover, when wives are employed outside of the home, husbands do not significantly increase the amount of time they spend on housework (Berk, 1985; but see Coltrane & Ishii-Kuntz, 1992). Although the amount of time spent on housework decreases for the wife when she has outside employment, apparently the overall amount of housework she performs does not decrease. Rather, she simply accomplishes the work more quickly.

Perhaps as a function of the amount of time spent "working" in marriage, married partners report engaging in comparatively fewer maintenance activities that are companionate or intimate in nature (Dainton & Stafford, 1993). We doubt that couples prefer to engage in household activities over more pleasurable ones, however. Indeed, Huston et al. (1986) found that married couples were dissatisfied with their amount of interaction, including the amount of time spent talking to each other and the amount of self-disclosure.

Further, Huston et al. (1986) found that married couples only spend a little over an hour a day talking to each other. Much of the content of these conversations concerns decision making and conflict resolution (Sillars & Wilmot, 1989). Apparently, married couples find little time to talk to each other, and when they do their conversations focus on "business" rather than "pleasure." The demands of marital and family life leave little time to engage in companionate talk.

Not only is marriage comprised of chores and task-oriented talk, but it is also a breeding ground for conflict. Marriages (and families) have been characterized as systems of natural conflict (Sprey, 1969). As individuals become more intimate and interdependent the potential for conflict becomes greater (Roloff & Cloven, in press). Paradoxically, the investment and commitment inherent in marriage seems not only to foster conflict but also to provide strong incentives to avoid conflict (Turner, 1970). Couples find themselves in a no-win situation; unaddressed conflicts often remain unresolved conflicts, which may have detrimental consequences on a relationship (Duck, 1988; Lloyd & Cate, 1985). At the same time, the romantic/passionate dimension of marriage appears to promote the use of destructive conflict management styles, which are also associated with detrimental consequences for the relationship (Fry, Firestone, & Williams, 1983). Even more reflective of this lose–lose position are the findings of Rcloff and Cloven (1990); these researchers have found that both voiced and unaddressed conflicts were negatively associated with marital satisfaction.

Most adults recognize that matrimony does not guarantee living "happily ever after," and that conflict is inevitable. Nonetheless, people tend to believe in the power of "good" communication, despite the fact that "good" communication is simply a stereotype (Fitzpatrick & Badzinski, 1985). These stereotypes may "set expectations for a relationship that cannot be met and hence may lead to dissatisfaction" (p. 696).

For example, in discussing prevailing beliefs concerning openness, Fitzpatrick (1991) noted that "the proverbial visitor from Mars would be convinced that competent marital communication in our milieu was accomplished solely through self-disclosure or the revealing of private thoughts and feelings" (p. 74). Yet, counter to expectations, couples often are not disclosive. Self-disclosure may actually comprise little of a couple's interaction (Dindia, Fitzpatrick, & Kenny, 1989). Further, Baxter and Wilmot (1986) found certain topics were considered relational "taboos." Taboo topics were avoided due to fears of embarrassment, fear that talking about the relationship may have a negative impact on the relationship, or due to an individual's desire to protect his or her own privacy (see Petronio, this volume, on privacy). Finally, openness is in dialectical tension with closedness (Bochner, 1984). It seems that not being open is as fundamental as being open.

Marital skills programs endeavor (in part) to train couples to alter negative communicative patterns in favor of stereotypes of good communication such as self-disclosure. Several problems with such approaches exist. The basic premise of marital communication skills programs is that communication leads to understanding, which in turn enhances relational satisfaction. Yet, knowing how to appropriately and effectively communicate does not ensure that an individual will do so. For example, Sillars and Weisberg (1987) argued that marital conflict is often so emotional, so ambiguous, and so "messy" that it is unlikely partners will even remember to use such oft-touted strategies as *I statements* (i.e., say "I" before each attribution) and validation (i.e., acknowledge the partner's communication).[3] Skill is also difficult to use even in nonconflictual situations. Garland (1981), for example, found that although individuals knew how to engage in "active listening," they often did not do so with their spouses. Similarly, individuals in unhappy marriages have the ability to decode nonverbal messages when interacting with strangers, but this "skill" mysteriously disappears when decoding the spouse (see Noller, 1984). The contention that partners' possess "better skills" than they use with their spouses is also supported by the work of Birchler, Weiss, and Vincent (1975), who found that even happily married spouses are much nicer when talking to strangers than when talking to each other. Specifically, Birchler et al. found that married individuals verbalized more complaints, criticisms, denials, excuses, put downs, interruptions, and disagreements with each other than when talking to strangers. In a similar vein, married partners ignored each other more and paid less attention to each other than did stranger dyads.

In sum, marriage is replete with less-than-expected and less-than-desirable interaction, and the communication in marriage rarely conforms to the cultural stereotype of "good communication." The next section highlights the dark side of interaction between parents and children.

---

[3]The standard practice of teaching the use of *I statements* (Gordon, 1970, 1975) may not be as beneficial as initially thought. Such statements may in fact be destructive and distancing. Burr (1990) proposes that couples desiring egalitarian relationships should strive to use *we statements* (which acknowledge the interdependence of the relational partners) in place of *I statements*.

Parent–Child Relationships

Communication between parents and children retains the potential to be damaging to both parents and children. Numerous examples of the darker elements of communication between parents and children could be offered. Of course, these elements change with the course of development of the child and the development of the family (see Nussbaum, 1989, on life-span perspectives). In order to limit our scope, however, we focus primarily on early childhood. Two topics serve as our examples: self-esteem and child compliance (or lack thereof).

A caveat should be offered first. Much of the evidence discussed has been generated from a unidirectional research approach, which is based on the premise that parents do something to children that "causes" a given outcome in the child. In reality, the paths of influence are not one way. For example, some researchers suggest that children with high self-esteem behave in ways that elicit more favorable communication from their parents (Felson & Zielinski, 1989). Or, similarly, children who are mild in temperament are less likely to provoke coercive compliance tactics (Stoneman, Brody, & Burke, 1989). Alternatively, children who engage in problematic behaviors elicit more high-power controlling strategies from parents than their less problematic counterparts (Mash, 1984).

Moreover, a systemic orientation adheres to the principle that families set up patterns of reciprocal influence. Thus, although our major focus is on parents' influence on children, it must be acknowledged that children greatly influence parental self-concept and self-esteem as well (Demo, Small, Savin-Williams, 1987; Stryker & Statham, 1985). Cyclically, parents with low self-esteem tend to engage in more self-esteem damaging behaviors with their children than parents with high self-esteem (Small, 1988).

Self-Esteem. Symbolic interactionists such as Mead (1934) and Cooley (1902) posited that an individual's sense of self is formed through interaction with significant others. There are no others more "significant" in a young child's life than his or her parents. Accordingly, a child's self-esteem emerges, in part, through everyday parent–child communication. An accumulation of daily damaging messages may eventually discourage and disconfirm a child's sense of self. Three types of potentially damaging messages are discussed: invalidating remarks, including disconfirmations and disqualifiers; labeling; and double binds.

Children, like all people, need validation of their self-worth (Satir, 1988). However, children often experience an abundance of invalidations as evidenced through disqualifiers and disconfirmations. Definitions of disqualifications are prolific, yet, "there has never been a single 'true' or 'original' definition" (Bavelas, Black, Chovil, & Mullett, 1990, p. 21). Nevertheless, the central characteristic of disqualifying messages seems to be that they say something without really saying it (Bavelas et al., 1990; also see Chovil, this volume). In short, disqualifying messages ignore the child as a person.

Disconfirming messages also diminish a child's sense of self. However, disconfirming messages are a direct invalidation. Let us offer a real-world example to distinguish between disqualifiers and disconfirmations. At the end of the day, when a parent picks up a child at day care, and the child desires to show the parent the art he or she created, the child is seeking validation. The parent may be confirming by saying, "What a good picture." Alternatively, the parent may explicitly disconfirm the child by saying, "That doesn't look like a dog to me." On the other hand, disqualifying may take place; the parent might respond, "Get your coat on, I'm late starting dinner." Without explicitly saying it, the parent is saying to the child, "Your picture, and hence you, are not worth my time nor attention."

If the child's environment is filled with disqualifying and disconfirming remarks, if these are the parental voices to which the child has grown accustomed, the child's sense of self will undoubtedly suffer (Satir, 1988). The evidence accumulated thus far indicates that children are bathed in parental disqualifying and disconfirming messages. Although the study of such messages began with pathological families, parental disqualification occurs quite often in everyday, normal interaction (Bavelas et al., 1990; Weakland & Fry, 1962).

The second type of damaging message is labeling. Labeling reflects the power of words. Satir (1988) pointed out how parents "hang labels" on their children and set pessimistic goals for them. Yet, parents are taken aback when the child indeed behaves in a manner consistent with the unfavorable parental label or goal. Margolin, Blyth, and Carbone (1988) found that parental expectations about a child's competencies were strongly related to the child's self-esteem. Children strive to live up (or down) to parental expectations. Thus, parental admonishments of "bad" or "selfish" or "shy" often serve as self-fulfilling prophecies.

The final type of damaging messages is the use of double binds (see also Wilder & Collins, this volume). Although the concept of double binds originated with the Palo Alto group's study of pathological families, double binds occur quite regularly in everyday conversation (Knapp & Vangelisti, 1992; Watzlawick, 1963). Double binds are messages that carry two contradictory meanings; in essence, people are left feeling that they are damned if they do and damned if they don't (see Watzlawick, Bavelas, & Jackson, 1967). Further, such double meanings are confusing to a child. A parent who says "I love you" verbally, but pushes the child away, is sending a very mixed message to this child. The child probably does not comprehend the perhaps perfectly practical purpose of protecting an expensive suit from paint, play-dough, or pudding.

Compliance Gaining. A second domain in which parents' communication evidences shades of darkness is in compliance gaining. Within this section a brief overview of compliance is offered, and three basic styles of gaining compliance and the relationship of these styles to long-term goals are reviewed.

Compliance occurs when a child obeys an adult directive immediately or in the short term (i.e., until the authority figure leaves the room). Child compliance is considered essential for socialization. Indeed, compliance may well lay the foundation for the internalization of parental values and the development of a moral conscience (Lytton, 1980). Accordingly, the internalization of parental values and beliefs is a principal goal of parenting, and compliance is seen as a requisite for that goal (Kochanska, 1991). Yet, the same parental compliance-gaining attempts that foster the immediate cessation of a sanctioned behavior are not necessarily the same ones that promote internalization or moral consciousness. Unquestioning compliance is not the long-term goal; we generally do not want children to grow up to deferentially and blindly obey authority.

Though child noncompliance occurs within disturbed (i.e., clinical) families, some degree of noncompliance is also completely normal (Kuczynski & Kochanska, 1990). In fact, parents report that a lack of child compliance is the most problematic issue they face (Forehand, 1977). Ironically, however, children receive virtually no support when they do comply. Ideally, we praise children and tell them when they do well. Nevertheless, the most common response to compliance is no response at all (Lytton, 1979). Conversely, children do receive a great deal of attention for disobedience. Fathers tend to react to disobedience in overt physical manners, whereas mothers use more admonishments, criticisms, and verbal threats (Hetherington, Cox, & Cox, 1978; Lytton, 1980).

Parents may draw from a wide variety of strategies to "persuade" a child to comply. Most of these tactics are encompassed by three general categories: coercion, love withdrawal, and induction (Rollins & Thomas, 1979). Coercion is a high-power assertive technique that reflects a clash of wills as the parent exerts pressure on the child to "mind." Tactics may include physical punishment, deprivation of privileges, and verbal threats and criticism. Though many of us were raised with the philosophy of "spare the rod and spoil the child," research indicates that such a philosophy does not appear to be in the best interest of either the child or the parent. After a decade of research in numerous disciplines, the most robust conclusion to date is that the greater the parental coercion, the less the child compliance over time (Stafford & Bayer, 1993). In other words, although such techniques are effective in the short run to gain initial compliance, chains of negative interaction develop in time. Aggression toward, and avoidance of, the parent is promoted (see Crockenberg

& Litman, 1990; Peterson, Rollins, & Thomas, 1985). As summarized by Stafford and Bayer (1993), coercive techniques restrict the child's development of high self-esteem, internal locus of control, sense of autonomy, and development of a moral conscience. Nevertheless, despite enlightenment by some, coercive punishment remains a significant part of many family discipline practices.

Love withdrawal is the second general control strategy invoked by parents. Love withdrawal, like coercion, also has been found to be effective to bring the child into line in the short run. However, many have argued that the long-term effects of love withdrawal may be devastating (e.g., Hoffman, 1970). Maccoby and Martin (1983) suggested that love withdrawal promotes child anxiety, lowers self-esteem, and fosters a lack of cooperation. Empirical findings concerning love withdrawal have been mixed. This is perhaps due to the differences in the operationalization of love withdrawal; the term has been used for everything from "time outs" to locking a child in a dark closet (Stafford & Bayer, 1993).

Despite the potential adverse effects of such techniques, love withdrawal remains the most frequently used strategy in day care settings and by many parents. The popular conception is that love withdrawal lacks the negative consequences of coercion; hence, it is used more by "enlightened" parents. As Stafford and Bayer (1993) propose, the issue is tied into the label itself. Researchers, not children, labeled the strategy *love withdrawal*. It may well be that the child does not infer a withdrawal of love when such techniques are combined with supportive messages and explanations. The effects of love withdrawal may depend on the manner in which it is implemented, as well as whether or not it is combined with coercive or inductive strategies.

The third strategy, induction, is likely invoked least frequently by parents. This strategy refers to the use of reasoning and explanation. Induction seems to promote immediate compliance, as well as long-term internalization and the development of a moral consciousness (see Stafford and Bayer, 1993, for a review). This strategy has been found to be effective with children as young as 2 (Marion, 1983), and anecdotal evidence shows its success at an even earlier age. Yet, the notion of explaining to a child is foreign to many parents. Consequently, the other two strategies, despite potential negative consequences, are much more likely to be utilized.

In sum, parents often invalidate a child's sense of worth. They disqualify them, hang dooming labels on them, and utilize adverse compliance strategies with them. As illustrated earlier, parents frequently treat their children with very little respect. Parents are rude, ignore their children, are too busy for them, and forget to even say "thank you." In sum, parents, in their own busy lives, tend to forget the ramifications of the way they talk or simply do not talk to and with their children.

Children and the Marital Relationship

> In fact, children do not have to be problem children to be stressful, they just have to be children. (Mash, 1984, p. 65)

The birth of a child is stressful. The child's arrival transforms the dyad into a triad and necessitates major changes in the couple's routine (Parke & Tinsley, 1987). Accommodating a child into the family system changes the status quo, upsetting the system's prior equilibrium (Kreppner, 1989).

Further, parents have what may be the toughest job in the world (Satir, 1988), especially because parenting involves daily hassles that create a great deal of stress (Crnic & Booth, 1991). During any typical day parents experience nagging, whining, complaining, continuously cleaning the same messes, and a host of other minor irritations and annoyances. In addition, parents must become time-management experts as they routinely coordinate activities such as soccer practices, piano lessons, and orthodontic appointments. The difficulties in time management increase exponentially with the number of children. Finally, parents experience difficulty in obtaining privacy and finding time (for anything), and they also face chronic fatigue (Crnic & Booth, 1991; Sillars & Wilmot, 1989).

Although the nature of routine hassles changes with the age of the child, parents report that such aggravations increase as the child gets older, at least until age 3 (Crnic & Booth, 1991). However, stressful parent–child relationships continue well into the often stormy period of adolescence (Rosenberg, 1985). For parents, antagonizing agents shift from minor stresses, physical exhaustion, and concerns for the child's immediate safety to more emotionally stressful concerns over issues such as peer pressure, potential substance abuse, academic performance, and the like. In brief, hassles have an unfavorable effect on marital satisfaction (Crnic & Booth, 1991).

Indeed, after the birth of a child the prognosis for the course of the marital relationship is unequivocally grim (Belsky & Rovine, 1990; Engfer, 1988). Communication between spouses changes with the addition of a child (Sillars & Kalbfleisch, 1989). In fact, the fundamental premise of much research on the link between children and marital satisfaction is that the child disrupts communication in the marriage, which in turn results in a decline in marital quality (Belsky & Rovine, 1990). Sillars and Wilmot (1989) proposed that the transition to parenthood engenders a decrease in companionate talk. Providing empirical support for this proposition, Belsky and Rovine (1990) found that from pregnancy to 3 years after the birth of the first child marital partners reported a decrease in feelings of love and amounts of open communication. Moreover, they found that the amount of conflict increased, as did ambivalence about the marriage.

Although children certainly have an effect on marriage, marital interaction also has an effect on the child. Numerous studies support the claim that unhappy marriages play a formative role in the development of numerous less desirable child "outcomes" (Mash, 1984). To illustrate, parental disagreement on childrearing practices and inconsistent discipline between parents appear to perpetuate child misbehavior and noncompliance (Block, Block, & Gjerde, 1986). Yet, disagreements about how to raise children is one of the most common problems that married couples encounter (Gottman, 1979; Sillars, Pike, Jones, & Redmon, 1983). Of concern here is the direct, linear relationship that has often been found between marital discord and child behavior problems (see, e.g., Peterson & Zill, 1986).

Marital conflict affects children in a variety of ways. For example, it is not uncommon for parents to draw children into parental conflict, which in turn seems to facilitate problematic child behavior (Johnston, Gonzales, & Campbell, 1987) and lower self-esteem (Bartle, Anderson, & Sabatelli, 1989; Satir, 1988). Minuchin and Fishman (1981) have suggested that when one parent sides with a child, or brings a child into a marital dispute, inappropriate coalitions are formed. These coalitions are inappropriate because placing a child in a parental role (i.e., mediating conflict between parents) gives the child a sense of power in the family, which in turn serves to promote disobedience (Adler & Furman, 1988). These coalitions are not uncommon (see Wilmot, 1987). The danger is not so much in the occasional siding of a child with a parent, but rather when a stronger bond exists between a parent and a child than between the marital partners.

In sum, when married individuals become parents, the marriage inevitably becomes strained and conflict ridden. Reciprocally, strained and/or conflict-ridden marriages adversely affect children. Generally, although the direction of causality is unknown, unhappy marriage and unhappy children co-occur (Belsky & Pensky, 1988; Belsky, Youngblade, Rovine, & Volling, 1991). The next section focuses on what happens when there is more than one child in a family system.

The Sibling Relationship

Jealousy and rivalry among siblings can be traced through mythology, literature, history, and religion (Dunn, 1988a). Throughout all of these accounts, the birth of a second child has been portrayed as traumatic to a first-born child. It also has been argued that sibling rivalry is on the increase, as couples are having fewer children, and smaller families might experience more of these problems. Gudykunst, Yoon, and Nishida (1986) found that when only two children are present there is more intensive rivalry between siblings. Furthermore, Dunn (1988b) noted that parents often feel responsible for the communication of hostility or aggression between children. Many parents feel distress and an inability to intervene.

Though some have argued that "traumatic" is too strong a word, research does indicate that "most first-born children showed signs of disturbance following the sibling's birth" (Dunn, 1988b, p. 170). A commonly used phrase is that the first-born experiences emotions of displacement. Reports concur that there is a marked drop in the frequency of communication between the mother and the first-born child after the arrival of the second child (Dunn & Kendrick, 1982). More specifically, mothers initiate fewer conversations and engage in shorter conversations with the first-born after the arrival of a second. First-born children react differently to these communicative changes; some become clingy and sad, others belligerent and demanding, and some simply withdraw from communication with the mother altogether.

Over time immediate feelings of displacement can change in a variety of ways. Dunn (1988a) reported a series of longitudinal studies that found that some pairs eventually developed positive affect and communicated in friendly and affectionate ways. Other pairs became increasingly negative and hostile in their interactions. Dunn and Stocker (1989) speculated that the sibling–sibling relationship is mediated by the first-born child's emotional well-being. That is, insecure first-borns have a more difficult time accepting and incorporating the new child into the family system.

Parents can and do exacerbate sibling rivalry and jealousy, however. The most robust conclusion to date is "the greater the maternal involvement in play and attention to either child, the less friendly the interaction between the siblings" (Dunn, 1988b, p. 172). Children are quite sensitive to maternal differences. Children monitor parental favoritism and any communicative act that may signal favoritism (Dunn, 1988b).

The manner in which parents differentially discipline children is one way favoritism is "communicated" to the child. When two siblings are engaged in a misdeed, the parent is far more prone to punish the child perceived to be the stronger of the two. This occurs regardless of which child initiates the transgression (Dunn & Munn, 1986; Felson & Russo, 1988). For example, Dunn and Munn (1986) found that mothers were more than twice as likely to discipline the older child and to lure the younger child away with a more pleasant activity. After all, the older child is "old enough to know better." The same holds true in opposite-sex sibling pairs. Boys are punished more often and more severely than girls, because they are stereotypically the stronger sibling. It comes as little surprise that such parental attempts to maintain peace do just the opposite. The "weaker" child increasingly expects and receives parental support, which in turn increases the child's aggressive behavior (Dunn, 1988b; Minuchin, 1988). Due to the perception of unfair treatment, the "stronger" child becomes more noncompliant as well (Dunn & Stocker, 1989). Such noncompliant children increases parent–child conflict. Thus, through either indirect or direct means, both parent–child conflict and sibling conflict is higher when siblings perceive partiality (Adler & Furman, 1988).

In sum, certain normative patterns of parent–sibling communication can have long-standing and deep effect on the children, the relationships between the parent and the children, and the relationships between the children (Dunn & Stocker, 1989).

The Family as a System

We have segmented the traditional family by dyadic and triadic interactions, but a systematic view holds that all interactions and relationships influence all others. For instance, Belsky (1981) asserted that "parenting affects and is affected by the infant, who both influences and is influenced by the marital relationship, which in turn both affects and is affected by parenting" (p. 3). Therefore, although discussing the segments of the family separately does provide some insight into the dark side of family interaction, such examinations fail to capture the complexity of family interaction and the detrimental systemic patterns that are embedded within the relationships between relationships. Accordingly, a few examples of such complex interaction are offered.

First, it should be clear by now that the birth of a child, whether the first child or a subsequent child, resounds throughout the entire system. Rules, boundaries, and communication patterns must be renegotiated between the parents, between the parents and older siblings, between any already present siblings, and between the newborn child and all of these individuals and their relationships with each other (Collins, 1990). Because, from a systemic view, families strive to maintain a homeostatic state, the birth of a child creates stress for all.

To further illustrate the intricacy of family patterns, we turn to the work of Stoneman et al. (1989), who posit that stress from child noncompliance escalates marital dissatisfaction. This dissatisfaction in turn lessens spousal support and communication, which further increases dissatisfaction and increases conflict. Moreover, this conflict further divides the parents on issues such as child discipline strategies, and the result is even less success at modifying a child's disobedient behavior, which leads to increases in parental dissatisfaction with the child, and so on.

In a similar vein, Belsky et al. (1991) examined family interrelationships. They found that as men's marital satisfaction declined in terms of their love for the spouse and in terms of increased ambivalence, they became more negative in interaction with their children. Children experiencing such negativity likewise reciprocated negativity to their fathers. These negative interactions were proposed to further contribute to the father's dissatisfaction with the marriage, which would lead him to decrease involvement in parenting. Lessened paternal involvement in childrearing in turn would decrease the mother's marital satisfaction, and the pattern continues.

In sum, family communication patterns are systematically and dynamically interwoven. These patterns function to perpetuate spirals of negativity, that is, the dark side of normal family interaction.

RECONSIDERING THE FAMILY

The history of the family is a furtive affair, marked by manipulation, dishonesty, and sophistry—as well as by cruelty and indifference to individuals. (Mount, 1982, p. 10).

Perhaps because of the widespread belief of the myths described earlier in this chapter, many Americans are lamenting the "death" of the family, especially in terms of traditional family values. These doomsayers cite increasing divorce rates, single-parent families, and out-of-wedlock childbirth as evidence that the family is a dying institution. Regardless of historical data that indicate that this is not the case, there are a number of scholars who are anxious to dance on the symbolic grave of the family system.

These scholars not only recognize the negative effects of the family discussed thus far, but further propose that the family system in and of itself is the cause of individual and cultural problems. A stance taken by many is that "the family is a subversive organization. In fact, it is the ultimate and only consistently subversive organization" (Mount, 1982, p. 1).

The primary criticism offered by these scholars focuses on beliefs concerning what the family does to the individual. This stance takes two principal forms: social-political and feminist critiques. Although there are many variations of each genre, only the fundamental issues representing each view is offered here.

First, most social-political critiques are grounded in Marxism. Marxist critiques of the family condemn the family for serving as an "ideological conditioning device" that exploits the individual (Cooper, 1970, p. 3). From this perspective, the primary problem with the family as a social form is its ultimate suitability in denying individualism and in maintaining oppressive social conditions. The family, in essence, sustains the power of the ruling class by teaching children "not how to survive in society, but how to submit to it" (Cooper, 1970, p. 24). Normal family interactions, then, serve as an hegemonic force in creating and preserving class distinctions.

Feminist critiques emphasize not only how the family structure represses individualism, but particularly how it represses the individualism of women. "The family remains a vigorous agency of class placement and an efficient mechanism for the creation and transmission of gender inequality" (Barrett & McIntosh, 1991, p. 29). Historically, feminists have rejected traditional forms of marriage and family because they have been offered as the only legitimate avocation for women. Certainly, there have been legal (e.g., no-fault divorce) and ideological (e.g., increasing acceptance of career wives) changes in marriage because the feminist movement gained a voice in the early part of this century. Barrett and McIntosh (1991) observed that "shorn of its more obviously oppressive features, it is often thought that marriage is now a harmless or neutral institution" (Barrett & McIntosh, 1991, p. 54). Not so, say Barrett and McIntosh. Instead, they argue that current ideology stresses the companionate and romantic elements of marriage, elements that fuse two individuals into a unit wherein each partner is the other's "better half." Marriage, then, manufactures half people.

Both Marxist and feminist scholars of the family structure usually admit that the family does meet fundamental human needs such as affection, security, and intimacy. However, the family's repression of other human needs such as the need for individuality and a sense of wholeness is seen as the basic problem. For example, Cooper (1970) argued that "bringing up a child in practice is more like bringing down a person" (p. 10), and the socialization is ultimately the "chronic murder" of a sense of self (p. 11).

Given the proposed problems with the family, what is to take its place? Most critics fail to address this crucial question. Others offer a rather vague answer; for example, Barrett and McIntosh (1991) contended:

> What is needed is not to build up an alternative to the family—new forms of household that would fulfill all the needs that families are supposed to fulfill today—but to make the family less necessary, by building up all sorts of other ways of meeting people's needs. (p. 159)

SUMMARY AND CONCLUSIONS

There is likely no more mythical a creature than a "normal" family. Despite the fact that the family is often idealized as a "haven in a heartless world," the research reviewed in this chapter provides some initial evidence that there is indeed a dark side to family interaction. Members of normal families routinely fight with each other, ignore each other, disconfirm each other, criticize each other, are rude to each other, and generally treat each other in a manner as heartless as anything experienced in the outside world. Indeed, "failure, hostility, and destructiveness are as much a part of the family system and the relationships among family members as success, love, and solidarity" (Rossi, 1968, p. 29).

Some scholars have taken a broader yet dimmer cultural view of the family: They propose that the family as a social form is the source of many individual and cultural woes. Compelling arguments have been made that the family functions to squelch individualism and promote gender and class inequalities (Barrett & McIntosh, 1991; Cooper, 1970).

Regardless of the ubiquitous dark side of family interactions, a dialogic stance proposes that the bright side occurs hand in hand with the dark. Although all families experience at least some of the negative communication patterns described in this chapter, we would be remiss not to mention that most people do not suffer severe adverse effects as a result. Families may even offer tangible benefits to their members, perhaps because of the balancing effect of the bright side of family interaction. For example, married people are happier, less stressed, and experience fewer mental and physical impairments than single people (see Coombs, 1991). Indeed, most of us have survived and flourished thanks to (or despite) our families.

REFERENCES

Adams, B. N. (1988). Fifty years of family research: What does it mean? *Journal of Marriage and the Family, 50,* 5–17.

Adler, F., & Furman, W. (1988). A model for children's relationships and relationship dysfunction. In S. W. Duck (Ed.), *Handbook of personal relationships* (pp. 211–232). New York: Wiley.

Barrett, M., & McIntosh, M. (1991). *The anti-social family* (2nd ed.). New York: Verso.

Bartle, S. E., Anderson, S. A., & Sabatelli, R. M. (1989). A model of parenting style, adolescent individuation and adolescent self-esteem: Preliminary findings. *Journal of Adolescent Research, 4,* 283–298.

Bavelas, J. B., Black, A., Chovil, N., & Mullett, J. (1990). *Equivocal communication.* Newbury Park, CA: Sage.

Baxter, L., & Wilmot, W. W. (1986). Taboo topics in close relationships. *Journal of Social and Personal Relationships, 2,* 253–269.

Beer, W. R. (1989). *Strangers in the house: The world of siblings and halfsiblings.* New Brunswick, NJ: Transaction Books.

Bellah, R. N., Madsen, R., Sullivan, W. M., Swidler, A., & Tipton, S. M. (1985). *Habits of the heart: Individualism and commitment in American life.* Berkeley: University of California Press.

Belsky, J. (1981). Early human experience: A family perspective. *Developmental Psychology, 17,* 3–23.

Belsky, J., & Pensky, E. (1988). Developmental history, personality, and family relationships: Toward an emergent family system. In R. A. Hinde & J. Stevenson-Hinde (Eds.), Relationships within families: Mutual influences. New York: Oxford University Press.

Belsky, J., & Rovine, M. (1990). Patterns of marital change across the transition to parenthood: Pregnancy to three years postpartum. *Journal of Marriage and the Family, 52,* 5–19.

Belsky, J., Youngblade, L. Rovine, M., & Volling, B. (1991). Patterns of marital change and parent–child interaction. *Journal of Marriage and Family, 53,* 487–498.

Berk, S. (1985). *The gender factory: The apportionment of work in American households.* New York: Plenum.

Billig, J. (1987). *Arguing and thinking.* Cambridge, UK: Cambridge University Press.

Birchler, G. R., Weiss, R. L., & Vincent, J. P. (1975). Multidimensional analyses of social reinforcement exchange between maritally distressed and nondistressed spouse and stranger dyads. *Journal of Personality and Social Psychology, 31,* 348–360.

Block, J. H., Block, J., & Gjerde, P. F. (1986). The personality of children prior to divorce: A prospective study. *Child Development, 57,* 827–840.

Bochner, A. P. (1984). The functions of human communication in interpersonal bonding. In C. C. Arnold & J. W. Bowers (Eds.), *Handbook of rhetorical and communication theory* (pp. 544–621). Boston: Allyn & Bacon.

Burr, W. R. (1990). Beyond I-statements in family communication. *Family Relations, 39*, 266–283.

Canary, D. J., & Stafford, L. (1992). Relational maintenance strategies and equity in marriage. *Communication Monographs, 59*, 243–267.

Collins, R. (1988). *Sociology of marriage and the family: Gender, love, and property* (2nd ed.). Chicago: Nelson-Hall.

Collins, W. A. (1990). Parent–child relationships in the transition to adolescence: Continuity and change in interaction, affect, and cognition. In R. Montemayor, G. R. Adams, & T. P. Gullotta (Eds.), *From childhood to adolescence: A transitional period* (pp. 85–106). Newbury Park, CA: Sage.

Coltrane, S., & Ishii-Kuntz, M. (1992). Men's housework: A life course perspective. *Journal of Marriage and the Family, 54*, 43–57.

Cooley, C. H. (1902). *Human nature and the social order.* New York: Scribner's.

Coombs, R. H. (1991). Marital status and personal well-being: A literature review. *Family Relations, 40*, 97–102.

Cooper, D. (1970). *The death of the family.* New York: Pantheon Books.

Crnic, K. A., & Booth, C. L. (1991). Mothers' and fathers' perceptions of daily hassles of parenting across early childhood. *Journal of Marriage and the Family, 53*, 1042–1050.

Crockenberg, S., & Litman, C. (1990). Autonomy as competence in 2-year-olds: Maternal correlates of child defiance, compliance, and self assertion. *Developmental Psychology, 26*, 961–971.

Curran, D. (1983). *Traits of a healthy family.* Minneapolis: Winston.

Dainton, M., & Stafford, L. (1993). Routine maintenance behaviors: A comparison of relationship type, partner similarity, and sex differences. *Journal of Social and Personal Relationships, 10*, 255–271.

Dainton, M., Stafford, L., & Canary, D. J. (1991, November). *Maintenance strategies and physical affection as predictors of love, liking, and satisfaction in marriage.* Paper presented at the Annual Meeting of the Speech Communication Association, Atlanta.

Demo, D. H., Small, S. A., & Savin-Williams, R. C. (1987). Family relations and the self-esteem of adolescents and their parents. *Journal of Marriage and the Family, 49*, 705–715.

Dindia, K., Fitzpatrick, M. A., & Kenny, D. A. (1989, May). *Self-disclosure in spouse and stranger dyads: A social relations analysis.* Paper presented at the meeting of the International Communication Association, San Francisco.

Duck, S. W. (1988). *Relating to others.* Chicago: Dorsey.

Duck, S. W. (1990). Relationships as unfinished business: Out of the frying pan and into the 1990s. *Journal of Social and Personal Relationships, 7*, 5–28.

Duck, S. W. (1992). *Human relationships* (2nd ed.). Newbury Park, CA: Sage.

Dunn, J. (1988a). *The beginnings of social understanding.* Oxford, UK: Basil Blackwell.

Dunn, J. (1988b). Connections between relationships: Implications of research on mothers and siblings. In R. A. Hinde & J. Stevenson-Hinde (Eds.), *Relationships within families: Mutual influences* (pp. 168–180). New York: Oxford University Press.

Dunn, J., & Kendrick, C. (1982). *Siblings: Love, envy, and understanding.* Cambridge, MA: Harvard University.

Dunn, J., & Munn, P. (1986). Sibling quarrels and maternal intervention: Individual differences in understanding and aggression. *Journal of Child Psychology and Psychiatry, 27*, 583–693.

Dunn, J., & Stocker, C. (1989). The significance of differences in siblings' experiences within the family. In K. Kreppner & R. M. Lerner (Eds.), *Family systems and life-span development: Issues and perspectives* (pp. 289–302). Hillsdale, NJ: Lawrence Erlbaum Associates.

Elder, G. H. (1974). *Children of the great depression.* Chicago: University of Chicago Press.

Engfer, A. (1988). The interrelatedness of marriage and the mother–child relationship. In R. A. Hinde & J. Stevenson-Hinde (Eds.), *Relationships within families: Mutual influences* (pp. 104–118). New York: Oxford University Press.

Engram, E. (1982). *Science, myth, reality: The Black family in one-half century of research.* Westport, CT: Greenwood.

Felson, R. B., & Russo, N. (1988). Parental punishment and sibling aggression. *Social Psychology Quarterly, 51,* 11–18.

Felson, R. B., & Zielinski, M. A. (1989). Children's self-esteem and parental support. *Journal of Marriage and the Family, 51,* 727–735.

Fitzpatrick, M. A. (1991). A microsocietal approach to marital communication. In B. Dervin & M. J. Voight (Eds.), *Progresses in communication sciences* (Vol. 10, pp. 67–101). Norwood, NJ: Ablex.

Fitzpatrick, M. A., & Badzinski, D. M. (1985). All in the family: Interpersonal communication in kin relationships. In M. L. Knapp & G. R. Miller (Eds.), *Handbook of interpersonal communication* (pp. 687–736). Beverly Hills: Sage.

Forehand, R. (1977). Child noncompliance to parental requests: Behavior analysis and treatment. In M. Hersen, R. M. Eisler, & P. M. Miller (Eds.), *Progress in behavior modification* (Vol. 5, pp. 111–247). New York: Academic Press.

Fry, W. R., Firestone, I. J., & Williams, D. L. (1983). Negotiating process and outcome of stranger dyads and dating couples: Do lovers lose? *Basic and Applied Social Psychology, 4,* 1–16.

Galvin, K. M., & Brommel, B. J. (1991). *Family communication: Cohesion and change* (3rd ed.). New York: Harper Collins.

Ganong, L. W., Coleman, M., & Mapes, D. (1990). A meta-analytic review of family structure stereotypes. *Journal of Marriage and the Family, 52,* 287–298.

Garland, D. R. (1981). Training married couples in listening skills: Effects on behavior, perceptual accuracy and marital adjustment. *Family Relations, 30,* 297–306.

Gordon, T. (1970). *P.E.T.: Parent effectiveness training: The tested new way to raise responsible children.* New York: Plume.

Gordon, T. (1975). *P.E.T. in action.* New York: Bantam.

Gottman, J. M. (1979). *Marital interaction: Experimental investigations.* New York: Academic Press.

Gudykunst, W., Yoon, Y. C., & Nishida, T. (1986). The developmental tasks of siblingship over the life cycle. *Journal of Marriage and the Family, 48,* 703–714.

Hareven, T. K. (1982). American families in transition: Historical perspectives on change. In F. Walsh (Ed.), *Normal family process* (pp. 446–466). New York: Guilford.

Hetherington, E. M., Cox, M., & Cox, R. (1978). The aftermath of divorce. In J. H. Stevens, Jr. & M. Matthews (Eds.), *Mother–child, father–child relations* (pp. 110–155). Washington DC: National Association for the Education of Young Children.

Hinde, R. A., & Stevenson-Hinde, J. (1988). *Relationships within families: Mutual influences.* New York: Oxford University Press.

Hoffman, M. L. (1970). Moral development. In P. H. Mussen (Ed.), *Carmichael's manual of child psychology* (Vol. 2, 3rd ed., pp. 261–360). New York: Wiley.

Huston, T. L., McHale, S. M., & Crouter, A. C. (1986). When the honeymoon's over: Changes in the marriage relationship over the first year. In R. Gilmour & S. W. Duck (Eds.), *Emerging field of personal relationships* (pp. 109–132). Hillsdale, NJ: Lawrence Erlbaum Associates.

Huston, T. L., & Vangelisti, A. L. (1991). Socioemotional behavior and satisfaction in marital relationships: A longitudinal study. *Journal of Personality and Social Psychology, 61,* 721–733.

Johnston, J. R., Gonzales, R., & Campbell, L. E. G. (1987). Ongoing postdivorce conflict and child disturbance. *Journal of Abnormal Child Psychology, 15,* 493–509.

Kirchler, E. (1988). Marital happiness and interaction in everyday surroundings: A time-sample diary approach of couples. *Journal of Social and Personal Relationships, 5,* 375–382.

Knapp, M. L., & Vangelisti, A. L. (1992). *Interpersonal communication and human relationships* (2nd ed.). Boston: Allyn and Bacon.

Kochanska, G. (1991). Socialization and temperament in the development of guilt and conscience. *Child Development, 63,* 1379–1392.

Kreppner, K. (1989). Linking infant development-in-context research to the investigation of lifespan family development. In K. Kreppner & R. M. Lerner (Eds.), *Family systems and lifespan development: Issues and perspectives* (pp. 33–61). Hillsdale, NJ: Lawrence Erlbaum Associates.

Kuczynski, L., & Kochanska, G. (1990). Development of children's noncompliance strategies from toddlerhood to age 5. *Developmental Psychology, 26*, 398–408.

Lasch, C. (1977). *Haven in a heartless world: The family besieged.* New York: Basic Books.

Lloyd, S. A., & Cate, R. M. (1985). The developmental course of conflict in premarital relationship dissolution. *Journal of Social and Personal Relationships, 2*, 179–194.

Lytton, H. (1979). Disciplinary encounters between young boys and their mothers and fathers: Is there a contingency system? *Developmental Psychology, 15*, 256–268.

Lytton, H. (1980). *Parent–child interaction: The socialization process observed in twin and singleton families.* New York: Plenum.

Maccoby, E. E., & Martin, J. A. (1983). Socialization in the context of the family: Parent–child interaction. In E. M. Hetherington (Ed.), *Handbook of child psychology: Vol. 4. Socialization, personality, and social development* (pp. 1–101). New York: Wiley.

Margolin, L., Blyth, D. A., & Carbone, D. (1988). The family as a looking glass: Interpreting family influences on adolescent self-esteem from a symbolic interaction perspective. *Journal of Early Adolescence, 8*, 211–224.

Marion, M. (1983). Child compliance: A review of the literature with implications for family life education. *Family Relations, 32*, 545–555.

Mash, E. J. (1984). Families with problem children. In A. Doyle, D. Gold, & D. S. Moskowitz (Eds.), *Children in families under stress* (pp. 65–84). San Francisco: Jossey-Bass.

McCall, G. J. (1988). The organizational life cycle of relationships of relationships. In S. W. Duck (Ed.), *Handbook of personal relationships* (pp. 467–484). New York: Wiley.

McKenry, P. C., Everett, J. E., Ramseur, H. P., & Carter, C. J. (1989). Research on black adolescents: A legacy of cultural bias. *Journal of Adolescent Research, 4*, 254–264.

Mead, G. H. (1934). *Mind, self and society.* Chicago: University of Chicago Press.

Minuchin, P. (1985). Families and individual development: Provocations from the field of family therapy. *Child Development, 56*, 289–302.

Minuchin, P. (1988). Relationships within the family: A systems perspective on development. In R. A. Hinde & J. Stevenson-Hinde (Eds.), *Relationships within families: Mutual influences* (pp. 7–26). New York: Oxford University Press.

Minuchin, S., & Fishman, H. C. (1981). *Family therapy techniques.* Cambridge, MA: Harvard University Press.

Mount, F. (1982). *The subversive family: An alternative history of love and marriage.* London: Jonathan Cape.

Noller, P. (1984). *Nonverbal communication and marital interaction.* New York: Pergamon.

Nussbaum, J. F. (Ed.). (1989). *Life-span communication: Normative processes.* Hillsdale, NJ: Lawrence Erlbaum Associates.

Offer, D., & Sabshin, M. (1966). *Normality: Theoretical and clinical concepts of mental health.* New York: Basic Books.

Parke, R. D., & Tinsley, B. J. (1987). Family interaction in infancy. In J. D. Osofsky (Ed.), *Handbook of infant development* (pp. 579–641). New York: Wiley.

Peterson, G. W., Rollins, B. C., & Thomas D. L. (1985). Parental influence and adolescent conformity: Compliance and internalization. *Youth and Society, 16*, 397–420.

Peterson, J. L., & Zill, N. (1986). Marital disruption, parent–child relationships, and behavior problems in children. *Journal of Marriage and the Family, 48*, 295–307.

Rollins, B. C., & Thomas, D. L. (1979). Parental support, power, and control techniques in the socialization of children. In W. R. Burr, R. Hill, F. I. Nye, & I. L. Reiss (Eds.), *Contemporary theories about the family: Research-based theories* (Vol. 1, pp. 317–362). New York: Free Press.

Roloff, M. E., & Cloven, D. H. (1990). The chilling effect in interpersonal relationships: The reluctance to speak one's mind. In D. D. Cahn (Ed.), *Intimates in conflict: A communication perspective* (pp. 49–76). Hillsdale, NJ: Lawrence Erlbaum Associates.

Roloff, M. E., & Cloven, D. H. (in press). When partners transgress: Maintaining violated relationships. In D. J. Canary & L. Stafford (Eds.), *Communication and relational maintenance.* New York: Academic Press.

Rosenberg, M. (1985). Self-concept and psychological well-being in adolescence. In R. L. Leaky (Ed.), *The development of the self* (pp. 205–246). Orlando, FL: Academic Press.

Rossi, A. S. (1968). Transition to parenthood. *Journal of Marriage and the Family, 30,* 26–39.

Satir, V. (1988). *The new peoplemaking.* Mountain View, CA: Science and Behavior Books.

Schaefer, M. T., & Olson, D. H. (1981). Assessing intimacy: The PAIR inventory. *Journal of Marriage and the Family, 43,* 47–60.

Sillars, A. L., & Kalbfleisch, P. J. (1989). Implicit and explicit decision making styles in couples. In D. Brinberg & J. Jaccard (Eds.), *Dyadic decision making* (pp. 179–215). New York: Springer-Verlag.

Sillars, A. L., Pike, G. R., Jones, T. S., & Redmon, K. (1983). Communication and conflict in marriage. In R. N. Bostrom (Ed.), *Communication yearbook 7* (pp. 414–429). Beverly Hills, CA: Sage.

Sillars, A. L., & Weisberg, J. (1987). Conflict as a social skill. In M. Roloff & G. Miller (Eds.), *Interpersonal processes: New directions in communication research* (Vol. 14, pp. 140–171). Newbury Park, CA: Sage.

Sillars, A. L., & Wilmot, W. W. (1989). Marital communication across the life-span. In J. F. Nussbaum (Ed.), *Life-span communication: Normative processes* (pp. 225–253). Hillsdale, NJ: Lawrence Erlbaum Associates.

Skolnick, A. S., & Skolnick, J. H. (1989). *Family in transition* (6th ed.). Boston: Scott, Foresman and Co.

Small, S. A. (1988). Parental self-esteem and its relationship to childrearing practices, parent–adolescent interaction, and adolescent behavior. *Journal of Marriage and the Family, 50,* 1063–1072.

Sprey, J. (1969). The family as a system in conflict. *Journal of Marriage and the Family, 31,* 699–706.

Stafford, L., & Bayer, C. L. (1993). *Interpersonal communication between parents and children.* Newbury Park, CA: Sage.

Stafford, L. & Canary, D. J. (1991). Maintenance strategies and romantic relationship type, gender, and relational characteristics. *Journal of Social and Personal Relationships, 8,* 217–242.

Stoneman, Z., Brody, G. H., & Burke, M. (1989). Sibling temperaments and marital and family functioning. *Journal of Marriage and the Family, 51,* 99–113.

Stryker, S., & Statham, A. (1985). Symbolic interaction and role theory. In G. Lindzey & E. Aronson (Eds.), *The handbook of social psychology* (Vol. 1, 3rd ed., pp. 311–378). New York: Random House.

Trost, J. (1990). Do we mean the same by the concept of family? *Communication Research, 17,* 431–443.

Turner, R. H. (1970). *Family interaction.* New York: Wiley.

Walsh, F. (1982). Conceptualizations of normal family functioning. In F. Walsh (Ed.), *Normal family process* (pp. 3–42). New York: Guilford.

Watzlawick, P. (1963). A review of the double bind. *Family Process, 2,* 132–153.

Watzlawick, P., Bavelas, J. H., & Jackson, D. D. (1967). *Pragmatics of human communication.* New York: W. W. Norton.

Weakland, J. H., & Fry, W. F., Jr. (1962). Letters of mothers of schizophrenics. *American Journal of Orthopsychiatry 32,* 604–623.

Wilmot, W. W. (1987). *Dyadic communication* (3rd ed.). New York: Random House.

12

PHYSICAL AND
PSYCHOLOGICAL ABUSE

Linda L. Marshall
University of North Texas

Perhaps the darkest side of communication is evident when physical violence or psychological abuse occurs. Unfortunately, these forms of communication are all too common in intimate relationships. Vangelisti's chapter (this volume), showing that hurtful messages are remembered for a long time, suggests that a one-time, overtly hurtful message may have some type of long-term effect on the target. Violence and verbal aggressiveness, which are overtly hurtful messages, usually occur more than once and have implications of immediate and long-term harm to the target.

Although investigators usually examine physical violence in the context of conflict, with few exceptions (e.g., deTurck, 1985, 1987; Infante, Chandler, & Rudd, 1989; Spitzberg & Marshall, 1990, 1991) they have not explicitly conceptualized violence as a type of communication or influence. However, some investigators have implicitly begun to take a communication perspective by examining communication and relational variables in couples who have and have not experienced violence. Adoption of a similar perspective facilitated a new approach to psychological abuse described in this chapter, which is broader than the dominance and verbal aggression perspectives usually used.

Little attention has been paid to psychological abuse, even though the body of research on physical violence in adult dating, cohabiting, and marital relationships is very large. This author's files contain more than 1,200 articles and chapters, approximately two-thirds of which report or review violence research. Until about 10 years ago, research on violence was sparse, which is the current state of affairs for knowledge about psychological abuse.

A selected overview of research on violence is presented before focusing on psychological abuse. One issue in the violence literature revolves around the appropriateness and implications of using the terms *abuse, aggression,* or *violence.* Whether research should continue to use the most popular measure or gender-specific measures (the second issue addressed) is relevant for the discussion of prevalence and incidence and gender differences in violent behavior. The few studies on communication-related variables are also summarized before the focus shifts to psychological abuse. The typical perspective and available measures are of psychological abuse as it relates to violence and dominance. A new perspective is presented which broadly conceptualizes psychological abuse as a form of harmful influence resulting from common, day-to-day communication and interaction with a partner. Finally, research based on this new approach is presented which suggests that much of the harm previously associated with violence may actually be a result of subtle forms of psychological abuse.

PHYSICAL ABUSE

Because the body of research on physical violence in close relationships is so large, this chapter focuses on the pervasiveness of the problem and studies which most closely relate to communication. Reviews and theoretical articles are readily available (Ellis, 1989; McHugh, Frieze, & Browne, 1990; O'Leary & Vivian, 1990; Pagelow, 1992; Russell, 1988; Strube, 1988; Widom, 1989), including issues related to the criminal justice system (Archer, 1989; Dutton, 1988; Frieze & Browne, 1988). Several books also are informative (Dickstein & Nadelson, 1989; Ohlin & Tonry, 1989; Pirog-Good & Stets, 1989; Sonkin, 1987; Yllo & Bograd, 1989), including a cross-cultural perspective (Levinson, 1989). For research on batterers see Barnett and Hamberger (1992), Barnett, Fagan, and Booker (1991), Edleson, Eiskovits, and Guttman (1985), Hastings and Hamberger (1989), and Tolman and Bennett (1990), among others. Marshall and Vitanza (1994) reviewed research for purposes of dispelling or qualifying common myths. Unfortunately, a heterosexual bias is present in this literature. Few studies have examined violence in the relationships of gay men or lesbians (Lie, Schilit, Bush, Montagne, & Reyes, 1991; Renzetti, 1988).

Terminology

The terms *abuse, aggression,* and *violence* have been used to conceptualize acts which may result in physical harm. The term *physical abuse* is subjective and laden with negative connotations. An act perceived as abusive to one person may not be to another. When studies have used this term, results have generally shown lower rates than when questions require participants to report specific acts. Thus, use of the term *abuse* has become relatively rare.

Conceptualizng acts with the potential for physical harm as aggression has been a limiting factor. Basic research on aggression is relevant and very useful for researchers attempting to understand physical force in close relationships. However, the fit between aggression research and violence research is less than perfect. Applying a term from basic social psychological research, especially one in common usage by laypeople, is at best awkward. Also, the concept of aggression makes some aspects of these acts more salient than others.

There is evidence of the less than perfect fit between aggression and violence research from a metaanalysis of aggression research. Eagly and Steffen (1986) showed that across studies men were more aggressive than women, especially when measures assess physical aggression ostensibly producing pain and injury. Men are also more aggressive on psychological and verbal aggression measures, albeit to a lesser extent. Yet, studies on physically forceful acts in close relationships show that more women report using more of these acts than do men.

Definitions of aggression include the intent and perceived intent to harm. In addition to the lack of clarity about whose perception of intent is important, research on motives for engaging in these acts is sparse and equivocal. It is conceivable that potentially harmful acts may occur without a conscious or even nonconscious intent to harm the partner. Basic research distinguishes two types of aggression. Instrumental aggression is used in the service of another goal (e.g., to remove an obstacle). When aggression is expressive of an underlying emotion or arousal, the intent may be to cause harm. In close relationships, forceful acts are sometimes instrumental (e.g., to gain compliance), sometimes expressive (e.g., anger related), and sometimes a mixture of both.

Notions of expressive aggression underlie most research on violence in relationships (e.g., Stets, 1992). Participants typically are told to report how they and their partner behave during conflicts. The assumption has been that these acts occur during conflict and that conflict elicits the acts, presumably because strong emotions may be present. However, anecdotal evidence from battered women indicates that sometimes they are hit "out of the clear blue sky" without a prior or concurrent conflictual interaction.

Berkowitz (1989, 1990; Berkowitz & Heimer, 1989) and Zillman (1988, 1989) provided useful perspectives for close relationships. In simplified form, these theorists argue that emotions and cognitions interact as determinants of aggression. An aversive event may lead to arousal and negative affect which, coupled with an aggressive impulse and aggression-related thoughts and memories, may lead to higher order cognitive processes (e.g., attributions about cause and intent) related to aggression, which then result in an aggressive act. Arousal may be triggered by thoughts of current or past events. The primary point is that an aggressive act may result from an arousing (e.g., exercise, certain types of music) or aversive event unrelated to the partner in the present situation (e.g., what the boss said at work, the hunger pangs she or he had for an hour, a relational conflict two weeks ago, being hot or cold). Focusing on physically forceful acts only in the context of conflict limits the way violence in close relationships is conceptualized and examined. A violent act performed in an emotional or conflictual situation may result in very different attributions and have different implications for the target than the same act performed in a previously neutral or pleasant situation.

The term *aggression* also leads to considerations of the actor as aggressor, but an act which may result in harm to the partner may be used for retaliation or self-defense. These forms of aggression have very different meanings which are not captured by the general term. Retaliatory violence may be expressive aggression and a forceful act to prevent the partner from using more physical force is clearly instrumental aggression. Although technically accurate, the term *aggression* is awkward when considering that a potentially harmful act may be done in self-defense.

The term *aggression* implies there is an aggressor and victim. Determining whether an individual considers himself or herself a victim or aggressor (e.g., Makepeace, 1986; Richardson, Leonard, Tyler, & Hammock, 1985) is important because of the different implications involved. It may be argued that because men are generally larger and stronger, they are more likely to be the aggressor and women are more likely to be the victim. Research shows that women are more likely than men to be harmed by physical force in a close relationship (e.g., Stets & Straus, 1990), but consider the situation of a woman initiating the violence. By doing so, she would be the aggressor, but if she is more harmed as a result of her partner's physical force, she may be considered the victim. Use of a term without these implications may facilitate a broader understanding and less awkward conceptualizations.

For these reasons, the best term for physically forceful acts is *violence*. With this term, basic research on aggression can be applied without the associated problems of implying intent, purpose, effects, or victimization. These problems then, are no longer conceptual issues, they become empirical questions. The major problem with the term *violence* is that it implies a high level of intensity and severity, but most physically forceful acts in close relationships are performed at a low or moderate level of intensity and severity. This problem may be overcome by the use of simple modifiers (e.g., mild or severe violence). Further, use of the term *violence* is appealing from a feminist perspective because it does not minimize the potential for harm nor does it imply that the acts are acceptable.

Measures

The most often used instrument to assess violence is the Conflict Tactics Scale (CTS; Straus, 1979) with subscales for reasoning, verbal aggression, and violence. Although the CTS is a generally sound instrument (Barling, O'Leary, Jouriles, Vivian, & MacEwen, 1987; Straus, 1990), it has several problems. Only 8 items assess violence, some of which contain acts with differing potential for harm. Researchers have separated the acts, added items, or modified the rating scale. The acts are ordered based on frequency of occurrence rather than severity. Also, the CTS does not take gender into account. The recipient of a violent act may be differentially affected based on gender (Arias & Johnson, 1989; Makepeace, 1986; Pirog-Good & Stets, 1989). Although different levels of violence may have different implications and different relationships with other variables, the violence subscale is unidimensional. However, researchers have begun to differentiate "minor" or "common" violence ("threw something at"; "pushed, grabbed, or shoved"; and "slapped") from severe violence ("kicked, bit, or hit with a fist"; "hit or tried to hit something"; "beat up"; "threatened with a knife or gun"; and "used a knife or gun").

To address some of these problems, the Severity of Violence Against Women Scales (SVAWS; Marshall, 1992a) and Severity of Violence Against Men Scales (SVAMS; Marshall, 1992b) were developed. To develop the SVAWS (SVAMS), females (males) rated how violent, serious, abusive, threatening, and aggressive it would be if a man (woman) inflicted each act on a woman (man). Severity scores, the mean of the ratings, were submitted to factor analysis procedures. The SVAWS has 9 dimensions, differing in level of severity. Data from community samples were used to identify the second-order factor structure and provide weights to approximate physical and emotional harm for use with community samples. Symbolic violence and threats of mild, moderate, and serious violence comprise the second-order factor representing threats of violence. Acts of mild, minor, moderate, and serious violence and sexual violence formed the second-order factor actual violence. Eight dimensions were found for the SVAMS. The symbolic violence items did not load together. The second-order factor analysis showed that sexual violence loaded with threats rather than actual violence among the men. Items on the SVAWS and SVAMS are ordered based on the perceived severity of the acts. Thus, the factor structure may not replicate because subdimensions are based on the severity of the acts, and the rating scale assesses the frequency with which they occur. However, use of these scales permits researchers to make relatively fine distinctions between levels of severity or to differentiate threats of violence, acts of violence, and sexual violence.

Prevalence and Incidence

The first major study of violence in close relationships was conducted in 1975 (Straus, Gelles, & Steinmetz, 1980). A large-scale survey of people in relationships with at least one child found a prevalence rate of 28%, showing that violence was a widespread problem in the United States. Straus and Gelles's (1986) second national survey of intact relationships found little change in prevalence. Approximately 12% reported at least one act of violence during the year (see Straus & Gelles, 1990, for more results from this study). The consistency across time may be a function of the similarity of the studies because other random surveys show very different rates. O'Leary (1988) asserted that half of the population are likely to sustain at least one act of violence from a partner during their lifetime. A recent study of couples drawn from the general population in Calgary, Canada, reported an incidence of 38% for at least one violent act. Almost 22% reported an act of severe violence during the previous year (Brinkerhoff & Lupri, 1988). It is not clear whether more Canadian than United States couples are violent or whether the difference results from other factors (e.g., methodology, year of survey).

Sugarman and Hotaling (1989) summarized results of studies on premarital violence. Prevalence rates averaged about 30%, ranging from a high of 66% to a low of about 9%. A recent study using student versions of the SVAWS and SVAMS found that over 75% of the sample had expressed threats of violence to their partner, and over 75% had sustained threats (Vitanza & Marshall, 1993). Using violent but not sexual acts, 55% had been violent to a partner, and 56% reported having sustained at least one act of violence. Earlier studies on the same campus using the CTS reported similar rates (Marshall & Rose, 1987, 1990). Some discrepancies may be due to urban–rural (Sugarman & Hotaling, 1989) or regional differences. For example, White and Koss (1991) reported higher rates in the Great Lakes area and the Southeast than in the Rocky Mountains area, Plains States, and Far West.

Relational violence is also more likely in some samples than in others. Marshall's research on psychological abuse and violence is described later in the chapter.[1] She recruited community women in "bad" or "stressful" relationships. Of 620 women screened for participation on the SVAWS, 84% reported that their partner had inflicted at least one act of violence on them during their relationship. Sixty percent of the volunteers had sustained at least one act of moderate or serious, potentially life-threatening violence.

---

[1]This study was funded by the National Institute of Mental Health, Grant number 1 R29 MH44217 to the author of this chapter. The research is described in more detail later in the chapter. NIMH funds also supported portions of the research to develop the SVAWS.

Gender Differences

Females are more likely to be harmed by violence in close relationships than are males (e.g., Cascardi, Langhinrichsen, & Vivian, 1992; Stets & Straus, 1990) and are more likely to report using violence (e.g., Stets, 1992). One hypothesis holds that men underreport and women overreport their own violence. Social desirability is related to reports of inflicting (especially among men), but not to sustaining violence (Arias & Beach, 1987; Dutton & Hemphill, 1992; Riggs, Murphy, & O'Leary, 1989). Some researchers advocate using reports in which an individual describes violence inflicted by the partner, or base the determination on whether either person reports inflicting or sustaining any violent act. These solutions may work well when groups differing by the presence of violence are studied, but these procedures obscure relevant gender differences. With the common size and strength difference and the likelihood that acts inflicted by males differ from those inflicted by females in physical and emotional implications (Marshall, 1992a, 1992b) and meanings (Makepeace, 1986), it is important to explore how men and women differ in their likelihood of inflicting or sustaining specific violent behaviors.

Approximately 11% of Straus and Gelles's (1986) national sample reported at least one act of husband-to-wife violence, and 12% reported wife-to-husband violence during the preceding year. In Sugarman and Hotaling's (1989) review, the range for students inflicting violence was from 14% (Makepeace, 1983) to 54% (Sigelman, Berry, & Wiles, 1984) among men and from 10% (Makepeace, 1983) to 59% (Marshall & Rose, 1987) among women. For sustaining violence, the range was from 10% (Makepeace, 1983) to 59% (Sigelman et al., 1984) among men and from 11% (Makepeace, 1983) to 57% (Marshall & Rose, 1987) among women. In a recent study of students using the SVAWS (Vitanza & Marshall, 1993), 77% of males and 76% of females had expressed threats of violence to their partner, whereas 72% of males and 79% of females had sustained threats. Using only acts of violence (not including sexual violence), 65% of males and 54% of females had been violent to a partner, whereas 53% of males and 58% of females had sustained at least one act of violence.

Some variations in results on gender differences may be a function of using limited measures of violence. Even modifications of the CTS include only a small range of acts. To begin to determine whether males and females differ in the acts they report, data from two studies by Vitanza (1991; Vitanza & Marshall, 1993) were combined. Results in Table 12.1 include only individuals who reported either partners' use of threats or violence. The acts are listed in increasing order of severity within threats and actual violence for female students on the SVAWS. Differences of approximately 5% and greater in Table 12.1 are worth noting.

Several points should be mentioned. More males than females reported

TABLE 12.1
Prevalence by Gender on Specific Acts*

	Males (n = 208)		Females (n = 229)	
	Express %	Receive %	Express %	Receive %
Threats of Violence				
hit/kick wall/furniture	56.5	35.6	38.0	57.2
threw/smash/broke an object	32.9	27.9	36.7	38.9
drove dangerously	43.5	28.9	28.4	45.4
thrown object at	12.1	23.6	24.5	14.4
shook a finger	52.7	57.7	60.7	59.8
threatening gestures/faces	44.4	52.4	48.5	53.7
shook a fist	18.4	26.0	20.5	25.8
acted like a bully	35.7	23.1	29.7	44.5
destroy something	11.6	15.4	18.8	20.5
threaten harm/damage things	8.2	15.4	10.9	14.0
threaten destroy property	5.8	10.1	6.6	11.8
threaten someone care about	6.8	7.7	2.6	7.0
threaten to hurt	9.7	18.3	12.7	16.6
threaten to kill self	6.3	10.6	11.4	14.9
threaten with clublike object	2.4	5.3	2.6	3.1
threaten with knife or gun	1.9	2.4	2.6	2.6
threaten to kill	3.4	6.3	3.5	6.1
threaten with weapon	1.9	2.9	2.6	3.9
act like wanted to kill	5.3	9.6	7.9	11.8
Acts of Violence				
held down, pinning in place	29.8	9.6	10.0	34.9
pushed or shoved	28.8	36.5	47.2	38.0
shook or roughly handled	30.3	18.8	18.3	35.8
grab suddenly/forcefully	37.5	26.4	27.1	43.7
scratched	5.8	33.7	23.1	7.9
pulled hair	9.6	14.9	13.5	15.3
twisted arm	13.0	8.2	5.7	18.3
spanked	14.4	13.0	6.1	8.7
bit	9.1	19.7	17.0	7.9
slapped with palm of hand	12.5	29.3	29.7	13.1
slapped with back of hand	5.3	7.7	5.2	6.1
slapped face and head	12.0	18.3	18.3	10.9
kicked	5.8	13.5	15.3	6.6
hit with an object	3.8	10.6	8.7	4.8
stomped on	2.4	1.9	3.1	1.8
choked	3.4	2.4	2.2	5.2
punched	3.9	22.1	14.4	7.9
burned	1.9	2.4	2.2	1.3
used clublike object	1.9	2.4	2.2	1.3
beat up	1.9	1.0	4.4	3.1
used a knife or gun	1.9	1.9	1.7	.4

*Note: Data were collected by Vitanza (1991) and Vitanza and Marshall (1993). Subjects were included if they had either expressed or received a threat or act of violence. Items are ordered by the degree of severity for female students.

inflicting three types of threats and five acts of violence. In contrast, more females reported expressing four threats and eight acts. More males than females reported receiving one threat and seven acts of violence, whereas more females reported sustaining five threats and four acts.

Although couples were not used in the studies, comparing acts males report performing with those females report receiving (and vice versa) is one way to begin to identify specific acts associated with gender. Males were more likely to hit or kick a wall, door, or furniture; drive dangerously; act like a bully; hold and pin; shake or roughly handle; grab; and twist an arm, whereas more females sustained these acts. Females were more likely to throw an object, scratch, bite, slap with a palm, slap around his face, kick, and punch, whereas men sustained these acts. Most proportional differences between the genders were relatively small (e.g., almost 10% more females than males reported kicking their partner, and about 7% more males than females reported receiving this act). However, some differences seem more substantial. Almost 20% more males than females reported holding and pinning a partner, but 25% more females than males reported their partner had done this to them. The largest difference may be a function of interpretations. Only 6% more males than females reported having acted like a bully, but 21% more females than males reported that a partner had acted like a bully.

A final point to note is that more females reported beating up a partner. When typical physical differences are considered, it seems odd that so many females would be physically capable of beating up males, unless they caught them completely off guard. Findings such as these may result from differing interpretations or perceptions. Males' and researchers' notions of beating up may consist of repeatedly hitting someone with resulting visible injuries. In contrast, females' concept may include repeated hits, regardless of evident injury.

These figures are certainly not definitive, but they do suggest that males and females exhibit different behaviors which may have been obscured previously by use of the CTS. For example, one CTS item includes a behavior that may be more characteristic of females (pushing or shoving) and one that males may be more likely to perform (grab). Although there was general agreement across the genders on only four types of threats, they broadly agreed on almost half of the violent acts. Too few individuals reported expressing or sustaining the more serious threats and acts of violence to gain a sense of whether males or females are more likely to exhibit these behaviors.

Communication-Related Variables

Relatively little research examines the relationship between violence and other forms of communication. Most research has focused on individuals rather than partners and/or has paid little attention to relational variables.

For example, studies focus on intrapersonal variables such as stress and family of origin violence (e.g., MacEwen & Barling, 1988; Malone, Tyree, & O'Leary, 1989). There are a few notable exceptions.

O'Leary and his colleagues (e.g., Arias & O'Leary, 1985; Murphy & O'Leary, 1989) conducted a longitudinal study from 6 weeks premarriage to 30 months after marriage. O'Leary et al. (1989) found that only 25%–30% of people who had sustained violence at each of three times indicated relational distress, and almost 10% of those who were stably nonviolent scored as distressed. Because most people in stably violent relationships were not dissatisfied, factors other than violence must be responsible for relational distress.

These and similar results have led researchers to begin to focus more on relational and communication variables. For example, Vivian and O'Leary (1987) observed discussions among a subsample of the engaged couples. Negative affect and negative content discriminated violent and nonviolent couples, but both groups showed positive and negative reciprocity during their interaction. O'Leary and Curley (1986) found less spouse-specific assertiveness among men and women in violent relationships than among those in distressed or satisfied relationships.

Morrison, Van Hasselt, and Bellack (1987) compared couples who were violent, distressed and nonviolent, and not distressed and nonviolent. Males and females in violent relationships showed more speech disturbances than people in distressed relationships. The violent couples also used compromise more and made more problem-solving suggestions than satisfied couples. In comparison to their satisfied counterparts, women in violent relationships were more compliant, and their partners used less praise and appreciation. These findings suggest violent couples may have tried harder to resolve problems than those who were satisfied.

Smith, Vivian, and O'Leary (1990) observed discussions and compared couples in which violence had occurred with those who were maritally distressed but nonviolent. There were only moderate group differences. Couples did not differ on positive or negative verbal messages and the expression of positive and negative emotions, nor was there a gender difference. Violence was associated with a reduced likelihood of reciprocating positive messages and a greater likelihood of reciprocating negative verbal messages and negative affect. The distressed couples showed more agreements than did those who were violent.

Margolin, John, and Gleberman (1988) compared violent, verbally aggressive, and withdrawing distressed couples with those who were not distressed, aggressive, or violent. In comparison to other distressed groups, violent men made more offensive negative statements, used more negative voice, showed more subtle anger cues, and felt more attacked, but there was no difference in escalation patterns. In contrast, women in violent relationships initially escalated then deescalated negative offensive tactics. Women in the verbal aggression group did not show this pattern. Margolin and her colleagues found more group differences for men than for women.

Spitzberg and Marshall (1991) were interested in relational outcomes. Among college students, commitment, intimacy, length of relationship, and trust were partially a function of tactics individuals used to influence their partner. Common influence tactics (integrative, distributive, and psychological abuse tactics) were more important variables than violence. Commitment and intimacy were negatively related to the use of distributive tactics, possessiveness, serious violence, and physical escalation tactics consisting of acts of mild and symbolic violence.

Lloyd (1990) interviewed distressed (violent and nonviolent) and nondistressed (violent and nonviolent) couples about their typical conflicts. Nondistressed groups used more problem-solving tactics than distressed groups who reported more heated conflicts. Nonviolent groups had more squabbles without solutions. The distressed nonviolent group was least likely to initiate discussion, and the nondistressed nonviolent group was most likely to do so. The violent distressed group had the fewest people who reported negotiation tactics, all reported verbal attacks, and almost all reported anger. More individuals in the nondistressed violent group reported anger and verbal attacks than in the nondistressed nonviolent group. Everyone in the violent distressed group and most in the distressed nonviolent and nondistressed violent groups reported withdrawal tactics. The violent distressed group was least likely and the distressed nonviolent group was most likely to apologize to their partner. The distressed nonviolent group was most likely to report a total lack of resolution to typical conflicts.

A clear conclusion from these studies is that the mere presence of violence may not have a direct association with relational variables. The relationship violence has with relational variables is likely to be indirect, through its effect on another variable. Thus, a worthwhile endeavor would be to identify variables which may moderate or mediate the relationship between violence and relational and personal outcomes. For example, Canary and Cupach (1988) and Canary and Spitzberg (1987, 1989, 1990) offered strong evidence that perceptions of an actor's competence mediate the link between the actor's conflict behavior and relational outcomes (e.g., trust, satisfaction).

Further evidence that violence itself is not the critical event for relational disturbance results from the difficulty finding comparison groups who are distressed but not violent or generally satisfied and not violent. Many people recruited for comparison purposes have experienced violence (Barling & Rosenbaum, 1986; Dutton & Strachan, 1987; Lloyd, 1990; O'Leary & Curly, 1986). This may not be surprising when couples seeking marital therapy are recruited, but violence occurs among couples reporting relational satisfaction. For example, Holtzworth-Munroe et al. (1992) found that 23.5% of husbands recruited for a "satisfied" group had inflicted violence on their partner, almost 12% had done so in the preceding year. Unfortunately, many investigators recruited "clearly" nonviolent couples, but did not report tests of that assumption (Goldstein & Rosenbaum, 1985; Hastings & Hamberger, 1989; Rosenbaum & O'Leary, 1981).

Although the most salient aspect to an outsider is the fact that violence occurs, that does not seem to be the case for those in the relationship. This should not be surprising because people have many more interactions with their partner in which violence does not occur than in which it does occur. On the other hand, it is very clear that women who sustain serious violence from their partner feel a great deal of emotional distress. To date, most of women's physical and emotional problems reported in this literature have been assumed to be a result of the violence. Studies of couples suggest this assumption may be inaccurate.

The pervasiveness of violence in relationships is clear. Additionally, a large body of research shows that women in violent relationships experience serious personal consequences. Their mental and physical health is poorer than for women in nonviolent relationships. Further, in seriously violent relationships women are in danger of killing their partner or being killed by him (Browne, 1987; Goetting, 1988, 1989, 1991; Mann, 1990; Parker & Toth, 1990; Saunders & Browne, 1991; Stout, 1991). Despite women's physical and emotional vulnerability to violence, anecdotal evidence indicates that severely battered women believe the emotional and psychological abuse they receive is worse than the violence. However, very little research has been conducted to address this issue. Most articles have been directed to counselors with a focus on therapy and case histories.

PSYCHOLOGICAL ABUSE

The primary approach has focused on psychological abuse as it reinforces or results from violence. This perspective and its limitations are addressed before an alternative approach is described. The new approach argues that the effectiveness of abuse results from normal interpersonal and intrapersonal processes occurring through everyday communication. In this view, psychological abuse is not intrinsic to specific behaviors, although certain acts (e.g., yelling or swearing at) are almost always abusive. Rather, it is the content of the message conveyed during interactions that constitutes abuse. Day-to-day, subtle messages may be more harmful than more serious, less frequent, and more salient acts. The essence of this approach is that some psychological abuse occurs in all close relationships. The point at which it becomes clearly harmful, undermining the target's psychological, emotional, and/or behavioral competence, is an empirical question. Although women also psychologically abuse men, conceptualizations have focused on male-to-female acts, in part, because anecdotal evidence resulted from interviews with battered women. Because the focus has been on the association with violence, especially life-threatening violence, it is difficult to consider a male being physically terrorized over a long period of time by a female. A further reason for the bias may result from gender-difference research. The sex-role training women receive may make them particularly vulnerable to abuse because of their expressive and interpersonal orientation. For these and other reasons, there is a gender bias in this literature which is reflected in the remainder of the chapter.

The Violence Approach

When an interest in psychological abuse derives from battered women and the association between violence and abuse, the logical approach is to consider abuse another form of dominance or control. Terms include *environmental abuse* (Gondolf, 1985), *psychological abuse* or *battering* (Edleson, 1984; Okun, 1986), *psychological torture* (Russell, 1982), *confined abuse* (Star, 1982), *assaultive behavior* (Okun, 1986), *maltreatment* (Hudson & McIntosh, 1981; Tolman, 1989, 1992) and *social abuse* (Walker, 1979). These authors focused on psychological abuse as it accompanies and results from violence. Partly because violence can readily be conceived of as resulting from a desire to control a partner, conceptualizations have focused on overtly dominating and controlling behaviors.

To some extent the focus on psychological abuse as an overt form of control has been in response to the question, "Why do battered women remain in a violent relationship?" From this approach, women stay because they are dominated by a violent and abusive man (Gelles, 1976). They have been forced to submit to control and dominating tactics exhibited by a violent man. For example, one prevalent notion is that once violence occurs, the threat of further violence is always present. This threat is viewed as a powerful form of psychological abuse a man uses to obtain what he wants from a woman. The underlying assumption is that women remain in violent relationships because they are afraid to terminate them due to the possibility of future violence, and because they have been "beaten down" psychologically and emotionally. Some women stay because they fear for their life and some have been "beaten down" by their partner, but there is much more to psychological abuse than overt domination and fear of worse violence.

Hilberman and Munson (1977–78) were the first to describe behaviors that may constitute psychological abuse. They interviewed 60 battered women referred for psychiatric evaluation at a rural health clinic. Although violence played a major role in women's psychiatric symptoms, nonphysical acts were addressed. For example, Hilberman and Munson reported that men's "morbid jealousy" when women left the house usually resulted in violence. Partners embarrassed the women, refused to allow them to work, monitored their activities, isolated them from others by overtly preventing communication, and so on. Psychological abuse was usually a precursor to violence. Hilberman and Munson argued that women's physical and psychological symptoms resulted from the constant threat of violence.

According to Walker (1979, 1984), battered women in her sample experienced acts that correspond to Amnesty International's definition of torture. These forms of abuse include: (a) isolation; (b) induced debility (limiting food or sleep, physical exhaustion); (c) obsessiveness and possessiveness to monopolize perceptions; (d) vague and specific threats of violence and death; (e) degradation (e.g., humiliation, name calling); (f) forced alcohol or drug use; (g) "altered states of consciousness produced through hypnotic states"; and (h) occasional indulgences (1984, pp. 27–28). Walker (1986) argued that most of these psychologically abusive behaviors occur in a context of anger, expressed through cold silence, yelling, sarcasm, abrupt movements, and so forth. The underlying message of the abuse is that the woman must always be vigilant, with most of her energy devoted to trying to keep the batterer from becoming violent. Thus, Walker believes that abuse, like violence, is another way of expressing dominance and control, and it occurs during conflict.

This dominance approach is evident in the available studies. Murphy and Cascardi (1993) reviewed research, but few types of psychological abuse have been examined. Psychological abuse has been operationalized as verbal aggression (e.g., Lebov-Keeler & Pipes, 1990; Mason & Blankenship, 1987) or other dominating, overt forms of control (Follingstad, Rutledge, Berg, Hause, & Polek, 1990; Stets, 1990; Stets & Pirog-Good, 1990). Tolman (1992) discusses several categories of abuse from this dominance and violence perspective. Types of abuse include the creation of fear, isolation, economic abuse, monopolization, degradation, rigid sex-role expectations, withdrawal, contingent expressions of love, and psychological destabilization which occurs when men's behavior challenges women's perceptions of reality. Many types of psychological abuse have been neglected as a result of the focus on overt acts, the context of conflict and anger, and the association with violence.

Measures

Three scales assess psychological abuse from the violence perspective. Hudson and McIntosh (1981) devised the Index of Spouse Abuse (ISA). The violence dimension contains nonviolent (e.g., "becomes surly if I tell him he is drinking too much") and sexually aggressive acts ("makes me perform sex acts that I do not enjoy or like"). Items on the emotional abuse dimension assess sexual aggression, assume the presence of children, and assume co-habitation. Other problems relate to item wording and specificity. For example, "My partner feels that I should not work or go to school" is problematic because the opposite (being forced to work, often to support a partner) also may be abusive and not uncommon according to women in Marshall's current study. Item specificity is problematic because events researchers think are relevant may not be relevant for a subject. For example, a woman may not endorse the item "does not want me to socialize with my friends" because her partner only tries to control access to her family, not her friends.

Tolman's (1989) Psychological Maltreatment of Women Inventory (PMWI) contains dimensions representing dominance/isolation and emotional/verbal abuse. Several items assume effectiveness of control, rather than attempts to control. This implies an act is abusive only if it "works," but it may be the fact that he tries to control her or the manner in which he does so which actually constitutes abuse. For example, Stets and Pirog-Good (1990) found that six items relating to control of a partner formed two dimensions: attempts and successful control. Further, men may abuse from a dependence rather than a dominance position, or their dominance may be exerted in a manner that makes a woman feel she has to take care of the man. Ten items did not have clear or strong factor loadings. Several items assume cohabitation, male control of finances, and the presence of children which limits their usefulness for dating, separated, or divorced women. There are also item specificity problems. The PMWI has been adapted and expanded for use with dating samples (Kasian & Painter, 1992), but limitations remain.

The most recent instrument is the Abusive Behavior Inventory (ABI) by Shephard and Campbell (1992). The violence subscale includes sexual aggression which may have different meanings than other acts of violence. For example, the sexual violence items formed distinct dimensions on the SVAWS and SVAMS (Marshall, 1992a, 1992b). Shephard and Campbell do not clearly show which items are indicative of violence or psychological abuse. Several items constitute threats of violence which may differ in effects from other types of psychological abuse as shown in the results of Marshall's study described later. Some items also assume cohabitation and the presence of children. However, the specificity problem is not as serious as on the ISA and PMWI, and some items do not necessarily assume that the man is effective in his attempts to control a woman.

Items for these scales were based on descriptions by clinically identified battered women, usually from shelters. Women in these samples differ from other battered women in a number of ways. The psychological abuse they receive may also differ from that received by women drawn from community samples or campuses. Research on violence with nonidentified, nonclinical samples does not support some of the results found with sheltered women, even when women have sustained similar levels of violence. If psychological abuse is examined from the same perspective, research may miss many pervasive forms of abuse, and the results may not generalize. The most serious problem with this approach is that it implies that psychological abuse is overt and is important because it accompanies violence. Few researchers have addressed psychological abuse in its own right, and even those who have, they have not examined subtle forms of abuse.

A New Perspective

The new approach began with the question, "Why do women leave violent relationships?" Although little research has directly addressed this question (Bowker, 1986), some women do terminate a relationship after their partner is violent. Undeniably, some battered women remain with a partner because they fear he will kill them, and some women leave a partner as a result of the same fear. If the same level of serious violence is assumed to exist for women who do and do not terminate their relationship, some factors must differentiate these women. One possibility is that women who remain in violent relationships have partners who are effective psychological abusers. In contrast, women who leave violent relationships may be with partners who are ineffective psychological abusers, or they may be highly skilled communicators who readily deflect or cope with the abuse. This, then, raises the question: What would make psychological abuse effective and ineffective? A brief description of several bodies of research suggests some possible answers.

During interaction partners affect and react to each other. These factors have been examined using terms such as *power, compliance, persuasion*, and so on. Research shows that overtly coercive compliance tactics are used less frequently than "milder" or socially desirable traits. For example, deTurck found an increased likelihood of punishment (1985) and physical aggression (1987) when subjects were faced with resistance. Unfriendly responses appear to increase a persuader's verbal aggression, and strong resistance rapidly increases verbal aggression (Lim, 1990). The point is that overtly dominating and coercive tactics as well as violence may occur only when more subtle or less effortful tactics fail. Thus, to "get his way" or make his partner behave and think as he wants her to, a man may begin with the least effortful or least coercive tactics, then escalate his tactics as necessary. The extent to which psychological abuse or violence is used by a man to affect his partner's behavior is not yet known. However, this view suggests that subtle or less violent tactics will be used more frequently, with escalation to more overt and forceful coercion occurring when "milder" or "lesser" tactics fail.

Application of the sexual harassment literature suggests that harm can result from acts performed in a positive context as well as from acts in an aversive or coercive context. For example, research shows that women feel harmed from acts and statements performed in a "joking" context as well as in more overtly coercive situations (Koss, 1987; Paludi & Barickman, 1991). By extension, there is no reason to necessarily assume a conflict when examining psychological abuse.

Consider a woman who typically confronts problems directly. Confrontation may be associated with short-term emotional distress, but problems are more likely to be resolved resulting in less distress over time. Her confrontive behavior may make her partner worry about retaliation against her or may annoy him. Whether motivated by caring for her or by a selfish desire to make life easier by suppressing her confrontive behavior, he may repeatedly point out how upset she gets when she confronts people. She could begin to focus on these negative feelings which may lead her to confront fewer problems, leaving more problems unresolved. Unresolved problems may keep reappearing which could result in stress and her beginning to feel inadequate in some way. Thus, the woman's competence could be undermined by her partner focusing on a negative side effect of her style of problem solving.

Now, suppose that he also points out how upset he becomes when she is distressed. He says he loves her so much that he hates to see her like that or that it makes him feel helpless because he wants her to be happy. Although this woman's sense of self is being undermined, she is feeling loved and valued by her partner. She may even feel grateful to him for recognizing something she had "missed," that confronting problems upsets her. Clearly, some acts may be psychologically or emotionally harmful, yet not be perceived as coercive or even overt. It is also possible that subtle psychological abuse may be more harmful than that which is overt because people may be more readily able to defend themselves against a clear attack.

Beginning to think in these terms opens the possibility that it is the message conveyed during interactions and, at times, the style with which messages are conveyed that constitute psychological abuse. When the messages undermine a woman's personal or social competence, she is being psychologically abused. If the hypothesized partner in the previous example pointed out how effective she was by the way she confronted problems, the woman's sense of self might be enhanced. Thus, over time, day-to-day nonconflictual interactions may result in a woman feeling very good about herself, believing she has specific positive personality characteristics, and feeling little emotional distress. Alternatively, similar interactions with a different content may result in a woman feeling bad about herself, believing she has negative personality characteristics, and feeling a great deal of emotional distress. By removing issues of dominance from a conceptualization of psychological abuse, it becomes clear that a relationship may be high in psychological abuse, but not violent.

Many people have been in a relationship in which they "discovered" they had changed. When asked for explanations about how it may have occurred, they talked about the person in negative terms, but focused on their own weakness in letting it happen. There appeared to be no consistency in whether these relationships were high or low in conflict or whether they had ever argued about the particular characteristics involved. There was also no consistency in whether they thought the person had actually loved them or been selfish, caring mostly for himself or herself. Some of the ex-partners were characterized as strong and dominating, but some were considered self-effacing or very vulnerable. Thus, it seemed unlikely that psychological abuse occurred only in an obvious or overt way.

In contrast, many people have also been in relationships in which their partner somehow made them feel better about themselves. This, too, often seems mysterious to the person involved. People have difficulty explaining why or how one person can make them feel good about themselves and how another person can make them feel bad about themselves. It is my contention that both results occur through common interpersonal and intrapersonal factors related to social influence. The content and pattern of interactions differentiate relationships that are satisfying from those that are psychologically abusive.

From this perspective, an effective psychological abuser would be a person who effectively undermined a partner's sense of self. This could be accomplished purposefully with the intent of causing harm. It could also be accomplished out of a sense of love and caring, to help the person become healthier and happier. It may occur without either person being aware of the changes. Some individuals simply may be especially good at influencing their partner.

To determine the degree to which a woman is psychologically abused, the pattern of messages must be considered in the context of the relationship. It is clear from the research reviewed earlier (e.g., Smith et al., 1990) that a combination of positive and negative messages and positive and negative affect is communicated in all relationships. Therefore, it is not likely to be the mere presence of negative messages that identifies a relationship as psychologically abusive to the woman any more than violence is necessarily associated with relational distress. It is unclear exactly when a relationship becomes psychologically abusive. The critical point of distinction may be reached via a cumulative impact for negative messages from a partner, a certain imbalance of positive and negative message, a particular pattern of negative messages, or in some other way. To identify the critical point for serious harm rather than transitory hurt, research will have to consider communication within the context of the entire relationship. In the meantime, psychological abuse can be thought of as a floating continuum. To some extent, the resulting harm depends on the threshold of the target, which may differ depending on the characteristic targeted in the message(s), her sense of self, the relational context, and other factors at the time the abuse occurs.

To address these issues, this perspective drew on bodies of research related to social influence (e.g., tactical communication). For example, recent approaches to self-concept are important to this conceptualization. Some of these include Higgins (1989; Higgins, Klein, & Strauman, 1987) on self-discrepancies, Pelham and Swann (1989) on self-worth, McGuire and McGuire (1986) on the self versus others, Tesser's (1988) Self Evaluation Maintenance Model and the role of emotion (Tesser, Pilkington, & McIntosh, 1989), and Steele (1988) on self-affirmation. These approaches address the effects others may have on an individual's self-concept. Taken together, results suggest that normally occurring interpersonal and intrapersonal processes can have major consequences on a woman's self-concept, depending, in part, on the content of her partner's communication to her and the aspects of her self-concept he criticizes overtly as well as covertly.

Also, research on the role of uncertainty in self-concept (Baumgardner, 1990; Epstein, 1986; Pelham, 1991), relationships (Berger, 1988; Cupach & Metts, 1987; Noller & Gallois, 1988), behavior (Weinstein, 1989), coping (Folger, 1986; Janoff-Bulman, 1988; Lopes, 1987), and cognitive processes (Chaiken, Liberman, & Eagly, 1989; Masters & Keil, 1987) are important to this approach. The primary implication is that the more uncertain a woman is about herself or her partner, the more discomfort and anxiety she will feel, and the more effect this uncertainty will have. This suggests that one way in which a man can psychologically abuse a woman is by increasing her uncertainty about herself, about him, or about their relationship. It may be more effective to undermine a woman's feelings of uncertainty through subtle, ambiguous, or mixed messages (see chapters by Chovil, and Wilder and Collins, this volume) than through overtly dominating or verbally aggressive messages.

This view does not preclude the possibility that psychologically abusive acts can be overt and dominating. It should be obvious that coercive and aversive acts can be harmful, especially over time. Primarily, the new perspective broadens the range of possibilities to be considered when examining psychological abuse.

Research

The need to initially examine a wide range of potentially abusive acts and include subtle as well as overt abuse can be seen in results from a recent study (see fn. 1; Marshall, 1993a, 1993b, in prep.). The results reported here show that the pattern of correlations for psychological abuse and emotional distress are likely to differ, depending on the presence and level of violence sustained by a woman. More importantly, the results show that some effects reported in the violence literature are more closely associated with psychological abuse than with violence.

A list of types of psychological abuse was drawn from the literature on maltreatment of children, clinical and case studies on violence, and shelter workers' perceptions. Another source was discussions with others as described earlier. Table 12.2 lists the content categories developed for psychological abuse. Many categories overlap, but to begin to understand the effects of psychological abuse it was important not to eliminate types of abuse a priori, because there was no evidence upon which to decide which types may be more or less harmful.

An exploratory study of seriously psychologically abused women has begun to differentiate harmful effects associated with violence from those associated with psychological abuse. A primary goal was to assess the usefulness of conceptualizing psychological abuse as consisting of many types of subtle and overt acts occurring in everyday conflictual and nonconflictual interactions.[2] Flyers, advertisements, and announcements requested women in "bad or "stressful" long-term relationships to call the project. A screening instrument was based on the types of abuse listed in Table 12.2. Although the items were more general than those on the ISA, PMWI, and ABI and covered both subtle and overt acts, the scale was not designed to identify women who had been the victim of only a moderate level of psychological abuse.

Participants. Only 14% of 640 women screened for participation had not sustained any act of violence from their partner. Anecdotal evidence from the screening interviews suggests that one difficulty in recruiting women in nonviolent relationships resulted from terminating interviews if women spontaneously mentioned co-dependence. These women and others with extensive or recent therapy may have a different perspective and be unable to express how they had felt before gaining the new perspective.

To qualify, all women had to score over 200 on 51 items assessing the psychological abuse categories. This score reflected a mean of approximately 4 on a 7-point scale (never to very often). Three groups of women were chosen based on SVAWS (Marshall, 1992a) scores. Women in the serious violence group (SV; $n = 32$) scored over 25 on the violent acts subscale, indicating that they had sustained a great deal of violence, including potentially

---

[2]Two points regarding data analysis should be made. First, when performing a series of statistical tests, it capitalizes on chance to use a $p < .05$ as the criterion for reporting significance. For confirmatory purposes, a more stringent criterion is necessary. However, the purpose of exploratory research is to detect effects if they exist. Discovery is the goal of this study. Consequently, $p < .05$ was used as the criterion to show the potential importance of each type of abuse. Second, the number of subjects varies greatly across correlations because the number of women reporting that their partner had exhibited a particular type of abuse varied. This factor also affected the strength of the correlation necessary to reach the .05 level of significance.

TABLE 12.2
Types of Psychologically Abusive Acts

Control—Activities	Fear & Anxiety—Physical	Omnipotence
Control—Emotions	Fights or Conflicts	Possessiveness
Control—Information	Humiliate	Punish
Control—Thinking	Induce Debility—Emotional	Reject
Corrupt	Induce Debility—Physical	Rules
Degrade	Induce Guilt	Sabotage
Denigrate	Induce Powerlessness	Secrecy
Dominate—Emotionally	Intrude—Activities	Self-Denunciation
Dominate—Physically	Intrude—Privacy	Shift Responsibility
Double Binds	Isolate—Emotionally	Surveillance
Embarrass	Isolate—Physically	Threats—Emotional
Encourage Dependence	Jealousy	Threats—Physical
Exploit	Loyalty	Verbal Aggression
Fear & Anxiety—Mental	Monopolize Perception	Withdraw

life-threatening acts from their partners. The moderate violence group (MV; $n = 30$) scored between 5 and 15 on the violence dimension. The abuse only group (A; $n = 31$) scored between 0 and 5 on these items. Statistical tests comparing women in the latter group who had and had not experienced violence found no differences on any variable examined.

Procedures. Women read a description of the types of abuse listed in Table 12.2 (except embarrassment, threats of violence, and verbal aggression) as well as several types of partner behavior that women may consider positive (showing love and caring, dependence, helping their self-concept). They then completed a set of scaled items describing how they usually feel when their partner exhibits each type of behavior (e.g., does something that makes them feel guilty). The impact of each type of abusive behavior was the mean of 8 ratings on a 7-point scale (e.g., relaxed–tense, not–very afraid, not–very upset). The lowest means (5 or below) were on possessiveness, jealousy, dominance-physical, monopolize perception, and encourage dependence. The relatively low impact of the first three types of abuse suggests that these acts may not be as problematic for women as heretofore has been assumed. The frequency of men's verbal aggression was assessed with Infante and Wigley's (1986) instrument. The frequency of men's threats and acts of violence and their sexual violence were assessed with the SVAWS.

Results. Not all women reported all types of abuse. Less than half of the sample reported their partner had tried to corrupt them (44.1%), tried to control their access to information (46.2%), or denigrated them (48.4%). In contrast, more than 85% reported typical and serious fights, guilt, isolation-emotional, rejection, shifting responsibility onto them, and withdrawing from them. The frequency of men's verbal aggression correlated with the impact of 36 of the 39 types of abuse listed in Table 12.3 (mean $r = .37$). In contrast, the frequency of men's threats of violence correlated with only 6 types of abuse, their violence with 8 types of abuse, and their sexual violence with the impact of only 7 types of abuse. Although threats and violence may be psychologically abusive in their own right, they may not be directly related to the impact of most types of psychologically abusive acts. This contrasts with the violence perspective on abuse which assumes that the impact is increased because of the violence.

On an 11-point labeled scale women's partners often ($M = 8.87$, about weekly) appeared to depend on them. The frequency of men's dependence was significantly correlated (mean $r = .31$) with the impact of 27 of the 39 types of psychological abuse listed in Table 12.3 and frequency of verbal aggression, but not with men's threats or acts of violence or sexual violence. Women's partners showed love and caring more than once a week ($M = 9.57$) and tried to help women's self-concept about twice a month ($M = 7.75$). The frequency of men showing love and caring was related to the impact of 15 types of abuse (mean $r = .26$), and the frequency with which they tried to help women's self-concept was related to the impact of 11 types (mean $r = .32$). The frequency of verbal aggression, threats and acts of violence, and sexual aggression were unrelated to these positive behaviors. This contrasts with the cycle theory of violence which posits the importance of a loving phase.

These results show that abusive men also frequently behave in endearing or helpful ways. The frequency of these positive behaviors correlates significantly with the impact of many types of psychological abuse. The more often these men behaved positively, the stronger was the negative impact of their abuse. This underscores the importance of considering many factors in a relationship. A combination of positive and negative messages may be especially harmful to women, in part because it could increase their uncertainty about themselves and their perceptions as well as about the effects of men's more harmful acts. Uncertainty is uncomfortable and may increase a woman's distress directly as well as indirectly by focusing her attention on what may be wrong with her.

The SCL90R (Derogatis, 1983) measured emotional distress. On all dimensions (somatization, obsessive-compulsive, interpersonal sensitivity, anxiety, depression, hostility, phobic anxiety, paranoia, psychoticism, and global distress) each group had mean T scores of 60 or higher, indicating more serious distress than 84% of the nonclinical female norm. The exception was the abuse-only group's T score of 59 on phobic anxiety. A MANOVA on SCL90R subscales was not significant, showing that the groups did not differ. Because all groups were very high on psychological abuse, these results suggest that emotional distress is more closely associated with psychological abuse than with violence.

TABLE 12.3
Correlations Between the Impact of Abuse and Emotional Distress*

	SCL90R Somatization				"Nerve" Medication				Past Hosp.	
	All	A	MV	SV	All	A	MV	SV	All	A
Abuse-Impact										
cntrl-activity	.24		.48	.43	.37		.53	.34	.35	.54
cntrl-emotion	.39			.50	.28				.21	.52
cntrl-info	.27						.67		.31	.72
cntrl-thinking	.21				.26				.32	.42
corrupt	.33			.58	.32			.51	.30	.68
degrade	.28	.36			.26		.39			.35
denigrate					.34		.48	.47	.36	.65
dom-emotional	.51	.54	.63	.36	.31	.56			.21	
dom-physical	.25									.47
double binds	.29		.57	.42					.39	.55
encrg-depndce	.22			.39	.29		.40	.31	.47	.58
exploit	.25	.54			.33	.57	.63			.48
fear-mental	.30		.53		.33		.56		.34	.42
fear-physical	.27		.55		.35			.34	.30	.53
fights-serious	.40	.46	.48	.37						
fights-typical	.27	.34	.48							
humiliate	.27			.46	.32	.36			.27	.42
induce-debility			.37							.46
induce-guilt	.25		.40		.29		.36		.33	.48
ind-powerless							.34		.21	
intrude-act	.25		.40		.34		.41		.23	.60
intrude-priv	.37		.64	.39					.29	.65
isolate-emot			.50		.29	.58				
isolate-phys	.28			.41	.27				.27	.43
jealousy	.28		.41		.21					.53
loyalty	.34			.36	.47	.40	.54	.52	.38	.44
mon perception						.64				
omnipotence			.36							.37
possessive					.27	.41			.20	
punish	.22	.37			.26		.43		.30	.45
reject	.34	.32		.52				.34	.23	.37
rules					.28			.37	.33	.51
sabotage					.23		.42		.33	.56
secrecy	.22		.47							
slf-denunc	.28			.56	.30		.53			.56
shift respon	.22		.49							
surveillance	.32	.45			.49	.55	.62			.48
thrts-emot	.35	.35	.46		.33	.38	.67		.32	.57
withdraw	.33	.31	.35	.42					.20	
mean *r*	.28	.40	.48	.45	.30	.49	.50	.40	.27	.51
Frequency Scores										
verbal agg	.23		.34		.25		.39	.35		
threats-viol	.22									− .34
violence	.27									
sexual viol	.30		.46		.18		.33			

Note: Only significant correlations, $p < .05$, are reported.

The within-group correlations show that the pattern of relationships between the impact of abuse and emotional distress indicators differ, depending on the presence and level of violence. The significant correlations reported in Table 12.3 show some of these differences. These results support the hypothesis that subtle acts of psychological abuse are at least as harmful and, in some instances, more harmful to women than are overt types of abuse and violence.

Somatization on the SCL90R had a mean correlation of .29 for the impact of 30 of 39 types of abuse and with the frequency of verbal aggression, threats, violence, and sexual violence for the whole sample. Correlations in the table show that the relationships differ for the three groups. The largest number of correlations and the strongest ones were found for the moderate violence group

Similarly, women having taken medication for their "nerves, the way [they] feel emotionally," had low correlations for the impact of almost all types of abuse as did having been hospitalized for emotional problems when the whole sample was considered. However, the correlations for medication were higher and the patterns differed, depending on group membership. The largest number of correlations were found for the moderate violence group. Their correlations and those for the abuse group were stronger than for women who had received serious violence. The more impact abuse had, the more likely women were to have taken medication.

A history of hospitalization for emotional problems related to almost all types of abuse in correlations for the whole sample, but the relationships were only important for the abuse group. Women who had received serious violence from their partner had 6 significant correlations between the impact of abuse and hospitalization and the moderate violence group had only 1. The impact of abuse women received when overt acts of violence were not present was related to hospitalization for emotional distress. When overt acts of violence occurred (MV and SV groups), these relationships were not significant. The only negative correlation in the table showed that the more overt threats of violence women received from their partner, the less likely they were to have been hospitalized. These findings support the possibility that women may be more able to engage in self-defensive cognitive processes when a partner's harmful acts are overt, which makes them readily recognizable as aversive and potentially harmful.

Conclusions. Because women used general descriptions, the problem of women making fine distinctions between whether or not their partner performed a specific act was alleviated. However, during interviews when individualized descriptions were given, it was clear that many women had experienced some acts they had not reported in the questionnaires. For example, about half the interviews were completed before we realized that an explanation involving "tit for tat" and "getting even" elicited more recognition than did the term *punishment*.

Several conclusions can be drawn from these results. They underscore the importance of examining many different types of behaviors to understand psychological abuse. Acts thought to be most harmful from a violence perspective (e.g., jealousy) did not show consistent patterns. Further, the impact of some acts most likely to be overtly dominating or controlling (e.g., some types of control, degradation, dominance-physical) were not associated with distress indicators in the severe violence group. Findings such as these give credence to this new approach to psychological abuse. Behaviors that are subtle and difficult to identify may have at least as much association with distress as do overtly harmful acts.

The most important conclusion is that it is premature to limit the types of acts examined to those which have been addressed in the past. Psychological abuse should not be conceptualized as dominance or as it is related to violence. Psychological abuse must be addressed in its own right. Preliminary examination of results from coding the transcripts of 4-hour interviews in the study supports the hypothesis that much of the psychological abuse these women experienced was performed in a subtle way. This subtlety may prove to be more harmful than acts that are overtly dominating, in part because they may encourage women to feel there is something wrong with them. With an overtly dominating act, women may more readily be able to recognize that they feel distressed because of what their partner does and says, rather than because of something about themselves.

In summary, this chapter reviewed research showing that violence is prevalent in close relationships. This dark side of communication is all too common. Results reported here show that males and females may differ in the specific acts of violence they inflict and sustain. Although observers would expect most relational and communication variables to be affected by the presence of violence, the violence itself may have little direct effect on other aspects of the relationship.

Defining psychological abuse as messages that are harmful and undermine the partner's personal and/or interpersonal competence yielded a different perspective on the dark side of communication. The more narrow definition of psychological abuse as control or dominance may not capture a broad enough view of communication within the relationship to fully understand the nature or effects of abuse. The perspective introduced here and results from the exploratory study suggest that psychological abuse may be more harmful than is violence. Because psychological abuse appears to occur during normal, everyday interactions, it is also likely to be more prevalent than violence. The point at which psychological abuse becomes darkest or most harmful remains to be determined.

REFERENCES

Archer, N. (1989). Battered women and the legal system: Past, present and future. *Law and Psychology Review, 13*, 145–163.

Arias, I., & Beach, S. R. H. (1987). Validity of self-reports of marital violence. *Journal of Family Violence, 2*, 139–149.

Arias, I., & Johnson, P. (1989). Evaluations of physical aggression among intimate dyads. *Journal of Interpersonal Violence, 4*, 298–307.

Arias, I., & O'Leary, K. D. (1985). Semantic and perceptual discrepancies in discordant and nondiscordant marriages. *Cognitive Therapy and Research, 9*, 51–60.

Barling, J., & Rosenbaum, A. (1986). Work stressors and wife abuse. *Journal of Applied Psychology, 71*, 346–348.

Barling, J., O'Leary, K. D., Jouriles, E. N., Vivian, D., & MacEwen, K. E. (1987). Factor similarity of the Conflict Tactics Scales across samples, spouses and sites. *Journal of Family Violence, 2*, 37–56.

Barnett, O. W., Fagan, R. W., & Booker, J. M. (1991). Hostility and stress as mediators of aggression in violent men. *Journal of Family Violence, 6*, 217–241.

Barnett, O. W., & Hamberger, L. K. (1992). The assessment of maritally violent men on the California Psychological Inventory. *Violence and Victims, 7*, 15–28.

Baumgardner, A. H. (1990). To know oneself is to like oneself. *Journal of Personality and Social Psychology, 58*, 1062–1072.

Berger, C. (1988). Uncertainty and information exchange in developing relationships. In S. W. Duck (Ed.), *Handbook of personal relationships* (pp. 239–255). New York: Wiley.

Berkowitz, L. (1989). Frustration-aggression hypothesis: Examination and reformulation. *Psychological Bulletin, 106*, 59–73.

Berkowitz, L. (1990). On the formation and regulation of anger and aggression: A neoassociationistic analysis. *American Psychologist, 45*, 494–503.

Berkowitz, L., & Heimer, K. (1989). On the construction of the anger experience: Aversive events and negative priming in the formation of feelings. *Advances in Experimental Social Psychology, 22*, 1–37.

Bowker, L. (1986). *Ending the violence: A guidebook based on the experience of 1000 battered wives.* Holmes Beach, FL: Learning Publications.

Brinkerhoff, M. B., & Lupri, E. (1988). Interspousal violence. *Canadian Journal of Sociology, 13*, 407–434.

Browne, A. (1987). *When battered women kill.* New York: Free Press.

Canary, D. J., & Cupach, W. R. (1988). Relational and episodic characteristics associated with conflict tactics. *Journal of Social and Personal Relationships, 5*, 305–325.

Canary, D. J., & Spitzberg, B. H. (1987). Appropriateness and effectiveness in the perception of conflict strategies. *Human Communication Research, 13*, 93–118.

Canary, D. J., & Spitzberg, B. H. (1989). A model of competence perceptions of conflict strategies. *Human Communication Research, 15*, 241–268.

Canary, D. J., & Spitzberg, B. H. (1990). Attribution biases and associations between conflict strategies and competence outcomes. *Communication Monographs, 57*, 139–151.

Cascardi, M., Langhinrichsen, J., & Vivian, D. (1992). Marital aggression: Impact, injury and health correlates for husbands and wives. *Archives of Internal Medicine, 152*, 1178–1184.

Chaiken, S., Liberman, A., & Eagly, A. H. (1989). Heuristic and systematic information processing within and beyond the persuasion context. In J. S. Uleman & J. A. Burgh (Eds.), *Unintended thought* (pp. 212–251). New York: Springer-Verlag.

Cupach, W. R., & Metts, S. (1987, May). *Perceived cues associated with relationship change and stability.* Paper presented at the Iowa/International Network on Personal Relationships Conference, Iowa City, IA.

Derogatis, L. R. (1983). *SCL90-R Administration, scoring and procedures manual*. Towson, MD: Clinical Psychometric Research.

deTurck, M. A. (1985). A transactional analysis of compliance gaining behavior: Effects of noncompliance, relational contexts, and actors' gender. *Human Communication Research, 12*, 54–78.

deTurck, M. A. (1987). When communication fails: Physical aggression as a compliance-gaining strategy. *Communication Monographs, 54*, 106–112.

Dickstein, L. J., & Nadelson, C. (Eds.). (1989). *Family violence: Emerging issues of a national crisis*. Washington, DC: American Psychiatric Press.

Dutton, D. G. (1988). *The domestic assault of women: Psychological and criminal justice perspectives*. Boston: Allyn and Bacon.

Dutton, D. G., & Hemphill, K. J. (1992). Patterns of socially desirable responding among perpetrators and victims. *Violence and Victims, 7*, 29–39.

Dutton, D. G., & Strachan, C. E. (1987). Motivational needs for power and spouse-specific assertiveness in assaultive and nonassaultive men. *Violence and Victims, 2*, 145–156.

Eagly, A. H., & Steffen, V. J. (1986). Gender and aggressive behavior: A meta-analytic review of the social psychological literature. *Psychological Bulletin, 100*, 309–330.

Edleson, J. L. (1984). Working with men who batter. *Social Work, 29*, 237–242.

Edleson, J. L., Eiskovits, Z., & Guttman, E. (1985). Men who batter women: A critical review of the evidence. *Journal of Family Issues, 6*, 229–247.

Ellis, D. (1989). Male abuse of a married or cohabiting female partner: The application of sociological theory in research to research findings. *Violence and Victims, 4*, 235–255.

Epstein, S. (1986). Anxiety, arousal and the self-concept. *Stress and Anxiety, 10*, 265–305.

Folger, R. (1986). A referent cognitions theory of relationship deprivation. In J. M. Olsen, P. Herman, & M. P. Zanna (Eds.), *Relative deprivation and social comparison* (pp. 33–55). Hillsdale, NJ: Lawrence Erlbaum Associates.

Follingstad, D. R., Rutledge, L. L., Berg, B. L., Hause, E. S., & Polek, D. S. (1990). The role of emotional abuse in physically abusive relationships. *Journal of Family Violence, 5*, 107–120.

Frieze, I. H., & Browne, A. (1988). Violence in marriage. In L. Ohlin & M. H. Tonry (Eds.), *Crime and justice—an annual review of research: Volume on family violence* (pp. 1–46). Chicago: University of Illinois Press.

Gelles, R. J. (1976). Abused wives: Why do they stay. *Journal of Marriage and the Family, 38*, 659–668.

Goetting, A. (1988). Patterns of homicide among women. *Journal of Interpersonal Violence, 3*, 3–20.

Goetting, A. (1989). Men who kill their mates: A profile. *Journal of Family Violence, 4*, 285–295.

Goetting, A. (1991). Female victims of homicide: A portrait of their killers and the circumstances of their deaths. *Violence and Victims, 6*, 159–168.

Goldstein, D., & Rosenbaum, A. (1985). An evaluation of the self-esteem of maritally violent men. *Family Relations, 34*, 425–428.

Gondolf, E. W. (1985). Fighting for control: A clinical assessment of men who batter. *Social Casework, 66*, 48–54.

Hastings, J. E., & Hamberger, L. K. (1989). Personality characteristics of spouse abusers: A controlled comparison. *Violence and Victims, 3*, 31–48.

Higgins, E. T. (1989). Self-discrepancy theory. *Advances in Experimental Social Psychology, 22*, 93–136.

Higgins, E. T., Klein, R., & Strauman, T. (1987). Self-discrepancies. In K. Yardley (Ed.), *Self and identity psychosocial perspectives* (pp. 173–186). New York: Wiley.

Hilberman, E., & Munson, K. (1977–78). Sixty battered women. *Victimology, 2*, 460–470.

Holtzworth-Munroe, A., Waltz, J., Jacobson, N. S., Monaco, V., Fehrenbach, P. A., & Gottman, J. M. (1992). Recruiting nonviolent men as control subjects for research on marital violence: How easily can it be done? *Violence and Victims, 7*, 79–88.

Hudson, W. W., & McIntosh, S. R. (1981). The assessment of spouse abuse. *Journal of Marriage and the Family, 43,* 873–888.

Infante, D. A., Chandler, T. A., & Rudd, J. E. (1989). Test of an argumentative skill deficiency model of interspousal violence. *Communication Monographs, 56,* 163–177.

Infante, D. A., & Wigley, C. J. (1986). Verbal aggressiveness. *Communication Monographs, 53,* 61–69.

Janoff-Bulman, R. (1988). Victims of violence. In S. Fisher & J. Reason (Eds.), *Handbook of life stress, cognition and health* (pp. 101–113). New York: Wiley.

Kasian, M., & Painter, S. L. (1992). Frequency and severity of psychological abuse in a dating population. *Journal of Interpersonal Violence, 7,* 350–364.

Koss, M. P. (1987). Changed lives: The Psychological impact of sexual harassment. In M. A. Paludi (Ed.), *Ivory power: Sexual harassment on campus* (pp. 73–92). Albany: State University of New York Press.

Lebov-Keeler, K., & Pipes, R. B. (1990, August). *Psychological abuse among college women in exclusive heterosexual dating relationships.* Paper presented at the American Psychological Association, Boston.

Levinson, D. (1989). *Family violence in cross-cultural perspective.* Newbury Park, CA: Sage.

Lie, G-Y., Schilit, R., Bush, J., Montagne, M., & Reyes, L. (1991). Lesbians in currently aggressive relationships: How frequently do they report aggressive past relationships? *Violence and Victims, 6,* 121–135.

Lim, T. (1990). The influences of receivers' resistance on persuaders' verbal aggressiveness. *Communication Quarterly, 38,* 170–188.

Lloyd, S. A. (1990). Conflict types and strategies in violent marriages. *Journal of Family Violence, 5,* 269–284.

Lopes, L. L. (1987). Between hope and fear. *Advances in Experimental Social Psychology, 20,* 255–293.

MacEwen, K. E., & Barling, J. (1988). Multiple stressors, violence in the family of origin and marital aggression: A longitudinal investigation. *Journal of Family Violence, 3,* 73–87.

Makepeace, J. M. (1983). Life event stress and courtship violence. *Family Relations, 32,* 101–109.

Makepeace, J. M. (1986). Gender differences in courtship violence victimization. *Family Relations, 35,* 383–388.

Malone, J., Tyree, A., & O'Leary, K. D. (1989). Generalization and containment: Different effects of past aggression for wives and husbands. *Journal of Marriage and the Family, 51,* 687–697.

Mann, C. R. (1990). Black female homicide in the United States. *Journal of Interpersonal Violence, 5,* 176–201.

Margolin, G., John, R. S., & Gleberman, L. (1988). Affective responses to conflictual discussions in violent and nonviolent couples. *Journal of Consulting and Clinical Psychology, 56,* 24–33.

Marshall, L. L. (1992a). Development of the severity of violence against women scales. *Journal of Family Violence, 7,* 103–121.

Marshall, L. L. (1992b). The severity of violence against men scales. *Journal of Family Violence, 7,* 189–203.

Marshall, L. L. (1993a, April). *Coping and health in psychologically and physically abused women.* Paper presented at Women's Psychological and Physical Health: A Scholarly and Social Agenda, Lawrence KS.

Marshall, L. L. (1993b, June). *Psychological abuse, violence and emotional distress.* Paper presented at International Network on Personal Relationships, Milwaukee, WI.

Marshall, L. L. (in prep.). *Psychological abuse of women: Six distinct patterns.*

Marshall, L. L., & Rose, P. (1987). Gender, stress and violence in the adult relationships of a sample of college students. *Journal of Social and Personal Relationships, 4,* 299–316.

Marshall, L. L., & Rose, P. (1990). Premarital violence: The impact of family of origin violence, stress and reciprocity. *Violence and Victims, 5,* 51–64.

Marshall, L. L., & Vitanza, S. A. (1994). Physical abuse in close relationships. In A. L. Weber & J. H. Harvey (Eds.), *Perspectives on close relationships.* Boston: Allyn & Bacon.

Mason, A., & Blankenship, V. (1987). Power and affiliation motivation, stress and abuse in intimate relationships. *Journal of Personality and Social Psychology, 52*, 203–210.

Masters, J. C., & Keil, L. J. (1987). Generic comparison processes in human judgment and behavior. In J. C. Masters & W. P. Smith (Eds.), *Social comparison, social justice and relative deprivation* (pp. 11–54). Hillsdale, NJ: Lawrence Erlbaum Associates.

McGuire, W. J., & McGuire, C. V. (1986). Differences in conceptualizing self versus conceptualizing other people as manifested in contrasting verb types used in natural speech. *Journal of Personality and Social Psychology, 51*, 1135–1143.

McHugh, H. C., Frieze, I. H., & Browne, A. (1990). Research on battered women and their assailants. In M. Paludi & F. Denmark (Eds.), *Handbook on the psychology of women*. New York: Greenwood Press.

Morrison, R. L., Van Hasselt, V. B., & Bellack, A. S. (1987). Assessment of assertion and problem-solving skills in wife abusers and their spouses. *Journal of Family Violence, 2*, 227–256.

Murphy, C. M., & Cascardi, M. (1993). Psychological aggression and abuse in marriage. In R. L. Hampton, T. P. Gullotta, G. R. Adams, E. H. Potter, & R. P. Weissberg (Eds.), *Presentation and treatment* (pp. 86–112). Newbury Park, CA: Sage.

Murphy, C. M., & O'Leary, K. D. (1989). Psychological aggression predicts aggression in early marriage. *Journal of Consulting and Clinical Psychology, 57*, 579–582.

Noller, P., & Gallois, C. (1988). Understanding and misunderstanding in marriage. In P. Noller & M. A. Fitzpatrick (Eds.), *Perspectives on marital interaction* (pp. 53–77). Newbury Park, CA: Sage.

O'Leary, K. D. (1988). Physical aggression between spouses: A social learning approach. In V. B. Van Hasselt, R. L. Morrison, A. S. Bellack, & M. Hersen (Eds.), *Handbook of family violence* (pp. 31–55). New York: Plenum.

O'Leary, K. D., Barling, J., Arias, I., Rosenbaum, A., Malone, J., & Tyree, A. (1989). Prevalence and stability of physical aggression between spouses: A longitudinal analysis. *Journal of Consulting and Clinical Psychology, 57*, 263–268.

O'Leary, K. D., & Curley, A. D. (1986). Assertion and family violence: Correlates of spouse abuse. *Journal of Marital and Family Therapy, 12*, 281–289.

O'Leary, K. D., & Vivian, D. (1990). Physical aggression in marriage. In F. D. Fincham & T. N. Bradbury (Eds.), *The psychology of marriage: Basic issues and applications* (pp. 323–348). New York: Guilford.

Ohlin, L., & Tonry, M. (Eds.). (1989). *Family violence*. Chicago: University of Illinois Press.

Okun, L. (1986). *Woman abuse: Facts replacing myths*. Albany: State University of New York Press.

Pagelow, M. (1992). Adult victims of domestic violence. *Journal of Interpersonal Violence, 7*, 87–100.

Paludi, M. A., & Barickman, R. B. (1991). *Academic and workplace sexual harassment: A resource manual*. Albany: State University of New York Press.

Parker, R. N., & Toth, A. M. (1990). Family, intimacy and homicide: A macro-social approach. *Violence and Victims, 5*, 195–210.

Pelham, B. W. (1991). On confidence and consequences. *Journal of Personality and Social Psychology, 60*, 518–530.

Pelham, B. W., & Swann, W. B. (1989). From self-conceptions to self-worth. *Journal of Personality and Social Psychology, 57*, 672–680.

Pirog-Good, M. A., & Stets, J. E. (Eds.). (1989). *Violence in dating relationships: Emerging social issues*. New York: Praeger.

Renzetti, C. M. (1988). Violence in lesbian relationships: A preliminary analysis of causal factors. *Journal of Interpersonal Violence, 3*, 381–399.

Richardson, D., Leonard, K., Tyler, S., & Hammock, G. (1985). Male violence toward females: Victim and aggressor variables. *The Journal of Psychology, 119*, 129–135.

Riggs, D. S., Murphy, C. M., & O'Leary, K. D. (1989). Intentional falsification in reports of interpartner aggression. *Journal of Interpersonal Violence, 4*, 220–232.

Rosenbaum, A., & O'Leary, K. D. (1981). Marital violence: Characteristics of abusive couples. *Journal of Consulting and Clinical Psychology, 49,* 63–71.

Russell, D. E. H. (1982). *Rape in marriage.* New York: MacMillan.

Russell, D. E. H. (1988). Wife assault theory, research and treatment: A literature review. *Journal of Family Violence, 3,* 193–208.

Saunders, D. G., & Browne, A. (1991). Domestic homicide. In R. T. Ammerman & M. Hersen (Eds.), *Case studies in family violence* (pp. 379–402). New York: Plenum.

Shephard, M. F., & Campbell, J. A. (1992). The abusive behavior inventory: A measure of psychological and physical abuse. *Journal of Interpersonal Violence, 7,* 291–305.

Sigelman, C. K., Berry, C. J., & Wiles, K. A. (1984). Violence in college students' dating relationships. *Journal of Applied Social Psychology, 5,* 530–548.

Smith, D. A., Vivian, D., & O'Leary, K. D. (1990). Longitudinal prediction of marital discord from premarital expressions of affect. *Journal of Consulting and Clinical Psychology, 59,* 790–798.

Sonkin, D. J. (Ed.). (1987). *Domestic violence on trial.* New York: Springer.

Spitzberg, B. H., & Marshall, L. L. (1990, July). *The topography of relational violence and abuse.* Paper presented at the Fifth International Conference on Personal Relationships, Oxford.

Spitzberg, B. H., & Marshall, L. L. (1991, October). *Courtship violence and relational outcomes.* Paper presented at the International Communication Association, Chicago.

Star, B. (1982). Characteristics of family violence. In J. P. Flanzer (Ed.), *The many faces of family violence* (pp. 14–23). Springfield, IL: Thomas.

Steele, C. M. (1988). The psychology of self-affirmation. *Advances in Experimental Social Psychology, 21,* 261–302.

Stets, J. E. (1990). Verbal and physical aggression in marriage. *Journal of Marriage and the Family, 52,* 501–514.

Stets, J. E. (1992). Interactive processes in dating aggression: A national study. *Journal of Marriage and the Family, 54,* 165–177.

Stets, J. E., & Pirog-Good, M. A. (1990). Interpersonal control and courtship aggression. *Journal of Social and Personal Relationships, 7,* 371–394.

Stets, J. E., & Straus, M. A. (1990). Gender differences in reporting marital violence and its medical and psychological consequences. In M. A. Straus & R. J. Gelles (Eds.), *Physical violence in american families: Risk factors and adaptations to violence in 8,145 families* (pp. 151–165). New Brunswick, NJ: Transaction Books.

Stout, K. (1991). Intimate femicide: A national demographic overview. *Journal of Interpersonal Violence, 6,* 476–485.

Strauss, M. A. (1979). Measuring intrafamily conflict and violence: The Conflict Tactics (CT) Scales. *Journal of Marriage and the Family, 41,* 75–86.

Strauss, M. A. (1990). Measuring intrafamily conflict: The Conflict Tactics (CTS) Scales. In M. A. Straus & R. J. Gelles (Eds.), *Physical violence in american families: Risk factors and adaptations to violence in 8,145 families* (pp. 29–45). New Brunswick, NJ: Transaction Books.

Straus, M. A., & Gelles, R. J. (1986). Societal change and change in family violence from 1975 to 1985 as revealed in two national surveys. *Journal of Marriage and the Family, 48,* 465–479.

Straus, M. A., & Gelles, R. J. (Eds.). (1990). *Physical violence in american families: Risk factors and adaptations to violence in 8,145 families.* New Brunswick, NJ: Transaction Books.

Straus, M. A., Gelles, R. J., & Steinmetz, S. K. (1980). *Behind closed doors: Violence in the american family.* Garden City, NY: Doubleday.

Strube, M. J. (1988). The decision to leave an abusive relationship: Empirical evidence and theoretical issues. *Psychological Bulletin, 104,* 236–250.

Sugarman, D. B., & Hotaling, G. T. (1989). Dating violence: Prevalence, context and risk markers. In M. A. Pirog-Good & J. E. Stets (Eds.), *Violence in dating relationships: Emerging social issues* (pp. 3–12). New York: Praeger.

Tesser, A. (1988). Toward a self-evaluation maintenance model of social behavior. *Advances in Experimental Social Psychology, 21,* 181–228.

Tesser, A., Pilkington, C. J., & McIntosh, W. D. (1989). Self-evaluation maintenance and the mediational role of emotion. *Journal of Personality and Social Psychology, 57*, 442–456.

Tolman, R. M. (1989). Development of a measure of psychological maltreatment of women by their male partners. *Violence and Victims, 4*, 159–177.

Tolman, R. M. (1992). Psychological abuse of women. In J. Campbell (Ed.), *Assessing the risk of dangerousness* (pp. 290–310). Newbury Park, CA: Sage.

Tolman, R. M., & Bennett, L. W. (1990). A review of quantitative research on men who batter. *Journal of Interpersonal Violence, 5*, 87–118.

Vitanza, S. A. (1991). *The relationship of stress, cognitive appraisal and dating violence.* Unpublished master's thesis, University of North Texas, Denton, TX.

Vitanza, S. A., & Marshall, L. L. (1993). *Dimensions of dating violence, gender and personal characteristics.* Manuscript under review.

Vivian, D., & O'Leary, K. D. (1987, July). *Communication patterns in physically aggressive engaged couples.* Paper presented at the Third National Family Violence Research Conference, University of New Hampshire, Durham.

Walker, L. E. (1979). *The battered woman.* New York: Harper & Row.

Walker, L. E. (1984). *The battered woman syndrome.* New York: Springer.

Walker, L. E. (1986). Psychological causes of family violence. In M. Lystad (Ed.), *Violence in the home: Interdisciplinary perspectives* (pp. 71–97). New York: Brunner/Mazel.

Weinstein, N. D. (1989). Effects of personal experience on self-protective behavior. *Psychological Bulletin, 105*, 31–50.

White, J. W., & Koss, M. P. (1991). Courtship violence: Incidence in a national sample of higher education students. *Violence and Victims, 6*, 247–256.

Widom, C. S. (1989). Does violence beget violence? A critical examination of the literature. *Psychological Bulletin, 106*, 3–28.

Yllo, K., & Bograd, M. (Eds.). (1989). *Feminist perspectives on wife abuse.* Newbury Park, CA: Sage.

Zillman, D. (1988). Cognition-excitation interdependencies in aggressive behavior. *Aggressive Behavior, 14*, 51–64.

Zillman, D. (1989). Transfer of excitation in emotional behavior. In J. T. Cacioppo & R. E. Petty (Eds.), *Psychophysiology: A sourcebook* (pp. 215–239). New York: Guilford.

FETCHING GOOD
OUT OF EVIL

13

Dark Side Dénouement

Brian H. Spitzberg
San Diego State University

William R. Cupach
Illinois State University

This book is built on the notion of the dark side of interpersonal reaction. What is the dark side? Is it a place? A state of mind? A force within nature? An ideology? It can be any of these things, but essentially it is simply a metaphor—a vantage point adopted to gain insight into phenomena. In this volume the metaphor is employed to advance understanding about human communication. Metaphors are useful to the extent that they are meaningful, quite literally. In our judgment, the dark side metaphor is useful for understanding interpersonal relationships because it focuses on important, yet neglected, phenomena and helps to discern new and useful connections among concepts. The dark side metaphor is only one among many that can be applied to the study of communication and relationships. Yet, it is one that manifests multifarious meanings and offers a fecund source of scholarly insight. The chapters in this volume clearly evidence that the dark side metaphor is provocative, revealing, and heuristic.

The dark side metaphor conjures up several shades of meaning. The most fundamental sense of dark simply suggests dimly lit, concealed, or obscured. Many of the topics covered in this volume constitute familiar but complicated situations that are particularly challenging or problematic, both for the social actors who experience them and for the social researchers attempting to explain and predict them. The dark side metaphor stimulates us to consider these pervasive but elusive and neglected areas of inquiry. Whatever the dark side consists of, it begs for enlightenment.

Perhaps the most salient semantic aspect of the dark side metaphor is its insinuation of something evil, sinister, depressing, and forbidding. In fact, some undoubtedly will criticize our adoption of the dark side metaphor as itself being overly pessimistic, or even inimical. They will contend that to dwell on the negative is to affirm it; to employ the dark side metaphor is to reify and perpetuate it. (Perhaps such debates are the stuff of the dark side of scholarship—a topic beyond the scope of this book, but one that could usefully be taken up in another forum.)

Of course, there is nothing inherently evil about the metaphor. It simply directs us to investigate the slimy, seamy underbelly of human interaction, such that it may be. It does not a priori presume what is dark or what should be dark or what should be done about darkness. The dark side metaphor does not imbue researchers with a sense of what is good or bad, but it does suggest that the existence of a sense of darkness is an inherent part of our lived experience. We can all identify with the dark side of interpersonal communication. Confronting and exploring the darkness helps us cope with it and adapt to it accordingly.

As many of the chapters in this book reveal, the dark, difficult, disruptive, and distressing elements of social interaction deserve close empirical scrutiny. The authors in this volume have illustrated a number of important nuances about the dark side of interpersonal communication—whatever darkness implies. Exploration of the dark side reveals, for example, that messages we often assume superficially to be negative and destructive are sometimes positive and constructive when we consider their consequences more fully. Moreover, what constitutes a dark side of interaction is not always obvious. It is, by its dark nature, frequently hidden, secret, and therefore elusive.

From the standpoint of scholarship, the dark side metaphor has been liberating as well as enlightening. This book began with a vague yet haunting suspicion that the field of interpersonal communication has been unduly dominated by an overly benevolent ideology. Standard interpersonal textbooks seem littered with topics such as disclosure and openness, intimacy, love, cooperation, empathy, assertiveness, "win–win" orientations, and a host of pollyannish skills and processes. Implicit in much of this work, as well as the more scholarly original research of the discipline, are presumptions about what constitutes "good" interpersonal relationships. One of the ironies of these ideological presumptions is that they seem to be based on the notion that what is "normal" is preferred, yet what is truly normal is far from the cultural ideal of good interpersonal relations.

There are many ideological presuppositions that seem to underlie the study and discussion of interpersonal relationships. Such ideologies have been identified and their changes charted in historical studies (Kasson, 1990; O'Neill, 1980; Wine, 1981) and recent cultural paradigms reflected in the rhetoric of popular media (Hubbard, 1985; Kidd, 1975; Megli & Morgan, 1991; Prusank, Doran, & DeLillo, 1991), as well as therapeutic regimens and movements

(Dillon, 1986). Efforts at deconstructing some of these ideologies (e.g., Bochner, 1982; Eisenberg, 1984; Kursh, 1971; Lannamann, 1991; Lawrence, 1991; Parks, 1982) have helped to reveal the often subtle influences of these values. Although there are many such ideologies, a few seem to have been prominently identified in the chapters of this text.

For example, a common yet generally unarticulated assumption seems to be that closer relationships are better than more distant or detached relationships (cf. Knapp & Vangelisti, 1991; Rook & Pietromonaco, 1987). Relationships represent a growing together, a merging, a bonding, and an intertwining of selves into new unities and entities that are considered nonsummatively more than the independent personas involved. Relationships are considered "on track" if they are progressing toward intimacy and togetherness, and are disintegrating, decaying, dissipating, deescalating, declining, dissolving, or dying if they are moving away from intimacy. Yet, as chapters on the dark side have argued, closeness often breeds undue influence, loss of identity, loss of privacy, frustrations of individual goals and personal projects, and the possibilities of great psychological and even physical harm. Furthermore, nonintimate relations with others may represent the modal form of interaction in everyday encounters. Intimacy may not be the halcyon fields it is often presumed to be.

Closely related to this ideology is the presumption that openness and expressiveness are better than closedness and privacy (cf. Bochner, 1982; Parks, 1982). At least since the 1960s, the afterglow of Rogerian therapeutic assumptions, the influence of Jourard's (1971a, 1971b) work on self-disclosure, and a general eurocentric cultural move toward self-actualization through the exposure of the self to relational experiences, have moved the ideological pendulum toward openness and expressiveness. Yet, as chapters on the dark side have indicated, privacy and the bolstering of one's separate identity are integral to personal, and often relational, well-being.

Also closely related to openness and expressiveness is the assumption that such disclosures should be veracious. A common ideology is that accuracy, clarity, consistency, and mutual understanding are better than distortion, deception, obfuscation, and symbolic dilemmas (cf. Cerulo, 1988; Eisenberg, 1984; Kursh, 1971; Lawrence, 1991). Yet, the unification of divergent factions, the management of failed identities or identities at risk, and the mere greasing of the gears of everyday interaction appear to require a substantial degree of equivocation and dishonesty. Generally, even the most fervent advocates of a higher moral order in relationships concur that honesty and accuracy in the extreme would be devastating to the functioning of everyday relational interaction.

To discuss the "functioning" of relationships is to fall back on a machine or structural metaphor. Such metaphors tend to suggest that systems function best when they function as they were intended to function. The ideological equivalent of this metaphor in relationships seems to be that maintenance of face and relationship is better than falling from either personal or relational grace (cf. Baumgardner & Brownlee, 1987; Helmreich, Aronson, & LeFan, 1970; Jones, 1989). Most people have experienced the mortal fear of embarrassment, discovery of transgression, and the loss of desired identity. Less examined, however, are the potential saving graces of such falls from grace. Such lapses of projected social identities, though generally unintended, may jolt individuals into realizations of new identities, new relational definitions, and may even have a favorable humanizing influence on social actors.

The machine, computer, and team metaphors that often inspire our visions of relationships lead to another ideology: Cooperation is better than competition, coercion, and aggression (cf. Felson, 1978, 1981). Smooth, steady, and tranquil interactions are considered more satisfying, in which the gears of interrelating mesh with less friction and resistance. Yet, as chapters on the dark side have suggested, there are times when a shock to the relational system may bring forth a recognition of hidden relational whirlpools, stimulate creative sources of relief for an acerbic climate, and forge bonds that are stronger for having weathered the storm.

This latter ideology is perhaps the most culturally intransigent of these value systems. The devastation of international conflicts, the realization of the horrors of torture and terrorism, and the rise of "enlightened" civilizations, along with the liberating influences of feminism and civil rights groups, have all drawn attention to the repressive, coercive, and "dehumanizing" influences of violence. Certainly, we would agree that there will likely always be means of interpersonal interaction that are potentially more ideal than violence and aggression. Yet, it is scientifically and academically reckless to define a priori such forms of interaction as either evil or beyond the scope of scholarly inquiry as an objective phenomenon.

For example, research indicates that the average college female has experienced an average of one to two episodes of violence. These episodes are typically mild forms of aggression, such as shoving, slapping, pushing, or verbal threats. As distasteful as such actions may be, it is at least arguably possible that such behaviors become turning points for the participants. The individuals involved may realize deeper problems that otherwise may not have been recognized or managed. Is it at least possible, therefore, that such violence occasionally serves to advance the relationship toward more mutually satisfying relational definitions and patterns of interaction, in ways that other more traditional forms of interaction would not have allowed?

To suggest that the first onset of mild violence or aggression in an established relationship may occasionally function to enhance the relationship in the eyes of the participants is not to say that it is desirable, competent, or preferable to more ratiocinative means of resolving differences. It is to suggest that such behavior may function in complex ways to stimulate relational evolution that otherwise would not have been within the normal means of the participants. To either exclude such possibilities from the realm of concern, or to ideologically define such actions as incapable of serving such functions, is to do damage to scholarly inquiry into the complexities of the human condition. In claiming this, we are not attempting by this question to recommend violence, but only to argue that such questions regarding the value and function of the darker strains of human interaction deserve to be asked and investigated. This is the primary motivation of this dark side compilation: to redress the imbalance of scholarly and popular attention to the benevolent forms of human intercourse.

Of course, the dark side was only barely explored in this volume. Numerous other topics litter the landscape of the scholarly alleyways. Jealousy, possessiveness, revenge, loneliness, depression, schizophrenia, enemyship, hassles, insult and invective, conflict, divorce, stalking, harassment, child abuse, incest, failure of support, unrequited love, and a host of other topics have received scholarly attention, yet have yet to be brought under the light of the dark side metaphor. We expect such topics to complete yet other volumes of dark side research. In the interim, it is hoped that the chapters here have begun to tip the scales back into a balance that places the darker sides of human nature into a more integrated picture of interpersonal interaction. As Duck indicated in this volume, the dark side is not a separate corner in the ballroom of human interaction, but an integral part of the architecture of daily interaction, and as such, needs to be conceptualized and understood in its own right.

REFERENCES

Baumgardner, A. H., & Brownlee, E. A. (1987). Strategic failure in social interaction: Evidence for expectancy disconfirmation processes. *Journal of Personality and Social Psychology, 52,* 525–535.

Bochner, A. P. (1982). On the efficacy of openness in close relationships. In M. Burgoon (Ed.), *Communication yearbook 5* (pp. 109–124). New Brunswick, NJ: Transaction/ICA.

Cerulo, K. A. (1988). What's wrong with this picture? Enhancing communication through distortion. *Communication Research, 15,* 93–101.

Dillon, G. L. (1986). *Rhetoric as social imagination: Explorations in the interpersonal function of language.* Bloomington: Indiana University Press.

Eisenberg, E. M. (1984). Ambiguity as strategy in organizational communication. *Communication Monographs, 51,* 227–242.

Felson, R. B. (1978). Aggression as impression management. *Social Psychology, 41,* 205–213.

Felson, R. B. (1981). An interactionist approach to aggression. In J. T. Tedeschi (Ed.), *Impression management theory and psychological research* (pp. 181–199). New York: Academic Press.

Helmreich, R., Aronson, E., & LeFan, J. (1970). To err is humanizing—sometimes: Effects of self-esteem, competence, and a pratfall on interpersonal attraction. *Journal of Personality and Social Psychology, 16,* 259–264.

Hubbard, R. C. (1985). Relationship styles in popular romance novels, 1950 to 1983. *Communication Quarterly, 33,* 113–125.

Jones, E. E. (1989). The framing of competence. *Personality and Social Psychology Bulletin, 15,* 477–492.

Jourard, S. M. (1971a). *Self-disclosure: An experimental analysis of the transparent self.* New York: Wiley-Interscience.

Jourard, S. M. (1971b). *The transparent self* (revised ed.). New York: Van Nostrand Reinhold.

Kasson, J. F. (1990). *Rudeness and civility: Manner in nineteenth-century urban America.* New York: Hill and Wang.

Kidd, V. (1975). Happily ever after and other relationships styles: Advice on interpersonal relations in popular magazines, 1951–1973. *Quarterly Journal of Speech, 61,* 31–39.

Knapp, M. L., & Vangelisti, A. L. (1991). *Interpersonal communication and human relationships* (2nd ed.). Boston: Allyn & Bacon.

Kursh, C. O. (1971). The benefits of poor communication. *Psychoanalytic Review, 58,* 189–208.

Lannamann, J. W. (1991). Interpersonal communication research as ideological practice. *Communication Theory, 1,* 179–203.

Lawrence, S. G. (1991, November). *Is fidelity a goal of communicators?* Paper presented at the Speech Communication Association Conference, Atlanta, GA.

Megli, J. M., & Morgan, L. G. (1991, May). *How to get a man and other advice: Articulation of the rhetorical visions present in popular women's magazines from 1974–1989.* Paper presented at the International Network on Personal Relationships Conference, Bloomington, IL.

O'Neill, Y. V. (1980). *Speech and speech disorders in Western thought before 1600.* Westport, CT: Greenwood Press.

Parks, M. (1982). Ideology in interpersonal communication: Off the couch and into the world. In M. Burgoon (Ed.), *Communication yearbook 5* (pp. 79–108). New Brunswick, NJ: Transaction/ICA.

Prusank, D. T., Duran, R. L., & DeLillo, D. A. (1991, May). *Interpersonal relationships in women's magazines: Dating and relating in the 1970's and 1980's.* Paper presented at the International Network on Personal Relationships Conference, Bloomington, IL.

Rook, K. S., & Pietromonaco, P. (1987). Close relationships: Ties that heal or ties that bind? In W. H. Jones & D. Perlman (Eds.), *Advances in personal relationships* (Vol. 1, pp. 1–36). Greenwich, CT: JAI.

Wine, J. D. (1981). From defect to competence models. In J. D. Wine & M. D. Smye (Eds.), *Social competence* (pp. 3–35). New York: Guilford.

Author Index

A

Abbey, A., 27, *41*
Abeles, G., 85, *100*
Adams, B. N., 261, *276*
Adams, G., 245, *256*
Adams, R. M., 7, 12, *20*, 39, *41*
Adler, F., 271, 272, *276*
Agarie, N., 77, *81*, 168, *178*
Alberts, J. K., 28, *41*
Albright, L., 28, *45*
Alexander, E. R., 36, *47*
Allan, G., 8, *20*
Allen, C. M. B., 14, *21*
Altman, I., 241, 242, 245, *256*
Amato, P. R., 28, *41*
Amirkhan, J., 64, *82*, 168, *180*
Andersen, E. L., *157*
Andersen, J. F., 190, 191, *211*
Andersen, P. A., 14, *22*, 186, 189, 193, *211*
Anderson, C., 91, *100*
Anderson, E. L., 135, *157*
Anderson, S. A., 271, *276*
Andrews, B., 66, *78*
Angrosino, M. V., 119, *122*
Applegate, J. L., 35, *41*
Archer, N., 282, *306*

Argyle, M., 27, 28, *41*, 160, 163, 164, 168, *176*, 220, 226, *238*
Arias, I., 285, 287, 290, *306*, *309*
Aristotle, 86, *105*, *122*
Aronson, E., 164, *176*, *177*, 318, *319*
Asher, S. R., 7, 12, *20*
Athay, M., 35, 36, *42*
Atwater, L., *238*
Aune, R. K., 197, *211*, 230, *238*
Austin, J. L., 53, *78*
Averill, J. R., 54, *78*
Avery, P. B., 224, *239*

B

Badzinski, D. M., 260, 264, *278*
Bandura, A., 41, *42*
Barickman, R. B., 297, *309*
Barling, J., 285, 290, 291, *306*, *308*, *309*
Barnes, K. J., 14, *23*
Barnett, O. W., 282, *306*
Baron, R. A., 38, *42*
Barrett, M., 274, 275, *276*
Bartle, S. E., 271, *276*
Bateson, G., 83, 84, 89, 90, 94, 95, *100*, 106, 111, *122*, 128, *157*

Subject Index